Women in the
American Revolution

Women in the American Revolution

Sudie Doggett Wike

McFarland & Company, Inc., Publishers
Jefferson, North Carolina

LIBRARY OF CONGRESS CATALOGUING-IN-PUBLICATION DATA

Names: Wike, Sudie Doggett, author.
Title: Women in the American Revolution / Sudie Doggett Wike.
Description: Jefferson, North Carolina : McFarland & Company, Inc., Publishers, 2018. | Includes bibliographical references and index.
Identifiers: LCCN 2017052890 | ISBN 9781476671963 (softcover : acid free paper) ∞
Subjects: LCSH: United States—History—Revolution, 1775–1783—Women. | United States—History—Revolution, 1775–1783—Participation, Female.
Classification: LCC E276.W54 2018 | DDC 973.3082—dc23
LC record available at https://lccn.loc.gov/2017052890

ISBN 978-1-4766-7196-3 (print)
ISBN 978-1-4766-3087-8 (ebook)

BRITISH LIBRARY CATALOGUING DATA ARE AVAILABLE

© 2018 Sudie Doggett Wike. All rights reserved

No part of this book may be reproduced or transmitted in any form or by any means, electronic or mechanical, including photocopying or recording, or by any information storage and retrieval system, without permission in writing from the publisher.

On the cover: *Molly Pitcher firing cannon at Battle of Monmouth,* E. Percy Moran artist, 1911 (Library of Congress)

Printed in the United States of America

McFarland & Company, Inc., Publishers
Box 611, Jefferson, North Carolina 28640
www.mcfarlandpub.com

For our daughter, Dr. Martha Wike, our son, Sidney Wike, Jr.,
our grandchildren, Abigail and Miles Wike and Katie and Christopher Lyne.

Acknowledgments

A special thanks to my husband, ophthalmic surgeon Sidney Wike, for critiquing the entire manuscript. Select sections of the work have also benefitted from the careful reading, comments and questions of our son, Sidney Wike, Jr., and our grandson, Christopher Lyne. I am grateful to Dr. John S. Gaines, former dean of faculty and professor emeritus of King University, for his guidance and encouragement. Books and articles from his extensive personal library have enriched this work. Thanks to Myra Orr-Ashbrook for sharing her exhaustive research through DAR files. The writing of this history was inspired initially by the enthusiastic cooperation of our local Fort Chiswell Chapter of the National Society of Daughters of the American Revolution (DAR) located in Bristol, Tennessee-Virginia. Each member was eager to know how her particular Patriot (a direct ancestor who fought, provided service, or furnished supplies for the American cause) fit into the panoramic puzzle of the Revolution. The description of each of these DAR members regarding her Patriot's service in the Revolution, as proven by primary documents, formed the root for researching this book.

Table of Contents

Acknowledgments	vi
Preface	1
Prologue: George III and Queen Charlotte of Mecklenburg	7

PART ONE. WAR IN THE NORTH

1. Founding Mothers in the First Days of Revolution	11
2. Correspondence Committees, the Tea Party and Coercive Acts	27
3. Siege of Boston and the Canada Campaign	35
4. New York and New Jersey Campaigns	56
5. Saratoga Campaign, Ben Franklin and French Aid	73
6. Valley Forge, Monmouth Battle and Sullivan's Raid	87

PART TWO. WAR IN THE SOUTH

7. Regulators and Wataugans	99
8. Pontiac's War, Boundaries and Treaties and Dunmore's War	106
9. Transylvania, Great Bridge Battle and Kentucky County, Virginia	123
10. Snow Campaign, Moore's Creek, Sullivan's Island and the Cherokee War	131
11. Northwest Territory, Chickamauga Expedition and Mid-Tennessee	145
12. Georgia Invades Florida, and the Savannah and Augusta Campaigns	153
13. Charlestown Campaign, Camden Battle and Fishing Creek	164
14. Militiamen Cross the Blue Ridge and Face Ferguson in Tryon County	173
15. Watauga, Kings Mountain and the Journey Home	183
16. Cornwallis Reverses Course and Confronts Greene in the South	200
17. British and American Strategy in the Virginia Campaign	219
18. The Virginia Campaign and the American Victory at Yorktown	230
19. The Last Pockets of Revolution and the Treaty of Paris	239

Chapter Notes	245
Bibliography	253
Index	259

Preface

In Upper New York Bay stands a colossal statue of a woman holding a tablet inscribed JULY IV MDCCLCCVI, the day the nation that became the United States of America declared its independence from Great Britain—July 4, 1776. Her uplifted hand holds a torch, a universal symbol lighting the way through the harbor to freedom and a path to liberty, one of hope and opportunity. She stands on the same spot where General William Howe, commander in chief of the British Army in America and Vice Admiral Lord Richard Howe, commander of the British navy in America, sailed into the harbor to subdue the British colonies in America. The massive incursion caused Lucy Knox to panic, gather up her children and flee along with scores of other families. Almost a decade later a defeated British military departed this same spot and sailed back to London, leaving America independent.

Much has been written about the men who fought on the battlefields or in Congress to counter the British incursion during the revolutionary period. A good bit has been written about a few educated women—Mercy Warren, Abigail Adams, Hannah Winthrop and British historian Catherine Macaulay, all of whom corresponded with each other and influenced prominent political and military leaders like General George Washington, General Henry Knox, and congressmen Thomas Jefferson and John Adams. Relatively little, however, is known about the contributions of a colossal number of ordinary women without whom the symbolic Statue of Liberty would not exist. Oral history is all that remains of the majority of women who faced hardships on the home front or exerted a steady influence in the background of the battlefields. Their contributions were of such magnitude that the war would not have been won without their support.

These enormous contributions of women were crucial not only behind the lines on the battlefields but also on the home front. Most colonial women worked at home, caring for large families, weaving and mending clothing, plowing, planting and harvesting crops, milking cows, feeding, killing and cooking chickens at the hearth over an open fire. Some ladies melted lead and molded bullets; some made saltpeter for gunpowder. If they leveled a rifle, it was to defend against Indian attacks or to shoot varmints. These wives and daughters freed up their men to fight on the battlefield. Without the womens' sacrifice, the men would have been unable to go to war to fight for independence.

Women wrote letters, raised funds for the army, and sewed fringed hunting shirts for soldiers. They spied and carried messages on horseback. Some cannonaded alongside their men on the battlefield or masqueraded in men's clothing to fight as soldiers. If they were successful at that, some received pensions. If caught, they were expelled.

Women camp followers—wives, children and other women seeking work, food and security—accompanied the Continental Army. They usually walked, or sometimes rode, in the rear with the baggage train. In 1777 Washington asked commanding officers to recruit women followers as nurses, to be paid $2.00 per month and one full ration per day. Nurse supervisors earned $4.00 per month. Nurses' duties included feeding and bathing the wounded, scrubbing and sanitizing wards, emptying chamber pots, and sometimes cooking special foods for patients. The medical occupation was hazardous; disease was everywhere and nurse mortality was high. They handled the jobs usually performed by men and so freed up the men to fight. Camp followers included cooks who hung heavy iron kettles on trammels suspended on cranes, cooked over open campfires, and ladled boiled beef, squash or corn meal into the tin container each man carried with him. Some officers requested that their wives be permitted to accompany them. Some valuable soldiers simply would not go on campaigns without their wives.

At the end of the American Revolution, the legal status of women and inheritance laws began to change. Petitioning the legislature was a constitutional tradition brought to America by the English colonizers. "Petitioning was the only formal political channel accessible to women during the revolutionary era." Most petitions involved requests for a widow's pension or back pay for services rendered by a deceased husband.[1] As in English common law, colonial laws during the American Revolution considered a husband and wife to be one person. Each household had only one vote and that vote was cast only by the property owner—the man. Under the existing coverture, the legal status acquired by women upon marriage, a married woman could own no property and sign no legal documents. She was allowed neither to enter into contracts nor to acquire an education against the wishes of her husband. She could keep no wages for herself. Only the property owner—her husband—had political clout. Women were assumed to have absolutely no "separate interests of their own that needed to be represented in politics." Hence, "the welfare of women was completely in the hands of men," and the law offered them little protection from oppressive men.[2] This was the legal status of women when Abigail Adams told her husband, Congressman John Adams, to "Remember the Ladies." Her famous letter to him on March 31, 1776, urged, "Do not put such unlimited power into the Hands of the husbands."

A spinster or a widow was allowed to own property. She could run a business and act as head of her household until she married. Upon marriage, however, her property legally belonged to her new husband. For that reason, when the wealthy widow Martha Custis married George Washington, he received ownership of her estate. The same was true of widow Mary Jameson when she married guerrilla fighter Thomas "Gamecock" Sumter, and of wealthy spinster Mary Esther Videau when she married Francis "Swampfox" Marion.

The primogeniture law, an inheritance law, favored the first-born son. It was he who received almost all of the valuable real property—the land and buidings—but not the personal belongings. Younger sons received family support to pursue military, ecclesiastical or governmental positions. That's why younger sons were attracted to Berkeley's colony at Jamestown, Virginia, where they were given the opportunity to own land. A daughter received a dowry to present to her husband in lieu of any rights to her father's estate. If she separated from her husband her dowry was returned to her family. In 1777 Georgia was the first state to abolish the practice of primogeniture and provide equal inheritance to all the children.

Entailment, another inheritance law, was a legal device to limit property inheritance to the owner's biological descendants. Entailment prevented lands from being broken up. It kept all the land in one chunk and preserved large estates, which provided social status for the whole family. Land was the basis of wealth and therefore the aristocracy. If a father had only daughters, however, his estate was divided equally among his daughters and his widow. All of them, including his widow, had to eke out a living from just one estate. Entailment was an important concept for the Bennet family and their five daughters in Jane Austen's classic novel *Pride and Prejudice*. The state of Virginia abolished entailment in 1776 at the beginning of the Revolutionary War and eliminated primogeniture after the end of the war, in 1785.

Mercy Warren wrote little about the great nonwhite minority, black Americans, except for criticizing colonists for bringing slaves to America in the first place and thereby making themselves vulnerable to slave revolts.[3] Regarding black slaves, Thomas Jefferson wrote to his plantation overseer: "My first wish is that the labourers may be well treated." Another time he wrote, "I consider a woman who brings a child every two years as more profitable than the best man of the farm." In 1820 he remarked, "What she produces is an addition to the capital (the value of his holdings) while his labors disappear in mere consumption."[4] Jefferson provided 85 slaves as dowries for his sisters and daughters and as occasional gifts to members of his family.

Slaves were considered to be the property of their master. Black Americans made up 20 percent of the colonial American population. Most lived in the Chesapeake Bay area of Virginia and Maryland. Neither the enslaved black female nor her counterpart, the black male, had any rights at all in colonial America. They were allowed to own no property and had no right to assemble. It was against the law to teach a black to read or write. Blacks could not testify in court against whites. In 1781—the year after Massachusetts law declared all men free and equal—a black American, Elizabeth Freeman ("Mum Bett"), brought the first legal test of the constitutionality of slavery in Massachusetts. Both "Mum" and a male slave named "Brom" were set free.

In the matriarchal Iroquoian society of the Six Nations and the Cherokee Nation, women and men enjoyed equal social and political status. Regarding the relationship between British colonists and Native Americans, Mercy Warren's contemporaneous *History* blames British general Burgoyne for the brutal murder of Jane McCrae by Indian allies of the British in Upstate New York. Warren also notes the atrocities of American general Sullivan against the Six Nations when he attacked people "enjoying domestic quiet in the simplicity of nature." Her surprising solution for the "barbarity of the borderers" was to build a "Chinese wall" along the Appalachians, a "price" far less that than "paid by the lives of young heroes." In that way the lives of both whites and Native Americans would be spared.[5]

Wives of Loyalists made valuable contributions to family farms and businesses while their husbands were fighting away from home. After the Revolution, most widows of Loyalists were allowed a one-third share of their husband's estate so that they would not become a burden on the Whig society. However Mercy Bedford, the wife of Jonas Bedford, was particularly vulnerable. That's because wealthy Loyalists who had held public office in the colonial government were considered traitors. Hence all their property was confiscated. After Jonas escaped the gallows and fled to England, Mercy—through the help of Whig friends and a good lawyer—furnished supplies to the Patriot cause and obtained a voucher to prove it. Declaring herself a Patriot and a widow, as Jonas was in exile in England, she took her case through many court proceedings and all the way to the General Assembly of the State of North Carolina, where she succeeded in changing the law. Mercy's Law—"An Act for the Relief of Mercy Bedford"[6]—helped women win back their husbands' confiscated or stolen estates for themselves and their children to be passed down in perpetuity.

Mercy Bedford of the western frontier of North Carolina and Mercy Otis Warren of the city of Boston, Massachusetts, had much in common. Both were Mayflower descendants, married to educated, affluent men, and politically active during the Revolution. And each was determined to achieve for women what was rightfully theirs—whether equal education or the right to own property.

This book is divided into two parts: War in the North and War in the South. Unsung women heroes served in every campaign and every battlefield of the American Revolution. They stood by their husbands, brothers and sons or acted independently as passionate Patriots. This book shows cameos of many of these women, both valiant and vulnerable, documented and anecdotal, in whatever situation they happened to be caught or passionately chose to confront. It is a holistic view of the Revolution in that it describes well-documented campaigns and battles while simultaneously focusing, through whatever lens is available, on the women who supported those campaigns. Whether doing the emotionally and physically exhausting work of nurses or mothers and farm women keeping the home fires burning or serving on the battlefields, the women of this book take their rightful places alongside men. That's where they belong. Here, on these pages, integrated with men in each phase of the war, women receive a token of the credit they deserve.

The need to show adequate appreciation for the contributions of women within the context of each battle became apparent to me when I was registrar of our local chapter of the Daughters of the American Revolution. I began researching the battles and campaigns in which each DAR Patriot had been involved. Most proven Patriots were males because households were registered in their names and they received a voucher or a pension for supporting the Revolution by supplying provisions or serving in public office or fighting on the battlefield. A woman could not receive a voucher (a legal document to prove her patriotism) unless she was head of a household or filed pension papers proving that she served in battle. Soon the project became so fascinating that I catalogued the information chronologically, year by year, battle by battle. It became a huge jigsaw puzzle. The accumulated pieces comprise this book, which is written for sister DAR members, our spouses, children, grandchildren and other interested persons. It tells how each particular battle—the Battle of Kings Mountain, the Battle of Saratoga—or the actions of Congress fit into the whole scheme of the war and how each individual ancestor is woven into the cycloramic tapestry of the Revolution.

Sources for this history include Mercy Otis Warren's contemporaneous history of the American Revolution, which was the first history of the Revolution written by a woman. This book also benefits from the works of Elizabeth Fries Lummis Ellet. Born in 1818, four years after the death of Mercy Warren, Ellet was the first historian to write specifically about the females, in *Women of the American Revolution*. Ellet's main sources were primary documents, unpublished letters and diaries preserved by Mercy Otis Warren's descendants. Other primary sources are excerpts from documents found at the Library of Congress:

contemporaneous letters, logs, and diaries, pension papers of Revolutionary War Patriots, and Pension Memorials of Loyalists. Secondary sources include published works of creditable authors and historians in books, magazines and newspapers. This author's experience in research and scholarship and her awareness of the need to document sources comes from years of studying science in college and medical school and in working as a physician in clinical research at a pharmaceutical company.

Prologue: George III and Queen Charlotte of Mecklenburg

George III (r 1760–1820) became the king of England near the end of the French and Indian War and continued to rule throughout the American Revolution. He was the first native English-speaking monarch to sit on the throne since Queen Anne died in 1714. The robust, blue-eyed, auburn-haired George III was crowned in 1760 when he was 21 years old. The following year the friendly young king married 17-year-old Sophia Charlotte of Mecklenburg-Strelitz, a German princess of part-African descent. On her three-day sea trip to England, the poorly schooled but intelligent Charlotte had practiced English tunes on the harpsichord. The first time the couple met was on their wedding day, six hours before their wedding. A contemporary writer describes the bride:

When she first saw the palace she turned pale….

The Duke of York gave her his hand at the garden-gate: her lips trembled, but she jumped out with spirit. In the garden the King met her; she would have fallen at his feet; he prevented and embraced her, and led her into the apartments, where she was received by the Princess of Wales and Lady Augusta: these three Princesses only dined with the King. At ten the procession went to chapel, preceded by unmarried daughters of peers, peers, and peeresses in plenty. The new Princess was led by the Duke of York and Prince William; the Archbishop married them; the King talked to her the whole time with great good-humour, and the Duke of Cumberland gave her away. She is not tall, nor a beauty; pale, and very thin; but looks sensible, and is genteel. Her hair is darkish and fine; her forehead low, her nose very well, except the nostrils spreading too wide; her mouth has the same fault, but her teeth are good. She talks a good deal, and French tolerably.[1]

Charlotte had been trained as a singer and, according to Haydn, played the keyboard passably well. She quickly learned English, which she spoke with a heavy German accent. As an amateur botanist, she collected exotic plants brought to England by British explorers and helped establish the Royal Botanic Gardens. At a party for children on Christmas Day 1800 the queen delighted the youngsters by introducing to England the Christmas tree from her native Germany. Dominating the center of the room, the glowing tree was anchored in a huge tub. A yew tree, its branches were hung with fruits, packets of raisins and almonds, candy and toys, and it was illuminated by tiny wax candles. Walking in wonder around and around the tree, each wide-eyed child received sweetmeats and a toy.

George was passionately devoted to his family and faithful to his wife, Queen Charlotte, who gave birth to their 15 children. The king was "deeply religious, sincerely patriotic and an exuberant talker."[2] A man of simple tastes, he was content to inspect his farm, peruse his lifetime collection of 65,000 books—which became the backbone of the British Library—play the violin and piano and ride horseback, as shown by his equestrian statue that once stood in Bowling Green, New York. The statue was melted down by Whigs and used as bullets during the Revolutionary War. George delighted in organ concerts by the boy composer Wolfgang Amadeus Mozart. He encouraged Joseph Haydn and resurrected the music of his favorite composer, George Frederick Handel.[3]

While "some of the noblest English statesmen drank their gallon of strong wine daily, or sat late at the gambling table, or lived in scarcely hidden concubinage, George III was decorous in personal habits and pure in domestic relations, and no banker's clerk in London applied himself to the details of business more industriously than he. He had a genuine talent for administration."[4] His vast 18th-century British Empire encompassed sugar fields and the slave trade of the Caribbean; cod fishing villages and fur trading posts on the eastern seaboard of Canada and Massachusetts; tobacco plantations in Virginia; and cotton fields, indigo and rice in the Carolinas and Georgia. The busy southern seaports of Charlestown and Savannah exported furs and timber on British ships flying the Union Jack. King George's mighty empire stretched out to engulf the pungent aroma of British trading posts in India, where pepper and cinnamon—once more valuable than gold—were loaded under the billowing sails of His Majesty's ships already aromatic with cloves, mace, and nutmeg from the Spice Islands and redolent with cassia, cardamom, ginger, and turmeric from India and Ceylon.

When George III became king he was politically inexperienced. He did not initiate the colonial policies that precipitated the American Revolution. His decisions depended on the advice of his prime ministers. He chose ministers who could win support in Parliament and stabilize the government. Over the first decade of his reign, six successive prime ministers introduced the colonial policies that caused the Revolution. Between 1763 and 1765 Prime Minister George Grenville engineered three policies that were direct causes of the American Revolution. First, the Sugar Act of 1764 was imposed to stop smuggling and to collect more tax money on sugar, and second, the Stamp Act of 1765 taxed almost all printed matter from documents to dice. The Grenville government's third main cause of revolution, the Quartering Act of 1765, established a standing British military in America.

The government of George III was politically unstable until 1770, when the king chose Lord North, who served as prime minister during the height of the Revolutionary War. Awkward and ungainly, North was corpulent, with thick lips, bushy eyebrows, and "large eyes that rolled about and gave him the air of a blind trumpeter." But the king was fond of him. Even North's opponents liked his self-deprecating humor, jovial manner, quick wit and literary anecdotes. They tolerated his occasional weeping before the House of Commons when the war was not going well and when he "lost faith in the British effort to recover America." Although "North inherited a revolutionary situation," he was "ultimately responsible for the policies that precipitated the American Revolution with the East India Tea Act which aimed to remedy the financial problems of the East India Company ... and uphold the right of Parliament to tax America."[5] When neither King George III nor Parliament responded to colonists' complaints against the ministers, the Americans held Parliament responsible and sent their appeals directly to the king. When this avenue failed, the colonists declared independence and "laid the blame squarely on the shoulders of George III himself."[6]

The American Revolutionary War focused on the concept of Tories and Whigs. But in America, unlike in England, these were not political parties. The terms defined one's stance on the question of revolution. Loyalists were American colonists who remained loyal to the British crown and disagreed with the revolutionists. Loyalists were also called Tories, Royalists or King's Men. Their opponents, the Whigs, were American colonists who supported the Revolution. Whigs were also called Rebels or Patriots. The term Patriot, however, was not commonly used until after the war. At the beginning of the war, almost every American was a Loyalist (Tory), including Benjamin Franklin, George Washington and Thomas Jefferson. As the Revolution wore on, the first Rebels (Whigs, Patriots) were Sam Adams, the Sons of Liberty and Patrick Henry. During most of the war, Tories and Whigs were evenly split. One-third of Americans were Tories, one-third were Whigs and one-third vacillated between the two.

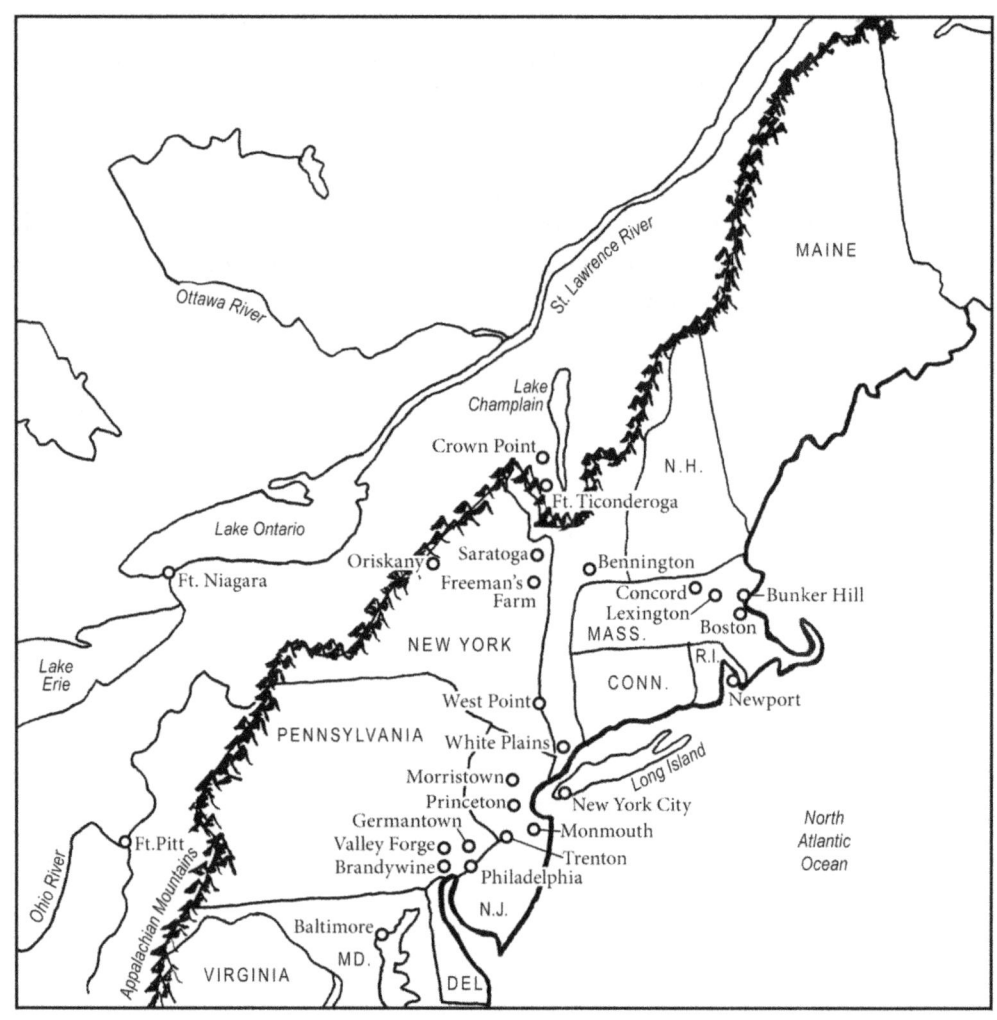

Revolutionary War in the North (Glen McCroskey).

PART ONE. WAR IN THE NORTH

1

Founding Mothers and Politics in the First Days of Revolution

In the city of Barnstable, in Plymouth Colony, Massachusetts, Mercy Otis Warren (1728–1814) penned notes that would become a book like no other. Not only was it the first history of the American Revolution written by a woman (a fact that diminished its popularity then but enhances its appeal today)[1] but its author was also witnessing events as they happened. And she personally knew the people—the soldiers, the founding fathers and the brave women—she wrote about. Her three-volume book, *The History of the Rise, Progress and Termination of the American Revolution*, was published in 1805 when she was 77 years old. She had worked on it for 40 years (1761–1801). In ordering copies of Warren's history for himself and his cabinet, Thomas Jefferson anticipated that her truthful and insightful account of the last thirty years "will furnish a more instructive lesson to mankind than any equal period known in history."[2] Although she married a prominent man who agreed with and supported her writings, Mercy was not dependent on her husband for her identity. She became famous and influential in her own right, writing poetry and essays and recording American history day by day as it happened.

In the days when it was not customary to educate girls, Mercy Otis was privileged. Her father, Colonel James Otis, had encouraged her to study alongside her brothers under a private tutor. An intelligent and diligent scholar who relished history and politics, Mercy held her own in lively family conversations. At home she sparred verbally with her adored bright older brother, James Otis, Jr., who encouraged and accepted her as an intellectual equal. Throughout her life Mercy's conservative opinions would be solicited and respected, so much so that after the Revolution, when her book charged her long-time friend Federalist John Adams of forgetting "the principles of the American revolution" and of being "beclouded by a partiality for monarchy ... by living long near the splendor of courts and courtiers,"[3] he was hurt and angry. She implied that as president Adams threatened to bring the country to autocratic rule. When he repeatedly responded in writing, she considered his ten letters of retaliation not as constructive criticism but as devastating attacks on her character and her family. However, John Adams and Mercy Warren eventually patched up their lifelong friendship.

While Mercy pictured women of the Revolution as essentially weak and helpless in the war, both she and Abigail Adams advocated for equal opportunity in education for women as a source of attaining strength. A woman's formal education in the North was almost as deficient as that of the frontierswoman of the South, where "a country school had but two classes in it, viz: the big boys and the little boys, and sometimes a third—the girls."[4] In adolescence, Mercy was disappointed when her father insisted that she practice her needlework rather than learn Latin and Greek with her brothers. But what she hated most was that when the boys were allowed to enroll in Harvard College she could not attend. College was for men only; females were not accepted. So Mercy read Sir Walter Raleigh's *History of the World* and pondered global events while she pursued the proper colonial girl's domestic duties of cooking and sewing. That is how "Mercy Otis learned to move easily between an intellectual world inhabited primarily by men and a household world run largely by women."[5]

When she was 26 years old in 1754, Mercy Otis married farmer and merchant James Warren, a Harvard graduate. The couple would have five sons. James Warren, a political radical, adored Mercy and promoted her self-esteem. Watching her dip feather quill into ink, he fondly called her a "scribble" and said, "God has given you great abilities; you have improved them in great Acquirements. You are possessed of eminent Virtues and distinguished Piety. For all these I esteem I love you in a degree that I can't express. They are all now to be called into action for the good of Mankind, for the good of your friends, for the promotion of Virtue and Patriotism."[6] James often sent his wife's "scribbles," her political satires and poetry, to his fellow Congressman John Adams for help in publishing them. A lover of books, Adams—who enjoyed Shakespeare and Swift, and usually carried a volume of English poetry or Cervantes with him on trips—found Mercy's ideas and writings fascinating.

Having similar backgrounds, both Mercy Otis and James Warren were from wealthy and prominent families. Mercy's maternal lineage traces back several generations to Edward Doty, a 1620 *Mayflower* Pilgrim who came to Plymouth Colony as Stephen Hopkins' servant and signed the Mayflower Compact. Another of Mercy's ancestral grandfathers immigrated to America in 1630 with the Great Puritan Migration to the Massachusetts Bay Colony. On the other hand, one of James Warren's ancestral grandfathers was Pilgrim Richard Warren, who also sailed to America on the 1620 *Mayflower*. Richard received his acreage in the first (1623) Plymouth Colony Division of Land and his allotment of heifers and "two shee-goats" in the 1627 Division of Cattle. His descendent James Warren inherited what Mercy would name Clifford Farm, which was part of the original Warren estate from the *Mayflower* Pilgrims' division of land. There Mercy would give birth to and nurture five boys, perform domestic as well as hospitality duties, and design a card table using pressed flowers from her garden as a pattern. Having a powerful intellect, she spent much of her lifetime reading books, recording history, writing letters, plays and poetry, and hosting political get-togethers beside her hearth. Her rich correspondence with great Patriots of her era "includes letters from Samuel and John Adams, Jefferson ... and Knox and others,"[7] men who sought her opinion and valued her judgment.

Knowing Mercy Otis Warren's Puritan heritage, it is not surprising that the first chapter of her history challenges Americans to "look back with due gratitude and respect on the fortitude and virtue of their ancestors who left England, not as adventurers for wealth and fame, but for the quiet enjoyment of religion and liberty." It was essential to the preservation of the liberties of Englishmen, wrote Mercy, "that no grants of monies should be made, by tolls, talliage, excise, or any other way, without the consent of the people by their representative voice." Yet, "numberless restrictions had been laid on the trade of the colonies ... and every method had been taken to ... prevent the growth of their manufactures."[8]

1. Founding Mothers and Politics in the First Days of Revolution

When Parliament passed laws that restricted colonial trade and levied import duties on goods except for those produced in Britain or her colonies, smuggling became a common method for merchants to avoid restrictions and duties. Parliament clamped down on illegal trade by enacting the Writs of Assistance in 1760. The Writs were vague general search warrants that allowed government officials (customs inspectors) absolute power to enter private homes wherever they chose on the least pretext in order to search for contraband and catch smugglers. Not Quakers or Puritans or Anglicans considered smuggling a sin.

Parliament's Writs of Assistance was a tinderbox ready to fuel the flame of revolution. Mercy Warren's brother—a political activist, lawyer and firebrand—James Otis, Jr., of Massachusetts was outraged by the warrants. He resigned his post as Britain's advocate general, the official legal advisor for the British-controlled colonial government. Instead of advocating for England he began delivering incendiary speeches in court against Parliament's Writs of Assistance. In February 1761 James Otis, Jr.—one of America's first Patriots—a "plump, round faced, smooth-skinned, short-necked, eagle-eyed young politician,"[9] was in the courtroom and wearing the lawyer's conventional wig and black gown. Near the beginning of his five-hour speech, he reminded the court, "I was solicited to argue this cause as Advocate-General (to defend the legality of the Writs of Assistance); and, because I would not, I have been charged with desertion from my office." When Otis refused to defend the Writs as advocate general, the merchants of Boston urged him to oppose the Writs, which he did. He refused payment for arguing against a law he so ardently opposed. Speaking with "fiery eloquence" before the Massachusetts Superior Court—and witnessed by the young and "awestruck" lawyer John Adams—James Otis harangued that the Writs, which were "valid in English law and commonly used in England, were null and void because they violated the natural rights of Englishmen."[10]

The upstairs council chamber of the royal governor in the Old State House where the argument took place overlooked the Long Wharf and the Boston Harbor. The room was frequently used by Patriots speaking and debating against the British Crown, but none of those speeches were more fiery or famous than the one taking place at this moment. Onlookers listened transfixed as Otis presented his argument attacking the legality of the warrants (Writs) before the State Superior Court of the British Province of Massachusetts:

> Now, one of the most essential branches of English liberty is the freedom of one's house. A man's house is his castle; and whilst he is quiet, he is as well guarded as a prince in his castle. This writ, if it should be declared legal, would totally annihilate this privilege. Custom-house officers may enter our houses when they please; we are commanded to permit their entry. Their menial servants may enter, may break locks, bars, and everything in their way; and whether they break through malice or revenge, no man, no court can inquire. Bare suspicion without oath is sufficient.[11]

Considered by many observers and historians to be the opening scene of the American Revolution, Otis's masterful "a man's house is his castle" argument questioned whether colonists should comply with laws that were made without their knowledge or consent. Leaving the courtroom with notes in hand, Lawyer John Adams wrote, "Every man of a crowded audience appeared to me to go away, as I did, ready to take arms against Writs of Assistance. Then and there was the first act of opposition to the arbitrary claims of Great Britain, then and there the child of Independence was born.... The masses of the people caught the word from his lips, and hence forth it came to be a common maxim in the mouths of all that taxation without representation is tyranny."[12]

The next year, although Otis had coined the phrase "taxation without representation is tyranny," England confirmed the legality of the Writs and five years later would reauthorize them as part of the Townshend Acts. The Writs then became a major prerevolutionary grievance. Though Otis's inflammatory "a man's house is his castle" speech failed to win his case against the Writs of Assistance in the Massachusetts Superior Court, it lit the imagination of the people, made Otis an instant celebrity, and got him elected to the Massachusetts General Court (legislature). In 1762 he again appealed to the law and logic of Britons everywhere, both in the British colonies and in the United Kingdom, when he "maintained that the rights of a colonial assembly as regarded the expenditure of public money, were as sacred as the rights of the House of Commons."[13]

Samuel Adams, a Boston maltster, joined Otis in opposing British authority in the colonies. While Otis used the spoken word Adams wrote pamphlets and letters, and the influence of Samuel Adams soon rivaled that of Otis. One weapon in pamphleteer Samuel Adams' arsenal to foment revolution involved the possibility of England sending bishops to the colonies. The very thought of establishing bishops in America caused great anxiety for many colonists. They knew the history of the Bishops Wars when the Presbyterian people of Scotland rose up in arms against the religious intolerance of King Charles I and William Laud, Archbishop of Canterbury, who tried to impose Anglican ceremonies upon them. For voicing his opinion, one unfortunate Scot was "pilloried, whipped, branded in the cheek, and had one of his ears cut off and one of his nostrils slit."[14]

When the head of the Church of England, the Archbishop of Canterbury, informed colonists that a movement was underway to send Episcopal bishops to America, the Reverend Mayhew, a Boston Congregationalist minister and anti–Royalist, objected. Mayhew's pamphlet to his congregation had great influence in setting the ball of revolution rolling. It reminded colonists how their ancestors had suffered persecution during the reigns of the Stuart Kings. John Adams wrote, "If any gentleman supposes this controversy to be nothing to the present purpose, he is grossly mistaken. It spread a universal alarm against the authority of Parliament. It excited a general and just apprehension that bishops and dioceses and churches and priests and tithes were to be imposed upon us by Parliament."[15]

In general, the episcopacy was intimately related, through the Mother Church, to the throne, and the "Episcopal Clergy, as a body, were active or passive Loyalist." For years Puritans had resisted a movement to send bishops to America. They objected because they believed that if Parliament and the throne could create dioceses, appoint bishops and demand tithes, it could also mandate that everyone attend the Anglican Church or else be persecuted as a heretic. The archbishop replied in writing to Minister Mayhew's pamphlet and tried to allay the fears of non–Episcopalians. He assured them that the Church of England did not desire in the least that the Episcopal clergy "should hold courts to try material or testamentary causes, or be vested with any magisterial authority, or infringe or diminish any privileges or liberties."[16] The archbishop's letter nevertheless put fear into the hearts of New Englanders whose forefathers had come to America to escape the tyranny of the Church of England.

Two years later pamphleteer Samuel Adams and the Sons of Liberty, his newly formed muscle for protesting the Stamp Act, would use the issue of the episcopacy to propagandize and bring Presbyterian and Congregational ministers and most of the colonial clergy into the camp of revolutionists—the Whigs or rebels now known as Patriots. Adams would soon earn the epithet "Father of the American Revolution," but when former Massachusetts governor William Shirley retired to England he had never heard of him. Shirley remarked, "Mr. Cushing I knew, and Mr. Hancock I knew; but where the devil this brace of Adamses came from, I know not." Historian Theodore Parker has responded: "Had [the governor] lived a little longer, he might have found out where they went to, taking the nation with them."[17]

During the time Samuel Adams was floundering in business, failing as a bank teller, failing in the beer industry, failing to finish law school, failing as a tax collector, he finally found his niche. Influenced by Boston lawyer James Otis in 1761, Sam became a fierce opponent of British authority in the colonies. John Adams, a younger second cousin of Sam, observed that Samuel Adams had a "most thorough understanding of liberty." He was "zealous and keen in the cause," "a man of steadfast integrity and universal good character."[18] A decade later Sam's pamphlet *The Natural Rights of Colonists* was published by Benjamin Franklin. Even later John Adams would call Jefferson's Declaration of Independence a recapitulation of Samuel Adams' *Natural Rights* pamphlet.

Before Samuel Adams was the founding father of anything, he was a son influenced by his parents. His mother was a rigidly pious Puritan. Owner of a large Boston estate with a waterfront mansion, his father was a justice of the peace, a deacon of Old South Church, a selectman, and an assemblyman whose son "Sam," as he was called by his contemporaries, studied law for a time. But in those days law was not recognized as a profession and Sam's mother preferred that he be a merchant. His father wanted him to enter the ministry. Sam did neither. Although he studied law briefly at Harvard, where he ranked a respectable fifth in a class of 22, he entered the world of business where he struggled unsuccessfully for a toehold. Working in a countinghouse and spending too much time talking politics instead of adding up numbers, he found the job uninteresting and difficult. He then received from his father, the elder Samuel Adams, 1,000 pounds sterling to set up his own business. But soon young Sam lent half of the stake to a friend who never repaid it; the other half he lost in his own business operation. For him, vying with competitors in trade was obnoxious. Afterward, he and his father set up a malt house—turning barley into malt to blend with beer—on the Adams estate. The father died in 1748, leaving one-third of his estate to young Sam, who then married Elizabeth Checkley, the daughter of a family friend. When Elizabeth died, Samuel Adams wrote this tribute in the family Bible: "To her husband she was as sincere a friend as she was a faithful wife.... She ran her Christian race with remarkable steadiness and finished in triumph! She left two small children. God grant they may inherit her graces!"[19]

Adams served on committees in offices both large and small—chimney inspection, fire wards, and monitoring of smallpox isolation. During the French and Indian War, he was elected annually as one of the tax collectors, a job he did most inefficiently. He often failed to collect any taxes at all. When people were slow to pay, the tax collector was indebted to the town. The general public did not question Adams' honesty; his failure to collect taxes was blamed on his feeling of sympathy for the poor.

Samuel married his second wife, Elizabeth Wells, seven years after his first wife died. Elizabeth Wells' father—an Anglican merchant and wine distiller who owned a pew in Boston's Old North Church—became friends with Samuel Adams through business transactions. "In the year 1764," writes James K. Hosmer, his biographer, "Samuel Adams had reached the age of forty-two." He continued:

Even now his hair was becoming grey, and a peculiar tremulousness of the head and hands made it seem as if he were already on the threshold of old age. His constitution, nevertheless, was remarkably sound. His frame of about medium stature was muscular and well knit. His eyes were a clear steel grey, his nose prominent ... his face ... wearing a genial expression. Life had brought him much of hardship ... [and] his wife had died.... Misfortune had followed him in business. The malt house had been an utter failure; his patrimony had vanished little by little, so that beyond the mansion on Purchase Street, with its pleasant harbour view, little else remained. His house was becoming rusty through want of means to keep it in repair. On the sixth of December of this year he married ... Elizabeth Wells, a woman of efficiency and cheerful fortitude, who, through the forty years of hard and hazardous life that remained to him, walked sturdily at his side. It required indeed no common virtue to do this, for while Samuel Adams superintended the birth of the child Independence, he was quite careless how the table at home was spread, and as to the condition of his own children's clothes and shoes. More than once the family would have become objects of charity if the hands of his wife had not been ready and skillful.

"Betsy," as Sam Adams called his wife to distinguish her from his first wife, whose name also was Elizabeth, was a loving stepmother for Sam's two children, Samuel and Hannah. In the following letter to Sam, Betsy admitted to being "low in cash":

Cambridge, Feb. 19, 1775.
  MY DEAR—I received your affectionate Letter by Fesenton and I thank you for your kind Concern for my Health and Safty.... I beg you to Excuse the very poor Writing as My paper is Bad and my pen made with Scissars. I should be glad (My dear), if you shouldn't come down soon, you would Write me Word Who to apply to for some Monney, for I am low in Cash and Every thing is very dear.
  May I subscribe myself yours,
  ELIZAH ADAMS.

Low in cash or not, Betsy's "fine sewing skills" coupled with Hannah's "exquisite embroidery" kept food on the table and the bills paid, and she maintained a hospitable home. Abigail Adams, whose intellect and socioeconomic standing were quite different from Betsy's, genuinely liked her and often traveled many miles to visit her.[20]

Abigail and John Adams' wedding was another auspicious marriage of a founding mother and father, which occurred in 1764. Samuel Adams' second cousin John Adams, five-foot, eight-inch, slightly portly, square-shouldered and fit, had met Abigail Smith when she was a 15-year-old, shy, petite and frail girl busily educating herself by reading books in her father's library. Five years later, when John was 28 and she was a poised and pretty young lady, he married her. In the interim, when his father died John experienced a "want of strength and courage" but gained an inheritance—a farmhouse in Braintree with 40 acres. Abigail's mother, a Quincy, opposed Abigail's marriage. John had low social standing and her mother thought Abigail would be marrying beneath her. But John knew that their bond to each other was like "magnet and steel." He was a studious lawyer. He was also a farmer whose rough hands "were accustomed to pruning his own trees, cutting his own hay and splitting his own wood." As his wife, Abigail did her own sewing, cooking over the open hearth, baking, feeding ducks and chickens, and churning her own butter. She was as talkative and strong-minded as her husband and was his equal in all respects. Competently managing the family's finances, she exerted on him a steady influence. One year after their marriage, news of the Stamp Act reached the American colonies. Years later John Adams would say that revolution began in the minds of colonists long before the shot was fired at Lexington. Soon he would draft the *Braintree Instructions* "from the freeholders of the town to their delegates to the General Court, the legislative body of Massachusetts"[21] advising them how to respond to the Stamp Act of 1765.

Sam Adams, John's cousin, led a revolt against the Stamp Act, and Mercy Warren wrote about it. Sam declared, "It does not take a majority to prevail ... but rather an irate, tireless minority, keen on setting brushfires of freedom in the minds of men." Recently remarried and penniless, Adams found his passion in local politics. Austere and implacable, a "genuine revolutionary," Adams was master of the town meeting, a wizard at propaganda and "the western world's first orchestra-leader of revolution."[22] He was one of the first to oppose British authority in the colonies and one of the first to see independence as the goal. A skilled organizer, he arranged the election of men who agreed with him, spurred committees to act as he wished and to pass resolutions that he wanted. His newspaper letters and essays were powerful tools for Adams in leading the colonies along the dangerous road to independence. Writing under various pseudonyms, he gave the appearance that great numbers of Americans wanted independence. Through letters, articles, and writings read at Boston town meetings, he led the opposition against the king, Parliament's Sugar Act of 1764, and the Stamp Act of 1765.

The Sugar Act imposed duties on molasses, refined sugar, and rum. It was an attempt by the British Parliament to stop colonists from smuggling sugar and molasses into American colonial ports from non–British Caribbean sources, such as the French and Dutch West Indies. The purpose of the Sugar Act was to raise money by selling more sugar to the colonies; the act granted a virtual monopoly of the rum trade to sugar planters of the British West Indies whose largest export to the America colonies was rum.

The Stamp Act, imposed by Parliament, required almost all printed materials except books and personal letters to carry revenue stamps, some quite expensive. As with the Sugar Act, the purpose of the Stamp Act was to defray the costs of colonial wars. The tax applied only to printed items originating internally within the colonies but not to external (imported) goods—such as lead, glass, and paper itself—shipped from England.

The Stamp Act imposed a direct tax on colonial commercial papers, contracts, licenses, wills, and all other legal documents, as well as almanacs, pamphlets, dice, and playing cards. It mandated that every piece of skin, parchment or vellum on which these items were printed should be stamped. The stamps were required to be purchased from official stamp distributors for the British government. The cost ranged from 10£ for attorney's licenses to smaller amounts for everything else. The stamps were one-inch-tall impressions made on paper by a die similar to today's notary seal. If a skin (parchment) would not hold an impression, a piece of paper containing the stamped impression was affixed to the parchment with a metal staple and glue.

In 1764 Mercy Otis Warren began chronicling the "memorable era" of the Stamp Act. "It was," she said, "the first innovation that gave general alarm through the continent." As soon as Americans became aware of it, a "universal murmur" arose:

> While the judicious ... thought it time to make a resolute stand against the encroachment of power, the resentment of the lower classes broke out into ... excesses of riot and tumult.... Multitudes assembled in the principal towns and cities. Houses of abettors and suspected abettors of the legislation were razed to the ground. The more judicious and discrete characters were exceedingly apprehensive that the general clamor might terminate in the extremes of anarchy. Heavy duties had been laid on all goods imported from such of the West India islands as did not belong to Great Britain. These duties were to

be paid into the exchequer, and all penalties incurred were to be recovered in the courts of vice-admiralty, by the determination of a single judge, without trial by jury, and the judge's salary was to be paid out of the fruits of the forfeiture.[23]

In opposition to the Stamp Act, revolutionary leaders everywhere began to surface. Because the stamp tax on newspapers was one shilling per sheet, there was "almost total erosion of newspaper support for Parliamentary rule." Colonial newspapers were united in eroding "royal support among the reading public."[24] The problem was not that Americans refused to pay any taxes at all. Americans objected to the stamp tax passed by Parliament, but they did not refuse to pay taxes imposed by their own legislatures. When the colony of Pennsylvania ran up a debt of a "half million pounds during the French and Indian War," Pennsylvania levied property taxes, business taxes, and poll taxes to pay for it. "From New Hampshire to Georgia the same tax system prevailed." It was this system of passing their own laws to pay their own debts that colonists fought to preserve. The general sentiment was to let the Crown and Parliament govern foreign relations and trade but to make them stay out of local business.[25]

Virginia and Massachusetts opposed Parliament's measure on different grounds: "Virginians ... asserted their rights as men. The Massachusetts generally founded their claim on the rights of British subjects."[26] Patrick Henry of Virginia, Samuel Adams from Massachusetts, and Christopher Gadsden in South Carolina decried the Stamp Act. American lawyers and young merchants objected, but even more vehement opposition came from English merchants "who realized that the Act imperiled the recovery of their commercial debts."[27] Some members of the British Parliament's House of Commons spoke in support of the Stamp Tax. Other House members opposed it. Despite opposition, the Stamp Act was passed in March 1765 to become effective in November.

In America the House of Burgesses of the Colony of Virginia passed a series of resolutions denouncing the Stamp Act. The Massachusetts general court (provincial assembly) met regularly in the statehouse at Boston. Assembly members were delegates elected from each town at a town meeting (folkmoot). General court was scheduled to meet in Boston in early fall of 1765 to formulate the colony's response to the Stamp Act. In preparation for general court, each town meeting appointed a committee to instruct newly elected delegates on how to air their concerns before the general court. Boston's five-man committee elected one of its members, Samuel Adams, to draft instructions regarding the stance that Boston delegates to the general court should take.

The instructions from each town meeting centered around the rationale of Samuel Adams from Boston, his cousin John Adams from Braintree, and other town leaders who followed suit. Their logic was that American legislative bodies had not been asked to consent to the Stamp Act. As there was no direct representation of the colonies in Parliament, the act violated the Magna Carta, the British constitution and the "Natural Rights of Man." Most colonists, in the early days of revolution, however, simply wanted their rights as Englishmen, and not independence from England. Their quarrel was with Parliament, not with the king.

Samuel submitted his instructions at the Boston town meeting on May 24, 1765. He recommended that Boston's representatives deny Parliament the right to put into operation Prime Minister George Grenville's "scheme of the Stamp Act." Sam Adams' delicate but firm handwriting asserts, "These unexpected Proceedings may be preparatory to more extensive Taxation upon us. For if our Trade may be taxed, why not our Lands, the Produce of our land, and in short everything we possess or make use of? This, we apprehend, annihilates our Charter Rights to govern ourselves.... His instructions paper was important because it was "the first public denial of the right of British Parliament to put into operation the Stamp Act, and it suggested for the first time that the colonies should form a union to redress grievances."[28]

Andrew Oliver, secretary of the Massachusetts province, was charged with distributing the tax stamps in his state. It was a sad day full of apprehension when the ships carrying the stamps docked at American harbors in October 1765. Flags were lowered to half mast; tolling bells and beating drums were muffled; crowds of protesting citizens assembled in a mood of great agitation.

The Stamp Act—legalizing the practice of stamping every piece of printed paper for a fee—was "the first direct, internal tax ever to be laid on the colonies by Parliament; indeed, the first tax of any sort other than customs duties. It was a heavy tax, bearing on all classes and sections in America."[29] It was not uncommon for Parliament to tax citizens of Britain living within the British Isles, citizens who had representatives in Parliament. But it was the first time that Parliament had directly taxed the colonies in an attempt to raise revenue. The Stamp Act was significant because it solidified colonial resistance to taxes. Such resistance unified the colonists and fortified them in their fight for independence a decade later.

By protesting the Stamp Act—a tax that was, in the colonists' opinion, both exorbitant and unfair—the colonists stubbornly upheld their rights as Englishmen to be taxed only by their own consent through their own representative assemblies as they had been doing for years. Fearing that Parliament would extend the taxation of sugar and paper by imposing taxes on land and who knows what else, outraged colonists heatedly protested "taxation without representation." So frenzied were the protests that a mob hanged stamp collector Andrew Oliver in effigy. They carried his dangling image to his home and burned it in a bonfire on Fort Hill in front of his house. Swilling rum, the drunken mob proceeded angrily to torch his home and send his barn and garden fence up in flames as well. Oliver resigned as tax collector. Still protesting the Stamp Act, a Boston mob looted and destroyed the home of Andrew Oliver's brother-in-law Thomas Hutchinson, the lieutenant governor of Massachusetts.

Patrick Henry of Virginia also slammed the Stamp Act. At Virginia's capitol in Williamsburg, Henry, a new member of the House of Burgesses, astonished people with his oratorical eloquence in denouncing the Stamp Act. Criticizing the king in his famous "treason speech" of 1765, Henry thundered, "Caesar had his Brutus, Charles the First his Cromwell and George the Third…" At that point he was interrupted by cries of "Treason!" from delegates who easily recognized the reference to assassinated leaders. Henry paused briefly, and then calmly finished his sentence: "… may profit by their example. If this be treason, make the most of it."[30] High treason—betrayal, inciting resistance to, or insurrection against the king of England—was the most serious of all felonies in 18th-century England. Today in America, treason, the attempt to overthrow the government of the United States, remains the most serious of all crimes.

Spurred on by the protests of the Sons of Liberty and the rousing rhetoric of Patrick Henry, colonial leaders solicited the aid of America's emissary to Britain, Benjamin Franklin, in petitioning Parliament to abolish the Stamp Act. Franklin, a loyal supporter of the king, vacillated. At first he agreed with the Stamp Act. He realized that British troops stationed in America needed to be paid, but he failed to realize the full extent of American resentment toward the act. By condoning the Stamp Act, he showed how out of touch he was with American opinion. He had gone to England to try to abolish Penn's charter and convert Pennsylvania to a Crown colony. He represented discontented Pennsylvanians who were fed up with the refusal of William Penn's descendant, who was governor of the province, to pay taxes to local government on hundreds of thousands of acres of proprietary lands. Tax money was essential for the colonial government to establish schools and maintain a military for defense.

As time went on and tension mounted during the crisis, Franklin began to see that "Englishmen no longer considered Colonists as equal to themselves." The Englishman began to think of Americans as "unrefined, if not barbarous and ... degenerate ... persons," an idea that Franklin, at least at first, had reacted to with "reason, humor and satire" rather than with "self-protective outrage." Dr. Franklin "was the celebrated American Philanthropist and Scientist noted everywhere for his practicality and reasonableness," and if anyone could convince Parliament to repeal the Stamp Act, he could. When Franklin ultimately testified against the Stamp Act in the British House of Commons, Americans credited him for its prompt repeal in 1766 just as they had blamed him for its passage in the first place. Following the repeal, however, Franklin continued to envision "an empire in which all the colonies were tied to Great Britain solely through the King, at least until some sort of fair and equal representation of the colonies in Parliament could be worked out." Americans at that time remained suspicious of Franklin's loyalist leanings, wondering just whose side he was on.[31]

News of Parliament's repeal of the Stamp Act early in 1766 brought jubilant celebrations in the colonies. Barbecue, with free beer and grog, was served in New York. Massachusetts heard the news in May when John Hancock's brig *Harrison* brought the word to Boston: "Great was the general joy ... [and] the Sons of Liberty gathered under their favorite tree, drank toasts, and fired guns.... Every debtor in the jail was ransomed and set at liberty.... On the Common the Sons of Liberty erected a magnificent pyramid, illuminated by two hundred and eighty lamps.... John Hancock, Esq., gave a grand and elegant entertainment.... Mr. Otis, and some other gentlemen ... kept open house the whole evening."[32] Although the Stamp Act was quickly abolished, significant damage had been done. Colonists had taken up the battle cry "taxation without representation is tyranny," which led to the organization of the Sons of Liberty. In that same year, 1766, Parliament again caved in to colonial objections and lowered the tax on sugar and molasses.

The Stamp Act was dead, but the Sons and their battle cry lived on. Opposing the Stamp Act, radical leader Samuel Adams was instrumental in founding the secret society called the Sons of Liberty, a group of Boston radicals who actively demonstrated against the Crown. Voluntary organizations opposing unjust British practices and naming themselves Sons of Liberty soon sprang up throughout the colonies. Persuasive in preventing the enforcement of the Stamp Act, the Sons used petitions, assemblies, propaganda, and sometimes violence to rally support for colonial resistance against British officials. Their symbol was the Liberty Tree, an old elm tree on Boston's Hanover Square, where they gathered to protest the Stamp Act. They ended their meetings by hanging a tax collector in effigy from the tree. Flying beside the dangling dummy was a flag whose nine alternating red and white stripes symbolized the spirit of liberty.

When young John Hancock, a rich and popular Boston ship magnate and merchant, joined the Sons of Liberty, both Sam and John Adams welcomed him aboard. Hancock, a future signatory of the Declaration of Independence, developed an especially close working relationship with Samuel Adams and served as the main financier of the Sons of Liberty. Dorothy Hancock, the wife of John Hancock, who was "one of the greatest men of his age," moved in the best social circles and became a leader in taste and fashion. In this illustrious station, she was a dignified and gracious hostess. Not only was Mrs. Hancock "admirable in the pleasing duties of mistress of her household, but in hours of disease and pain soothed her husband and calmed his sensitive and irritable temper."[33]

John Hancock, a descendent of several prominent Congregational clergymen, was sole heir to his uncle Thomas Hancock's estate. Thus the orphaned John, a Harvard graduate, became one of the wealthiest men in New England. Two years after John Hancock joined the Sons of Liberty, a British warship sailed into Boston harbor. Its arrival emboldened customs officials to seize Hancock's merchant ship *Liberty* and charge him with smuggling. Built at the Boston shipyard, ships like those of Hancock sailed through the world carrying "timber, tobacco, tar, rice from the Southern Colonies, wheat from Maryland, sugar and molasses from the West Indies.... The laws of trade were oppressive; but every skipper was more or less a smuggler and knew well how to brave or evade authority."[34] John Adams defended John Hancock in court. The charges were dropped, but the incident endeared Hancock to people throughout the colonies.

Sons of Liberty organizer Samuel Adams was no orator. Like Thomas Jefferson and Benjamin Franklin, Sam was never highly successful as a speaker but "relied on his pen rather than his tongue in public debate."[35] Samuel made little if any attempt to move the crowds with oratory. Instead he, being educated in Greek and Roman classics and a master of propaganda, swayed the crowds with forceful pamphlets and theatrics. An astute politician and skilled manipulator of the town meeting, Adams employed emotion, drama, classic symbols, and ritual rather than logic to reach the people. His props were the Phrygian cap (a conical headdress symbolizing freedom), a liberty song, dancing around the liberty tree, and hanging unpopular officials in effigy. Working through pamphlets and symbolism, agitator Adams encouraged the Sons of Liberty to use oratory and street theatre to protest unfair taxes and oppressive acts of Parliament. His clear, fiery and logical political writings and his vast numbers of newspaper articles written under a plethora of pseudonyms were hugely persuasive.

The Sons of Liberty expanded their goals to oppose other taxes. Usually backed by merchants and working mainly in seaport towns from Portsmouth, New Hampshire, to Savannah, Georgia, the typical Sons were well-educated, middle-class citizens who wore silk stockings and agitated Tories. But sometimes the Sons masqueraded in mobs like that of the Boston Tea Party to make their point. Protesting British taxes, the Sons demonstrated how organizing and standing together as a unified group could accomplish change. This lesson proved valuable in achieving independence.

Even though the colonists had objected to the Stamp Act, an "internal" tax on printed materials, Benjamin Franklin held the mistaken premise that Americans would not object to "external" taxes on imported goods. Acting on Franklin's advice, Chancellor of the Exchequer (secretary of the treasury) Charles Townshend sponsored the series of acts bearing his name. Still trying to balance the budget and simultaneously keep the colonies in check, Parliament passed the Townshend Acts in 1767. The first Townshend Act enforced the Quartering Act by suspending the New York legislature until it complied with the Quartering Act of 1765; the second act, the Townshend Duties, imposed customs duties (taxes) on imported British goods including lead, glass, paper, paint, and tea. It was payable at colonial ports and enacted solely to raise revenue for the British Treasury. The third act enforced the collection of customs and hired extra officers, searchers, and spies, and the fourth act lifted commercial duties on tea and allowed tea to be exported to the colonies free of all taxes levied in Britain.

Not only did Townshend levy customs duties on many British products shipped to the colonies, but he also increased British authority over the colonies by expanding organizations for collecting customs. Thus, Sam Adams again led the opposition. This time he supported the Sons in opposing Parliament's Townshend Acts. James Otis wrote, "Taxes on trade, if designed to raise revenue, were just as much a violation of their rights as any other tax." The Otis pamphlets prepared colonists and colonial newspapers for opposing such taxes when Parliament actually enacted them. When Parliament passed all four Townshend Acts, Americans perceived them as threatening the established traditions of colonial self-government. Especially threatened was the practice of taxation through representative provincial assemblies. The Townshend Acts were universally resisted with violence, evasion of duties, nonimportation agreements among merchants, and hostility toward British enforcement agents.

The Massachusetts General Assembly assigned a committee to "consider the state of the province" and petition the king, although—as Mercy Warren pointed out—in the past "their petitions to the throne had been suppressed without even a reading."[36] Samuel Adams and James Otis drafted a circular letter the assembly adopted in February 1768. Addressed to all the colonies, the letter proclaimed that the Acts violated the British Constitution and the natural rights of the colonists. Natural rights, said John Locke, a prevailing political philosopher of the time, embraced the idea that no human should harm "the life, the liberty, health, limb or goods of another." This translated into the God-given, inalienable rights of life, liberty and property. The tone of the Adams-Otis letter was loyally respectful to the king, but it also pointed out that the "new taxes were unconstitutional."[37] Learning about the letter, Lord Hillsborough, the Crown-appointed secretary of state for the colonies, instructed Massachusetts governor Francis Bernard to demand that the assembly rescind its resolutions listed in the circular letters. If they refused, the governor was to dissolve the assembly.

During the assembly meeting, James Otis spoke out against rescinding the letter. Tories—friends of the British government—called Otis's speech "the most violent, insolent, abusive, and treasonable declaration that perhaps ever was delivered." Otis responded, "'When Lord Hillsborough knows that we will not rescind *our* acts, he should apply to Parliament to rescind theirs. *Let Britons rescind their measures, or they are lost forever.*" For nearly an hour Otis harangued the assembly until even the Sons of Liberty trembled lest he should be accused of treason.[38]

In a vote of 92 to 17, the Massachusetts assembly refused to rescind the letter and held fast to their stance that the Townshend Acts violated the colonists' natural rights of life, liberty and property. Sam Adams and the Sons seized the opportunity to propagandize. Silversmith-minuteman Paul Revere fashioned a silver bowl dedicated to "the immortal

92" assemblymen who deemed the Townshend taxes unconstitutional. To the English House of Commons, the Sons of Liberty sent "two turtles, one weighing 45 pounds, the other 47 pounds, making the whole 92 pounds which is the Massachusetts patriotic number."[39] Angry about their refusal to rescind the letter, Bernard dissolved the Massachusetts assembly. The assembly recognized that Britain's royal governor had struck the first blow against freedom of discussion in the colonies. Thus, before they adjourned, they compiled a list of grievances against the governor and petitioned the king to remove him. Other colonies sympathized with Massachusetts.

In Boston a group of 50 young women, the "Daughters of Liberty," met at a minister's house and spun skeins of fine yarn. They ended the meeting by singing anthems and liberty songs. The Daughters boycotted the imported British products and manufactured goods. Making cloth with their own threads and yarns, the Daughters of Liberty became the first society of working women in colonial America. Both men and women wore homespun clothing during the Revolution. In a 1768 meeting New York ladies protested the Townshend Act that taxed imports. They resolved to spend their time spinning skeins of yarn. Boycotting at teatime, the ladies refused to drink "poisonous bohea" tea but instead drank tea brewed from leaves of the raspberry plant. One New York woman described the ladies gathering for spinning bees as "a fighting army of amazons ... armed with spinning wheels."[40]

Nevertheless, Britain proceeded toward war by enforcing the unpopular Townshend Acts, beginning with the Quartering Act. Lieutenant General Thomas Gage, commander in chief of the British Army in America (1663–1775), sent an officer to prepare Bostonians for housing British troops in their homes. A Boston impromptu town meeting appointed a committee of inquiry. James Otis, Samuel Adams, John Hancock, and John Adams met with Governor Bernard to verify Parliament's intention. The governor admitted that troops would soon be quartered in Boston. But pending further orders from Gage he refused the committee's request to call a special meeting of the assembly for September 1768. To assuage concerns of the powerful committeemen, however, the governor attempted to bribe them. All of them refused in disgust.

"The American war may be dated from the hostile parade of this day," the first of October 1768, when the king's troops arrived from Halifax, Novo Scotia, wrote Mercy Warren. The whole province was astonished: "To the grief and consternation of the town of Boston ... several regiments were landed, and marched sword in hand through the principal streets of their city." Yet no one among the "gazing multitudes" attempted to resist the authority of the king of Great Britain. The people were totally subdued by the first appearance of military power. With "a standing army thus placed in their capital, their commerce fettered, their representative body prevented meeting," their petitions rejected by the governor, and threatened with the arrival of more troops "little hope remained of a peaceful accommodation."[41]

Watching red-coated soldiers pouring into Boston, Samuel Adams with trembling, palsied hands not only seized the propaganda opportunity, but he also literally grabbed coat collars of people on the streets. In his "quavering voice" he urged citizens "to take up arms *and be free and seize the king's officers.*"[42] As soon as British soldiers took up quarters in Boston, Samuel Adams whirled into action, publishing a series of letters signed "Vindex." He argued that to keep "a standing army within the kingdom in time of peace, without the consent of Parliament, was against the law; that the consent of Parliament necessarily implied the consent of the people ... and that the Americans ... were not represented in Parliament (and) were therefore suffering under military tyranny."[43] His "unswerving devotion to public service" is virtually without parallel, his "sole source of income ... the small salary he received as clerk of the Assembly." By the good management of his wife, Elizabeth "Betsy" Wells, their home life was comfortable. "The children grew up happy ... well trained and cared for."[44]

Like Samuel Adams, the Patriot James Otis, Jr., Esq., continued speaking, even ranting, against British policy until he was assaulted in a public place in 1769. He was badly beaten by a commissioner of customs abetted by British officers armed with swords and bludgeons. The great Patriot lived, though he was seriously impaired. The would-be assassins escaped to one of the king's ships. Mercy Warren was convinced that blows to her brother's brain caused his progressive mental and emotional deterioration. But even in 1765 John Adams had watched the mental decline of his hero James Otis, who talked endlessly without stopping for anyone to get a word in. "Otis is in confusion yet," Adams noted. "He rambles and wanders like a ship without a helm."[45] The only therapy that could calm his lunacy and stop his violent destructiveness was the sound of Mercy's soothing voice. Later, when he was struck dead by a lightning bolt, she wrote this eulogy: "Mr. Otis lived to see the independence of America, though in a state of mind incapable of enjoying fully the glorious event which his own exertions had precipitated. After several years of mental derangement, as if in consequence of his own prayers, his great soul was instantly set free by a flash of lightning, from the evils in which the love of his country had involved him. His death took place in May, one thousand seven hundred and eighty-three, the same year the peace was concluded between Great Britain and America."[46]

Back in 1765 Parliament's Quartering Act had triggered a feud between the New York colonial assembly and royal officials. At first the assembly refused to allocate the full measure of funds requested by Parliament to supply food, drink, quarters, fuel, and transportation for British troops stationed in New York City. Later the assembly refused to allocate any funds at all for quartering. Tension tightened when Parliament enacted the Quartering Act of 1767 as part of the Townshend Acts. The New York Sons of Liberty erected a liberty pole for radicals to rally around and express their discontent. New assembly members, however, not having participated in the refusal to fund troops two years earlier, voted to allocate money for housing British soldiers. A broadside circulated by the Sons stirred up the smoldering emotions against quartering. Aroused residents clashed with British troops in New York City streets. British authorities then dispatched soldiers to tear down the liberty pole.

The redcoats taunted women as well as men. One soldier lunged with a bayonet at a woman at the entry of her home; another bullied a woman on her way to the market. On January 19, 1770, violence erupted as redcoats began posting their own broadsides in the form of British handbills titled *God and Soldier*. Citizens tried to stop them from doing so. The ensuing skirmish was called the War of the Broadsides, or the Battle of Golden Hill. A mob of citizens confronted the British with cutlasses and clubs, then retreated to a wheat field called Golden Hill and continued to taunt them. British soldiers charged the jeering crowd with fixed bayonets. Blood was spilled—some call it the first blood of the American Revolution—but no deaths resulted. Thus, in New York City, six weeks before the Boston Massacre, there occurred what some consider the first significant encounter between British officers and armed American colonists.

1. Founding Mothers and Politics in the First Days of Revolution

To enforce the Quartering Act, Lord Hillsborough, British secretary of state for the colonies, dispatched two regiments of British soldiers, to be quartered in Massachusetts to keep order. Great groups of citizens, mostly local workers and sailors, gathered in protest. The Boston Massacre erupted near the custom house on the moonlit, cold and snowy night of March 5, 1770, when protestors fired insults, rocks, and snowballs at the redcoats. With loaded muskets, fixed bayonets and the captain's drawn sword, the British soldiers returned fire, killing five. Among the five was Crispus Attucks, a black sailor and former slave. His body was carried to Faneuil Hall, where it lay in state for many days and then was buried in a common grave with the other four victims.

From his post in England, emissary Benjamin Franklin, who had done everything within his power to defuse the tension, considered both Massachusetts and Pennsylvania his home. He sympathized with Massachusetts and regarded the British soldiers as murderers. The Massachusetts assembly then named Franklin as its agent, or lobbyist, in London to petition the Department of American Affairs. Franklin was already serving in this position for the colonies of Pennsylvania, New Jersey, and Georgia. But several Massachusetts Patriots, notably Samuel Adams, opposed Franklin's appointment because they were not sure whether his loyalties lay with Britain or with America.

In the aftermath of the melee at Boston, the two Adams cousins played complementary roles. John ensured that the soldiers had a fair trial while Samuel "squeezed every ounce of propaganda out of the Boston Massacre." Samuel and the Sons of Liberty turned the slain citizens into "martyrs" and promoted the incident itself as a "massacre." Sons of Liberty member Paul Revere engraved a picture, *The Bloody Massacre*, showing a distressed woman in the crowd and displayed it in his window. Even though the British soldiers who fired into the mob were defended by John Adams and acquitted in a fair trial by jury, the Sons staged parades. They reenacted the shooting, orated against it and perpetuated the name massacre every successive March 5 for the next six years. The celebration was finally replaced by the Declaration of Independence and its subsequent anniversaries every July 4.[47]

No lawyer, except John Adams, who was whole-heartedly supported by Abigail, wanted to represent the British troops who had shot the five citizens on the streets of Boston. John—acting on his belief that every man in a free country deserved the right to counsel and a fair trial—defended the British soldiers and their captain, who had fired the shots. "The reason is," said Adams, "because it's of more importance to community that innocence should be protected, than it is that guilt should be punished."[48] Representing the accused, Adams argued that the Boston mob, by pummeling the soldiers with sticks, stones, and snowballs, had provoked the killings; that the mob itself had resulted from Britain's policy of quartering troops in the city; and therefore, that Parliament rather than the soldiers, was responsible for the murders. John Adams won the case, and the British soldiers were found not guilty.

On the very day of the Boston Massacre, Parliament coincidentally repealed the Townshend Acts, including the Quartering Act. Only the revenue tax on tea remained effective and continued to brew. British troops were removed from the streets of Boston. News of the repeal of the Townshend Acts silenced the opposition throughout the colonies and delighted Boston merchants who lifted their boycott of English imports in order to restock their shelves with fresh goods. "By mid 1770 reconciliation seemed complete except in Boston...." Samuel Adams "feared that the resistance of the colonies would crumble and the British would reassert their authority unless more trouble was stirred up"[49] and that's exactly what he and other radicals proceeded to do. Samuel Adams maintained that Parliament had no right whatsoever to legislate for the colonies on any occasion. He therefore tried to split the colonies away from British rule by writing letters, saying, "It is to be feared that the people will be so accustomed to bondage as to forget they were ever free. Every day strengthens the opponents and weakens us."[50]

George III supported eliminating the duties on imports imposed by the Townshend Acts, with one important exception. By retaining the (customs duties) tax on tea, the king asserted Parliament's right to tax colonists. He insisted that the customs duties on tea must still be collected at colonial ports. The tea tax then remained as a symbol for the supremacy of Parliament.

From 1770 to 1773, the three years after the repeal of the Townshend Acts—with the exception of the tea tax—the American economy flourished. On the northern seaboard, even Sam Adams, with his arsenal of pamphlets, drama and theatrics, was hard put to whip up resentment against Britain.

2

Correspondence Committees, the Tea Party and Coercive Acts

> And be it known unto Britain, even American daughters are politicians and patriots, and will aid the good work with their female efforts.
> —Hannah Winthrop[1]

The Massachusetts Provincial Assembly appointed Samuel Adams to draft a letter for Benjamin Franklin to submit to British officials. His letter sought redress for a long list of grievances. Among the issues were "the quartering of troops on the people in time of peace; ... the enormous extension of the jurisdiction of the Admiralty Courts, in violation of the clause of Magna Charta by which every freeman on trial was entitled to the "judgment of his peers on the law of the land"; ... the threatened bestowal by the king of salaries upon the attorney general, judges, and governor of the Province, thus removing their dependence upon the people."

Adams sent the letter to Franklin, the new agent to England for the province of Massachusetts. Franklin also served as the agent from Pennsylvania. But the deeply devout and Puritanical Sam Adams harbored suspicions about the worldly Franklin, who declared himself "a thorough Deist."[2] Adams knew the story about Franklin advising his father to say grace once for all over the whole barrel of beef in the cellar, and so avoid the necessity of blessing at table over each separate piece. There were political as well as religious differences. Samuel Adams was a radical revolutionary. Franklin, on the other hand, adamantly opposed revolution. He earnestly wanted to keep the whole British Empire together. He often compared it to a magnificent china bowl that would be ruined if a piece were broken out of it. As a Loyalist, he warned Boston against "violent spirits" who favored "a rupture with the mother country."[3] Franklin held the Crown-appointed position of postmaster general. His Loyalist son, William Franklin, was the royal governor of New Jersey.

Thomas Hutchinson, royal governor of Massachusetts, sent a copy of the Assembly's letter to England, naming Samuel Adams as the author and denouncing him as the great incendiary leader. John Adams, like many colonial leaders and unlike Sam, opted to keep mum and mind his own farm and his own business. Ben Franklin opined that Prime Minister North, by rescinding almost all of the Townshend Acts, had already made an ample concession and that America could well afford to pay the small remaining taxes. Sam Adams, however, maintained that the British government was using customs duties as a tool to tighten control on American liberties; that the mechanics of collecting taxes and customs duties allowed Britain to put more and more "Crown appointees on the royal payroll"; and that people growing accustomed to British control was perilous. It was dangerous for Americans to say "it was all right with them if the king paid the governor. Samuel needed a spectacular, emotional issue"[4] to awaken people to the dangers of tyranny. He therefore searched for issues as sharply effective as weapons to put into his revolutionary arsenal.

Mercy Warren fingered the governor. "It was at this time well known," said Mercy, "that Mr. Hutchinson had so far ingratiated himself as to entitle him to peculiar favor from the crown; and by a handsome salary from the king, he was rendered entirely independent of the people." One of the first issues that caught Samuel Adams' attention was judges' salaries. And rumors circulated that judges of the Massachusetts Superior Court, as well as Governor Hutchinson, were on the royal payroll. Adams organized town meetings and rallied orators James Otis and Dr. Joseph Warren—not related to Mercy's husband, Congressman James Warren—as well as radical students, to ask the governor if the rumor was true that judges were paid by the king. Hutchinson replied, in essence, that it was none of their business. Hutchinson, a staunch Loyalist, exhibited deep enmity towards rebel hotheads such as Samuel Adams. Resisting colonial movement toward independence, the governor favored repressive measures to show Parliament's supremacy over the colonies. Mercy Warren noted that Massachusetts governor Hutchinson, a native of Boston, "was the principal author of the sufferings of the unhappy Bostonians, previous to the convulsions which produced the revolution." Warren's contemporaneous history presents a scathing characterization of Hutchinson:

> All who remember his pernicious administration ... agree, that few ages have produced a more fit instrument for the purposes of a corrupt court. He was dark, intriguing, insinuating, haughty and ambitious, while the extreme of avarice marked each feature of his character.... Though bred a merchant, he had looked into the origin and the principles of the British constitution, and made himself acquainted with the several forms of government established in the colonies; he had acquired some knowledge of the common law of England, diligently studied the intricacies of Machiavellian policy, and never failed to recommend the Italian master as a model to his adherents.[5]

When Parliament legislated that the governors and law officers of each colony would be paid by the Crown, independent of colonial assemblies, Hutchinson announced the news to the Massachusetts assembly. The assembly members and colonists viewed Parliament's paying a salary to the governor and judges as bribery. Sam Adams reinforced his *Boston Gazette* articles that were written earlier under his penname Vindex. Later writing under the name Valerius Poplicola, Adams continued to insist that the colonial assembly and not the crown should pay the salaries of the colonial governor and judges. Bostonians who had been indifferent the previous year at a town meeting were now more receptive to the idea of setting up a Committee of Correspondence to promote union among Americans. The *Boston Record* reported: "It was then moved by Mr. Samuel Adams that a Committee of Correspondence be appointed, to ... state the rights of the colonists and ... to communicate and publish the same to several towns and to the world." The motion was debated and carried.

"Perhaps no single step," observed Mercy Warren, "contributed so much to cement the union of the colonies, and the final acquisition of independence, as the establishment of committees of correspondence. This supported a chain of communication from New Hampshire to Georgia, that produced unanimity and energy throughout the continent."[6] The correspondence committees were assigned three duties. One was to draft a statement of the rights of the colonists; this writing was assigned to Samuel Adams. Another was to present a declaration of the infringement and violation of those rights; this list was penned by Dr. Joseph Warren. A third duty was to compose a letter to be sent to towns of the province and to the world; this letter was drafted by Benjamin Church. These reports compiled by the various committees were presented to a town meeting by James Otis. Church, who was a Son of Liberty as well as a member of the provincial Congress, turned out to be a paid spy. Six weeks prior to the Battle of Lexington, Church would send detailed letters to British general Thomas Gage. The letters divulged military and political secrets of American rebel forces, the Sons of Liberty and the Provincial Congress of Massachusetts.

As a founder and member of the committee on colonists' rights, Adams lost no time in writing his famous pamphlet titled *A Report to the Committee of Correspondence to the Boston Town Meeting, Nov. 20, 1772*. This document contained not only Samuel Adams' own *Natural Rights of the Colonists* but also a long list of grievances against the king written by Joseph Warren. Among Warren's grievances was condemnation of Parliament's plan to establish bishops in the colony and their policy of paying salaries of judges and the governor. The tenth entry on the list was the Dockyard Act, which sentenced those accused of vandalizing His Majesty's vessels to be sent to England for trial. This violated the Magna Carta right to a just and fair trial, which, as reinterpreted through the years, came to mean the right to a speedy trial by one's peers.

Samuel Adams' pamphlet was, and remains, "important, not only as a platform upon which were afterwards built many of the celebrated state papers of the Revolution, but as the first fruits of the Committee of Correspondence.... The report was the boldest exposition of the American grievances which had hitherto been made public."[7] Influenced by English philosopher John Locke, Samuel Adams called the first section of his *Rights* pamphlet "The Natural Rights of the Colonists as Men" and opened it with these words: "Among the natural rights of the Colonists are these: First, a right to life; Secondly, to liberty; Thirdly, to property; together with the right to support and defend them in the best manner they can. These are evident branches of ... the duty of self preservation, commonly called the first law of nature." In the remaining two sections Adams addressed "The Natural Rights of the Colonists as Christians and as Subjects." The pamphlet listed colonial grievances and ended with the following words:

> Hitherto, many of the Colonists have been free from quit rents; but if the breath of a British House of Commons can originate an act for taking away all our money, our lands will go next, or be subject to rack rents from haughty and relentless landlords, who will ride at ease, while we are trodden in the dirt. The Colonists have been branded with the odious names of traitors and rebels only for complaining of their grievances. How long such treatment will or ought to be borne is submitted.

Adams' *Rights* pamphlet caused a sensation, both in America and in England. At first it was attributed to Franklin, who had republished it. Within three months, 80 intra-colonial committees sprang up throughout Massachusetts. Almost four years later Thomas Jefferson's Declaration of Independence would draw heavily from Adams' declaration *Rights of the Colonists* and Warren's list of grievances.

When Rhode Islanders faced charges regarding the *Gaspee* Affair they sought the advice of Sam Adams. The incident had occurred on June 9, 1772, when a small revenue cutter, the HMS *Gaspee*, was patrolling the waters off the Rhode Island coast. The cutter carried customs commissioners who seized American vessels, confiscated cargo and caught smugglers. Rhode Islanders sympathized with the smugglers. While chasing a smuggler, the *Gaspee* ran aground. Rhode Island patriots boarded the cutter, captured her officers and crew, dragged them ashore, beat them up, and burned the ship. Local courts failed to prosecute the offenders, who made no effort to hide their identities. England sent a special commission to round up the attackers and ship them to England for trial, although no arrests were ever made. The threat of taking accused miscreants to England became a rallying point: doing so denied the accused their right of being tried by a jury of their peers, which had been a sacred right of English law ever since King John granted that liberty under the Magna Carta in 1215 and upon which the Habeas Corpus Act was based.

On Christmas Day 1772 Rhode Island deputy governor Darius Sessions sent a desperate letter to Samuel Adams seeking his "assistance and advice" on how the colony should respond to King George III's commission of inquiry into the burning of the *Gaspee*. In particular, the Sessions letter asked Adams how to answer the king's demand that involved persons be delivered to the Royal Navy and transported to England for trial and execution. Adams mailed a detailed answer to Sessions on January 2, 1773. He agreed with Hutchinson that someone had been asleep. It was not the British Lion, however but the colonists who had been "too long dozing upon the brink of ruin"; the *Gaspee* Affair should unite the colonies by making them realize that an attack on one colony was an attack on all. Adams' postscript to his January 2, 1773, letter innovatively suggested sending circular letters to communicate with other colonies: "P.S. I beg just to propose for Consideration whether a circular Letr from your Assembly on this Occasion, to those of the other Colonies might not tend to the Advantage of the General Cause & of R Island in particular; I should think it would induce each of them, at least to injoyn their Agents in Great Britain to represent the Severity of your Case in the strongest terms." Circular letters then became a common method of intercolonial communication. Circulated among the colonies, printed in newspapers or posted in public places, these letters served to coordinate action from colony to colony against Great Britain. Adams' postscript regarding expanding the Committees of Correspondence to include all the colonies via circular letters ultimately led to independence.

Women everywhere were concerned about the *Gaspee* Affair. In January 1773 Hannah Winthrop, wife of Dr. Winthrop—professor of mathematics, natural history and astronomy at Cambridge College—wrote to her intimate friend Mercy Warren: " I think one of the most extraordinary political maneuvers this century had produced, is the ministerial mandate to the Newportians for transporting them a thousand leagues for trial. Oh, America! You have reason to tremble and arouse, if we are not able to say to this Royal Vengeance— hitherto shalt thou come and no further: here shall thy proud waves be stayed!"[8]

The *Gaspee* Affair in Rhode Island and the presence of a standing army of redcoats in New York and Massachusetts prompted the Virginia legislature to select eleven members, including Thomas Jefferson and Patrick Henry, to act as a standing committee for *inter*colonial (between the colonies) correspondence. Samuel Adams—having already suggested that Rhode Island might consider formally objecting to the proceedings of the royal commission of inquiry—wrote to House of Burgesses member Richard Henry Lee of Virginia about the *Gaspee* Affair. Lee then advocated for the formation of intercolonial Committees of Correspondence, which the burgesses implemented on March 12, 1773. Thus Lee is credited with conceiving the idea. Rhode Island was the first colony to follow suit. Samuel Adams, Boston representative in the Massachusetts general court (Legislature), warmly welcomed the idea and said so in a letter to R.H. Lee.

"In spite of the Boston 'massacre,' the violence on the high seas, and the commercial squabbles, the agitations of Adams and his friends were beginning to peter out, when Lord North committed a fatal blunder": Parliament's 1773 Tea Act, which "legalized a new arrangement designed to relieve the British East India Company from the results of its own inefficiency."[9] It authorized the East India Company to ship vast amounts of surplus tea directly to the colonies. British tea agents could sell the tea directly to the consumer in America without paying import duties. Lord North's Tea Act "succeeded where Adams had failed: it united colonial opinion against the British."[10]

Nathaniel Hawthorne, in his *Grandfather's Chair* (historical nonfiction for children) expresses the view of many when he makes his character Clara say, "How odd it is that the liberties of America should have had anything to do with a cup of tea!" One explanation might start with the knowledge that taxes had been repeatedly enacted forcing the colonies to pay for the French and Indian War. Taxes also were repeatedly repealed at the insistence of British merchants and manufacturers whose businesses were hurt by the acts. Only one Townshend Act remained: the tax on tea. Between 1768 and 1773, the 13 colonies had imported and paid duty on two million pounds of tea. During the same period, many Americans evaded the expensive tea by buying less costly tea from Dutch smugglers. Thus 17 million pounds of unsold tea piled up in storehouses of Britain's East India Trading Company. The company, whose charter was granted in the 1600s by Queen Elizabeth I, was a monopolistic stock company comprising a group of London merchants and financiers for the exploitation of trade with East and Southeast Asia and India.

The 1773 Tea Act was passed by Prime Minister North's administration to help merchants of the nearly bankrupt British East India Company sell tea. The act also allowed Americans to buy tea more cheaply. This act imposed no new tax but merely kept in place the old Townshend Tea Tax and also granted the company a monopoly on the sale of tea to the colonies. It allowed Britain's India Tea Company to select a group of agents, cut out the middlemen, undersell smugglers and market tea directly to the colonists. The Tea Tax was small, but by keeping it in place Parliament retested Britain's right to levy taxes and raise revenue without colonial approval. The danger of this monopoly aroused resentment in the colonies because the Magna Carta stated that no taxes could be levied without the general consent of the realm.

Radicals in America turned the growing issue of monopoly—along with that of taxation without representation—into another musket ball to stuff into their arsenal of revolution. They began composing articles and poems about the illegal monopoly. When East India Company ships carrying half a million pounds of tea began to arrive at colonial ports in Charlestown, Philadelphia, New York, and Boston colonists refused to buy it. At Charlestown, South Carolina, the tea was unloaded into government warehouses, where it lay rotting until after the Revolution. At Philadelphia and New York, the ships were turned back before they entered port. But in Boston, first the ship *Dartmouth* and then two others laden with tea, most of which was Bohea black tea from China, sailed into harbor. On

December 5, 1773, Abigail Adams, John's wife, wrote to her friend Mercy Warren, the famed American author and sister of the firebrand James Otis. The strong, open and warm friendship between Abigail and Mercy stemmed from childhood and continued "through the vicissitudes of a long life." Abigail told Mercy, "The tea, that baneful weed, is arrived in Boston: Great, and I hope effectual opposition, has been made to the landing."[11]

The arrival of the tea registered waves of anger in the watchful eyes of the Sons of Liberty. "The town" said Governor Hutchinson, "is as furious as it was in the time of the Stamp Act."[12] In an attempt to prevent the unloading of the offensive cargo, Samuel Adams, John Hancock, Joseph Warren, Paul Revere and other leaders of the Sons of Liberty organized the Boston Tea Party. A secret meeting place for the Boston Sons was the Green Dragon Tavern, sometimes called the "headquarters of the American Revolution." Here the Boston Committee of Correspondence was formed; and here the North End Caucus organized the guard that saw to it that no tea ships were unloaded. Senior Grand Deacon of the Grand Lodge, Brother Paul Revere, was part of that guard. Revere also belonged to a guard called the Selectmen, who met at the Green Dragon Tavern. Taking an oath of secrecy on the Bible, Selectmen walked the streets of Boston, watched the movement of British troops and informed the Massachusetts Committee of Safety of any unusual activity. Minuteman Paul Revere would be alerted to the British move toward Lexington that spurred his famous midnight ride. A typical minuteman pledged to take up arms at a minute's notice. In some colonies he trained for two weeks and then met every two weeks for drill and instructions. Joseph "Warren and Revere met at the Green Dragon Tavern with the North End Caucus that sang the 'Rally Mohawks' song." The song tells that Warren and Revere were there, but it does not say who the "Chiefs" were. Nor does it say who the "Mohawks were."[13]

> Rally, Mohawks—bring out your axes!
> And tell King George we'll pay no taxes
> on his foreign tea!
> His threats are vain—and vain to think
> To force our girls and wives to drink
> His vile Bohea!
> Then rally boys, and hasten on
> To meet our Chiefs at the Green Dragon.
> Our Warren's there, and bold Revere,
> With hands to do and words to cheer....

Two Boston folkmoots resolved that the ships must return to England without the colonists paying duty. Samuel Adams and the Sons refused to acknowledge Parliament's right to tax colonists and refused to endorse the East Indian Tea Company's monopoly. When Samuel Adams' bitter enemy Governor Hutchinson refused to grant the request for the ships' return, "Adams arose from the mass meeting of Committees of Correspondence which he called ... and said: 'This meeting can do nothing further to save the country.'[14] Instantly the Sons of Liberty left the meeting."

Mercy Warren wrote that within an hour, on the evening of December 16, 1773, "A group of people clad like the aborigines of the wilderness, with tomahawks in their hands, and clubs on their shoulders, who without the least molestation marched through the streets with silent solemnity, and amidst innumerable spectators, proceeded to the wharves, boarded the ships, demanded the keys, and with much deliberation knocked open the chests, and emptied several thousand weight of the finest teas into the ocean."[15] Hannah Winthrop wrote to her friend Mercy Warren about the Tea Party: "We hope to see good accounts of the tea cast away on the Cape. The union of the Colonies, the firm and sedate resolution of the people, is an omen for good unto us. And be it known unto Britain, even American daughters are politicians and patriots, and will aid the good work with their female efforts."[16] Occurring three years after the Boston Massacre, the Boston Tea Party was the first openly rebellious act of the colonies against Britain in the American Revolution. In April 1774 a similar action occurred in New York. The great importance of the Tea Party and the Sons of Liberty masquerade was that "it goaded John Bull (Englishmen) into a showdown, which was exactly what Sam Adams and other radicals wanted."[17]

In reaction to the Boston Tea Party the king relieved Hutchinson as governor of Massachusetts and Parliament sent General Gage to succeed him. Gage was to command all of His Majesty's forces in North America and reduce the country to submission. He would also act as governor and commander in chief of the province of Massachusetts Bay. When he arrived in May 1774, Bostonians entertained Gage elegantly at Faneuil Hall. His first act of authority was to read a list of 28 counselors who had been unanimously elected by representatives of the people. He then erased 13, "leaving only a quorum as established by charter." Among those eliminated were James Otis and John Adams. "These gentlemen," wrote Mercy, "had been undoubtedly pointed out as obnoxious to administration by the predecessor of governor Gage."

Parliament soon passed the Coercive Acts. The colonists called them "Intolerable Acts." Designed to punish the defiant Bostonians, one of the acts closed the port of Boston. Most of the other acts also applied to Massachusetts. Only one applied to all the colonies: The Quartering Act demanded that British troops be quartered throughout the land to preserve order. The new Quartering Act of June 2, 1774, states, "[I]t shall ... be lawful for the governor of the province to order ... uninhabited houses, outhouses, barns, or other buildings as he shall think necessary to be taken ... and make fit for the reception of such officers and soldiers, and to ... quarter such officers and soldiers therein for such time as he shall think proper."[18] "The Coercive Acts accomplished what years of rhetoric and circulations by committees of correspondence had failed to bring about—union of the Thirteen Colonies."[19]

Lord North had been responsible for the East India Tea Act, which occasioned the Tea Party and precipitated the Revolution. He was also responsible for the Coercive Acts, which triggered the Revolutionary War itself. George III endorsed the Coercive Acts. Until the Boston Tea Party, the king supported a more conciliatory approach than did his ministers. After the Tea Party, however, George tightened his policy. He believed that the earlier concession of repealing the Stamp Act was too lenient and would be seen by the colonists as a sign of indulgence and weakness and would encourage further demands. He decided that crushing the rebellion was essential for maintaining order and upholding the supreme authority of Parliament. He then adhered to the earlier advice of his mother. When he came to the throne his mother, Augusta of Saxe-Gotha, namesake of Augusta Georgia, had said to him, "George, be king!" She undoubtedly referred to the powerful influence of "Prime Minister" Sir Robert Walpole during previous reigns. She meant that he should "rule forcefully." And so he did—after the Tea Party—with little compassion for colonials. George III ruled by statecraft, which meant gathering about him a group of "King's Friends" to whom he extended personal favors and thus manipulated Parliament. Facing the growing hostility from Americans over taxation, King George III "took a hard line, opposing moderates who urged conciliation; George's intransigence was a major factor in the outbreak of the Revolutionary War."[20]

Leading Virginians feared that the far-reaching effects of closing Boston harbor and the quartering of British soldiers posed a threat to the rights and liberties of all American colonists. The Virginia House of Burgesses called for a day of fasting and prayer on May 24, 1774. Two days later Virginia's governor, Dunmore, dissolved the assembly. The burgesses, however, continued to meet in Williamsburg at the Raleigh Tavern. There they resolved that "an attack made on one of our sister colonies is an attack made on all British America, and threatens ruin to the rights of all."[21] The burgesses, now acting as Virginia's legislative body, urged cooperation of all the Committees of Correspondence to exchange views and then send delegates to a Continental Congress. Virginians soon learned that Massachusetts and other colonies also favored forming a Continental Congress to discuss how the colonies would respond to Britain's Intolerable Acts.

3

Siege of Boston and the Canada Campaign

> America stands armed with resolution and virtue; but still recoils at the idea of drawing the sword against a nation from whence she derived her origin.
> —Mercy Warren

> The war is inevitable—and let it come!
> —Patrick Henry

Samuel Adams' Committees of Correspondence wasted no time. When Parliament and the king closed Boston Harbor as punishment for the Tea Party, other colonies sent supplies, food, and money to the blockaded countryside to aid their sister colony. Discovering that all 13 colonies empathized with Boston, the tall, slender, and mild-mannered Thomas Gage, the royal governor of Massachusetts, vacillated. A popular man of great integrity, Gage proposed that Parliament suspend the Coercive Acts. As military general of British troops in America, Gage despaired of solving the problem militarily without doubling the number of British troops in Boston. The next year the British government, tiring of Gage's equivocation on military decisions and thinking him tentative and weak, began to turn against him.

Just as Benjamin Franklin had predicted, the colonies were now organizing for their own defense—exactly what the British government had feared 20 years earlier. Before the French and Indian War Britain had decided that if colonial assemblies were allowed to unite and coordinate their own defense, then the colonies would become "too military, and feel their own strength."[1] Stronger colonies would weaken their ties with England and undermine England's ability to successfully tax Americans. When militiamen formed a human wall around Boston the crown governors, one by one, began to dissolve colonial assemblies. The king and Parliament were pushing the colonies too hard; Americans fought back, first with oratory, then with a bloodless insurrection, and ultimately with war.

Protesting the Coercive [Intolerable] Acts, Committees of Correspondence in Virginia and Massachusetts distributed letters and pamphlets throughout the colonies. They urged all to establish provincial congresses or other transitional governments, to elect delegates to meet in Philadelphia and form the First Continental Congress, forerunner of today's United States Congress, to undo the Intolerable Acts. North Carolina's first provincial Congress convened in August 1774 in New Bern. It was their first meeting held without the royal governor's permission. Like other colonies, North Carolina's provincial Congress protested taxation, the Boston Port Bill, and the sending of individuals to England for trial.

The convention also elected delegates to the Continental Congress and planned to organize Committees of Safety. Two to seven delegates from each colony, depending on the colony's population, were elected by the people via provincial congresses, colonial legislatures or correspondence committees. Twelve colonies—all except Georgia—sent delegates.

One of the Intolerable Acts, the Quartering Act, forced the unwilling colonists to provide lodging, food and supplies for British troops. These very same redcoats watched silently, without intervening, while the excited Bostonians gathered, cheered, and applauded the delegates on their way to meet in Philadelphia. The delegates were on their way to attend the seven-week (September 5 to October 26, 1774) First Continental Congress, which had been formed to unite the colonies.

Samuel Adams led the Massachusetts delegation. The usually plainly dressed and virtually impoverished Adams was sporting a new wig, red jacket, silk stockings, gold knee buckles, and silver shoe buckles. The Sons of Liberty had presented Adams not only with a little pocket money but also with the fine and fancy attire for him to wear to the First Continental Congress. Samuel Adams was nearly 60 when he left Boston to take his seat in Congress. "His morals" said his contemporary Benjamin Rush, "were irreproachable, and even ambition and avarice, the usual vices of politicians, seemed to have no place in his breast."[2]

Congressmen would decide how to deal with the Intolerable Acts, especially the Boston Port Act. They intended to stop Parliament from further infringing on the rights and liberties of Americans. The delegates spoke and acted for the people and became the federal government of a nation at war. The 55 delegates met at Philadelphia's Carpenters' Hall, which was built and owned by a group of master builders known as the Carpenters' Company. The hall rather than the state house (now Independence Hall) was chosen as a meeting place because it was more politically neutral. The delegates represented the gamut of public opinion, ranging from those such as George Washington, who favored reconciliation, to revolutionaries such as Patrick Henry, who demanded parliamentary change, to flaming radicals such as Samuel Adams, who actively sought independence. Peyton Randolph of Virginia was unanimously elected as its president and Charles Thomson of Pennsylvania as secretary. Randolph set the tone of the meeting with the refrain "I am not a Virginian, but an American."[3] A 38-year-old Virginia lawyer, Patrick Henry, picked up the tenor: "The distinctions between Pennsylvanians, New Yorkers and New Englanders are no more. I am not a Virginian, but an American." His fellow congressmen responded enthusiastically to Henry's opening except there were objections when he suggested that the number of votes allowed each colony should reflect a percentage of that colony's population. After debate, it was decided, for the sake of unity—since the smaller colonies disagreed with Henry's proposal—that each colony would cast one vote regardless of the size of its population. Throughout the debates the taciturn George Washington, a stony-faced delegate from Virginia, was a "masterful listener." His calm demeanor "could inspire confidence and serve as a unifying figure."[4]

A week after the First Continental Congress began, Bostonian Paul Revere galloped into Philadelphia. Hitching his horse at City Tavern, he unbuckled his saddlebag and brought out a document destined to make waves. The document was the Suffolk Resolves, which had been agreed to by "delegates of every town & district in the county of Suffolk," Massachusetts, and recorded by Dr. Joseph Warren. It was presented to Congress as a proposal. One article of the resolves recommended that citizens organize a Patriot militia and arm themselves. Another imposed economic sanctions: "Until our rights are fully restored to us, we will ... withhold all commercial intercourse with Great Britain, Ireland and the West Indies."[5]

The Suffolk Resolves was the first proposal to be ratified by Congress. It triggered an angry response from the king, who addressed Parliament and declared the colony of Massachusetts to be in a state of rebellion. Abigail Adams' letter of February 3, 1775, said to her friend Mercy Otis Warren, "The die is cast." The Suffolk Resolves led to the adoption of the 14 Articles of Association, often abbreviated as "the Association." With only a few exceptions the Association banned trade with Great Britain if the Coercive Acts were not repealed. The first few Articles of Association called for nonimportation, nonexportation and nonconsumption. Designed to put economic pressure on Parliament, this boycott demonstrated the anger of the colonies against Parliament and the king. Congress called for setting up Committees of Safety in every town and county throughout the colonies to enforce the prohibition.

In those 18th-century days when it was unusual for women to be attuned to affairs outside their home Mercy Warren wrote to the celebrated English historian-philosopher Catherine Macaulay in December 1774. Telling her about the closing of the port of Boston, the Coercive Acts and the First Continental Congress, Mercy wrote, "America stands armed with resolution and virtue; but still recoils at the idea of drawing the sword against a nation from whence she derived her origin. Yet Britain, like an unnatural parent, is ready to plunge her dagger into the bosom of her affectionate offspring."

In 1775 Pennsylvania, Massachusetts, Maryland and North Carolina organized Committees of Safety. These were private, paramilitary, guerrilla-type groups. North Carolina met in Hillsborough and placed Committees of Safety throughout the state: "With them rested the real executive power of the state.... They held a strict police and rigid censorship over their respective counties, and did not hesitate to put in jail, or to the whipping-post, all persons convicted of disrespectful language toward the cause of America. They executed all orders of the Continental Congress, the Provincial Council and the District Committees of Safety."[6]

When the royal governor of South Carolina, William Bull II, dissolved that colony's House of Commons for sending five delegates to the First Continental Congress, the old assembly simply reorganized as an extralegal provincial Congress. It began working through its Committees of Safety. The committees sent three Whig preachers to whip up compliance with the Articles of Association, the trade restrictions and the self-denial policy that the Association suggested. The religious leaders—the Reverend William Tennent, a Charlestown Presbyterian minister; the Reverend Oliver Hart, a South Carolina Baptist minister; and the Honorable William Henry Drayton, an Anglican lay minister—were accompanied by two German-speaking assistants. Blending politics with religion, this itinerant preaching trio stumped separately through the backcountry. Delivering nearly 30 sermons, they influenced Loyalists and independents alike to support the Patriot cause. Penelope Barker organized a boycott—a no-tea party. Unusual for its day, it was a women's political action group asserting, "We women have taken too long to let our voices be heard. We are signing our names to a document not hiding ourselves behind costumes like the men in Boston did at their tea party" (Penelope Barker 1774).[7]

In October 1774, the same month the First Continental Congress adjourned, 51 ladies of Edenton in the Albemarle-Pamlico Sound region of North Carolina signed a pledge to stop serving and drinking East India tea. Penelope Barker gathered the ladies at the home of Mrs. Elizabeth King to protest the Intolerable Acts and support the nonconsumption clause of the Articles of Association. By attending the party and boycotting tea, the women supported Bostonians denouncing taxation without representation. The *Morning Chronicle and London Advertiser* published this contemporaneous account of the Edenton Tea Party:

> Extract of a letter from North Carolina, Oct. 27 ... The Provincial Deputies of North Carolina having resolved not to drink any more tea, nor wear any more British cloth, &c. many ladies of this Province have determined to give a memorable proof of their patriotism, and have accordingly entered into the following honourable and spirited association. I send it to you, to shew your fair countrywomen, how zealously and faithfully American ladies follow the laudable example of their husbands, and what opposition your Ministers may expect to receive from a people thus firmly united against them.[8]

Women of Charlestown renounced the "baneful herb" and resolved to promote the boycott among their townswomen. Ladies throughout the land were inspired to discuss politics and disprove the conventional notion that females lacked political consciousness. "Women of Wilmington 'burnt their tea in a solemn procession' through the streets of their community."[9]

When Congress passed the Articles of Association, Prime Minister North realized that the rebellion in America was not limited to Massachusetts. He and Lord Dartmouth, secretary of state for the American colonies, then began leaning toward conciliation and a negotiated settlement with America. Other cabinet members and George III stood firmly in favor of coercion. North was criticized for wavering between coercion and conciliation. He hated confrontation but he wanted to maintain the right of Britain to tax America. The Intolerable (Coercive) Acts caused Prime Minister North to be despised in America. The closure of the Boston Port was called "Lord North's Act." He was blamed for blocking ships and for the inconvenience of moving goods by road, which became known as "Lord North's Road." Even a wagon wheel falling into a rut elicited the expletive "damn Lord North."[10]

In December 1774 Maryland was the first colony to approve the Articles of Association. A month later, Fincastle County on the western frontier was the first county in Virginia to endorse the Association. Fincastle's freeholders appointed a committee of safety just as Congress had suggested. The 15-member committee, which included militiamen—veterans of the 1774 Lord Dunmore's War against Shawnee Alliance on the Virginia-Indian border—drafted the Fincastle Resolutions. The Resolutions were then sent to the Virginia delegates of the Continental Congress, who would reconvene as the Second Continental Congress in Philadelphia in May. The Fincastle committee resolved:

> We heartily concur in your resolutions, and shall, in every instance, strictly and invariably adhere thereto.... We by no means desire to shake off our duty or allegiance to our lawful sovereign, but to the contrary ... if no pacifick measures shall be proposed or adopted by Great Britain, and our enemies will attempt to dragoon us out of those inestimable privileges, which we are entitled to as subjects, and to reduce us to a state of slavery, we declare that we are deliberately and resolutely determined never to surrender them to any power upon earth but at the expense of our lives.[11]

In February 1775 Parliament declared not just Massachusetts but all the colonies to be in a state of rebellion. In March delegates of the Second Virginia Convention met at Richmond and passed resolutions preparing the colonies for military action. Patrick Henry, who had railed against the Stamp Act more than ten years earlier in his daring "Treason Speech," spoke out again. This time he denounced the Intolerable Acts with his famous "give me liberty or give me death" speech, ending with these words:

> There is no retreat but in submission and slavery! Our chains are forged! Their clanking may be heard on the plains of Boston! The war is inevitable—and let it come! I repeat it, sir, let it come. It is in vain, sir, to extenuate the matter. Gentlemen may cry, Peace, Peace—but there is no peace. The war is actually begun! The next gale that sweeps from the north will bring to our ears the clash of resounding arms! Our brethren are already in the field! Why stand we here idle? What is it that gentlemen wish? What would they have? Is life so dear, or peace so sweet, as to be purchased at the price of chains and slavery? Forbid it, Almighty God! I know not what course others may take; but as for me, give me liberty or give me death![12]

Ralph Waldo Emerson's poem *Concord Hymn* summarized the coming events when he wrote that the Coercive Acts led to a "rude bridge that arched the flood" where "the embattled farmers stood and fired the shot heard round the world."

General Thomas Gage, governor of Massachusetts and commander in chief of the British Army in America, tried in vain to enforce British martial law throughout the colony. His 4,000 troops succeeded only in controlling the city of Boston. In areas surrounding Boston, Committees of Safety rallied 10,000 Patriot militiamen who began drilling, gathering arms, and stocking warehouses with gunpowder and ammunition. Twenty miles from Boston the Massachusetts assembly, which Parliament had declared illegal, was in session at the village of Concord. Gage ordered British troops to seize the ammunition from the stores at Concord and arrest the radical rabble-rousers Sam Adams and John Hancock.[13] The Sons of Liberty Selectmen, surveilling the streets of Boston, suspected the British plot.

The Sons placed two signal lanterns in the bell tower of Christ Church in Boston to warn Charlestown citizens that boatloads of British soldiers were crossing the Charles River on their way to seize the weapons at Concord. Dr. Joseph Warren, recorder of the Suffolk Resolves, sent express messenger Paul Revere to Lexington—11 miles from Boston—to inform Sam Adams and John Hancock that "the Regulars" were coming to arrest them. "On the eighteenth of April, in Seventy-five; Hardly a man is now alive, Who remembers that famous day and year," the poet Longfellow noted. Revere was joined by other riders, William Dawes and Dr. Samuel Prescott, to warn local minutemen. The next day, April 19, 1775, seventy-seven local minutemen gathered at Lexington and formed a human chain across the road to Concord. As the red-coated British regulars approached, one of their officers shouted, "Disperse, rebels! Lay down your arms and disperse." The provincial minutemen stood their ground. A musket ball whizzed past. Who actually fired it? Nobody knows. An answering volley killed eight colonists and wounded ten.

The shot metaphorically "heard 'round the world" was actually heard by Sam Adams and John Hancock. Hancock was the president of the extralegal Massachusetts General Court, which was meeting at nearby Concord. Hearing the volley Sam Adams "exclaimed … 'This is a glorious day for America!' It was what he had been working toward for years—a bloody clash that would bring on independence."[14] Forewarned by minutemen Dawes and Prescott—who were arrested by the British patrol and escaped—the citizens of Concord were able to stash away most of their stores before the British swarmed in and destroyed the remaining gun carriages, tools, and flour. Patriot militiamen on guard at Concord's North Bridge inflicted several casualties, causing the advancing British to reverse their direction and withdraw to Boston. Farmers shooting from behind barns and trees sniped at the retreating redcoats. The Americans lost 95 men; the British lost 273.

Recording her eyewitness account of the "horrors of that midnight cry, preceding the bloody massacre at Lexington," Hannah Winthrop wrote to Mercy Warren:

> We were roused from ... slumber ... by the beat of drum and ringing of bells, with the dire alarm that a thousand of the troops of George the Third had gone forth to murder the peaceful inhabitants of the surrounding villages ... the platoon firing assuring us that the rising sun must witness the bloody carnage. Not knowing what the event would be at Cambridge ... it seemed necessary to retire to some place of safety.... We were directed to a place called Fresh-pond ... but what a distressed house did we find it, filled with women whose husbands had gone forth to meet the assailants, seventy or eighty of these (with numberless infant children,) weeping and agonizing for the fate of their husbands ... [and] thus we began our pilgrimage, alternately walking and riding, the roads filled with frighted women and children: some in carts with their tattered furniture, others on foot fleeing into the woods ... passing through the bloody field at Monotong, which was strewed with mangled bodies. We met an affectionate father with a cart, looking for his murdered son, and picking up his neighbors who had fallen in battle, in order for their burial.[15]

The Provincial Congress of Massachusetts, even as the battles of Lexington and Concord were being fought, organized an army and appropriated the money to pay for it. In April 1775 ten thousand militiamen from Massachusetts picked up their muskets and converged at Boston for the eleven-month siege. Committees of Safety sent out circulars. Post rider Israel Bissell carried the alarm to Connecticut, asking all citizens along the way to supply him with fresh horses as needed. Riding almost nonstop for more than four days—"covering 345 miles" throughout the colonies from Watertown, Massachusetts, through Connecticut, New York, and New Jersey, to the Philadelphia city hall—Bissell cried the alarm: "To arms, to arms! The war has begun!"[16] Other couriers carried the rallying cry to New Haven, western Massachusetts, the Hudson Valley and the Hampton Grants. Even before the provincial legislatures or the Committees of Safety had acted, the army outside Boston had grown by thousands. "Everywhere the news of Lexington and Concord strengthened the hands and fired the hearts of the Patriots."[17] Responding to the Lexington alarm, 4,000 Connecticut militia began marching to Boston.

Mary Draper wasted no time in exemplifying the zealous patriotism of New England women when she heard of the bloodshed at Lexington. She responded quickly to the call to arms by helping her husband, militia captain Draper, hurry to Boston to fight for his country. She then strapped a knapsack and blanket on the back of her only son and exhorted the 16-year-old to do his duty. Mary said to her daughter, "Kate, you and I also have service to do.... Before tomorrow night, hundreds, I hope thousands, will be on their way to join the Continental forces.... You and I with Molly [the domestic] must feed as many as we can."[18] The prosperous Draper farm at Dedham, Massachusetts, had always been a haven for the destitute. The farm's granaries were overflowing and milk from the dairy was plentiful. In this time of crisis, the women kept the oversized ovens going full blast night and day. They kneaded dough in long wooden troughs to bake brown bread to feed the army of volunteers who trudged by on their way to Boston. Kate and Mary Draper and Molly, assisted by a disabled veteran of the French and Indian War, erected roadside tables. Tubs of cider from the cellar and heaping pans of bread and cheese refreshed the weary patriots. When supplies ran low, Mary solicited the aid of neighbors.

In the small town of Pepperell, Massachusetts, on the Nashua River, lived a Whig housewife, Prudence Wright, with her husband, minuteman David Wright, and their six children. On April 18, 1775—when David learned that Paul Revere and other alarm riders were racing through the countryside warning Sam Adams, John Hancock and all residents that the Concord arsenal was targeted for British attack—David rallied. He quickly marched with his unit toward the scene of action. Soon after the attack at Lexington, Prudence visited her widowed mother at Hollis. While there, she overheard her two brothers talking with their friend Leonard Whiting. She suspected all three of being Tories. They were speaking of spies who were coming down from Canada to deliver valuable information to the British troops in Boston. Leonard was planning to meet with English forces and guide them a few miles south to the town of Groton.

Alarmed by the news, Prudence was aware that the spies from Canada on their way to Groton and Boston would need to pass through Pepperell. She also knew the perfect place to block their plan was at the Pepperell covered bridge—the Jewett Bridge—across the Nashua River. When she returned to Pepperell, she quickly spread the news among her female friends. These Patriot women were already spinning their own yarn, weaving their own cloth and boycotting British tea. Forty of the friends met, chose Prudence as their captain and quickly changed into their husbands' and brothers' clothing. Masquerading as men and armed with guns and pitchforks, "Mrs. David Wright's Guard" proceeded to the Jewett Bridge. Through the dark of night they were hidden by a curve in the road near the bridge. They were determined to let no one pass over the bridge without being unhorsed and searched. One of the riders forced to dismount was her brothers' friend, Captain Leonard Whiting. A historical marker placed by the Pepperell Historical Commission reads:

> Near this spot a party of patriotic women under the leadership of Mrs. David Wright of Pepperell in April 1775 captured Leonard Whiting, a Tory who was carrying treasonable dispatches to the enemy at Boston. He was taken a prisoner to Groton and the Dispatches were sent to the committee of safety at Cambridge.[19]

Colonel Israel Putnam—a weather-beaten, poorly educated farmer so suspicious that he "always slept with one eye open"[20]—belonged to the Connecticut Sons of Liberty. He was plowing his fields the morning after the fight at Concord when a drum-beating messenger on horseback sounded the alarm. Putnam, who soon became General Putnam, unhitched his plough, took up arms, mounted his horse, and sent his boy home to tell the wife where he was going. "Old Put—with flowing gray locks and head like a canon ball ... who spoke with a lisp ... could barely write his name ... and ... feared nothing"[21]—mustered the militia. After choosing him as their leader the men immediately followed him 100 miles to Cambridge. The militiamen organized on their way to Boston. Putnam and Joseph Spencer headed Connecticut troops; Nathanael Greene commanded Rhode Islanders.

When the news reached John Stark, leader of the New Hampshire men, he was "sawing pine logs without a coat; he shut down the gate of his mill, and commenced the journey to Boston in his shirt-sleeves."[22] All the militia leaders from surrounding colonies agreed to recognize Massachusetts militia leader Artemas Ward as their commander in chief. Soon, 30,000 militiamen from the New England colonies converged and joined the farmers who were shooting at the retreating redcoats. Establishing a blockade, they surrounded Boston. The 20-mile-long human line stretched from Mystic River to the town of Roxbury. These militiamen would become the core of the Continental Army, which would be created two months later, on June 14, 1775.

Plying the seas along the New England coastline during the Siege of Boston, two American merchant ships, the *Unity* and the *Polly*, escorted by an armed British schooner, *Margaretta*, sailed into the harbor at Machias, Maine. The merchant vessels were laden with long-awaited supplies from Boston. The *Margaretta*'s captain demanded that the materials carried by the merchantmen be exchanged for lumber, which would be shipped back to Boston and used to build barracks to quarter British soldiers. He required the citizens of Machias to sign a petition promising to protect British property. Determined not to support the quartering of British troops, the people of Machias made plans to capture the officers of the escort ship when its crew left church. While the Loyalists knelt in prayer, people of Machias secretly unloaded supplies from the cargo ships. The British mates and officers, however, eluded their would-be captors and set sail on the *Margaretta*. A sea chase followed. On June 12, 1775, forty Patriot privateers armed with any weapons they could find, including pitchforks, boarded the *Unity* and set out in pursuit of the *Margaretta*. The *Unity* rammed the *Margaretta*. The *Unity*'s crew climbed aboard the *Margaretta*, slew her British captain, and won the first naval battle of the rebellion. The Battle of Machias started the tradition of recruiting merchant vessels for wartime service. Merchant ships and privateers were attracted to sea by bulletins. This one was excerpted from a Boston newspaper:

> An Invitation to all brave Seamen and Marines,
> The grand Privateer ship DEANE ... will Sail on a Cruise against the Enemies of the United States of America.... This therefore is to invite all those Jolly Fellows, who love their country, and want to make their fortunes at one Stroke, to repair immediately to the Rendezvous at the Head of His Excellency Governor Hancock's Wharf, where they will be received with a hearty Welcome by a Number of Brave Fellows there assembled, and treated with that excellent Liquor call'd GROG which is allow'd by all true Seamen, to be the LIQUOR OF LIFE.[23]

In the wake of the Battle of Machias, the U.S. Navy was born, on October 13, 1775, when the Second Continental Congress authorized the "procurement of two armed vessels ... to cruise in search of munitions ships supplying the British arms to America."[24] Congress created the U.S. Marine Corps one month later by resolving to raise two battalions of Continental Marines.

The rifle shots at Lexington and the gathering of Patriots for the Siege of Boston prompted Benedict Arnold, a Connecticut militia captain, to request permission to attack Fort Ticonderoga and secure its impressive store of weapons. Two governing bodies, the Connecticut Committee of Correspondence and the Massachusetts Committee of Safety, commissioned Arnold as a colonel, issued an order to muster 400 men, and financed his campaign. When Arnold learned that Ethan Allen also planned to attack Ticonderoga, the two joined forces. Allen was elected as a colonel by his militia unit, known as the Green Mountain Boys from New Hampshire Grants (now Vermont). Known as the "Gibraltar of America," Fort Ticonderoga was in disrepair but strategically located inland on a water route linking New York to Canada. On May 10, 1775, Allen and Arnold surprised its sleeping British garrison and easily captured the cannons and artillery that would become the backbone of the American arsenal.

Many members of the newly formed Congress were dismayed by Allen's and Arnold's seizure of two British forts in New York on Lake Champlain: Ticonderoga and, two days later, Crown Point. Conservatives had wanted to give the appearance of acting only on the defensive. Seizure of these forts meant that America was now on the offensive. But if these strongholds could be held they would block the logical invasion route of the British moving from Canada down the Hudson River to New York City.

Meanwhile, in Massachusetts, the redcoats, having dodged the gunfire of angry farmers on the road from Concord, returned to Boston, where they continued to enforce British closure of the port. Hot on their trail was a long line of New England farmers and merchants who surrounded the city. They "hemmed in Gage and the only British force on the Continent"[25] and confined them to the city of Boston. Gage played a dual role as governor of Massachusetts and commander in chief of the British Army in America.

Gage's reinforcement came on May 25, 1775, when three British major generals—William Howe, Henry Clinton and John Burgoyne—sailed into Boston Harbor aboard the HMS *Cerberus*, named for the three-headed watchdog of Greek mythology. The three had been selected by George III and Parliament as the best men in the British Army to support General Gage in crushing the rebellion in America. Bostonian Patriots greeted the ship with much doggerel. One "mocked the three new generals as mere pups"[26]: "Behold the *Cerberus* the Atlantic plough,/Her precious cargo, Burgoyne, Clinton, Howe/Bow, wow, wow." Not only was the fate of the *Cerberus* doomed, but also each of the three military dogs of war would hold senior command. Each, successively, was blamed for the British loss in America and each was recalled to England in disgrace.

Howe supervised the landing of 3,000 British regulars. Within a short time, the *Cerberus* and her reinforcement troops were followed by several regiments from Ireland, bringing the number of British soldiers garrisoned in Boston (and at Charlestown, Massachusetts) to 10,000. Faced with growing anti–British sentiment, the British planned to expand their Boston stronghold. First, they intended to capture Charlestown Peninsula with its two high hills, Bunker and Breed, overlooking Boston Harbor. Next, they hoped to seize the Boston Peninsula's Dorchester Heights with its commanding view of the harbor and downtown Boston. Securing these positions, plus the Charlestown and Boston necks, which were the only means of land access to the two peninsulas, would prevent colonial forces from climbing the hills and leveling artillery fire at both the harbor and the city where the British army was stationed.

Gage offered a pardon written by the playwright General John Burgoyne to all provincials who would lay down their arms. The governor, however, did not offer pardons to Samuel Adams and John Hancock, whose treachery against the Crown was too villainous to be forgiven. Instead of accepting the pardons and laying down their arms, the Massachusetts Committee of Safety went on the offensive. When the committee received intelligence that the British intended to fortify Bunker Hill, it instructed General Artemas Ward to foil the British plan. Ward sent Colonel William Prescott of Massachusetts to capture and fortify Bunker Hill.

Fifty-seven-year-old Israel Putnam, working under Prescott, became one of four commanders of a detachment of provincial militia—1,000 untrained farmers from New Hampshire, Rhode Island, Connecticut, and Massachusetts—who silently moved east from Cambridge under orders to set up an entrenchment on lofty Bunker Hill. The officers discussed whether to fortify Bunker Hill or Breed's Hill, which was closer to the British ships in the harbor. In the dark of night the detachment passed the British Army unobserved. Their wagons—carrying the building materials for the main fortification—bypassed the 110-foot-high Bunker Hill and continued to Breed's Hill, a smaller mound much closer to

Boston and the British. Laboring with great zeal and purpose, the force began throwing up a redoubt and digging an entrenchment.

At 4:00 A.M. a ship's captain in the Boston harbor noticed the flurry of activity on the hill and fired a series of cannonballs toward the construction site. Awakened by the boom of cannon, townspeople and English troops lit candles, threw open their shutters and watched in wonder to see the fortification magically appearing above the city. By dawn, militiamen had completed their work. Every housetop, church spire, and hill in Boston was crowded with people waiting for the showdown.

Colonial Patriots held their gunshot until they received the command to begin firing at the approaching enemy. General William Howe, second in command to Gage, courageously led three rows of redcoats up the slope of Breed's Hill. Fifty yards from the summit, streams of buckshot and bullets struck the attackers. Howe, with his trademark taciturnity, coolness and presence of mind, charged the provincial militia ploughmen on Breed's Hill again and again. "At one stage of the battle he was the only officer in the front rank left standing."[27] On the American side, "Putnam ... was everywhere among his men on the hill, commanding, pleading, cursing and swearing like a madman, in his determination to rally and hold steady his green, embattled troops. When his men ran out of ammunition they fought the British bayonets with clubbed muskets, frail militia swords, and even rocks snatched up from the rough ground where they stood."[28] At the base of Breed's Hill, Charlestown was torched. Flaming church steeples seemed to float suspended in midair, supported only by a fountain of fire clearly visible to spectators watching from rooftops around Boston.

The five-foot, brown-eyed beauty Abigail Adams, trapped with her four children in Boston, wrote to her husband, John, who was in congress at Philadelphia. Beginning as usual with "My dearest friend" she said, "The constant roar of the cannon are so distressing that we cannot Eat, Drink or Sleep." But the biggest threat was not the cannon's roar or the marauding British soldiers at the epicenter of a crowded, unsanitary and lawless war zone. It was smallpox and dysentery. John Adams wrote to Abigail, whom he called his Diana, referring to the Roman goddess of the moon: "The Small Pox has done Us more harm than British armies, Canadians, Indians, Negroes, Hanoverians, Hessians, and all the rest and now it is threatening my little babes." He later said, "Disease has destroyed ten men for Us where the Sword of the Enemy has killed one."[29]

On the battlefield the provincial militia inflicted heavy losses on General Howe's bayonet-wielding troops. A thousand redcoats fell on the slopes. Five hundred farmers were killed. When the Patriots ran out of ammunition and withdrew, the British won the battle at great cost of life. The proportion of British officers killed was startling. "Over one-eighth of all British officers killed in the Revolutionary War" were killed on Bunker Hill.[30] All night long chaises carried the English casualties to Boston. "The British captured the hill, but the Americans had won the glory."[31]

Coming early in the war, the June 17, 1775, battle at Breed's Hill, which has gone down as the Battle of Bunker Hill, was an important moral victory for Americans. It served as a symbol of national pride. Peter Salem, a former slave, has been called a "hero" for his role in the battle at Bunker Hill. He allegedly killed Major John Pitcairn, who had commanded the British advance guard marching to the battle of Concord and was the leader of the final assault on American lines at Bunker Hill. The battle fortified colonial resolve and proved that the British were not unconquerable. It was indeed possible for the puny American colonies to gather strength and fight a winning war against the powerful British mother country. Sam Adams' wrote from Philadelphia to his wife Elizabeth in Boston:

> My Dearest Betsy.... It is painful to me to reflect on the Terror I suppose you were under, on hearing the Noise of War so near.... The Death of our truly amiable and worthy Friend Dr. Warren is greatly afflicting.... Gage has made me respectable by naming me first among those who are to receive no favour from him. I thoroughly despise him and his proclamation. The Clock is now striking twelve. I therefore wish you good Night.
> Yours most affectionately, S. ADAMS.[32]

Joseph Warren had been a leading member of the Sons of Liberty, author of the Suffolk Resolves, and president of the Massachusetts Provincial Council. Silversmith Paul Revere went to the Bunker Hill battlefield after the British evacuation and identified the exhumed body of the esteemed physician. In one of the first known cases of postmortem forensic medicine Revere recognized Warren's dental bridge as one that he himself had constructed from ivory and affixed with a silver wire. While their countrymen were besieging Boston in an attempt to confine the British to that city, Massachusetts delegates Samuel Adams and John Hancock were bouncing along in carriages on their way to attend the first session of the Second Continental Congress, over which John Hancock would soon preside.

The Second Continental Congress opened in May 10, 1775. Like the first Congress, it was the nucleus of the new nation. It acted as the provisional government of the 13 colony-states and served as the sole source of authority behind the American Revolution. In London, Prime Minister North's government considered the congress illegal, grudgingly acknowledging it as "the meeting at Philadelphia."[33] Several new members in addition to those who had attended the first Congress were elected to the Second Continental Congress. Virginia delegates to the second Congress were George Washington, Patrick Henry, Benjamin Harrison, Richard Henry Lee, Edmund Pendleton and Thomas Jefferson, who was the youngest. The 32year–old Jefferson took Peyton Randolph's vacant seat as a Virginia delegate. Jefferson, said delegate Dr. Benjamin Rush, was "a genius of the first order," equally distinguished for his political, mathematical and philosophical knowledge. Known for his benevolence, he was a friend of his country as well as to all nations and religions.[34]

Arriving in Philadelphia, Jefferson purchased a special writing desk and Windsor chair (or "stick chair," as he called it) in which he sat, pondering philosophical thoughts of his French contemporary Jean-Jacques Rousseau and drafting the Declaration of Independence. Tall, lanky, muscular and red-haired, Jefferson was accompanied by his childhood friend and personal valet, Jupiter. As the most privileged of the Monticello slave hierarchy, Jupiter dressed stylishly in coat, waistcoat, linen shirt and cravat.

George Washington, riding in his chariot guided by a coachman, arrived in Philadelphia nattily dressed in his blue and buff uniform of the Fairfax militia. Lean and virile, with "martial air and magical aura," he was the only delegate in military attire. There was not a king in Europe, said physician and surgeon Benjamin Rush, "that would not look like a valet de chambre by his side."[35] Historian Ron Chernow pointed out that Washington, under his facade, was a passionate, sensitive, complex man, one of many moods and fiery opinions, a fierce, hard-driving perfectionist. But his emotion was cloaked under this tremendous reserve and the stoical, laconic aura that we are familiar with. What kept his speeches short were probably his false teeth, which were hinged together by springs anchored to one tooth and prone to fly out of his mouth when he talked. In addition, whether Washington was "trotting off to the House of Burgesses, the Continental Congress or Valley Forge, Billie Lee was always at his side." William Lee, a short, powerfully built and versatile mulatto manservant—butler, waiter, valet—was a dare-devil horseman "with a gift for gab, a rich fund of anecdotes and a wealth of opinions."[36]

During the first week, Washington was elected to a committee for planning defenses for New York City and preparing that city for British attack. The committee decided to enlist 3,000 men, secure King's Bridge on the Harlem River, and erect forts on both banks of the Hudson River. Congress approved these schemes. Next, Washington served as chair of the key committee on military supplies. Vividly impressive in uniform, dining in the evenings with other congressmen and getting to know them, the muscular Washington was a man of commanding physique. He told his tailor "my stature is six feet, otherwise rather slender than corpulent." His weight fluctuated between 175 and 225. He never wore a wig but powdered his reddish-brown hair, fluffed out the sides into puffy wings, and tied a black bow around the queue, in the contemporaneous military style, at the nape of his neck. His eyes were pale grayish-blue, his complexion fair and easily sunburned. Rough-hewn, strong and graceful, he was a laconic man of "granite self control" masking pent-up passions, erasing all spontaneity, a man of "outward calm" and "intense hidden emotions." With his "easy, soldier-like air and gestures, he spoke very modestly and in a cool but determined style and accent," observed delegate Silas Deane of Connecticut. Sizing up George Washington, Abigail Adams, the wife of Massachusetts delegate John Adams, said, "The gentleman and soldier look agreeably blended in him."[37]

The Second Continental Congress resolved that "a general be appointed to command all the continental forces raised or to be raised for the defense of American liberty."[38] Congress was convinced that success in the siege of Boston depended on support from all the colonies united under one military leader. Ideally the commander would come from Virginia, since that colony was five times more populous than Massachusetts and New York combined. John Adams, a renowned statesman of the Revolution and a key figure in the Continental Congress, assured Congress that he had one man in mind.

The small, paunchy, sharp-minded John Adams, a younger second cousin of Samuel, was largely responsible for at least three monumental decisions of the Second Continental Congress. The first was the suggestion that 43-year-old George Washington serve as commander in chief of the Continental Army. John Adams, with his farmer's hands and fluent speech, would be one of Washington's most avid "advocates in congress and one of his more severe detractors in later years."[39] Adams' second great contribution was that he engaged Thomas Jefferson as the main author of the Declaration of Independence. His third major choice was to name John Marshall to head the Supreme Court. All three decisions ceded power to others, despite Adams' personal ambitions.[40]

One of the first steps of the Second Continental Congress was to elect George Washington commander in chief of the newly created American Continental Army on June 15, 1775, just two days before the battle of Bunker Hill. Accepting the nomination, Washington bowed before Congress, pulled a paper from his pocket, and read: "Mr. President ... as Congress desires I will enter upon the momentous duty and exert every power I possess in their service for the support of the glorious cause.... As to pay, Sir, I beg leave to assure the Congress that as no pecuniary consideration could have tempted me to have accepted this arduous employment at the expense of my domestic ease and happiness I do not wish to make any profit from it."[41] A few days later, Washington wrote the following letter to his wife, one of only two of the general's letters that Martha saved. She destroyed the rest:

Philadelphia June 18, 1775,
My Dearest ...

It has been determined in Congress that the whole Army raised for the defence of the American Cause shall be put under my care, and that it is necessary for me to proceed immediately to Boston to take upon me the command of it. You may believe me my dear Patcy, when I assure you, in the most solemn manner, that, so far from seeking this appointment I have used every endeavor in my power to avoid it, not only from my unwillingness to part with you and the Family, but from a consciousness of its being a trust too great for my Capacity and that I should enjoy more real happiness and felicity in one month with you, at home, than I have the most distant prospect of reaping abroad, if my stay were to be Seven times Seven years.

Elizabeth Ellet's *Women of the Revolution* points out that Mary Ball Washington shaped the duty-driven, steadfast, and conscientious character of her son George: "Washington ever acknowledged that he owed everything to his mother—in the education and habits of his early life. His high moral principle, his perfect self-possession, his clear and sound judgment, his inflexible resolution and untiring application—were developed by her training and example."[42] George was 11 years old when his father, Augustine Washington, died. Seeing his father through a child's eyes, George held onto his vague memory of a tall, sturdy, laconic man with phenomenal physical strength. Allegedly he could lift a wagon filled with iron that would ordinarily require two men and a horse to move. Augustine, a tobacco planter and a slaveholder, owned and operated an iron mine and furnace on Accokeek Creek, a tributary of the Potomac River in Virginia. When he died at age 48, his property was divided among his sons. According to the existing primogeniture law, Lawrence, the eldest son of Augustine's first wife, inherited the lion's share: Mt. Vernon and the iron mines. George, the eldest son of Augustine's second marriage, received Ferry Farm and its slaves opposite the village of Fredericksburg on the Rappahannock River in eastern Virginia. George's mother, Augustine's second wife, Mary Ball Washington, managed Ferry Farm for her young son. Because of his father's early death, George was denied the classical education that his older half-brothers received.

Widowed at 35 and forced to be frugal, Mary Washington managed the farm, supervised dozens of slaves and raised five children ranging in age from six to eleven. Intelligent, industrious and self-reliant, she was a businesswoman who lived a Spartan lifestyle without frills. As the oldest son living at home, George functioned as an adult at an early age. "Mary displayed a powerful capacity to command, and one is tempted to say that the first formidable general George Washington ever encountered was his own mother."[43] An aged inhabitant of Fredericksburg remembered Mary Ball Washington "as seated in an old-fashioned open chaise she was in the habit of visiting, almost daily, her little farm in the vicinity of the town. When there, she would ride about her fields, giving her orders and seeing that they were obeyed. When on one occasion an agent departed from his instructions—she reproved him for exercising his own judgment in the matter: 'I command you,' she said: 'there is nothing left for you but to obey.'"[44]

Through her, the future commander in chief was taught the duty of obedience and was prepared to command. One of young George's playmates said, "Of the mother I was ten times more afraid than I ever was of my own parents; she awed me in the midst of her kindness, for she was indeed truly kind ... a majestic woman with an awe inspiring air and manner so characteristic of the Father of his country." She was the "presiding genius of her well-ordered household, commanding and being obeyed."[45] Although she was not wealthy, her charity to the poor was dependably benevolent and kind.

When George's brother Lawrence and Lawrence's only son died, George inherited the entire estate at age 20. He moved into Mt. Vernon, but his mother preferred to stay on the farm at Fredericksburg. The Marquis de Lafayette, meeting her there several years later, saw Mary working in the garden, dressed in domestic clothes. She was not moved by pride, glory, pomp or circumstance or even the accomplishments of her son George. When the marquis lavished praise upon the chief, the mother replied, "I am not surprised at what George has done, for he was always a very good boy."[46]

On August 2, 1775, less than two months after Washington took command, Mercy Warren wrote to Mrs. Macaulay: "I hinted that the sword was half drawn from the scabbard. Since that it has been unsheathed. Almost every tongue is calling on the justice of heaven to punish or disperse the disturbers of the peace, liberty and happiness of their country." Simultaneously to her friend John Adams Mercy wrote, "I cannot wish to see the sword quietly put up in the scabbard until justice is done to America." She also informed him "Generals Washington, Lee, and Gates and several distinguished officers dined with us three days since."[47] She also shared with Congressman Adams her opinion of each man.

Washington's first job as commander in chief was to support the siege of Boston. He must recruit and organize an army, march to Boston, and confront the British Army garrisoned there. He learned about the Battle of Bunker Hill during his 11-day journey from the Continental Congress at Philadelphia to Boston. Arriving on July 2, General Washington took command of those spirited farmer militiamen who, by an act of the Second Continental Congress, became charter members of the American Continental Army.

The American government—Continental Congress—had no money to create a military or to equip, feed and pay soldiers. Washington soon realized that it was not an army he commanded but a lax conglomeration of disorganized troops in civilian clothes with no way to distinguish the officers from the men with whom they freely fraternized. Working on the principle that "discipline is the soul of an army," he adopted the British organization and created regiments (battalions), brigades and divisions. Having no means to fund uniforms, he provided officers with colored ribands or cockades and demanded that those men be obeyed. Eventually the blue and buff uniform became standard.

There were differences between the Continental Army and the militia, but both were organizations that fought the land war in the American Revolution. Although it varied from state to state, the militia, ages 16 to 60, performed short-term duty and protected the home front. Militiamen were under the auspices of the state. Usually each man served no more than three months at any one time. Militia officers often were elected by popular vote. Some militia were poorly trained and poorly disciplined, while others were seasoned soldiers. Each militiaman was required to possess a musket, bullets and powder.

By 1775 most New England colonies had reorganized and strengthened their militia to muster at short notice and remain in the field for longer periods of time. The provincial assemblies, and later the state governors, appointed militia generals. The four New England colonies were already in a state of war when the Second Continental Congress met in May

1775. After appointing Washington commander in chief, Congress authorized major staff officers to assist him. Between June 17 and June 22 Congress appointed four major generals and eight brigadier generals to the Continental Army. By July 2, more major generals were appointed. Although delegates sought appointments for favorite sons, the delegates worked together "remarkably free of political strife."[48]

As directed by Congress, Washington organized the Continental Army to be made up largely of lines formed from militia regiments of infantry recruited from the colony-states. Each line was named for its home state. The New Jersey Line and the Massachusetts Line were firing lines, composed of men standing shoulder to shoulder and three deep. Continental Line soldiers belonged to the regular army and were indirectly governed by the Continental Congress, which had appointed Washington as commander in chief. At first, soldiers in the regular army served for one year; later the term was extended to three years. The Continental Army was small, lacking sufficient recruits because it kept men away from their homes and farms for long periods of time. The pay was uncertain, and the army competed with states that needed men in their own militias to protect their home fronts. In contrast, the British army was efficient, well-trained and disciplined.

Headquartered at Cambridge on the outskirts of Boston during the siege, Washington took command of the Continental Army. The first thing the new commander accomplished was to strengthen the barrier surrounding Boston. The blockade cut off the food supply to British troops by land so that all supplies reaching the city must be delivered by ships from distant ports. Upon hearing about the desperately low supply of gunpowder, Washington "was so stunned he did not utter a word for half an hour."[49] He then spread the alarming news that the ammunition supply was desperately depleted. Mary Draper—who had fed hundreds of soldiers at roadside tables—joined many other New England housewives in sacrificing their cherished and valuable pewter to help win American independence. They donated pewter spoons, plates, chargers and tankards to be melted down for bullets. Silver was not widely available in colonial New England, and housewives—even in the mansions of the wealthy—diligently polished their pewter for decorative as well as utilitarian purposes. Using a bullet mold, Mary melted and molded her pewter into metal balls. As winter approached, she and many other New England women sewed domestic cloth into coats, sheets and blankets for the soldiers. Mrs. Draper epitomized the patriotic spirit and the "aid rendered by women whose deeds of disinterested generosity were never known beyond their own neighborhoods!"[50]

At first, Washington's Continental Army was composed entirely of New Englanders. The group was, for the most part, irregular, undisciplined, unclean, un-uniformed, inexperienced and without even one trained engineer to oversee the building of defense. The leaders of the new army surrounding Boston were former New England militia officers: Nathanael Greene, the self-taught, "fighting Quaker" with piercing blue eyes and a limp, was from Rhode Island; Israel Putnam ("Old Putt") from Connecticut; John Stark and John Sullivan from New Hampshire; and the ebullient and hefty Henry Knox from Massachusetts. Soon troops from other colonies arrived: 3,000 from Pennsylvania, Maryland, and Virginia. Daniel Morgan, "the Old Waggoner," came with his rustic band of Virginia sharpshooters. His riflemen had trudged 600 miles, carrying rifles that were longer than muskets and took longer to load but were more accurate.

From England, Thomas Gage, commander in chief of the British Army in America

(1763–1775), was held accountable for the heavy British losses in the Battle of Bunker Hill—roughly half of his estimated 2,200 troops, and a disproportionately large percentage of officers. Gage was the first in a long line of "military commanders to be blamed for British defeat in the American Revolutionary War." In October, Gage handed over his command to General Sir William Howe and returned to England in disgrace.[51]

Generals Washington and Howe avoided confrontation for months. Washington's army kept watch on British troops and the British looked back. "It seemed," wrote a contemporary, "to be the principle employment of both armies to look at each other with spyglasses."[52] William "Billy" Lee, Washington's manservant, friend and constant companion, frequently removed the mahogany and brass spyglass from its leather case and handed it to Washington to surveil his enemy.

Meanwhile, the Continental Congress—angry with Parliament, but making one last effort to negotiate peace with the British government and avert war—had drafted the Olive Branch Petition. Delegate John Jay, a member of the Tory-dominated New York legislature, wrote the initial draft. Appealing directly to King George III, the petition asked that the Intolerable Acts be rescinded and the Port of Boston reopened in return for their olive branch: a pledge of loyalty to the crown. The final version of the petition was pushed through Congress in early July 1775 by delegate John Dickinson, a Quaker and the Pennsylvania leader of the "cool faction" of Congress. The "cool faction" favored petitioning rather than a more heated retaliation. John Adams objected, maintaining that because the British had trampled over colonists at Concord and Lexington, America's only effective response would be with "powder and artillery," not an obsequious petition.[53] Congress adopted and dispatched the Olive Branch Petition in July 1775. Because mail was transported by ship, Congress did not learn until November that King George III had ignored the petition. The Boston port remained closed. The Intolerable Acts were not abolished. The British objective was to suppress the rebellion, make the colonists submissive and continue to collect colonial revenue. If this failed, she would need to rule by military force and thus spend any revenue that might be collected. The Americans were fighting for a set of ideas. They wanted home rule, to force Britain to recognize their right to freedom, but it took Congress a year to decide if they wanted freedom within the empire or complete independence.

Patriot women fervently assisted Washington in America's fight for freedom. In September 1775, twenty-two-year-old Deborah Champion of New London, Connecticut, delivered important dispatches from her father, Henry Champion, the Continental Army's commissary general, to General Washington in Boston. Mounted on horseback with the family slave, Aristarchus, escorting her, Deborah headed due north to the Massachusetts border. Hiding the note under food in her saddlebag, Deborah changed horses at her uncle's farm and continued riding through the night. At daybreak she was stopped by a sentry and told to dismount. He intended to take her to his commanding officer. But Deborah quickly suggested that it was too early in the morning to awaken his superior. The sentry, thinking she really did not look like a spy, allowed her to ride on to Boston. She delivered the papers into the hands of George Washington. "The general," Deborah later reported to a friend, "was pleased to compliment me most highly as to what he was pleased to call the courage I had displayed and my patriotism."[54]

In October 1775, during the Siege of Boston while Washington was headquartered at Cambridge, he received a poem of praise from Phillis Wheatley, a black American. Miss

Wheatley, the first black poet in America to publish her work, was born in West Africa. When she was eight years old, she was brought on the slave ship *Phillis* to New England, where John Wheatley, a prosperous Boston tailor, bought her for his wife, Susanna, who named the child Phillis. The Wheatley's 18-year-old twins, a boy and a girl, were thrilled by Phillis's interest in learning the English language. The Wheatley daughter, Mary, taught Phillis to read and write. Phillis also studied Latin, Greek and the Bible. The whole family encouraged her to attend church at Old South Meeting House. Phillis published her first poem when she was 14. Another is titled "On Being Brought from Africa to America":

> 'Twas mercy brought me from my Pagan land,
> Taught my benighted soul to understand
> That there's a God, that there's a savior too....
> Once I redemption neither sought nor knew....[55]

Later, Susanna Wheatley found 18 prominent Bostonians—among them, Governor Hutchinson, Andrew Oliver and John Hancock—to endorse Phillis and advocate for publishing her poetry in a book. The book was to be published in England. Susanna sent Phillis, who suffered from asthma, to England for the publication of her book because she hoped an ocean voyage might improve the young lady's health. Soon after the book was published and Phillis returned to America, the Wheatley family granted Phillis her freedom. Phillis then nursed Susanna for three months until Susanna died. In early 1776, George Washington invited Phillis to visit him in Cambridge in appreciation for a poem that she had written for him a few months earlier. Phillis married a freedman, a grocer, two years later. She died when she was 31. "Phillis Wheatley used her pen as her means of action in the Revolutionary America. She wrote of and for America ... [and] her poems still matter."[56] Many of Wheatley's works were published as a broadside, a large piece of paper or handbill printed on one side and posted to a tavern, tree, or post. It was a popular and quick way of spreading ideas, news or advertisements through the colonies.

Meanwhile, Martha Washington, unhesitatingly responding to her husband's request, bounced in a frigid carriage across 600 miles of rutted roads to join the general at Cambridge in November 1775. Traveling luxuriously with five household slaves and leather trunks studded with brass, she was greeted in Philadelphia by a military escort and in Newark by pealing church bells. Over the course of the war Martha would spend a total of more than two years with her husband at campsites. "He couldn't afford to show weakness or indecision and needed a wife to whom he could reveal his frustrations." Martha adapted quickly to the austere camp life and avoided lavish consumption. George was more relaxed in his wife's presence and they were happy with each other. When Mercy Warren visited Martha at Cambridge, Warren reported to Abigail Adams, "I took a ride to Cambridge and waited on Mrs. Washington at 11 o'clock, where I was receiv[e]d with that politeness and respect shown in a first interview among the well bred and with the ease and cordiality of friendship of a much earlier date." The inadequately educated but well-bred Martha became fast friends with Mercy Warren. Knowing Martha's shortcomings in education, Washington or a secretary drafted her replies when she corresponded with Mercy Warren and other such intellectuals.[57]

Lucy Knox and Henry, who would soon go to Ticonderoga, also connected with the commander in chief at Cambridge. From a prominent family, Lucy Flucker—pampered, jolly and accustomed to having her own way—set her sights on Henry Knox. He was equally determined to win her. Knox, an ebullient, bulky and poor Scots-Irish bookstore clerk who supported his widowed mother, mounted his horse late one night and set out for Cambridge. Beside him rode his chubby new bride, 18-year-old Lucy, nee Flucker, daughter of the affluent royal secretary of the Province of Massachusetts, who objected to their marriage. Knox's sword was sewn inside her cape. Calling Lucy "the charmer of my soul," Henry "adored his big, bossy and brilliant new wife." Lucy, devoted to Henry, called him "her ever dear Harry," her "only friend in world."[58] She would soon tell him something that most 18th century women would never dream of telling their husbands: "You being long accustomed to command.... I hope you will not consider yourself as commander in chief of your own house, but be convinced ... that there is such a thing as equal command."[59] Though accustomed to luxury, Lucy and their children would stay by his side as camp followers from that day forward. Keeping a handkerchief around his left hand to disguise the absence of two fingers lost from a shotgun wound while hunting, her new husband was on his way to join the Revolutionary forces. Twenty-five-year–old Knox, a 300-pound, six-foot, self-taught artillery colonel from Boston, soon approached General Washington. He suggested to the general that artillery could be transported from Ticonderoga to force British troops to evacuate Boston. Washington embraced and implemented the idea, giving the big man a big order:

> [E]xamine into the state of the artillery of this army and take an account of the cannon, mortars, shells, lead and ammunition that are wanting ... to proceed to New York in the most expeditious manner.... [A]fter you have procured as many of these necessaries as you can there, you must go to Major -General Schuyler [commander of the Northern army] and get the remainder from Ticonderoga, Crown Point, or St. John; if it should be necessary from Quebec, if in our hands. The want of them is so great that no trouble or expense must be spared to obtain them.... I have given you a warrant to the Paymaster-General of the Continental Army, for a thousand dollars, to defray the expense ... an account of which you are to keep and render upon your return.
>
> Given under my hand at head-quarters at Cambridge this 16th day of November ... 1775. G. Washington.[60]

Knox removed the artillery that Arnold, Allen and his Green Mountain Boys had captured from the British at Fort Ticonderoga the preceding May. For 56 days during the winter of 1775–76, the giant, his army and 80 yoke of oxen dragged 42 loaded sleds[61] at a speed of five miles per hour. They slid 60 tons of artillery—59 brass and iron cannons and mortar, the largest gun weighing 1,800 pounds—across 300 miles of icy trails from upper New York to Washington's headquarters at Cambridge on the outskirts of Boston. There, the "Noble Train of Artillery" was welcomed with cheers and jubilation. Knox was outside Boston on January 25, 1776. Powder for the cannon arrived in March.

As time crawled by, the New England soldiers besieging Boston were idle, bored, and short on guns and powder. Vessels only occasionally brought ammunition from distant shores to ports remote from the blockaded harbor. Wagons then transported the powder to the Americans surrounding Boston. The city's shops closed. Food prices shot up. British soldiers and Tory families shivered from cold, hunger and sickness. During the deep snows and severe winter of 1775–76, Bostonians burned church pews, warehouse counters, and timbers from uninhabited houses for fuel. Blockaded by land, the town's fuel and food from the open sea were cut off not only by American privateers boarding and plundering supply ships but also by freezing ocean storms. Ships at sea, said one British admiral, had "ropes and sails quite congealed, and the whole ship before long one cake of ice."[62] Bone-chilling winds and driving snows hammered soldiers on watch until they froze to death standing in their tracks.

The American forces blockading Boston had grown from 9,000 at the end of 1775 to 14,000 by February 1776. The city was stalemated. Neither the American nor British troops attacked the other. Finally reinforced with cannon and powder, Washington was prepared to break the deadlock. Silently and unobserved 2,000 Americans guided 80 teams of oxen from Cambridge through the dark and windy night of March 2. Wrapping wagon wheels in straw to silence the sound, they pushed, pulled and heaved cannons up the slope to Dorchester Heights. Both the British and the Loyalist townspeople were astounded by the Patriots' speed in erecting batteries and fortifications. The hill had stood unoccupied until now. Neither side had seized and fortified it, although both the British and the Americans had long known it was a crucial vantage point overlooking the harbor.

Now the Americans began firing on Boston. Houses burst into flames as cannonballs blitzed the town brimming with Loyalists, British troops and ships in the harbor. Howe dispatched 3,000 redcoats to the foot of Dorchester Heights. On the hilltop Quartermaster General Thomas Mifflin loaded hogsheads (barrels) with stones and sand and rolled them downhill, hitting the British who were climbing up. Washington prepared to send generals John Sullivan and Nathanael Greene with 4,000 men to attack the city. Howe, however, decided that now was the time to follow Secretary of State Dartmouth's orders to leave Boston and secretly organize British troops for the invasion of New York. Sending a flag of truce to Washington, he promised to evacuate the city and leave it standing in return for assurance that British troops and Loyalists could embark unharmed. An agreement was reached.

The eleven-month Siege of Boston ended on March 17, 1776, when Major General Howe, with 6,000 British troops, 900 sick people and 1,100 Loyalists left Boston.[63] The vessels were so crowded that Howe was obliged to leave behind "two hundred and fifty pieces of cannon, four large mortars, one hundred and fifty horses, twenty five thousand bushels of wheat, and a quantity of barley, oats, and other provisions, which [the American] army then greatly needed."[64] Howe also dumped cannon and produce into the harbor so that artillery and supplies would not fall into Patriot hands. Chaotic crowds of British troops and disillusioned Loyalists desperately scrambled onto "an armada of 120 ships stretching nine miles out to sea and left Boston forever."[65] Among the Loyalists sailing away with Howe were Lucy Flucker Knox's parents, whom she would never see again. Loyalist Samuel Quincy, the lawyer who had opposed John Adams in the Boston Massacre trials, was also among the evacuees. Writing from a hilltop, Abigail Adams, who loved to read, quote and write poetry, described British warships "lifting canvas in a fair breeze and turning to the open sea.... You may count upwards of one hundred and seventy-sail.... They look like a forest."[66] The Ticonderoga weapons that forced Howe to evacuate the city became the backbone of artillery for the American Continental Line. Howe sailed away to Halifax, Nova Scotia, where he trained his troops and awaited reinforcements before putting out to sea again and plowing toward New York. As will be shown later, General Washington anticipated the British move. But currently he was still conducting the Canada Campaign.

In the early months of the Siege of Boston, George Washington had launched the Canada Campaign, which lasted from fall 1775 until mid-1776. It began after Benedict

Arnold and Ethan Allen had captured Fort Ticonderoga from the British. George Washington then met with Arnold and they discussed plans for launching a major military initiative—the invasion of Canada. Washington was acting under the direction of the Continental Congress. In mid–1775 Congress had received reports that Parliament had ordered General Sir Guy Carlton, Royal Governor of Canada, whose inhabitants were mainly French, to invade New York. Congress sought to invade Canada preemptively and thus foil Carlton's British Army attack. Once they were in military control of Canada, the Americans hoped to convince that nation to become the 14th state. Canada then would be America's ally against Britain in the Revolution. To this end, General Washington met with Arnold in Boston. Washington and Arnold talked of a plan for Continental Army general Richard Montgomery and Colonel Ethan Allen to capture Montreal, and they then would join forces with Colonel Arnold to capture Quebec.

A Scots-Irish immigrant to Connecticut, General Montgomery marched northward from Lake Champlain and seized Fort St. John to open the way for Americans to advance to nearby Montreal. Ethan Allen approached the town of Montreal on an October morning with a small group of soldiers to join forces with Montgomery. They were intercepted by British troops and French Canadians. Colonel Allen was taken prisoner and shipped in irons to England (he was released and exchanged three years later). General Montgomery captured Montreal on November 13 and then began marching to Quebec. But by the time Montgomery arrived in Quebec, he found that many under his command had deserted, leaving him with only 400 men.

Early in September, Arnold had begun a trek that has been compared to Hannibal's crossing of the Alps. Making his way from Cambridge to join Montgomery in Quebec, Arnold led 1,100 men through the dense forests and hazardous swamps of the Maine wilderness. Sweating in the daytime, feeling the sweat freeze on their bodies at night, and starving, with some eating shoe leather and dogs, Arnold and his army entered Canada.

The wives of Sergeant Joseph Grier and Private James Warner marched by their husbands' sides, struggling and enduring hardships. A journalist wrote the following: "Mrs. (Suzannah) Grier has got before me. Her clothes more than waist high, she waded before me to firm ground. No one, so long as she was known to us, dared to intimate a disrespectful idea of her. My mind was humbled, yet astonished, at the exertions of this good woman." Along the way, Jemima Warner, dedicated to her sick husband, sat beside him under a tree and sadly watched him die. She then took up his gun and walked 20 miles to catch up with Arnold's admiring and amazed army. Both women made it to Quebec City, where Jemima was killed by enemy fire. There it was recorded that Mrs. (Suzannah) Grier, belonging to the Pennsylvania troops, was killed by accident, "a soldier carelessly snapping his musket which proved to be loaded."[67]

During the march, 200 men had deserted Arnold's camp, taking most of the provisions with them. Later, 200 more turned back. With a diminished force, Arnold scaled the Heights of Abraham in mid–November and assembled his remaining men on the plains. Arnold's force was insufficient to storm the city, and the strong British Canadian garrison would not come out to fight. Hence Arnold retreated 20 miles from Quebec and awaited the arrival of Montgomery. Montgomery and Arnold, marching with 900 troops, intended to besiege Quebec. That city was held by General Carleton, the governor of Quebec. English sailors, Highland soldiers and mercenaries watched from the battery as the Americans approached and unwittingly walked into the mouth of cannon. In this great onslaught of December 31, 1775, Montgomery and several other officers were killed instantly while their men retreated in confusion. In another part of town Arnold, working with Captain Daniel Morgan and his elite rifle company, attacked a battery. When Arnold was wounded, Morgan took command and secured the fortification. The English and Canadians squeezed the Americans from all sides, blocking their retreat and forcing Morgan's troops to surrender as prisoners of war. Major General Schuyler, the commander of the Northern army, wrote to General Washington:

> Albany, January 13, 1776
> I wish I had no occasion to send my dear General this melancholy account. My admirable friend, the gallant Montgomery is no more. Brave Arnold is wounded. We have met with a severe check in an unsuccessful attempt on Quebec.... I am Sir, Etc. Philip Schuyler.[68]

Arnold recovered, retreated with the remnants of his army, and spent the winter upriver from Quebec. The American invasion of Canada did not command the popular support Congress had expected from Canadians and Arnold was driven back. The Americans evacuated Canada in June 1776.

Mercy Warren's satirical chastisements are well known, but her letters of sympathy to strangers outside her circle of friends are equally moving. On January 20, 1776, Mercy, as a Patriot and a Christian, wrote a condolence letter to Janet Montgomery, widow of General Richard Montgomery. In it she said, "The urn of the companion of your heart will be sprinkled with the tears of thousands who revere the commander at the gates of Quebec, though not personally acquainted with General Montgomery." In November Mercy wrote, "Your letters have convinced me that the brave Montgomery had a partner worthy of his character." Janet replied:

> My dear Madam, The sympathy that is expressed in every feature of your letter, claims from me the warmest acknowledgments; and the professions of friendship from one who so generously feels and melts at the woes of a stranger, not only soothe but flatter me.... As a wife I must ever mourn the loss of the husband, friend, and lover; of a thousand virtues, of all domestic bliss; the idol of my warmest affections, and in one word, my every dream of happiness. But with America I weep the still greater loss of the firm soldier and the friend to freedom. Let me repeat his last words when we parted: "You shall never blush for your Montgomery."[69]

4

New York and New Jersey Campaigns

Watching the British evacuate Boston in March 1776 and sail to Nova Scotia, Washington predicted that their next move would be to occupy New York City. Enemy control of that city would stop the interchange of communication and supplies between northern and southern colonies. This interruption would threaten the unification and security of America. Therefore Washington ordered Quartermaster General Thomas Mifflin to transport the Continental troops, supplies and artillery to New York.

Regiments of Washington's troops departed New England for the first time in their lives and began winding through Massachusetts, Rhode Island, and Connecticut. Washington had overcome his initial generic dislike of New Englanders and "relied on his keen judgment of character." He "pinned his hopes on Yankees"—Henry Knox, without whom there would have been no "miracle" victory at Dorchester Heights, and Nathanael Greene, the "ideal lieutenant" whose troops were "the best disciplined in the army."[1] Lucy Knox and Caty Greene would travel with their young children from New England to join their husbands in New York. Washington himself arrived at the Brooklyn headquarters in April. Martha arrived later, having received a smallpox inoculation in Philadelphia. The small dose caused only a low fever, a mild rash with only a few pustules, and no facial scarring. Her mild reaction soon ran its course and she emerged protected and able to spend more and more time nursing sick troops.

After the Siege of Boston, General Sir William Howe, commander in chief of the British Army, had taken Loyalists and his exhausted troops from Boston to Halifax, Nova Scotia. In June, leaving the exiled Boston Loyalists in Halifax, he sailed with his newly organized and refreshed army to Sandy Hook, New Jersey, an anchorage at the entrance of the New York Harbor. By that time Washington's army had built batteries on Manhattan and Long Island and fortified Brooklyn Heights. Greene was in command of Long Island. Knox placed 120 cannon about the city, whose population was 25,000.

On June 29, Lucy and Henry Knox were at breakfast overlooking the harbor when they saw General Howe's ships sailing in from Nova Scotia. Lucy panicked.[2] Riders spread the news that the British fleet was anchored off Sandy Hook. Women and children scrambled to exit New York City against a tide of incoming militia. Troops from Massachusetts and Connecticut poured into New York to reinforce Washington's short-handed Continentals and repulse the invading enemy. Having spent a month in the broiling summer sun, one-third of Washington's men were disabled by diseases: dysentery, typhoid fever, malaria and smallpox. The usually jolly Henry Knox complained of fatigue; the jaundiced Nathanael Greene turned as yellow as a pumpkin.

On July 2, while the Second Continental Congress in Philadelphia adopted its most significant resolution—proclaiming "that these United Colonies are, and of right ought to be, free and independent states," with "full power to make war" and "declare peace," an enormous enemy fleet loomed on the horizon of New York Harbor. The force was under the command of Vice Admiral Lord Richard Howe, commander of the British navy in America and brother of General William Howe, commander in chief of the British Army in America.

Intent on crushing the American rebellion, King George III and Parliament had contracted with several German princes to hire Hessian troops, many of whom had fought under Frederick the Great. Britain paid a hefty price for these mercenaries. By July 4 this massive armada—30 battle ships, 1,200 cannon, 30,000 soldiers (including 800 Hessian mercenaries), 10,000 sailors and 300 supply ships—arrived in New York Harbor. By mid–July the largest expeditionary force in English history had disembarked on Staten Island. Washington's troops numbered 10,500, three thousand of whom were sick.[3] Britain's Royal Navy was the best in the world, a formidable instrument of war; America's Continental Navy was newborn and anemic.

When Admiral Howe sailed his huge armada into New York Harbor to reinforce his brother, these two men together commanded all the British military in America. Tall, swarthy and brave, the Howe brothers were professional soldiers committed to carrying out the orders of Parliament and the king. Personally, however, they were ambivalent regarding the war with America. Each man was recklessly courageous and taciturn—as silent as a rock. They had dual roles in America. They were military commanders. They were also joint peace commissioners with limited authority. By mid–August, Howe had assembled an army of 31,000 British, Hessian, and Loyalist troops on Staten Island. Against this formidable crew Washington would courageously, but unsuccessfully, lead his army in defense of New York and the Hudson Valley. The British Union Jack would wave over New York longer than in any other American city.

Outnumbered three to one by British and Hessian troops, Washington ordered his men to leave Long Island before the enemy could surround them. Thus, the British won the Battle of Long Island, the first major battle of the war after the Declaration of Independence was signed. But the August weather saved Washington's army from capture. A typical sudden summer storm prevented British ships from sailing up the East River. A curtain of dense fog shrouded fishermen's boats as they ferried 9,500 Continental soldiers to Kip's Bay on Manhattan. Howe overran the American post at Manhattan, forcing the continued retreat of Washington's Army.

The British, having captured General John Sullivan in the Battle of Long Island, freed him and sent him to Congress with a proposal for a peace conference. Hence, in September, Congress sent Benjamin Franklin, John Adams, and Edmund Rutledge of South Carolina to Staten Island as ambassadors to meet with the joint peace commissioners William and Richard Howe. On the way to the conference, Adams and Franklin—long-time adversaries—bickered with each other. At a Perth Amboy tavern, where they were obliged to share a bed, they quarreled over closing a window. Franklin wanted to leave it open; Adams wanted it closed. Fortunately neither was defenestrated. While meeting at Staten Island, the American delegation realized that the Howe brothers—even as peace commissioners—had no authority to negotiate a meaningful compromise. They could only grant pardons. Adams informed Howe that Americans needed no pardons because they had done no wrong. The ambassadors also refused to renounce the Declaration of Independence as a condition for further talks. At the end of the conference, there was no doubt that the only alternative to war that Americans would consider was absolute independence. The war resumed. Bullets shattered bones and bayonets pierced flesh, but the spirit of the American people would not be broken. That spirit strengthened in 21-year-old Nathan Hale, a soldier of the Continental Army who volunteered to go behind enemy lines in New York City on an intelligence-gathering mission in September. Disguised as a Dutch schoolmaster, Hale was captured and hanged as a spy by the British. Just before the noose tightened around his neck, Hale allegedly said, "I only regret that I have but one life to give for my country."

After winning control of New York City, General Howe's forces moved north in hot pursuit of Washington's main army, whose base of supply was at White Plains, New York. In October 1776, along a three-mile stretch, Washington fortified the village of White Plains with a line of breastworks made mostly of cornstalks. The main line of the American army positioned itself on Chatterton Hill, a high bluff near White Plains. Scarsdale inhabitants near White Plains watched the colorful pageantry of British redcoats and Hessian blues in Howe's pursuit of Washington. The sound of drums and bugles called to battle thousands of British troops bivouacked around the countryside among the burgundy, red and yellow leaves of Indian summer. Ahead of the resplendent parade, and making way for British troops, prisoners of war cleared the roads and built bridges. Terrified, the local Scarsdale people hid their cows and fled. One Patriot farmer drove his cattle to a swamp and then hid himself, miring up to his neck in mud.

Chatterton Hill, where Washington took his stand, and the rivers and swamps surrounding the village of White Plains offered a natural barrier as the British attempted to encircle and capture the American army. During the five days of intermittent fighting, Washington's sick and hungry soldiers, without tents, kept warm under a colorful blanket of leaves during the cool autumn nights. Artillery fire would soon set those autumn leaves afire, creating a thick canopy of smoke.

Awaiting reinforcement, Howe delayed attacking Washington's breastworks on Chatterton Hill. But when the severe wind and rain abated at twilight, cannonballs tore through heads, arms, and bowels. Body parts, guns and packs were piled in a heap. Enemy soldiers were able to dislodge the American troops. And yet, British and Hessians suffered twice as many casualties as the Americans. "Once again General Howe dawdled after victory and bungled a major opportunity."[4] Sir William Howe's habitual delay in his campaign of pursuing Washington has been attributed to his hedonistic lifestyle. While his wife remained in England, Howe had an affair with the wife of an American Loyalist "whom Howe promoted to commissary for prisoners." The following ditty was written by a Loyalist:

> Awake, arouse, Sir Billy
> There's forage in the plain,
> Leave your little filly,
> And open the campaign.[5]

Retracing their steps from White Plains, both Washington and Howe continued to vie for command of the Hudson River. Washington had built several forts to protect New York City. One was Fort Washington, on the Hudson River at the north end of present-day Manhattan Island. Another, Fort Lee, stood almost opposite Fort Washington on the Jersey shore. Guarding the Lower Hudson River, these forts blocked ships of the Royal Navy from transporting British troops, supplies, and communications inland and then moving out to sea again. Both America and Britain knew the importance of controlling the Hudson River, a vital waterway connecting the Atlantic Ocean with Canada and the West. Whoever controlled New York City controlled the Hudson.

George Washington's humiliating and disastrous defeat by British and Hessian troops in New York and White Plains was followed by yet another redcoat victory: "The surrender of Fort Washington on Saturday, November 16, was the most devastating blow of all, an utter catastrophe."[6] Nevertheless, Margaret Cochran "Captain Molly" Corbin won accolades for cannonading at Fort Washington. She was the first combat veteran of the Revolution and the first woman to receive a military pension. When she was 25 years old Margaret's husband, John Corbin, joined the Pennsylvania military, and she went with him as a camp follower. At first she earned money as a cook and laundress and caring for sick and wounded soldiers. The next year, in November 1776, Margaret dressed as a soldier for the Battle of Fort Washington. There she helped John load his cannon and fire against the British. When her husband was killed she took his place. Grapeshot from enemy fire soon struck, wounding her in the shoulder, chest and jaw. Her left arm was permanently paralyzed. Margaret Corbin was captured, paroled and then taken by wagon to Pennsylvania, where she was hospitalized. On July 6, 1779, the Continental Congress recognized her brave service by awarding her a veteran's pension: "half the pay and allowances of a soldier in service."[7] When she died she was buried with full military honors. A plaque in Fort Tryon Park in Manhattan salutes her as the "first woman to take a soldier's part in the War for Liberty."

At the Battle of Fort Washington, General Howe and General Charles Lord Cornwallis made 3,000 Patriot soldiers surrender. Washington, standing on the opposite shore of the Hudson River at Fort Lee, New Jersey, tearfully watched the defeat of Fort Washington.[8] He knew that Howe's superior forces would soon cross the Hudson, scale the cliff, and attack Fort Lee. Departing Fort Washington on November 20, Cornwallis ferried 8,000 Loyalists, redcoats, and Hessian troops across the Hudson and headed toward Fort Lee. Rallying from his despair after watching the fall of Fort Washington, Washington escaped the advancing British Army. He ordered his army to evacuate Fort Lee and retreat across New Jersey, leaving the spoils of war—cannons, tents, and stores—and New York City in enemy hands. It would be seven years before the Continental Army would once again control Manhattan.

Earlier, Washington had put the able and cool "Fighting Quaker," General Nathanael Greene, his most trusted military subordinate and favorite general, in charge of Fort Washington and Fort Lee, the twin citadels guarding the Hudson. But instead of downgrading the defective Fort Washington, as Washington had suggested, Greene tried to strengthen it. Greene paid a price for his misjudgment in thinking that Fort Washington was impregnable. General Washington consequently assigned Greene the lackluster duty of serving as quartermaster at Valley Forge. (However, if Nathanael Greene blundered at Fort Washington, he made up for it in future years by concluding the war in the South.) James Monroe, a future U.S. president, standing on the road at nearby Newark, New Jersey, counted Washington's dwindling army as it evacuated Fort Lee and retreated across New Jersey. Thomas Paine—a journalist and soldier who fled Fort Lee with Washington's army—described the evacuation in the first essay of his powerful series, *The Crisis*, published anonymously in his popular pamphlet *Common Sense*:

December 23, 1776

> THESE are the times that try men's souls. The summer soldier and the sunshine patriot will, in this crisis, shrink from the service of their country; but he that stands by it now, deserves the love and thanks of man and woman.... I was with the troops at Fort Lee, and marched with them to the edge of Pennsylvania.... Our force was inconsiderable, being not one-fourth so great as Howe could bring against us.... Our ammunition, light artillery, and the best part of our stores, had been removed, on the apprehension that Howe would endeavor to penetrate the Jerseys, in which case Fort Lee could be of no use to us; for it must occur to every thinking man, whether in the army or not, that these kind of field forts are only for temporary purposes, and last in use no longer than the enemy directs his force against the particular object which such forts are raised to defend. Such was our situation and condition at Fort Lee on the morning of the 20th of November, when an officer arrived with information that the enemy with 200 boats had landed about seven miles above; Major General [Nathanael] Greene, who commanded the garrison, immediately ordered them under arms, and sent express to General Washington at the town of Hackensack, distant by the way of the ferry = six miles. Our first object was to secure the bridge over the Hackensack, which laid up the river between the enemy and us, about six miles from us, and three from them. General Washington arrived in about three-quarters of an hour, and marched at the head of the troops towards the bridge.... I shall not now attempt to give all the particulars of our retreat to the Delaware.... Voltaire has remarked that King William never appeared to full advantage but in difficulties and in action; the same remark may be made on General Washington, for the character fits him. There is a natural firmness in some minds which cannot be unlocked by trifles, but which, when unlocked, discovers a cabinet of fortitude....

Washington avoided entrapment at Fort Lee by leading 2,000 troops in retreat through New Jersey on a three-week–long race toward the Delaware River. Cornwallis, in close pursuit, successively captured the New Jersey towns of Newark, New Brunswick, Princeton, and Trenton.

Along the way, Cornwallis offered pardon and protection to all persons who, within 60 days, took an oath of allegiance to the British Crown. Cornwallis's offer ruffled a New Jersey woman, Hannah Arnette, a staunch Patriot. Hannah was in her home in Elizabethtown (now Elizabeth) near Fort Lee when she overheard a group of men talking with her husband. They were considering signing the Royal oath of allegiance in return for protection of life and property. Hannah burst into the room. She called the dispirited men cowards and traitors for even considering such a pledge. Her show of patriotism to America convinced the men to ally with Washington rather than Cornwallis—to become Patriot soldiers rather than Loyalists.

Washington needed to expand his army. His American troops were leaving in large numbers as their terms of service expired. Yet he was determined to defend the nation's capital city as he resolutely marched across New Jersey toward Philadelphia. The Second Continental Congress, however, expecting the British to cross the Delaware, had vacated Philadelphia and adjourned to Baltimore. They left General Putnam in charge of the Philadelphia militia, and he was busily constructing forts along the Delaware to the mouth of the Schuylkill River. Washington sent Colonel John Glover to ferry American men, artillery, and horses across the Delaware River. Glover's Continental Regiment—formerly known as the Marblehead Massachusetts Militia—commandeered boats by promising the protesting local ferry owner that the new Continental Congress would pay him for their use. The purpose of this first crossing of the Delaware into Pennsylvania was to use the river as a barrier between the Continental Army and Cornwallis's pursuing British Army.

In New York, Washington had divided his retreating army into three sections. Generals Charles Lee and Horatio Gates and Washington himself took separate routes with plans to meet near the Delaware River. Washington's division arrived first, expecting to be joined by

Lee and Gates. Washington knew he must stop the British before the river froze over and Cornwallis could move across the ice to attack the Americans. General Washington realized that American forces needed a victory to give them a moral boost following their forced retreat from New York. General Charles Lee, however, who had long irritated Washington, failed to rendezvous. He had been detained in mid-December by 22-year-old Banastre Tarleton and a band of British soldiers who surrounded the inn where Lee, only three miles from his army's camp, was dallying with a prostitute. Shooting bullets through the window, Tarleton threatened to burn the house down, capturing the soot-covered Lee as he emerged from his hiding place in the chimney above a fireplace. Lee spent 16 months in British captivity.

General Sir Henry Clinton, Howe's second in command, arrived on the New Jersey shore of the Delaware River, but, having no boats to pursue the Continentals, as Washington had secured all the ferries, Clinton stationed Hessian soldiers at Trenton, New Jersey. Just as Washington had suspected, Clinton planned to move the larger British Army across the Delaware River when it froze over and confront the American troops. The British then hoped to proceed 33 miles south to Philadelphia and take possession of that capital city. Washington, however, guarding the route to Philadelphia, planned to stop the British at Trenton. Military historians generally agree that Howe's decision not to pursue Washington more aggressively in October 1776 into New Jersey was a huge tactical blunder. Had Howe persevered, he could have crushed the weakened Continental Army, ended the war, and changed the course of American history.

Having crossed the Delaware, Washington, watching through a spyglass on the Pennsylvania bank, looked across the river and saw Hessian soldiers on patrol at Trenton. He knew it was only a matter of time until the river froze and the British could march across the ice and attack. He therefore resolved to cross the Delaware a second time on Christmas Eve 1776 and surprise the Hessians. Sleet and driving snow of blizzard force caused him to postpone his plan until the next night. Shortly before Washington's second and most famous crossing of the Delaware, he ordered Paine's essay from *The Crisis*, titled "December 23, 1776," to be read to his American troops. Henry Knox, colonel of artillery, supervised the crossing upon hearing these words: "These are the times that try men's souls. The summer soldier and the sunshine patriot will, in this crisis, shrink from the service of their country; but he that stands by it now, deserves the love and thanks of man and woman."

On that freezing-cold, dark Christmas night of 1776 Washington's army of 2,400 ragged, mostly shoeless young soldiers left bloody tracks in the snow up to the water as they boldly and silently set about getting the boats across the Delaware River. Washington's army used four crossing points. Rowing the boats through a swirling blizzard, navigating around chunks of ice, these shivering, barefoot troops crossed the 800-foot–wide river, finally climbing ashore near Trenton, New Jersey. The horses were loaded onto platforms rigged between boats. One of the greatest challenges was transporting Henry Knox and his artillery train. It took eight hours to ferry the artillery across the river. Further delays occurred when the cannon had to be hoisted across a deep ravine, probably by dragging the monstrous guns with ropes, lowering them into the gorge, and pulling them back up the other side.[9]

Crossing the Delaware with Washington on Christmas Night were several eminent soldiers and statesmen, including two future presidents of the United States, James Madison and James Monroe, and a future chief justice of the United States Supreme Court, John Marshall. Alexander Hamilton was also among them, as well as Hamilton's murderer, Aaron Burr.

(In Emanuel Leutze's famous symbolic painting of the event, Marshall is depicted holding the flag, which the artist pictured as a Betsy Ross flag although she did not make the flag until a few months later. Prince Whipple, the oarsman—an African immigrant who did not actually travel in Washington's boat—is pictured in the painting seated directly in front of Washington.) Chief Artillery Officer Henry Knox stood by Washington's side, shouting Washington's orders and directing the crossing until every man landed safely. They climbed ashore nine miles from Trenton, and the Battle of Trenton was fought the next morning.

The battle began with a surprise attack on 1,500 hired Hessian soldiers. Silently, Rhode Island's Brigadier General Nathanael Greene and New Hampshire's Brigadier General John Sullivan split their columns and surrounded the Hessians, trapping them inside the town. Henry Knox's cannon and howitzers cleared the narrow streets of the village "in the twinkling of an eye," said Knox to Lucy in his letter of December 28, 1776. Two days later Knox was promoted to brigadier general of artillery. Caught unawares, the Hessians responded to their training and counterattacked with great courage, plus that "special fury" characteristic of Germans. Unlike the stereotypical picture, Hessians were not drunkards; rather, "they were Calvinists who read their prayer books before battle."[10]

The attack would not have been a surprise had it not been delayed by the winter storm and by the difficult crossing of the Delaware. A spy embedded in Washington's camp had alerted the British to the general's plans, putting Hessians in the British army on guard for hours before the attack. But because the delay was so long the British relaxed their guard and the attack turned out to be a surprise after all. In addition to causing the postponement of Washington's attack, the blizzard favored the Patriots in another way. Washington's American army fought under cover from inside houses along the streets of Trenton while the Hessians fought in the open, with snow and rain soaking their muskets and wetting their powder. With his legendary immunity to bullets, his confidence-inspiring, granite composure, and his iconic solidity, Washington swung into action and mobilized his men. His army killed 600 Hessians and captured 900 of them. The prisoners would later be paraded through the streets of Philadelphia.

James Monroe, who would become the fifth president of the United States, crossed the Delaware with Washington and was badly wounded at the Battle of Trenton. Artist John Trumbull, who depicted Monroe lying on the ground, remarked that the bullet that brought Monroe down raised him to the presidency. Alexander Hamilton fought alongside Washington at both Trenton and Princeton. When Washington became president he appointed Hamilton as the first United States secretary of the treasury. General Washington described the Battle of Trenton in a letter to "Gen McDougal" dated 28 December 1776:

> I hope that the late Success at Trenton on the 26th and the Consequence of it, will change the face of Matters not only there but every where else. I crossed over to Jersey the Evening of the 25th about 9 miles above Trenton with upwards of 2000 Men and attacked three Regiments of Hessians consisting of fifteen hundred Men about 8 o'clock next Morning. Our Men pushed on with such Rapidity that they soon carried four pieces of Cannon out of Six, Surrounded the Enemy and obliged 30 Officers and 886 privates to lay down their Arms without firing a Shot. Our Loss was only two Officers and two or three privates wounded. The Enemy had between 20 and 30 killed. We should have made the whole of them prisoners, could Genl. Ewing have passed the Delaware at Trenton and got in their Rear, but the ice prevented him.

It has been said that, in general, for every soldier who died in a Revolutionary War battle eight died from noncombat causes. In addition to Washington's primary account of the Battle of Trenton, tradition tells us that two black slaves froze to death. One anecdote indicates that Tom Graves, a young black man, wanted to join the volunteer black American soldiers under Washington's command or the black soldiers of Glover's Marblehead Regiment (by early 1778, black Americans comprised 10 percent of Washington's forces). Washington said the boy was too young to fight but asked him to hold a lantern to light the way for troops crossing the freezing Delaware in the dark of night. The young man, memorialized as a boy called "Jocko," froze to death still bravely holding the lantern. The legend goes that Washington was so moved by the story of "Jocko" that he ordered a commemorative statue in his honor. It was a sculpture of the courageous and patriotic young man dressed as a jockey holding the ring of a hitching post in his hand. Oral history has it that the symbol of "Jocko" again served the cause of freedom, this time freedom from slavery, during the Civil War when his statue was used to mark safe houses for the Underground Railroad. Green ribbons tied to the arms of the statue signified a safe house; red ribbons meant keep going. Charles Blockson, historian/author/curator of the Blockson Black American Collection at Temple University, points out the following: "People who don't know the history of the jockey have feelings of humiliation and anger when they see the statue.... But this figure which was sometimes used in a clandestine nature, and sometimes without the knowledge of the person who owned the statue, was a positive and supportive image to Black Americans on the road to freedom." Sometimes, added Blockson, a flag was put into the hand of the statue to indicate safety.[11]

Having crossed the Delaware and won victory over Hessian soldiers at Trenton, Washington ferried across icy waters a third time and returned to Pennsylvania. Many American troops, knowing that their enlistments would terminate within a few days, were dreaming of returning home. When drums beat out a roll call for volunteers and no one stepped forward, Washington pulled up his horse and rode along the long line of men. In his reserved manner he said, "My brave fellows, you have done all I asked you to do and more than could be reasonably expected. But your country is at stake, your wives, your houses and all that you hold dear.... If you will consent to stay one month longer, you will render that service to the cause of liberty and to your country which you probably can never do under any other circumstances." One by one the soldiers were saying among themselves, "I will remain if you will." Finally, all 200 men reenlisted for six more weeks. During that time, one-half would die from wounds or illness.[12]

On December 30, 1776, Washington put into motion a secret plan. Confiding his covert mission only to his generals, the American commander in chief rowed his army across the Delaware a fourth time. He intended to camp at the now-deserted village of Trenton and then march on to attack the British rear guard in Princeton, but General Cornwallis got wind of the scheme. When Cornwallis heard that the Continental Army was encamped at Trenton, he advanced toward the American camp. Washington, however, foiled the enemy's plan. Arriving at Trenton after dark, Cornwallis saw the American campfires burning and assumed that the full Continental Army was there warming their hands over the fires.

Washington, however, had ordered a decoy of troops to tend the fires while the bulk of his army slipped behind enemy lines. With wheels wrapped in rags to muffle the rumble, the bulk of the army marched silently toward the college town of Princeton. Traveling with Washington were generals Nathanael Greene and Hugh Mercer, a Pennsylvania surgeon. Washington personally led the charge up the hill for the Battle of Princeton on January 3,

1777. A perfect target sitting on his white horse, he seemed impervious to bullets. The snow-white battlefield became soaked with blood when the Americans and the British clashed at Clark's Orchard. By the time Cornwallis left the deserted campfires Washington's army had won the Battle of Princeton and was again slipping away. Forty Patriots were killed. The British dead numbered 175.

Because Howe had failed to stop him in New Jersey, Washington had crossed the icy Delaware and triumphed at Trenton and Princeton. Neither was a major battle but each turned out to be a tremendous moral victory that revived the seemingly hopeless American cause and kept it alive. After the Battle of Princeton, the British army, now confined to the east side of the Delaware, wintered in New Jersey while their officers partied in New York society. As Washington's battle-weary troops marched toward Morristown after the Battle of Princeton, they were too tired to pursue enemy soldiers who made off with 20 wagon loads of clothing and linens near the village of Somerset Court House. Later that month, however, the New Jersey Militiamen and Continentals retrieved some of the stolen livestock, supplies, and wagons, as well as flour pilfered from Van Nest's Mill.

Washington set up quarters in Morristown, New Jersey, in early January 1777 and stayed there until June, guarding the road to Philadelphia. He twice chose Morristown as his winter headquarters because it was strategically located between New York, where the bulk of the enemy was quartered, and Philadelphia, where the Second Continental Congress was working. Morristown was easily defended, situated on busy communication routes and surrounded by a community of Patriots. That same month of January 1777, Washington ordered Dr. William Shippen, Jr., to inoculate the smallpox virus into every soldier who came through Philadelphia who had not had the disease, "for should the disorder infect the army in the natural way and rage with its usual violence, we should have more to dread from it than the sword of the enemy." Even so, smallpox caused 90 percent of disease-related deaths in the Revolution. Washington was familiar with the ravages of smallpox, as he had contracted it in Barbados when he was 19 years old.

Keeping up appearances before an enemy army almost twice the size of the Continental Army, although imperative, was nearly impossible. Washington, making good use of his "gift of silence," as John Adams called it, kept his army's lack of gunpowder a "profound secret." Benjamin Franklin suggested supplying the troops with bows and arrows. "Those were good weapons," he said, "not wisely laid aside." Though usually reserved, Washington occasionally "after a few glasses of champagne got quite merry and ... laughed and talked a good deal" at lengthy mid-afternoon dinners with intimate friends. Yet he demanded self-sacrifice—"early rising and almost perpetual duty"—from his officers, who were compelled to join him sleeping under single blankets on hard floors or in fields.[13] Washington's letter dated January 19, 1777, addressed to the "President of Congress" reported that American troops were "absolutely perishing" from want of clothing, "marching over Frost and Snow, many without a Shoe, Stocking or Blanket." "The cry of want of Provisions came to me from every Quarter," he said.

From his first encampment at Morristown, Washington supervised generals like Nathanael Greene, Anthony Wayne and Henry Knox and managed an active recruitment campaign. From there he also expanded the spy network he had started in 1775 at Cambridge. With his sphinx-like expression he was an artful spymaster, covering New York, "the fountain of intelligence," with informers disguised as Tories who often wrote secret messages in invisible ink, either on blank pages or between the lines of family letters.[14] Washington's intelligence-gathering network ranged from unknown persons of low status to military officers to members of Congress. He dispatched a letter authorizing New Yorker Nathaniel Sackett to set up a spy network and promised to pay him fifty dollars a month "for your care and trouble in this business."[15]

In 1778 Washington requested Benjamin Tallmadge to organize a spy network to infiltrate the Tory stronghold of New York City and gather military intelligence. Tallmadge, who had worked under the spymaster Nathaniel Sackett, became one of the founders of the first organized spy operation in America. His top-secret espionage ring operated under the code name Samuel Culper. The Culper Ring became Washington's primary source for military information in New York during the American Revolution. Culper was actually two men, Abraham Woodhull and Robert Townsend. Initially both men signed secret correspondence as Samuel Culper. Later the two distinguished themselves: Woodhull signed as Culper, Sr., and Townsend as Culper, Jr.

At the time, only Tallmadge knew the identities of the Culper gang. The spy ring's central figure, Robert Townsend, was a society reporter and a dry-goods store owner whose occupations provided perfect cover. Mingling clandestinely at social functions, he conversed with British soldiers and overheard confidential conversation. At his store Townsend was able to scoop up threads of secret information dropped by his unsuspecting customers as they picked up fabric, ribbons and lace. He communicated this intelligence in invisible ink in letters he dropped into certain customers' packages. On horseback or in carriages the customers were able to carry secrets across British lines. Much of the gathered information needed to be passed to whaleboat captain Caleb Brewster—Culper spy number 725—who was in the Continental Army and commissioned to raid British ships traveling the waters of Long Island Sound.

This is where Anna Smith Strong, another link in the chain of information, came in. Anna could see the waters off the Sound as she hung laundry for her six children on her clothesline. Brewster signaled Anna when he docked in one of the coves. In turn, Anna arranged her laundry on her clothesline to communicate which of the six coves, numbered one through six, Brewster occupied. A black petticoat meant Brewster was anchored. The number of white handkerchiefs beside the petticoat indicated which cove. In this way the neighboring farmer friend who gathered Townsend's information in a box knew Brewster's whereabouts and delivered the information to him.[16]

While Washington was still at Morristown, General William Tryon, a former royal governor of North Carolina but now military governor of New York, obeyed General Howe's command to destroy a Danbury storehouse filled with provisions and military supplies. The Connecticut cities of Norwalk and Danbury are separated from Long Island, New York, by Long Island Sound. Tryon, the last Crown governor of New York, commanded a combination of 2,000 British, Hessian, and Loyalist (American Tory) troops. In April 1777 he sailed on the East River across Long Island Sound, landed on the Connecticut shore, marched to Danbury and ransacked the Continental Army storage warehouses. Confiscating clothing, medicine, pork, flour, molasses, and ammunition, his troops burned the village and terrorized its citizens. Burning the village of Norwalk, the soldiers left only six homes intact.

On a lakeshore in Carmel, New York, stands a bronze statue of 16-year-old Sybil Ludington riding sidesaddle on her horse, Star. This commemorates her famous 40-mile gallop through the New York countryside to alert farmers, villagers and militiamen with a rousing cry: "The British are burning Danbury!" Four hundred militiamen mustered to join their regiment, commanded by Colonel Ludington, Sybil's father. They marched 25 miles to Danbury and crushed Tryon's troops.[17] Sybil's Paul Revere-type ride alerted Benedict Arnold, a native of Connecticut. Arnold then led a band of Patriots and erected a barricade in Ridgefield, a village of 50 homes, to trap Tryon on his return to Long Island. In the ensuing Battle of Ridgefield, Tryon rolled a cannon into Main Street and fired a cannonball into a tavern, where it remains lodged to this day. During the battle Patriot Benedict Arnold (before he betrayed America and turned Tory) entangled his foot in the stirrup when his horse was shot out from under him. A Tory soldier yelling, "Surrender!" charged toward Arnold, who disengaged his trapped foot, pulled out a rifle, and shot the Tory dead. Arnold then escaped to a swamp and later received from the Continental Congress not only an award for bravery but also a new horse and a commission of major general. In the Battle of Ridgefield, Connecticut's only inland battle, 20 Patriots and 26 British soldiers died.

Washington, still guarding Philadelphia, marched his army from his headquarters at Morristown, New Jersey, to Pennsylvania in a desperate attempt to save the nation's capital and Congress from British attack. General William Howe was also moving his army to Philadelphia, but instead of proceeding 60 miles from New York City across New Jersey he chose a circuitous route. A Maryland Historical Society marker at Howe's Landing says that on July 23, 1777, Howe and 15,000 British troops set sail from Sandy Hook, New Jersey, transported by a fleet of 300 warships under the command of his brother, Admiral Richard Howe.

Philadelphia Campaign of 1777 (Glen McCroskey).

The armada, the largest fleet ever assembled in American waters, was bound for Philadelphia. During the month-long ocean voyage soldiers were seasick and scores of horses died. Instead of approaching Philadelphia from the Delaware River, the Howe brothers sailed south in the Atlantic to the Chesapeake Bay and debarked at Head of Elk, Maryland, on August 25.

A Delaware Historic Commissions Iron Hill marker titled *Washington's Reconnaissance* reads as follows: "Generals Washington, Greene, and Lafayette came to Iron Hill, August 26, 1777, in hope of viewing the British Army then landing along Elk River. Only a few tents could be seen. A heavy storm coming up, they spent the night in a nearby farmhouse." The next day, when the thunderstorms subsided, Howe began his 50-mile inland march toward the nation's capital. "Howe must mean to reach Philadelphia by that route," Washington wrote to Israel Putnam, "though to be sure it is a very strange one."[18] Realizing that Howe's route was designed to lure the Continental Army into a major engagement with British troops in the countryside outside Philadelphia, Washington began to rally Continentals to oppose the British. Before going out to repulse Howe, however, he endeavored to encourage Patriots and discourage Tories. A large and graceful equestrian who enjoyed parading on a white horse, Washington rode through Philadelphia at the head of 12,000 Continentals. He asked each parading man to wear a sprig of green in his hat to symbolize victory. The tattered, undisciplined, and untrained troops were not able to march in time with the beat of drum and fife, which bothered Washington, who loved to dance. Whether parading on a horse or promenading on a dance floor, he always moved with grace and dignity.

On September 11 Washington—with 19-year-old Major General Marquis de Lafayette, the Frenchman, riding by his side, and Alexander Hamilton, Washington's aide, not far behind—assembled his ragged, courageous recruits on the banks of Brandywine Creek near Chadds Ford. The Americans attempted to block the anticipated onslaught of British troops, who fully intended to attack the nation's capital, where delegates of the Second Continental Congress were in session. As Howe approached Chadds Ford, Washington informed his men that the "upcoming battle might be decisive. Should the British be defeated 'they are utterly undone—the war is at an end....' Not trusting Patriotism alone, he reminded his men that fleeing soldiers would be instantly shot down as a just punishment to themselves and to others."[19]

General Howe, on his way to Philadelphia, silently advanced toward Brandywine Creek. But instead of crossing Brandywine at Chadds Ford, where Washington expected him to cross, Howe forded the creek north of Chadds Ford at an unguarded crossing. He then marched southward to confront Washington. Sneaking up on Washington through a cover of thick fog, Howe caught the unsuspecting general by surprise. "Washington's inestimable strength, whether as a general, a planter, or a politician, was prolonged deliberation and slow, mature decisions, but these were luxuries seldom permitted in the heat of battle"[20] and did not serve him well at this time.

Howe's German soldiers, led by General William von Knyphausen, charged the American front line. As the fog lifted and the sun began to blaze, Cornwallis crossed the creek and assaulted the Continental flank. Fighting at Brandywine under Cornwallis on September 11, 1777, was Major Patrick Ferguson, who deliberately avoided an opportunity to shoot a rebel officer and his escort, a French hussar. Thin, short, and good-looking in an elfish sort of way, Ferguson was known for his gentlemanly and chivalrous conduct. He wrote that he resisted in this instance because the act of shooting someone in the back disgusted him. Historians think that the officer was Washington and the French hussar was probably the Polish count Casimir Pulaski. Later, in this same battle, a bullet penetrated Ferguson's right elbow and paralyzed his arm, quite a loss for this famed marksman and inventor of the breech-loading rifle. Not deterred, the tenacious "Bulldog" Ferguson learned to fire with his left arm. But that one too would be injured, in a bayonet accident in Charlestown, South Carolina, nearly three years later.

At Brandywine, Howe's British and Hessian soldiers killed or wounded 800 Americans and captured 400. Among the wounded was a Virginia officer named John Marshall, who had fought with Washington at Trenton and would be a future chief justice of the U.S. Supreme Court. Retreating with the Americans from Brandywine, the Marquis de Lafayette felt blood running down into his left boot and realized he had been shot in the calf. He was carried off the field. Writing to his wife he said, "When [Washington] learned that I wanted to rejoin the army too soon, he wrote the warmest of letters, urging me to concentrate on getting well first."[21] American losses far exceeded those of the British. The Continental commander in chief sent a letter to John Hancock. "Sir," he said, "I am sorry to inform you that in this day's engagement, we have been obliged to leave the enemy masters of the field." Thomas Jefferson noted that Washington prepared thoroughly for battles and did extremely well if everything went according to plan but he lacked the gift of spontaneity: "If any member of his plan was dislocated by sudden circumstances, he was slow in readjustment."[22] Technically the British won the battle, but they failed to destroy Washington's Continental Army. By failing to win the Battle of Brandywine, the Americans left the door to Philadelphia wide open.

John Adams had fled with the Continental Congress to Lancaster, Pennsylvania, in south central Pennsylvania, for one day in September and then to York, Pennsylvania, where Congress would remain for nine months. Adams criticized Washington for his weak defense of the Philadelphia capital. The congressman wrote to his wife, Abigail: "I believe the two Howes have not very great women for wives. If they had, we should suffer more from their exertions than we do. This is our good fortune. A smart wife would have put Howe in possession of Philadelphia a long time ago."[23]

On September 18 Washington sent Hamilton to alert Hancock that the British might enter Philadelphia by daybreak and the Continental Army could not adequately protect the American capital. This news triggered a mass moonlight exodus of panicky citizens and congressmen. However, it was another week before the British entered the city, and this allowed time for Washington to send Hamilton and 100 men into the city to solicit blankets, clothing and ammunition for his destitute troops. He asked Hamilton to issue vouchers to the donors, hoping that someday they would be reimbursed.

After Brandywine, Washington moved his barefoot, exhausted and hungry main force to Reading to reequip and rest. Having reinforced his army, he then marched his troops across the Schuylkill River to encamp at Pennypacker's Mills near Skippack Creek 30 miles northwest of Philadelphia. In the process, he stripped a 50-mile radius clean of cattle, feed, fuel, and other materials necessary for the army.

Washington sent General Anthony Wayne and his Pennsylvanians to harass Howe's rear guard as the British marched triumphantly toward Philadelphia. At Paoli, 20 miles west of Philadelphia, the British rear reversed and retaliated with a surprise attack. Wielding sabers and shouting huzzahs they charged Wayne's sleeping forces at dawn before the Americans could grab their guns. The methodical slaughtering of Wayne's unarmed pickets created a grisly mess called the Paoli Massacre. Wayne's troops swore revenge with the rebel cries "Revenge Wayne's Affair" and "Remember Paoli." Washington was encamped at Skippack Creek when he learned of the September 20 massacre of Wayne's troops at Paoli.

General Howe, after defeating Washington at the Battle of Brandywine, sent Cornwallis to Philadelphia. The well-nourished British troops under Cornwallis entered Philadelphia on September 26. They were met mainly by frightened women and children, the men having fled. Overpowering the city, Cornwallis's army and camp followers commandeered houses and pitched tents. While Cornwallis occupied Philadelphia, Howe kept the main British Army—9,000 men—at Germantown, on the Schuylkill River six miles northwest of Philadelphia. He diverted two regiments to attack American forts on the Delaware.

Washington was at Skippack Creek when he learned that Howe had sent a portion of the British army on a long trip to Head of Elk to load supply wagons. He told his generals, "It [i]s time to remind the English that an American army still exist[s]."[24] Taking advantage of the split British Army, Washington decided to attack Howe's remaining 9,000 troops at Germantown and recapture Philadelphia. When Howe learned that Washington had moved his entire ill-trained, recently defeated Continental Army to Skippack Creek, he knew that his 9,000 troops at Germantown could block the most likely avenues of approach Washington might use to recapture America's capital city.

Washington's complex and ambitious plan to attack Howe's forces at Germantown involved dividing his American forces into four columns. Each was to move at least 20 miles through the night in strict silence, by separate routes, and simultaneously strike British outposts at precisely 5:00 A.M. on October 4, 1777. Couriers would coordinate the timing between columns. Each man wore a piece of white paper in his hat for identification in the darkness. Washington's army started moving at 7:00 P.M. on October 3. Washington and Sullivan led a column of 3,000 soldiers down the Germantown Road; Greene led 5,000 men along a parallel path; Smallwood led 1,000 militiamen along an old Indian path; John Armstrong led 2,000 Pennsylvania militiamen to the south along the Schuylkill.

Somewhere in the darkness, both Greene's and Smallwood's columns got lost. When Washington and Sullivan arrived at their assigned position on time, they assumed that Greene had done the same. Sullivan then signaled his leading brigade to assault the British picket of light infantry at Chestnut Hill. Furious about the massacre at Paoli they shouted, "Avenge Wayne's affair!" as they fired a volley toward the British tents. The British fired back. The shots alerted the main British force in Germantown two miles to the south. Fearless as always, Washington rode his white horse into the midst of battle, miraculously impervious to cannonballs and grapeshot. "In hand to hand combat the Pennsylvanians pushed back the British.... Americans heard a British bugler sound retreat." Hurrying up the Germantown Pike and rallying the fleeing British, Howe himself appeared out of the fog shouting, "For shame, light infantry! I never saw you retreat before. Form! Form! It's only a scouting party."[25] But when a round of grape-sized lead balls whizzed by, Howe dived for cover. By sunrise the British 40th Foot under Colonel Thomas Musgrave rushed to Chestnut Hill to reinforce the light infantry.

Several Musgrave companies—120 men who were cut off by the American attack—ran for cover and barricaded themselves in the vacant Chew House, a stone house named Cliveden. Cliveden's owner, Judge Benjamin Chew, was in prison as a suspected Tory. Musgrave's men barricaded the oak doors and windows downstairs and sniped from the upstairs windows. Ignoring the small nest of holed-up men, Sullivan's and Wayne's divisions, barely able to see through the dense fog and gun smoke, spread out and moved over open fields, brooks and fences. Driving the British light infantry before them, they were heading for Market Square, the agreed-upon meeting point at the end of Germantown where the four attacking American columns were supposed to converge and recapture Philadelphia.

Along Germantown Road, winding through the two-mile stretch that comprised the hamlet of Germantown, the rallying British dived into a line of stone houses. From windows and behind walls they spat a steady stream of fire on Sullivan's and Wayne's men. While Sullivan and Wayne swept through Germantown, Washington reached the Chew House strongpoint where Musgrove's British were sniping from windows. Instead of following Sullivan to converge at the Market Square, General Henry Knox objected to leaving a fortress in the rear. He convinced Washington to bombard Cliveden and call the brigades out of reserve to storm the stone mansion. Knox's three-pound cannon balls were unable to break through the massive oak doors, and many of the assaulting reserve infantrymen were mowed down or bayoneted in the courtyard garden, which now was a battlefield filled with broken vases and headless marble statuary. Cannonballs struck more Americans than Englishmen.

In the smog, Anthony Wayne turned his Continental column around and came back to Cliveden. When Greene's column finally got back on the right road, Greene showed up on the battlefield at Cliveden. His subordinate, Adam Stephen, who would later face court-martial, lay drunk in the barn while his confused Virginia militiamen shot Wayne's countermarching Pennsylvanians. Friendly fire exhausted the ammunition of both columns. The British then opened deadly fire. The Americans backed away in pell-mell retreat. Greene withdrew when he learned that Sullivan's column was retreating. The British pursued both columns for nine miles. Hundreds of sick and wounded American soldiers returned to the Skippack area. A historical marker located on Germantown Avenue on the grounds of Cliveden in the Germantown neighborhood of Philadelphia, Pennsylvania, reads as follows:

> The Battle of Germantown occurred at Cliveden, the country home of Provincial chief Justice Benjamin Chew on Oct. 4, 1777. A British regiment occupied Cliveden and defended it from full assault by the colonials. Over 70 soldiers died on these grounds. Although it was an American defeat, Washington's bold strategy helped win French aid for the cause of independence.

For three hours Washington's troops had nearly routed the British and appeared to be winning. His troops, untrained in maneuvering under fire, were brave to have attempted such a difficult feat. British casualties were 500. An estimated 1,000 American were killed, wounded or missing, and 400 were taken prisoner.

Anna Maria Lane, masquerading as a soldier, was wounded at Germantown. Her approved pension record states, "In the garb, and with the courage of a soldier, [she] performed extraordinary military service and received a severe wound at the Battle of Germantown." Virginia state records indicate the governor entered a petition on behalf of Anna Marie Lane declaring, "She is very infirm having been disabled by a severe wound which she received fighting as a common soldier in one of our Revolutionary Battles" (Germantown). The state at the same time "pensioned a John Lane, possibly her husband or brother."[26]

The French court and Charles Gravier, Comte de Vergennes, who were on the verge of forming an alliance with the Americans, were not discouraged by the American defeat at Germantown. They were instead impressed that the Americans could raise a raw army gutsy enough to attack seasoned British troops. Howe missed chances to end the war when he failed to destroy the defeated American forces at Brandywine and Germantown. (Two days after the Battle of Germantown, Washington returned a lost dog with the following note to General Howe: "Sir William Howe: General Washington's Compliments to General Howe, does himself the pleasure to return him a Dog, which accidentally fell into his hands, and by the inscription on the collar, appears to belong to General Howe. October 6th. 1777.")[27]

General Howe, having captured Philadelphia in September and defended Germantown in early October, detached Hessian troops from his main army at Germantown and sent them to reduce three forts on the Delaware River: Fort Billingsport, Fort Mercer (Red Bank) and Fort Mifflin. Americans had built these forts on the river for the defense of the nation's capital at Philadelphia. Howe needed a safe supply route for the British navy to bring food, clothing and munitions to British-occupied Philadelphia. Hence, he soon forced the evacuation of Fort Billingsport. Forts Mercer and Mifflin, standing on opposite sides of the Delaware, remained as twin threats interrupting British shipping and navigation

New Jersey's Fort Mercer at Red Bank Plantation was placed under control of the New Jersey militia. In anticipation of a British attack, it was reinforced with the black American 1st and the 2nd Rhode Island regiments under the command of Colonel Christopher Greene. The Fort Mercer garrison sank destructive *chevaux de frise* ("frizzy horses," large timbers with branching iron-tipped arms) into the Delaware River. The sharp points of these underwater monsters pierced and splintered the wooden bottoms of British ships trying to navigate the waters between Fort Mercer and Fort Mifflin. In the Battle at Fort Mercer on October 22, 1777, the HMS *Augusta* bombarded the fort from the river, while three battalions of Hessians and a regiment of foot soldiers approached from the woods. The New Jersey and Rhode Island garrisons successfully defended Fort Mercer, causing many Hessian and British casualties. The day after the Fort Mercer battle, Patriots set fire to the anchored *Augusta* and watched it explode in the harbor. It was the same ship whose cannonballs had ripped through a home where a Quaker woman sat spinning. The very same Quaker woman nursed the ship's wounded Hessian soldiers, offering them water, changing dressings and bringing food while she scolded them for bombarding her house.[28]

The garrison of Pennsylvania's Fort Mifflin on the swampy Mud Island was outpowered and out-numbered by British cannon and men. On the night of November 15, 1777, the Patriot soldiers evacuated the fort. Rowing with muffled oars, they crossed the Delaware and reinforced New Jersey's Fort Mercer. Even so, a few days later Fort Mercer began evacuation. The withdrawing troops hurriedly set fire to the fort on November 21 just as Lord Cornwallis's 2,000 light infantry came into sight. Leaving Fort Mercer in ashes and Howe in control of the Delaware, the exhausted American soldiers of the Continental Army spent six weeks encamped at Whitemarsh, Pennsylvania, before going on to spend the bleak winter at Valley Forge.

Early in December General Howe failed to succeed in a surprise attack on Washington's Whitemarsh camp. Having been warned by spies, the Americans were well prepared and able to withstand the attack. After three days of skirmishing, the British returned to Philadelphia. Spymaster John André attempted to identify the informer who had warned Washington. One traditional version implicates Lydia Darragh. While occupying Philadelphia, General Howe commandeered a room for meetings at the Darragh house across the street from his headquarters. On December 2, 1777, housewife Lydia Darragh, a Quaker immigrant from Northern Ireland, courageously eavesdropped through a wall of the meeting room. She overheard a plan to attack Washington's army at nearby Whitemarsh, where Washington was temporarily encamped. Lydia obtained a pass from Howe to carry an empty flour bag and go to a mill to buy flour. She walked safely through British lines and hastened to American lines. She told a Patriot colonel what she had heard. The colonel relayed the information. Thus warned, Washington was prepared when the British appeared. After a few skirmishes, Howe withdrew.

Like most oral histories, Lydia Darragh's story has been discredited by some and believed by others. John André, the British spymaster who was later caught for conspiring with the traitor Benedict Arnold, allegedly knocked on the Darragh door on December 9 and asked if anyone had been up on the night of the second. Lydia, the female Patriot spy who wasn't caught, answered, "No, everybody went to sleep early that night." André then told Lydia, "One thing is certain, the Enemy had notice of our coming, was prepared for us, and had made us look like a parcel of fools. The walls must have ears."[29]

5

Saratoga Campaign, Ben Franklin and French Aid

The Saratoga Campaign raged in the North from June to mid–October 1777. Britain's General John Burgoyne had no idea that General Howe had leisurely sailed from New York to the Chesapeake Bay and captured Philadelphia. Burgoyne was expecting Howe to rendezvous with him at Albany, as Howe's cooperation was vital for the success of Burgoyne's Saratoga Plan. But the plan would go terribly wrong

In March 1777 Burgoyne was appointed commander of the Northern Army in Canada. It was a post that he had begun seeking the previous year when he devised his Saratoga Campaign. His divide-and-conquer strategy would join two British armies. One, led by himself, would move south from Canada. The other, led by General William Howe, commander of the British Army in America, would move north through New York. The two prongs would meet in Albany, New York. Once in control of the Hudson, they would isolate New England from the rest of the colonies. This would impede the movement of troops and supplies between North and South. Burgoyne sought to subdue the rebels in the populous Northeast. Three-quarters of America's three million colonists lived in a strip between Massachusetts and the northern boundary of Virginia. When the North surrendered, he hoped the other colonies would lose heart.

Glamorous and vain, Burgoyne was the "least aristocratic of the British commanders in America." He was plain "Gentleman Johnny," descended from the landholding gentry. He was also a famous, flamboyant, and popular playwright, as well as a politician and a soldier. But he proved to be a painfully deficient and overly confident commander. His paper, "My Thoughts for Conducting the War from the Side of Canada," was endorsed by King George III. The king assigned Lord George Germaine, the secretary of state for the colonies, to administer the plan. Germaine was the British "cabinet minister most responsible for the conduct of the war."[1]

The implementation of Burgoyne's "British strategic plan for 1777 was so bad as to be almost unbelievable."[2] Not one of its three main architects—Burgoyne, Howe, or Germaine—had adequate strategic ability. Making matters worse, the communication among the three was virtually nonexistent. The Burgoyne plan proposed to move British troops south by a lake-river route from Canada to rendezvous with Howe in Albany. Burgoyne further planned that Howe would capture the citadel at West Point on his way to Albany. Fort West Point was the key to the Hudson River, as it was strategically positioned to block the passage of enemy ships carrying supplies and troops. Burgoyne's ultimate "objective was to destroy Washington's army and kill or capture Washington."[3]

In May 1777, just before Burgoyne departed England, he wrote to Howe that he expected to meet up with him at Albany. Howe promptly replied that he would be unable to meet, that his force was too small to detach a corps along the Hudson, and that he would probably be in Pennsylvania. Earlier in 1777 Howe had described to Germaine a plan entirely different from that of Burgoyne. He proposed to capture Philadelphia, where Congress was protected by General George Washington, commander in chief of the American Continental Army. Incredibly, "Germaine approved Howe's plan in early March, at the moment he was giving final consideration to Burgoyne's plan."[4] He allowed the two British armies in America to split and travel in opposite directions. He permitted Burgoyne to move down the Hudson to Albany to establish communications with Howe from New York, but he also agreed that Howe's force could move away from New York toward the Delaware River. Perhaps Germaine thought Howe would have time to make the 100-mile (usually 12-day) overland trip to Philadelphia and capture the city in time to meet Burgoyne in Albany.

Burgoyne and Howe began their separate expeditions in June. Howe, however, seeking to hide his maneuver from Washington's Continental Army, delayed his trip for almost two months. Leaving behind in New York only a small force under his second in command, General Henry Clinton, Howe, as previously described, led the main force on a time-consuming, circuitous water route through the Chesapeake Bay to capture Philadelphia. "Instead of concentrating their strength, the British forces were now dispersed over eight hundred miles of country, and divided between Burgoyne in Canada, Howe on the Chesapeake, and Clinton in New York."[5] In June, when Burgoyne was planning his north-south, two-pronged invasion of New York, he was still expecting—as approved by Germaine—to meet Howe in Albany. Thus Burgoyne detached a small diversionary force, a third prong of attack from the west. He gave Colonel Barry St. Leger a brevet rank of brigadier general for the western expedition. General St. Leger was to leave from Montreal in Quebec Province and sail up the St. Lawrence River to Oswego on Lake Ontario. He was to liberate Loyalists in the Mohawk Valley, capture Fort Stanwix and then meet Burgoyne in Albany. Canadian governor Carlton raised 1,000 Indians for St. Leger and 400 for Burgoyne.[6]

The Six Nations of the Iroquois Confederacy played a significant role in the Saratoga Campaign, especially on St. Leger's route through the Mohawk Valley, where the Six Nations lived. Earlier in their history, the Iroquois had waged the Beaver Wars and conquered, driven out, or exterminated their neighboring Algonquin tribes, including the Illinois, the Shawnee and the Miami. Later, by right of conquest, the Six Nations claimed title to lands surrounding the Ohio River and southward to the Holston River in what became (East) Tennessee, which they recognized as their southern boundary separating them from the Cherokee. Calling themselves "the people of the Longhouse," the Six Nations lived in the northeastern woodlands of the Hudson and Mohawk valleys in what is now New York State. The hallway of the longhouse was the Mohawk River. The Mohawks guarded the longhouse door to the east. Then came the Oneidas and the Tuscarora, followed by the Onondaga, keepers of the sacred fire. To the west were the Cayuga and the Seneca, who were the gatekeepers of the west.

The Mohawk Valley was a principal passage between the Adirondack Mountains and the Appalachian Plateau. Fort Stanwix, the only fort in the Mohawk Valley, was crucial because it guarded the Oneida Carry. The Oneida Carrying Place was a three-mile portage path between the Mohawk River and Wood Creek, which through a series of waterways drained

5. Saratoga Campaign, Ben Franklin and French Aid

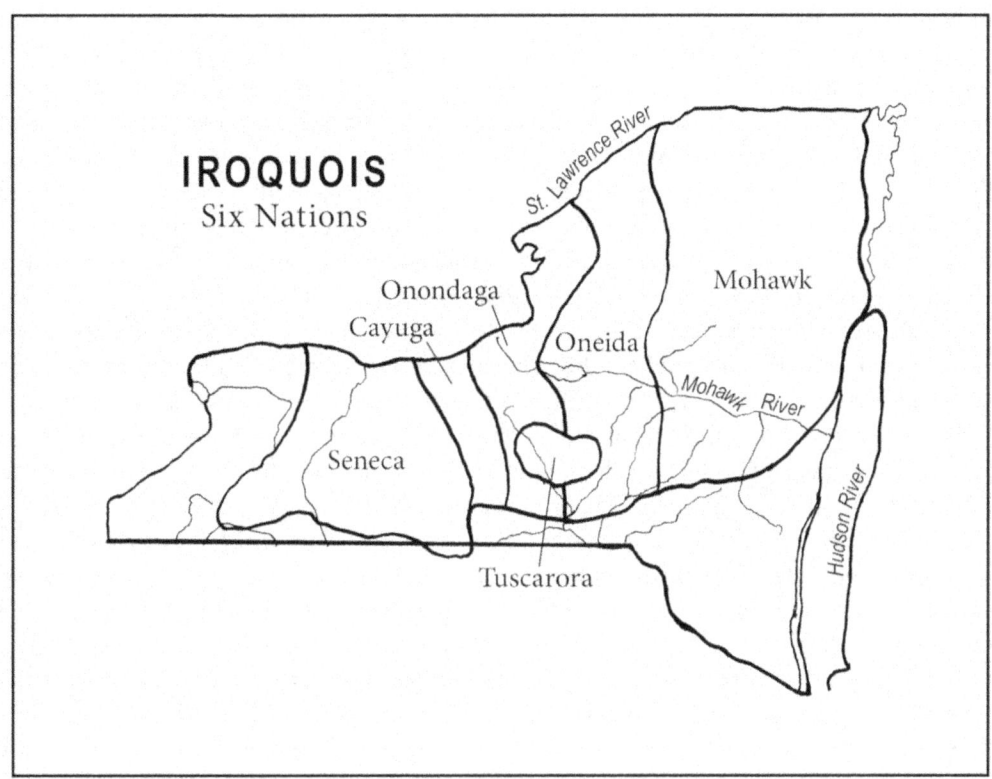

Iroquois Six Nations, Mohawk Valley (Glen McCroskey).

into Lake Ontario. Whoever controlled the Carry controlled the western gateway to the Great Lakes and the St. Lawrence River. The Six Nations split allegiances during the Revolutionary War: Four tribes, the Mohawk, Onondaga, Cayuga, and Seneca, allied with the British as Loyalists. Two tribes, the Oneida and the Tuscarora, joined the American Patriots.

Mohawk chief Joseph Brant joined St. Leger's Siege of Fort Stanwix. Joseph Brant's sister, Molly Brant, was the widow of the celebrated Sir William Johnson. A commemorative plaque honoring Molly Brant erected in Canada by the Ontario Heritage Foundation reads as follows:

> Born about 1736, Molly Brant (Degonwadonti) was a member of a prominent Mohawk family. About 1759 she became the wife of Sir William Johnson, Superintendent of Indian Affairs in the Province of New York and a powerful figure in that colony. Well-educated and a persuasive speaker, Molly Brant wielded great influence among the Iroquois and was responsible for much of Johnson's success in dealing with them. Following the outbreak of the American Revolution she and her younger brother Joseph played a leading role in persuading the Confederacy to support Britain. In 1777 she fled to Canada and after the war, in recognition of her services, was granted a pension by the government. She settled in Cataraqui (Kingston) where she died in 1796.

The Protestant Christian parents of Molly Brant were born in the Mohawk Valley town of Canajoharie. When Molly's father died while the family was living in the Ohio Valley her mother returned to Canajoharie, taking with her two children, Molly and Joseph. The mother then married a man who may have been part Dutch, or at least had some non-native ancestry. Molly and Joseph took their stepfather's surname of Brant, which was contrary to the matrilineal tradition of the Iroquois society, in which children usually take the name of their mother's clan. The Mohawk Nation was one of six members of the Iroquois Confederacy. Each nation had its own clans and each clan had a clan matron. Molly and Joseph's stepfather owned a large house, wore European-style clothing and befriended William Johnson. It was probably through this friendship that William became acquainted with Molly when she was an adolescent. Molly was formally educated in the European tradition, probably in an English mission school where she became fluent in writing and speaking in English. At age 18 she accompanied a delegation of Mohawk elders to Philadelphia to discuss fraudulent land deals. She also learned about Iroquois tradition and became a clan matron. Molly, along with other clan mothers, had great political power. These women chose the chief and had the authority to veto warriors' decisions. Also having economic power, the clan matrons controlled the use of agricultural land and therefore the food supply. At the end of the French and Indian War, William Johnson's German wife died and he began seeing the powerful Molly Brant.

When William Johnson, an Irish immigrant, first settled in the Mohawk Valley under the auspices of his wealthy uncle he became a New York landowner as well as a trusted mentor and mediator of the Iroquois, especially the Mohawks. Fluent in English, French and Iroquois, Johnson was equally at home reclining in a cushioned chair and chatting by the fireside with New York's royal governor or sitting cross-legged around a council fire and puffing a pipe with his Mohawk friends. The Mohawks called him *Warraghiygey*, "He Who Does Big Business."[7] In 1756 William Johnson became a colonel of the Albany County Militia and was appointed royal superintendent of Indian Affairs for the Northern Department of America. In the same year, he received a baronetcy from the king and became Sir William Johnson.

In 1759 widower William Johnson married Molly Brant, by whom he fathered eight children. Educated in a white school, Molly, the stepdaughter of a Mohawk chief and the sister of another, was equal in status to William and was a leader of Indian men in her society. She transitioned easily into the gracious hostess of William Johnson's manor. "Together, Molly and William became the most powerful political force in the Mohawk Valley, creating and sustaining links to both the White and the Indian societies around them.... While Britain ruled the colonies Molly Brant's two worlds, the White and the Indian seemed to be in harmony.... The Revolutionary War shattered that harmony."[8]

Molly's younger brother, Joseph Brant (Thayendanegea), became Johnson's protégé and grew up to be a famous Mohawk chief. William Johnson appointed John Johnson, his Anglo-German son by his first wife, and Guy Johnson, his nephew, as deputies for his Department of Indian Affairs. Because of William Johnson's influence the Mohawks, the easternmost Iroquois tribe, were pro–English in the French and Indian War. Johnson painted his face and dressed like a warrior when fighting alongside his Indian allies. He kept the other Iroquois neutral in the French and Indian War, except for the Seneca, the westernmost tribe, who occasionally fought as French allies.

When Sir William Johnson, the beloved superintendent of Indian Affairs in the North, died in 1774, his nephew and successor, Colonel Guy Johnson, appointed Mohawk chief Joseph Brant as his secretary. Brant received a captain's commission in the British Army and was assigned to unite the Iroquois with the British and Loyalists against Patriots in the

American Revolution. John Johnson's hereditary title of "sir" from his father, William, was confirmed in 1765 by George III, who knighted him. John also led Indian-Loyalist attacks on Patriots in the Mohawk Valley. Because of his Loyalist standing at the beginning of the Revolution, John fled the Mohawk Valley and moved to Canada, where he organized the King's Royal Regiment of New York, made up mostly of Mohawk Valley Loyalists. Sir John Johnson and his regiment allied with St. Leger's western prong of the Saratoga Campaign.

The relationship between the British and the Mohawk was so long-standing that the "British military leaders felt they could employ Mohawks as Mercenaries,"[9] just as they hired Hessian soldiers from the German princes. Lord Dartmouth, British secretary of state for the colonies, informed Colonel Guy Johnson, in a letter datelined Whitehall, 24 July 1775, "It is his majesty's pleasure that you ... induce the Six Nations to take up the hatchet against His Majesty's rebellious subjects in America."[10] The Guy Johnson-Joseph Brant connection was the glue that cemented the British-Mohawk alliance during the Revolution. Chief Brant, who joined the British army as an interpreter of native languages, influenced three other powerful Iroquois tribes—the Onondaga, Cayuga and Seneca—to ally with the British. American Patriots also needed to ally with indigenous peoples. Hence, in May 1776 the Continental Congress resolved to engage American Indians in the service of the united American colonies. The Iroquois-speaking Oneida and Tuscarora, plus some members of the Algonquian-speaking Mohican tribe, allied with the Patriots.

During Burgoyne's Saratoga Campaign, General St. Leger gathered 875 regulars and 1,000 Indians of the Iroquois Confederacy at Oswego, New York, and marched across the Mohawk Valley toward Fort Stanwix, the only American fortress in the Mohawk Valley. Although St. Leger's diversion was meant to encourage Tories to join the British, it had the opposite effect. The sight of a marching army of Iroquois painted for war panicked inhabitants of the valley. Approaching Fort Stanwix, St. Leger demanded surrender. The Patriot commander refused, and St. Leger laid siege to the fort. When General Nicholas Herkimer heard that the British were blockading Fort Stanwix, he gathered Patriot militia and allied Oneida scouts to reinforce the fort's defense. Upon learning that Herkimer was marching, St. Leger detached Sir John Johnson and Chief Joseph Brant and directed them to ambush Herkimer's men before they could reach Fort Stanwix. Johnson led the Royal New York Regiment and Brant led Loyalists of several Iroquois Nations of the Mohawk Valley.

Brant skillfully set a trap for Herkimer's Militia and Oneida Patriots. The ambush was set in a ravine at Oneida Creek near the Oneida village of Oriska (now Oriskany, New York) a few miles east of Fort Stanwix. En route to the fort, Herkimer led 600 Patriot soldiers, 15 wagons and 200 rear guardsmen down the slopes of the fateful ravine, where they were suddenly ensnared in the Battle of Oriskany. In a blaze of musket fire, the Indian Loyalists attacked Herkimer's troops in the gorge. Herkimer's right leg was shot through, and his horse was killed from under him. A few Patriots fled only to be chased by Joseph Brant's Mohawks and Senecas. "We killed most of the men in the American's army" recounted Seneca Chief Blacksnake. "The blood shed made a stream running down on the sloping ground."[11] Patriots carried Herkimer up the hill where, sitting on his saddle under a tree, he organized his remaining men in a circle for defending in all directions. The Fort Stanwix commander aided Herkimer by sending a sortie to create a diversion. The Patriot sortie raided the British-American Indian campsite, taking prisoners and wagonloads of booty. It was a civil war. Whigs fought Tories, brother shot brother, and Iroquois tribes attacked

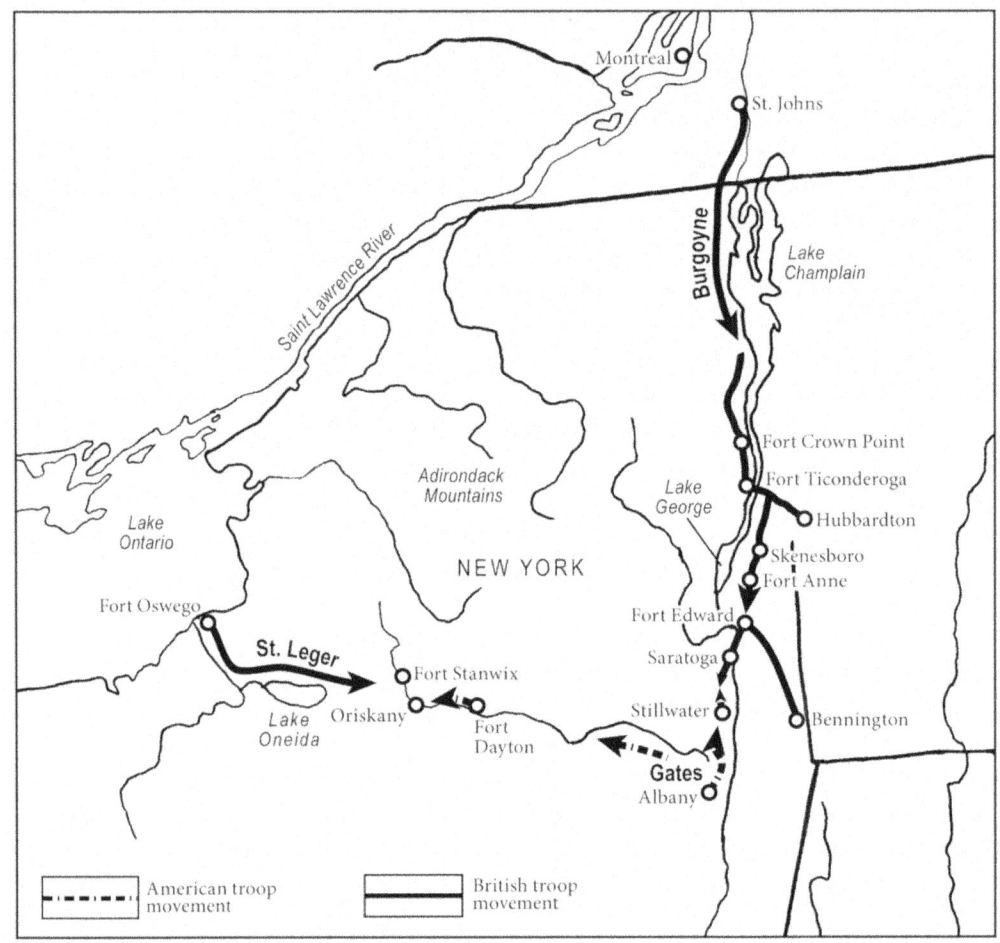

Burgoyne's Campaign June–October 1777 (Glen McCroskey).

each other. More than three-quarters of Herkimer's militia either died or were seriously injured. General Herkimer died within days after his leg was amputated. British losses were far fewer than Patriot losses.

A messenger carried news of the ambush to General Philip Schuyler, the commander of the Northern Department. Schuyler quickly dispatched Benedict Arnold and 900 regulars to reinforce the garrison at Fort Stanwix. Arnold cleverly sent a "half-witted Dutchman" to spread the word among the Indians that the Americans were as numerous as "the leaves on the trees."[12] Superstitions abounded among both colonists and Indians in 17th and 18th century America. Since many American Indians thought that mental defectives were possessed of spirits and had magical powers portending doom, the Indians defected en masse. When St. Leger, short on soldiers, returned to Oswego he ended the siege of Fort Stanwix and left Burgoyne without reinforcement. The fort's Patriot garrison then destroyed the village of Oriska and trampled its crops. Oneida and Patriot soldiers forced Molly Brant, Sir William Johnson's widow, to flee her manor home and take refuge in a nearby Cayuga village. She was accused of spying because she had warned St. Leger of Herkimer's approach.

Molly's home was then given to a Patriot Oneida chief who had fought as Herkimer's ally at Oriska.

Back when St. Leger was sailing up the Saint Lawrence to the Mohawk Valley and Howe's army still lingered in New York waiting to sail toward Philadelphia, Burgoyne and his army weighed anchor at St. Johns on the Richelieu River near Montreal and headed south toward Albany. Burgoyne's flotilla comprised 8,000 regulars and Hessians, 250 French Canadians and Tories, and 400 Indians. His forces were accompanied by wives—including German Baroness Von Riedesal—children, other camp followers, an abundant artillery collection, and a long, bulging baggage train. Bolstering Burgoyne's lavish lifestyle, the train included 30 carts of his fancy uniforms and personal supplies. He "was also accompanied by his mistress, the wife of a commissary officer."[13] General Burgoyne's soldiers were prepared for the trek through American forests. Having cut off the red tails of their uniform coats and trimmed the corners off their tri-cornered hats, turning them into caps, they could maneuver unencumbered through thickets and woods. Moving south on Lake Champlain, Burgoyne's army slapped, scratched and fanned their way through the gnat-infested forests of the Adirondacks and emerged exhausted near Fort Ticonderoga on July 1.

Ticonderoga was known by both British and Americans as North America's strongest fort. Its strength, however, was overestimated. Ticonderoga was undermanned. General Arthur St. Clair was in command of the two posts that Burgoyne was fast approaching—one Fort Ticonderoga, the other Mount Independence—housing a combined total of 3,000 Americans. St. Clair's superior officer, General Philip Schuyler, was stationed several miles south, at Fort Edward, on the Hudson. St. Clair had lost no time in evacuating Ticonderoga, New York, and Mt. Independence, Vermont, which was on Lake Champlain across from Ticonderoga. Burgoyne pursued the retreating American army through the woods, taking many prisoners and supplies. "St. Clair was court-martialed for retreating, but was exonerated as it was the only thing he could have done under the circumstances."[14] In their wake, however, St. Clair's withdrawing army left behind burned crops, burned bridges, roadblocks, and swamps created by altering the course of creeks. These obstacles impeded Burgoyne's progress.

The Battle of Hubbardton occurred when Burgoyne's forces caught up with St. Clair's rear guard retreating from Ticonderoga. Fighting took place at Hubbardton in the Green Mountains of Vermont. The courageous American rear guard consisted of the Green Mountain Continental Rangers (Ethan Allen's reorganized Green Mountain Boys), plus troops from New Hampshire and Massachusetts. The British, along with Hessian forces singing hymns during the battle, won a technical victory but losses were heavy on both sides. Although the Americans lost, their well-planned rearguard maneuver delayed the British. Therefore, the July 7, 1777, Battle of Hubbardton is counted as a successful defeat. It was the only Revolutionary War battle fought entirely on Vermont soil.

Burgoyne, blocked by the obstacles in his path, spent almost a month in marching the short distance down the Hudson from Ticonderoga to force the evacuation of Fort Edward. Knowing that General Schuyler's policy was to destroy all the crops along the British line of march, Burgoyne sent a detachment of German dragoons, Canadians and Indians toward the future state of Vermont to capture a large store of supplies that had been gathered for American forces. Their orders were to collect wagonloads of grain and to secure "large supplies of cattle, horses, carriages and crops and from there to proceed on the road between Manchester and Rockingham." Burgoyne's grain-gathering plan was thwarted, however, by

American militiamen from New Hampshire and Vermont. The August 14–16, 1777, Battle of Bennington, Vermont, was actually fought a few miles away in New York.

Having no uniforms, a group of Patriot militiamen disguised themselves by wearing rosettes like those worn by Loyalists. Infiltrating the British side, the victorious masqueraders killed or captured the entire raiding force. The savage trickery was unprecedented in traditional British warfare, in which good breeding dictated that the common soldier fire at the enemy common soldier and never at an officer, all of whom were considered to be gentlemen.[15] "The vigor of the Americans in the attack was described by a Hessian: 'The Americans fought with desperation, pressing within eight paces of the loaded cannon, to take surer aim of the artillerists.'"[16] The defeated Burgoyne and his surviving army delayed leaving Fort Edward until mid–September. Realizing that St. Leger would not meet him, that Howe was far away, and that the cautious Clinton could offer little aid, Burgoyne finally proceeded toward Albany, where he might at least sustain his army. After losing the Battle of Bennington, Burgoyne and his reduced force of soldiers slowly proceeded toward Saratoga on the way to Albany. His cumbersome wagon train advanced only one mile per day, hampered by the American army's device of felling trees and destroying bridges.

News of the American success at Bennington brought hundreds of Vermont militia to enlist at the Gates headquarters. They rallied to George Washington's rousing battle cry, "Let all New England rise and crush Burgoyne." On August 19, 1777, Washington assigned General Horatio Gates to replace General Schuyler as commander of the Continental Army's Northern Department. Gates—ruddy-complexioned and thick-set and with a "large aquiline nose and long hair flowing over his shoulders from a receding hair line"[17]—was a good administrator but a poor field general. He was fortunate to have under his command Benedict Arnold, hero of the 1775 capture of Ticonderoga and the Battle of Quebec. He was also lucky to have Daniel Morgan, the six-foot, 200-pound "Old Wagoner," leading his crack riflemen. Responding to orders sent out by the popular Washington, additional rifle-bearing troops swelled Gates' army to 11,000 against Burgoyne's force, which had shrunk to 7,000 men carrying smoothbore Brown Bess muskets with bayonets. Burgoyne had a tough choice. He could return to Canada and admit defeat or charge ahead to Albany with no or little help from General Clinton in New York or from General Howe. He could not survive a winter where he was. He decided to cross to the west side of the Hudson and march down to Albany.

Gates chose to intercept Burgoyne on the road to Albany. Knowing that Burgoyne would have to travel that road, Gates entrenched his Patriots in a fortified position on Bemis Heights, nine miles south of Saratoga. He built a strong line of defense reinforced by breastwork and fortified a barn at the apex of the line. Powerful batteries guarded the extremities of this position. Burgoyne's advancing British troops faced 9,000 Americans firmly entrenched under Gates' command at Bemis Heights overlooking Freeman's Farm. The first Saratoga battle, the Battle of Freeman's Farm, was fought on September 19 on the abandoned farm of Loyalist John Freeman.

Expecting to confront a ragtag bunch of rebel farmers, Burgoyne instead met a real American army led by General Benedict Arnold, assisted by General Philip Schuyler. Burgoyne held his ground but his British troops suffered stinging blows until finally they were reinforced by German troops. By nightfall, the American army still blocked Burgoyne's way to Albany. General Horatio Gates commanded the American's Northern Division.

Gates had grudgingly permitted Arnold to lead an attack commanding a New England regiment and Daniel Morgan's rifle brigade: "Through leadership, audacity, and tactical skill, Arnold beat Burgoyne badly in the First Battle of Saratoga. A Yankee soldier said of Arnold, 'There wa'n't no waste timber in him. It was "Come on, boys!" not "Go on, boys!" He didn't care for nothin. He'd ride right in.'"[18]

Meanwhile, General Clinton moved north from New York City and managed to capture West Point with a reduced force. Most of the British troops were with Howe on his expedition to Philadelphia. Clinton's small force then continued northward from West Point, but it was too late to help Burgoyne, who was surrounded. Burgoyne was trapped at Saratoga. His communications with Canada were cut off by New England militia under General Benjamin Lincoln, his Indian allies were deserting, and his field hospitals were overflowing with the sick and wounded. Yet he boldly launched another battle. Arnold took unauthorized command of the New England regiments. Without Gates' permission, on October 7, 1777, Arnold rushed into the Second Battle of Saratoga, also known as the Second Battle of Freeman's Farm and the Battle of Bemis Heights.

The precise drill and formations of Burgoyne's army did little good against the Americans, who fought from treetops and from behind rocks and bushes. Eventually Burgoyne's Hessian soldiers refused to fight any longer. As the victorious Arnold routed the Tories, he sustained a significant injury to his leg that required many months to heal and left him with a permanent limp (a monument to Arnold's legs stands at the battlefield of Saratoga today). After severe British losses in the Second Battle of Saratoga on October 7, Burgoyne returned to a fortified position at Saratoga to contemplate his next move. Ten days later, on October 17, 1777, he sent a flag of truce to Gates' headquarters and surrendered 6,000 officers and men and great stores of artillery. The American victory at Saratoga was a turning point in the war.

Before the battle, when Burgoyne was on his way from Fort Edward to Saratoga, Catherine Schuyler, complying with the policy of her husband, General Philip Schuyler, had burned her numerous wheat fields rather than have them available to feed the enemy. Soon the Schuyler's elegant country estate and its scorched wheat fields were destroyed by Burgoyne. After Burgoyne surrendered at Saratoga, his captive army was herded to Cambridge to board a ship for London. At her city mansion along the way, Mrs. Schuyler received the defeated army courteously when her husband brought the prisoners to spend the night at one of their estates. Catherine graciously fed them, made beds and spread mattresses on the floor for the officers. The German baroness Madame de Riedesel said their reception was not like that of enemies but of intimate friends: "All their actions proved, that at sight of the misfortune of others, they quickly forgot their own." Burgoyne told Schuyler, "You are too kind to me, who have done so much injury to you."[19] Catherine and Philip were the parents of the equally gracious Elizabeth Schuyler, the future wife of Alexander Hamilton.

At Saratoga, most of Burgoyne's army was taken prisoner, including camp followers. Prussian baroness Frederika von Riedesel, her husband (the general), and their three children were captured and treated comfortably in Boston. Riding in an attractive English carriage on their way to Virginia, the baroness found Lafayette courteous and agreeable. In Virginia she judged the Virginians lethargic because of the hot climate but believed they were always ready to dance. After serving a year on parole, General Von Riedesel was exchanged for General Benjamin Lincoln.

Mrs. Hannah Winthrop's November 11, 1777, letter to Mercy Warren describes the distressed circumstances of the townspeople when the captive army of Burgoyne entered Cambridge. There were no less than 7,000 prisoners to feed. The price of wood rose because "250 cords would not serve them for one week." The first captives to come into Cambridge were large numbers of British troops, followed the next day by Hessians: "The sight was truly astonishing ... poor, dirty emaciated men. Great numbers of women, who seemed to be the beasts of burden, having bushel-baskets on their backs, by which they were bent double. The contents seemed to be pots and kettles, various sorts of furniture, children peeping through gridirons—some very young infants, who were born on the road—the women barefoot, clothed in dirty rags. Such effluvia filled the air while they were passing." Preceded by an advance guard, Burgoyne, on horseback, headed this "terrible" group. Behind him were blue-cloaked generals—Hessians, Waldeckers, Anspackers, and Brunswickers. As they passed, the Hessians politely bowed to the people but "not so the British." The baggage wagons were drawn by "poor, half-starved horses."[20]

After his defeat, Burgoyne returned to England "to attack and be attacked by the Ministry."[21] He had soon recognized that the rumor of Loyalist strength was a myth, but Germaine kept on believing it. Both Howe and Burgoyne blamed Germaine, the secretary of state for the colonies, for the failure to win the Battle of Saratoga. Germaine held Carlton, the governor of Canada, responsible for not continuing his invasion of America from Canada and for abandoning the invasion of Crown Point. On the contrary, Carleton wrote, "This unfortunate event, it is to be hoped, will in the future prevent ministers from pretending to direct operations of war, in a country at three thousand miles distance of which they have so little knowledge."[22]

"In no small sense, however, the success of the American cause may be attributed to the skill of the colonial infantry who, under the daring leadership of Arnold and Morgan, had proved themselves more than a match for the British veterans."[23] Yet, the credit for Burgoyne's surrender at Saratoga was given to General Gates, commander of the Americans' Northern Department, rather than to Arnold, who deserved the honor because of his brilliant field leadership. "Nothing could exceed the bravery of Arnold on this day; he seemed the very genius of war. Infuriated by the conflict and maddened by Gates' refusal to send reinforcements, which he repeatedly called for, and knowing he was meeting the brunt of the battle, he seemed inspired with the fury of a demon," said one of his soldiers. "Arnold is the life and soul of the troops," wrote another. "They would, to a man, follow him to conquest or death ... [and] to Arnold alone is due the honour of our victory."[24] Gates despised Arnold after the Saratoga battle. Failure to give adequate credit to Benedict Arnold for the epochal American victory at Saratoga was one of the thorns that festered and eventually erupted in Arnold's betrayal of America. His Loyalist wife, Peggy Shippen Arnold, most likely also influenced his treachery. Credit for the Saratoga victory was also due Daniel Morgan and his rifle regiment, whose deadly rifle fire astonished both the English and the Germans. And General Washington's moving battle cry had rallied much support for Gates' Northern army

The enormity of the American Patriot victory at the Battle of Saratoga must be emphasized: "For the first time on North American soil, an entire British army—seven generals, 300 officers, and 5,600 noncoms and privates—surrendered at Saratoga."[25]

What was most significant was that the Patriot triumph over British troops at Saratoga in October 1777 provided Benjamin Franklin, at last, with a "substantial American victory to convince the French that the American cause was worth supporting with an open military alliance."[26] The Saratoga victory brought in not only France but also Spain and Holland to assist the cause of the hard-pressed colonists.

Despite General Washington's string of defeats at New York, Brandywine and Germantown, and Congress's growing discontent with his leadership, Washington remained "the idol of the whole army."[27] On the other hand, Americans knew that foreign aid would be needed to win independence from England, whose navy was the most powerful on earth. During the French and Indian War, the French foreign minister had predicted the American Revolution. When the French and Indian War ended he foresaw a chance for France to ally with America, get even with Great Britain and regain the territory it had lost in the war. But after sending secret agents to America to assess public opinion he reluctantly rejected the idea. In 1774, when Charles Gravier, Count de Vergennes, became secretary of state for foreign affairs under Louis XVI, he revived the former minister's idea that America was ripe for revolution.

Seeking an opportunity for vengeance, France sent secret agents to London's House of Commons to monitor tension between Britain and colonial America. At the same time, Britain, suspecting a French connection with American rebels, set up a British spy network in France. The next year, although France maintained a facade of disinterest, Vergennes sent an emissary to Philadelphia to hold secret meetings and assure the Continental Congress that France admired their work toward freedom and independence. It was this emissary who advised the Secret Committee of Congress to send Silas Deane on a diplomatic mission to France to encourage French merchants to deploy military supplies to America. In August 1775 Minister Vergennes's ambassador to Madrid discussed the possibility of both France and Spain recognizing American independence and officially opening their ports to American ships.

Vergennes pointed out what France had to gain by allying with America's colony-states. English power would diminish while French power would increase; English commerce would fall and French trade would rise; and France would regain some of the possessions she had lost by the humiliating treaty of 1763 that ended the French and Indian War. "She would recover fisheries of Newfoundland, the Gulf of St. Lawrence, the Isle Royale, etc. One does not speak of Canada." On the other hand, colonial America needed three things from France: "military supplies, ready cash and a good navy."

Minister Vergennes "persuaded Louis XVI to authorize one million livres for the Americans." He asked Spain for a similar amount and arranged for the merchant Beaumarchais to receive the French million in June 1776. Beaumarchais immediately established a private trading company that also acted as a front for secret French and Spanish aid to America. When Silas Deane arrived in Paris in July 1776 Beaumarchais informed him, through interpreter Conrad Gérard, that his firm would handle all transactions related to secret aid. By August Vergennes had forwarded Beaumarchais' company another million from Spain. According to the plan, American captains would deliver agricultural products to Santo Domingo or a port in France in return for military supplies, and "the transaction would be supervised by a merchant who would appear to have no connection with the French government." Subsequently, Beaumarchais sent shiploads of muskets, musket balls, tents, cannons, mortars, clothing and especially gunpowder. By the end of 1777 America had received from France 90 percent of the gunpowder they received from all sources, even though one of Beaumarchais' eight ships did not get through the British blockade.[28]

Again Vergennes proposed that Spain join France in declaring war on England and allying with Americans. Spain equivocated, fearing American expansionism once America became an independent nation. France wanted to weaken the British and restore a balance of power; Spain wanted only territory. Vergennes sent a dispatch to Madrid announcing his intention of forming a Franco-American alliance with or without Spain's agreement. The next day the American commissioners—Silas Deane, Benjamin Franklin and Arthur Lee—learned of Burgoyne's surrender at Saratoga. Still, although Spain was willing to provide secret aid, it was unwilling to recognize American independence.

France was impatient to enter the war for a reason more passionate than the victory at Saratoga: "the mass of Frenchmen were vehement to avenge" the defeats inflicted by Britain on France in the Seven Years' War (the French and Indian War). The three emissaries and the Beaumarchais interpreter, Gérard, signed the Treaty of Alliance with France on February 6, 1778. "Thus began another world war and Britain was without a single ally." Soldiers from one German army, Hessians from the Battle of Trenton, were prisoners of war at Philadelphia and "there were no more troops to be hired in Germany."[29] French financiers, encouraged by Benjamin Franklin, enabled Americans to continue their fight.

In Nathaniel Hawthorn's book *Grandfather's Chair*, his grandfather character points to a picture of Franklin and says, "Here we see the most illustrious Boston boy that ever lived.... This is Benjamin Franklin. But I will not try to compress into a few sentences the character of the sage, who, as a Frenchman expressed it, snatched the lightning from the sky and the sceptre from a tyrant." Benjamin Franklin (1706–1790), a 17-year-old printer's apprentice fleeing Boston, arrived in Philadelphia bedraggled and penniless. He had barely enough money to buy bread, three "great puffy rolls."[30] Stuffing one roll under each arm, he ate the third while walking around the streets of the Quaker City of Brotherly Love. From a doorway "his ridiculous, awkward appearance" was watched by his future wife, 15-year-old Deborah Read. Armed with knowledge of printing, amiability and modest diffidence, he became the prototype of the self-made man. Deborah and Benjamin were married by common law in 1730 when Benjamin was 24. Unlike the wives of other founding fathers, Deborah had neither wealth nor high social standing. She was "loud and lowly and scarcely literate." She might have been an embarrassment to him, but after their abrupt marriage she immediately took into their home, and became a mother to, Franklin's illegitimate son born to another woman whose name remains a mystery to this day. Deborah and Benjamin Franklin had two children—a daughter, Sara, who grew up to be an adept philanthropist, and a son who died in childhood of smallpox. The marriage did not help Franklin socially. Deborah was never included in his social invitations. She "did, however, help him economically; she was as shrewd and as frugal as he was, and she never ceased working to bring money into the household."[31] While Benjamin Franklin was out of the country on diplomatic missions for long periods of time, Deborah ran the family businesses, a book and stationary shop and a printing press. By the time of her death he seems to have forgotten about her: "Not a single friend or relative ever wrote him a note of sympathy or even referred to the death of his wife."[32]

After commanding a militia unit during the 1758–63 French and Indian War, Franklin was chosen as emissary to Great Britain, where he lived for 15 years. His mission in London was to oust the Lords Proprietor and make Pennsylvania a royal colony. Franklin opposed hereditary governors of the colony of Pennsylvania because they believed that their inherited property should be exempt from taxation. They refused to allow their personal estates to be taxed, even in order to finance the defense of the colony.[33]

Historian Gordon S. Wood's Pulitzer Prize winning *Americanization of Benjamin Franklin* states that Benjamin Franklin, in the early 1760s, was an American Tory, a Loyalist who believed in absolute monarchy. In contrast, at that time Whigs sided with Parliament, believing it to be a buffer against the tyranny of the Crown. Franklin—a Royalist allying with the king—envisioned a Great British Empire in which all the colonies were loyal solely to the king, at least until equal and fair colonial representation could be established in Parliament. As an avid Tory, Franklin supported the king against the "tyrannical Parliament that had passed the Stamp Act."

After the Boston Tea Party, Franklin, as emissary-lobbyist, tried to save the empire. He lobbied against the Intolerable Acts and "even offered to pay out of his own pocket the cost of the tea thrown into the harbor."[34] But he became increasingly irate throughout February and March 1775 as he listened to Parliament speaking arrogantly of Americans. At last he realized that his role as mediator in the crisis was over. American newspaper stories of reactions to the closed port of Boston brought tears to his eyes. He returned to America and became a passionate Patriot. Franklin, no longer a Tory but now a Whig, soon became a delegate to the Second Continental Congress and contributed to the drafting of the Declaration of Independence and the Articles of Confederation, which laid the foundation for the new union.

An international celebrity—inventor of the Franklin Stove, scientist experimenting with lightning and electricity, printer, publisher, author, and diplomat—Franklin was elected to the Congressional Committee of Secret Correspondence. His mission was to seek military and financial aid from France in America's fight for independence. In October 1777 he embarked for France and took with him his two grandsons. In France, Franklin dressed plainly in rustic white and brown linen as a simple Quaker, with spectacles and a fur cap that endeared him to Frenchmen. He contrasted sharply with the powdered wigs of Paris and the fancy dress of other diplomats. In the salons of Paris he was sought after and adored by diplomats, scientists, fellow Freemasons and fashionable ladies alike. He became the "hero of France ... personifying the unsophisticated nobility of the New World."[35]

John Adams, the ambassador to France in 1778–1779 and later to the Netherlands, was scandalized by Franklin's French lifestyle. Abigail was shocked by Franklin's behavior toward ladies in low-cut dresses. Disgusted, she called him the "old Deceiver" a "wicked unprincipled debauched wretch."[36] Obviously John and Abigail Adams did not understand that "in France, you did work socially." "Adams was clueless that it was through the dropped hints and seemingly offhand remarks at these salons that so much French diplomacy was conducted."[37] In March 1778 King Louis XVI welcomed the American delegation of Franklin at the Palais de Versailles. Franklin's achievements in France were even more remarkable than his popularity. He encouraged the monarchy of Louis XVI and Queen Marie Antoinette to side with American rebels and aid them against another monarchy. "Franklin was the person who stood for America," and it was "America's connection with France that gave the United States weight with England and the respect of Europe."[38] "The American Revolution could not have begun until France had been driven from North America, and it could not succeed until the French returned. Without French shipments of munitions "American military efforts of 1776 would not have been possible and the Revolution would have been over before France was ready to enter the war."[39] "The colonies could not survive without French supplies."[40]

In February 1778, four months after the Patriot victory over British troops at Saratoga, Franklin and others solemnly signed the French-American Treaty of Alliance pledging French military support for American independence. Substantial financial aid also was forthcoming. Franklin was the American envoy primarily responsible for convincing France to support America in the Revolution. Without military and financial support from France, America might never have won the War for Independence. Franklin had to continually apply to Vergennes for money and then ensure that Congress did not overdraft. Congress habitually overdrew on European loans, before they were negotiated. Franklin needed to keep asking France to cover these overdrafts.

During the war America's trade balance with France was favorable. After the war, however, America made peace with her parent country and resumed trade with England, leaving the French out. Without the hoped-for profits from trade that Vergennes and the French monarch had counted on to pay off loans that had financed French aid and military campaigns in America, France faced economic crisis: "It was this crisis, and the monarchy's clumsy attempts to deal with it, that helped trigger the French Revolution."[41]

In 1784 Thomas Jefferson succeeded Franklin as American minister to France. "You replace Dr. Franklin, then?" asked Vergennes. "I succeed," answered Jefferson. "No one can replace him."[42] After the war, upon learning that Americans were using profits from French trade to buy English goods, France—vexed with America's ingratitude—bought little more in large quantities from America than rice and tobacco.

Benjamin Franklin's distinguished legacy affirms that he was one of the greatest of the Founding Fathers. "His crucial diplomacy in the Revolution makes him second only to Washington in importance. But that importance is not what we most remember about Franklin." The image of Franklin as "the hardworking self-made businessman" has endured. It is the "symbolic Franklin—the man who personifies the American dream—who stays with us." "Franklin came to epitomize the new and radical notion of the *self-made man*." "By the early nineteenth century many ... successful businessmen no longer felt the need, as Franklin had, to shed their leather aprons in order to acquire respectability. They were proud of being self-made." Americans began to be "proud of pulling themselves up by their own boot straps" and, like immigrants to America, thought of America as a "place where anybody who works hard can make it."[43]

Wood's introduction to *The Americanization of Benjamin Franklin* notes, "Davy Crockett had ... with him when he died at the Alamo ... not the Bible but Franklin's *Autobiography* ... perhaps the most widely read autobiography in the world." Thomas Mellon, future founder of the great banking institute, as a poor 14-year-old farm boy read Franklin's *Autobiography* and *Poor Richard's Almanac* sayings and considered them the "turning point of his life." Mellon later placed Franklin's statue in front of his bank and bought a thousand copies of the *Autobiography* to distribute to young men who came "seeking his advice."[44] Nineteenth century schools began using the *Autobiography* to teach moral lessons to students.

6

Valley Forge, Monmouth Battle and Sullivan's Raid

While Franklin negotiated with the French in Paris and General Howe and the British celebrated their occupation of Philadelphia with galas and looting, General Washington, having gutsily fought the Battle of Germantown, returned to his camp on Skippack Creek. In December he marched his Continentals to Valley Forge. There in Pennsylvania on the west side of the Schuylkill River 20 miles northwest of Philadelphia they would spend the long, hard, hungry winter from December 1777 until June 1778. Eleven thousand soldiers and 500 women and children, many without shoes, stockings and blankets, entered the dense forest of Valley Forge in mid–December 1777. They began felling trees, notching logs and building redoubts. Covered with branches and earth to absorb cannonballs, the redoubts looked like giant molehills with a deep ditch in front. Located near the center of the encampment was an artillery park from which guns were issued. By mid–January 1,000 small log huts, six and one-half feet high, with a fireplace in the rear and a door facing the street, were ready to house most of the troops, 12 hungry, ragged, smelly soldiers to a cabin.[1]

There were 400 women at Valley Forge in December 1777. Within six years, the number of women camp followers—nurses, cooks, laundresses—would increase to one for every twenty-six males. The ratio of women to British forces in New York in May 1777 was one to eight. That of German forces was one to thirty. By 1781 there was one woman for every 4½ British soldiers. For Hessians, the ratio was one woman for every fifteen men.[2] Mercy Otis Warren's history of the Revolution gives a contemporaneous glimpse of the situation at Valley Forge, especially the plight of the ladies of the camp, many of whom she corresponded with and visited:

> The commander in chief, and several of the principal officers of the American army, in defiance of danger, either to themselves or to such tender connections, sent for their ladies from the different states to which they belonged, to pass the remainder of the winter, and by their presence to enliven the gloomy appearance of a hutted village in the woods, inhabited only by a hungry and half-naked soldiery. [Nothing but the inexperience of the American ladies and their confidence in the judgment of their husbands could justify this hazard to their persons, and to their feelings of delicacy.][3]

In February 1778 Martha Washington joined the general at Valley Forge. The barely five-foot Martha possessed social graces that put people at ease. At Mt. Vernon, the plump, winsome and wealthy Martha had kept the conversation, as well as the Madeira wine, flowing at official dinners. This was in sharp contrast to her six-foot, two-inch George, whose stern taciturnity and occasional tapping on the table with a spoon were intimidating.[4] Martha, who had bounced in a horse-drawn carriage over 600 miles of washboard roads in 1775 to spend the winter with her husband at Cambridge, often accompanied Washington at headquarters during the war years. At Valley Forge they lived in tiny quarters with a "small log cabin to dine in," wrote Martha. The cabin for dining was behind the Isaac Potts house, which was Washington's headquarters at Valley Forge. A woman who lived nearby said the following about Martha:

> I never in my life knew a woman so busy ... as was Lady Washington, providing comforts for the sick soldiers. Every day, excepting Sunday, the wives of officers in camp, and sometimes other women, were invited to Mr. Potts' to assist her in knitting socks, patching garments, and making shirts for the poor soldiers, when materials could he procured. Every fair day she might be seen, with basket in hand, and with a single attendant, going among the huts seeking the keenest and most needy sufferer, and giving all the comforts to them in her power.... On one occasion she went to the hut of a dying sergeant.... His case seemed to particularly touch the heart of the good lady, and after she had given him some wholesome food she had prepared with her own hands, she knelt down by his straw pallet and prayed earnestly for him and his wife with her sweet and solemn voice. I shall never forget the scene.[5]

Besides ministering to the sick and needy, Martha, as well as other officers' ladies, softened the cruel austerity by occasionally hosting evenings of elegant dinners and camp theater. Some of the wives were Lady Sarah Stirling, Lord Stirling's wife; Catharine (Caty) Greene, Nathanael's wife, with whom Washington danced three hours nonstop in Philadelphia when he and his retinue went there to meet with Congress; and Lucy Knox, Henry's wife. Lucy's amazing bulk was almost as massive as her husband's. "Her size is enormous," said Abigail Adams. "I am frightened when I look at her."[6] In Philadelphia, before waltzing the minuet with Caty Greene, Washington, an excellent dancer, opened the first dance with Lucy Knox. At Valley Forge, among the camp followers were women of all levels of society, from common whores to soldiers' wives. There was little prostitution in American camps, partly for religious reasons and partly because the soldiers had little money. Cooking, cleaning, sewing, mending and working as laundresses, seamstresses and nurses, women earned their meager food by caring for husbands and relatives.[7] Washington's valet, Billy Lee, courted Margaret Thomas, a free black (mulatto) cook and seamstress who was considered to be his common-law wife.

The starving army at Valley Forge was surrounded by a land of plenty. Describing his unclothed, unshod, unfed, and unpaid army, Washington wrote, "There are now in the army ... 4,000 men wanting blankets."[8] The lack of medical supplies was so shocking that after the war medical personnel came together and founded American medical schools. Washington and his quartermaster general, Greene, had always treated civilians fairly, but at Valley Forge the situation was so dire that Greene gave orders to strip the land naked of food, forage, horses, cattle and sheep. Hundreds of army horses actually starved to death. But even when the men had gone "seven days without meat and several days without bread," Greene was lenient with one farmer who begged him to return his pregnant mare, for she was "all of the Horse Kind" he owned.[9] While Washington's army starved, local farmers—whose greed outweighed their patriotism—drove their food-laden wagons to Philadelphia and sold their produce to British troops who paid in pounds sterling rather than debased Continental currency.

By the fall of 1779 hyperinflation would become rampant. Seeing corruption everywhere, Washington composed numerous screeds berating speculators and war profiteers and asking, "Is the paltry consideration of a little dirty pelf to individuals to be placed in

6. Valley Forge, Monmouth Battle and Sallivan's Raid

competition with the essential rights and liberties of the present generation and of millions yet unborn?"[10] Although the amiable yet slightly aloof Washington was frequently angered by the lack of patriotism of civilians and their lack of monetary support for the troops, he also was encouraged by the crowds of people who gathered to greet him. Once, when an adoring assembly of townspeople and children turned out to cheer him and called him their father, he pressed the hand of an aide-de-camp and said, "We may be beaten by the English; it is the chance of war: but behold an army which they can never conquer."[11]

According to Ellet's *Women of the American Revolution*, a Quaker woman by the name of Rebecca Biddle and her husband, Colonel Clement Biddle, were "read out of meeting" by the Society of Friends when the two joined the American army. Rebecca, like Lucy Knox, Caty Green, and Martha Washington, was a camp follower. She organized forages and cooked for the soldiers through the greater part of the war. Telling her children about the suffering of the army at Valley Forge, she recalled one providential day when a vast number of wild pigeons flew so close to the ground that the near-naked soldiers, swinging clubs and poles, were able to kill enough pigeons to feed many of the starving people at the Forge. Mrs. Biddle felt challenged to devise a variety of ways to cook the birds.

All through the long winter Washington readied his army for battle. He appointed 35-year-old General Nathanael Greene to the difficult and thankless job of quartermaster general. Greene complained that nobody ever heard of a quartermaster general in history, and yet he equitably and efficiently rationed the meager food supply to the starving thousands of troops encamped there. The jolly and paunchy Henry Knox instructed student artillerists in the punctilious skill of firing cannon. Another instructor, Friedrich Wilhelm Ludolf Gerhard Augustin, Baron von Steuben, was not really a baron. He was a tough, quirky mercenary "who liked to decorate himself with sonorous names."[12] A former Prussian army captain and aide-de-camp to Frederick the Great, Steuben—with his "drooping face, ample double chin and almost comical pomposity"[13]—came to America carrying a letter of introduction to Congress and to George Washington. The embellished letter was written by Benjamin Franklin and Silas Deane, American emissaries to France. Washington recommended that Congress appoint Steuben major general and inspector general of the Continental Army. Washington concentrated on creating a professional army. Bringing to Valley Forge the discipline and technical knowledge necessary to forge such an army, Steuben, sweating under his full military regalia, was the stereotypical disciplinarian. So meticulously did he instruct Washington's officers that every one of his 100 trained officers was able to teach each threadbare man under his command and turn him into a professional soldier.

Beloved by the troops, this delightful showman, with a greyhound trotting by his side, drilled the Continental Army eyeball to eyeball, yelling and swearing in German and French. When the trainees could not understand him, the baron got his aide to curse at them in English. Teaching his "School of the Soldier" from dawn to dusk, Steuben relied on interpreters (one was Lt. Colonel Alexander Hamilton, future secretary of the treasury) to translate his ideas from German-accented French to English. Performing in a grand review before the French ambassador and dignitaries of Congress he paraded his class, celebrating with grace and precision the new Franco-American alliance: "In the brilliant sunshine of a spring morning, they marched in perfect columns, quickly and precisely unwound into two parallel lines, and fired three rolling volleys of musketry to salute their awe-struck guests."[14] As the first inspector general of the United States Army, Steuben introduced new firing drills and regulations and monitored camp sanitation. During the winter of 1777–1778, while he was at Valley Forge, he wrote the basic plan for his *Regulations for the Order and Discipline of the Troops of the United States*, also known as the Blue Book. The drillmaster's practice ground, near the center of the camp was a showplace for his grand parade of precision-trained troops. General Von Steuben's imposing bronze figure commands attention there even today.

Of the 11,000 citizen soldiers at Valley Forge, approximately 3,000 died, 268 were court-martialed, and 1,134 deserted. "Spring and improved conditions brought about a change in attitudes."[15] As the climate turned warm in springtime 1778, Washington's army emerged reenergized from a winter of vigorous training, near starvation and freezing. After drilling under the stern General Steuben and shooting under General Henry Knox, a most dependable and able field commander, they had become trained, refreshed, and formidable soldiers ready to fight the 1778 battle at Monmouth.

The climate of the war was changing too, in favor of the Patriots. This was not only because Washington now had a real army, it was also due to the Franco-American Alliance. Conrad Alexandre Gérard, the English-speaking secretary of Foreign Minister Vergennes, conducted negotiations with Benjamin Franklin, Silas Deane and Arthur Lee for forming the Alliance. On February 6, 1778, Vergennes and Franklin accomplished this joint triumph: the signing of the landmark agreement, the Franco-American Alliance, which marked a turning point in the American Revolution. Franklin's enormous prestige and diplomacy, plus the huge American victory over Burgoyne at Saratoga, convinced France that it was possible for America to win the war and that an alliance with America would put France on the winning side. France was also frightened by the efforts of her long-time enemy, Britain, to pacify the colonies. France relished the idea of allying with America to get even with Britain. The possibility of an American reconciliation with Britain so concerned France that she took "hasty action without waiting upon her major ally, Spain."[16] By the Franco-American alliance, France agreed to furnish military and financial aid to the insurgent colonies.

In February 1778 John Adams, knowing nothing of European politics or diplomacy and unable to speak French, had embarked from Boston to join Benjamin Franklin and Arthur Lee as a minister to France. When Adams arrived in Paris some of the local people were disappointed that he was not Samuel, "le fameux Adams."[17] Vergennes disliked John Adams. He resented Adams' graceless and stubborn intrusion into the alliance negotiations so much that he ended all communication with him and urged the French minister to persuade Congress to recall him. Vergennes considered John Adams unsuited for the refined role of diplomat in a French court and wanted to deal only with Franklin. "Mr. Adams," explained Franklin, "has given offense to the Court here ... [and] he (Adams) thinks, as he tells me himself, that America has been too free in Expressions of Gratitude toward France."[18] This was unfortunate, because Americans depended on France for financial and military support. In May, John Adams suggested in a letter to Samuel Adams that a three-man commission to France was not necessary. One was sufficient. Not surprisingly, Congress chose Franklin. Adams was relieved of his position as minister plenipotentiary and assigned as minister to Amsterdam. There his successful mission gained recognition of America's independence and acquired a loan from Amsterdam bankers.

When news of the Franco-American agreement reached England, General William

Howe was recalled. Howe was succeeded by his second in command, General Sir Henry Clinton.

Meanwhile, a French admiral with a fancy name, Count Jean Baptiste Charles Hector d'Estaing, set sail for America in April 1778. Count d'Estaing's expeditionary force of 12 ships of the line escorted by four frigates carried 4,000 French soldiers. Two months later, when Clinton heard the news, he withdrew British troops from Philadelphia and moved his headquarters to New York City. He feared both the inflow of funds and the influx of French forces. He worried that the colonial militia might strangle Philadelphia by land and that a French blockade of the Delaware River would wipe out the water route to the capital city.

When Clinton left Philadelphia Washington gave Benedict Arnold military command there. Clinton also abandoned his Tory supporters in Philadelphia. But when the Patriots reclaimed their capital city, Washington levied no punitive taxes on the rich Tories. He said that a measure of this sort "would be looked upon as an arbitrary stretch of military power."[19] Revenue was greatly needed, however, to pay salaries and keep the American army fed and clothed. Esther de Berdt Reed and Sarah Franklin Bache became prominent Philadelphia fundraisers.

American women have long been known for their philanthropy. One of the first, the future Patriot philanthropist Ester de Berdt, was born in London of French Huguenot descent. She was the daughter of a British merchant involved in colonial trade. Because of her father's business relations with America, many young Americans traveling abroad were attracted to the de Berdt home in England. It was a place for discussing the Stamp Act and other British-American government affairs. At home, when she was 17, Esther met and fell in love with a bright 23-year-old student, Joseph Reed, from the colony of New Jersey. He was in London to finish his professional studies. Two years later, in 1765, he returned to America to practice law in Trenton. Joseph's and Esther's transatlantic correspondence flourished for five years. Miss de Berdt's letters, preserved by her descendants, show that she was a devoted American Patriot. Visiting the House of Commons in London, she enthusiastically applauded Mr. Pitt but did not hide her repugnance toward Prime Minister George Grenville because he was one of the "enemies to America."[20] Esther de Berdt became an American wife when she married Joseph Reed in St Luke's Church in the city of London. In November 1770 the newlyweds arrived in Philadelphia, which was then the heart of the nation. When news of Lexington and Bunker Hill alarmed the whole land, Esther Reed organized the first female voluntary association in America, one for the relief of the New England sufferers.

Joseph Reed became a soldier in General Washington's army, leaving Esther home with two babies. Joseph was appointed adjutant-general in 1776. With her household broken, her husband called away by war, Esther and the wives and children of other American soldiers thought their lives would be safer on the "perilous edge of an Indian wilderness, than in the neighborhood of the soldiers" commanded by noblemen such as Howe and Cornwallis, who had been sent by a "monarch to lay waste this land."[21] The safety and possessions of every Patriot family was threatened by gangs of armed Loyalists. Esther lost one of her children to smallpox in 1778, the same year her husband was elected governor of Pennsylvania. In 1780 the ladies of Philadelphia united for the relief of the suffering of soldiers by supplying them with clothing. Esther Reed, though feeble in health—plagued by a terminal illness and busily caring for her newborn baby—was elected head of this association. The ladies solicited money, did needlework, and contributed trinkets and jewelry to the charity. All ranks of society, from housemaids to the Marchioness de Lafayette and the Countess de Luzerne, joined in the effort. Deep sorrow was felt in Philadelphia in September 1780 when news of the death of the first lady of Pennsylvania circulated.

After the death of Mrs. Reed the project of collections and contributions fell to a committee of four women. One of the four was Sarah Bache, daughter of Dr. Benjamin Franklin. Like her father slightly above average height, with brown hair, blue eyes and simple in her manners, Sarah conducted guests through a room of her house filled with shirts made by the ladies of Philadelphia. These volunteers purchased the linen, brought it to Mrs. Bache's house, and then cut out and sewed 2,200 shirts for soldiers. Into each was stitched the name of the lady who made it.[22] Addressing circular letters to adjoining counties and states, Sarah raised $7,500 dollars. Ladies not only of Philadelphia but also of Maryland and Trenton, New Jersey, responded generously.[23]

When the British under General Clinton departed Philadelphia they marched through New Jersey to New York to protect the mouth of the Hudson. The trek took just 12 days, compared with the 60 days required for Howe's journey via the Chesapeake Bay the preceding year. On the way, Clinton's army halted at Monmouth Courthouse, New Jersey, where he left a small force behind. Washington planned to intercept the British en route to New York. He ordered his second in command, English-born General Charles Lee, commander of the Continental Army's advance guard, to attack General Clinton's small force left behind at Monmouth. Washington personally would lead the bulk of the Continental troops shortly thereafter and ram the British in a forceful attack. Initially obeying orders, Lee began to encircle the remnant of the small enemy army stationed at Monmouth Courthouse. When General Clinton learned about the American tactic he ordered General Charles Cornwallis to reverse his rear guard, backtrack to Monmouth, and reinforce the British force Lee's advance guard now surrounded. Surprised to see Cornwallis's rear guard returning to Monmouth, the arrogant General Lee—against orders and without notifying General Washington—committed the treasonous act of commanding the American advance guard to retreat.

Meanwhile, expecting Lee's advance guard to surround the small number of enemy soldiers at the courthouse and keep them in check as ordered, Washington, astride his great white horse, continued to move the Continentals toward Monmouth. Upon approaching Monmouth, he met his own advance guard retreating. Outraged by the treachery, Washington relieved Lee of command and personally ordered his advance guard to reverse their retreat and resume attack. The Battle of Monmouth ensued.

The marathon at Monmouth was the longest single battle of the Revolutionary War and was also the first clash to test the rigorous training of Washington's army at Valley Forge. It was fought throughout the hot summer day of June 28, 1778, from morning until 5:00 P.M. While winter weather had been Washington's enemy at Valley Forge, the sun now worked in his favor. Heatstroke from the 96 degree June heat killed 59 heavily uniformed British soldiers.[24] Washington's tattered but toughened Continental Army survived the furnace, but his own white charger dropped dead from the heat. Billie Lee trotted up and replaced the horse with a chestnut mare. There was no clear winner at Monmouth, but the Americans proved themselves to be respectable fighters, thus winning a moral victory. Sometime in the night the British left their campfires and continued on to New York.

6. Valley Forge, Monmouth Battle and Sallivan's Raid 93

The Americans might have won a decisive victory except for Lee's treachery. Washington was unaware that this strange, unpredictable man's loyalty was in doubt. The Mohawks, who inducted Lee into their tribe when he married a Mohawk woman, called him "Boiling Water" because of his quick temper. On June 4, 1778, two weeks after Charles Lee swore the oath of allegiance and rejoined the Patriot army after having been exchanged as a prisoner of war, he had written a letter to Clinton. In it, he congratulated Clinton on his promotion to succeed General Howe. The British had captured Lee in 1776 at a brothel. Fittingly, he was exchanged for a British major general who was also captured when lured by a nymph. The *London Chronicle* reported on it in this way:

> What various lures there are to ruin man;
> Woman, the first and foremost, all bewitches!
> A nymph once spoiled a General's mighty plan,
> And gave him to the foe—without his breeches.[25]

Brigadier General Charles Scott of Virginia recounted that at Monmouth Washington yelled at Lee until the leaves shook on the trees. Scott, though ordered by Major General Lee to retreat, had been the last to leave the field. A year later Washington appointed Scott as his intelligence chief. Because of Lee's betrayal, General Clinton was able to continue his march to Sandy Hook. Charles Lee was arrested, court-martialed, and convicted of insubordination and failure to follow orders. He was not sentenced to face a firing squad; instead he was simply suspended from command for one year. Lee then retired to his Virginia estate and wrote letters attacking Congress and General Washington. He offended so many Patriots that John Laurens challenged him to a duel and slightly wounded his left arm. It was enough of an injury to prevent Anthony Wayne from offering a similar challenge. Lee was formally dismissed from the army in 1780.[26]

Among the notables at Monmouth was Molly Ludwig Hayes McCauley (the symbolic "Molly Pitcher") known for carrying pitchers of water to the battlefield. Some say it was drinking water, and others say it was used for sponging and cooling the cannon. Upon seeing her gunner husband disabled, she took his place on the artillery squad and personally helped the team load and fire the cannon. Molly, whether fictional or real, represents many American women patriots who took their husbands' places on the battlefield. Another notable at Monmouth was General Anthony Wayne, who ruthlessly drilled and disciplined troops under his command. Legend has it that "Mad Anthony," so called because of his fiery temper and seemingly reckless courage, once told George Washington, "Give me the order, sir, and I will lay siege to hell."

One week after the Battle of Monmouth, d'Estaing's armada bringing French aid, ships and troops crucial to winning the war dropped anchor off Delaware Bay and began intercepting ships going to New York. Thus "ended Britain's undisputed dominance in sea power in the war."[27] England then drifted into open warfare with France. When Mercy Warren met d'Estaing she wrote, "While the errand on which the Count D'Estaing came out excites our gratitude, the dignity of his deportment commands respect; and his reserved affability, if I may so express it, heightens our esteem."[28]

After leaving Philadelphia and fighting at Monmouth, Clinton arrived in New York in July 1778 just in time to see his enemy, 48-year-old Admiral d'Estaing, and his fleet sailing near Sandy Hook lighthouse toward the harbor. Count d'Estaing had brought with him Conrad Alexandre Gérard, the first foreign minister from any country to the United States. Gérard entered Philadelphia in July 1778: "From then until the end of the war the French embassy was one of the central institutions of the American Revolution."[29] France entered the war to "damage Britain, not to aid America." In his November 14, 1778, letter to American ambassador Henry Laurens, Washington cautioned, "No nation is to be trusted farther than it is bound by its interest." Later, when Lafayette suggested invading Canada, the politically savvy Washington suspected that the idea originated in the French cabinet. He therefore warned that if the French occupied Canada, France would be in position to control the United States.[30] Admiral Richard Howe confronted the French forces in ocean waters outside Sandy Hook Harbor. There, French and English forces maneuvered for weeks. The British admiral successfully countered all efforts of Admiral d'Estaing and prevented the Franco-American attempt to seize Rhode Island, which the British occupied for another year. Abandoning the coast of America in October, d'Estaing's French squadron sailed to the West Indies, where they were again repulsed by Howe's fleet. Howe then established a British base at St. Lucia, but d'Estaing had delayed Clinton's campaign in the South by a year, proving that Britain was no longer in sole command of the sea.

In May 1779 Clinton amassed British troops at Kingsbridge, New York, in preparation for taking over the strategic American post at West Point, the "Key to the Continent," which controlled the Hudson. Clinton's superior force easily overpowered the Americans at Stony Point, just 12 miles south of West Point. The presence of the British garrisoned at Stony Point threatened West Point. To remove this threat, Washington ordered General Anthony Wayne to retake Stony Point. Wayne earned his epithet "Mad Anthony" by storming the heavily fortified British fort. Willard Church of the Connecticut Regiment of the Line told his grandson:

> [The m]ost memorable battle was the storming of Stony Point Fort on the Hudson on the night of July 15, 1779 under General Anthony Wayne. The attacking troops were massed at midnight two miles from the fort. A call was made for two hundred volunteers who with fixed bayonets were to proceed in front of the main attack force and draw the fire from the fort. The strategy was simple, the main assault was to be while the enemy were reloading their guns. The fort was captured, although the ruse was not a complete success. The first obstacle encountered was a two tier of abatis. As the advance party neared the foil their captain was observed to stumble. Asked if he was wounded, he gave a loud emphatic "No." He continued to lead the column, although it was soon learned that he had been shot in the thigh.... Church, was one of the two hundred volunteers, and one of the few that escaped the terrible ordeal unharmed.[31]

The victory won by Anthony Wayne and his American troops at Stony Point marked the last major battle in the North. Wayne captured 15 pieces of artillery and 500 British prisoners, among them 70 women and children.[32]

Throughout the War, both British and Americans took prisoners. Around New York City alone more than 11,000 Americans were taken prisoner by the British. Women everywhere nursed wounded soldiers and prisoners on both sides. "Few sites seemed too dangerous for women like Elizabeth Burgin."[33] Although she suffered anxiety and penury for engaging in a perilous rescue mission, Widow Burgin expressed no regrets. When one saw her distributing her basket of food among the sick, wounded and groaning American soldiers aboard a British prison ship floating in New York harbor, one might think she was an angel of mercy, certainly not a spy. Patriot Elizabeth Burgin was both. Working with George Higby, Elizabeth often carried not only bread but also secret messages to the starving prisoners, telling them the details of the next planned escape. Together with Higby she arranged the escape and rescue of 200 Patriot prisoners.

Her operation was discovered in June 1779 when a letter written by George Washington to spymaster Major Benjamin Tallmadge was intercepted. In the letter, Washington suggested that Tallmadge recruit George Higby to be part of the Culper Spy Ring, which Tallmadge headed. When the British arrested Higby, his wife attempted to lighten his punishment. She pointed to Elizabeth Burgin as his coworker. With a huge bounty on her head—a reward equivalent to 20 years' pay for a British soldier—Elizabeth went into hiding.[34] Escaping to Philadelphia, within a month she was able to move her children, but neither clothes nor possessions, out of New York. Having little means of support in Pennsylvania, she appealed to George Washington for financial aid. From his headquarters in Morristown, Washington wrote a letter, dated December 25, 1779, to the Continental Congress on behalf of Elizabeth Burger, an excerpt from which states, "From the testimony of different persons, and particularly many of our own Officers who have returned from captivity, it would appear that she has been indefatigable for the relief of the prisoners and in measures for facilitating their escape."[35] The letter prompted the Board of War to grant Elizabeth a pension of $53.50 per year.

On the northwestern frontier during 1778–79 some Loyalists from New York and Pennsylvania, as well as four of the six tribes of the Iroquois Nation living in the Mohawk Valley, decimated pioneer settlements. Led by Chief Joseph Brant, these Loyalists destroyed fields, houses, and cattle. They scalped, tortured and massacred Pennsylvania Patriot families from Wilkes Barre to Wyoming Valley and terrorized New York settlers from German Flats to Cherry Valley.[36]

Katherine Cole Gaylord's husband, Lieutenant Aaron Gaylord, was killed while defending Forty Fort in the Wyoming Valley of Pennsylvania. This occurred when 700 Loyalists and rangers allied with Seneca Indians attacked 5,000 inhabitants, mainly women and children who were seeking refuge within the fort. The Battle of Wyoming soon turned into the Wyoming Massacre when the attackers murdered and tortured those trying to escape. Many who evaded the assailants succumbed to exposure and starvation in the surrounding forest. Widow Katherine Gaylord gathered her three small children and fled on foot. Watching out for wolves and Indians and eating berries, bark, leaves and roots, Mary and her little ones walked for many weeks until they finally arrived at the home of her father in Connecticut.

Legend says that a part-white, part-Seneca woman, Queen Esther Montour—the power-wielding widow of a Munsee Delaware chief—angrily avenged the death of her son by massacring Patriot soldiers. Though "neither she nor any other woman took part in the events of July 1778"[37] rumors spread that she danced around a rock by firelight and bashed out the brains of many captives. Exaggerated tales of these Cherry Valley and Wyoming Valley massacres precipitated reprisals against the Six Nations the next year. In spring 1779 General Washington mounted a counteroffensive against the Iroquois Confederacy of Six Nations and their Loyalist allies. General John Sullivan led the retaliatory attacks. Four thousand Patriot troops converged on the Susquehanna River and systematically demolished Seneca towns, destroying women, children, homes, apple orchards and cornfields. Sullivan sent a detachment to Cayuga Territory and then returned to Pennsylvania.[38] General John Sullivan's official report to Congress mentioned Catherine Town, where he talked with an old woman who belonged to the Cayuga Nation. He stated that his goal in marching through the Iroquois towns was to destroy the "bread basket of both the Iroquois and the British." His army marched again through Catherine Town on the way back to Easton, Pennsylvania.[39]

Catherine Town was the namesake of Queen Catherine Montour (the sister of Queen Esther Montour), the part-French, part-Mohawk leader of the Senecas. Anticipating the appearance of Sullivan's force, Queen Catherine fled to Niagara, where she was welcomed by the British. But at least one woman remained. A journal entry of one of Sullivan's lieutenants written September 1 described seeing Madam Sacho alone at Catherine Town. She had "silver locks, wrinkled face, dim eyes" and a curved spine. On the next day, another officer wrote that the "very aged squaw" Sacho was found in a cornfield. "She told us," he said, "that the warriors had stayed in town till near night.... A great many squaws and children were over a hill somewhere near Seneca Lake four or five miles away.... A detachment of 400 men was unable to find them." On September 23 another of Sullivan's officers recorded that they found "the Old Squaw in the place we had left her ... [and] her provisions & wood was exhausted & she in tears & was not able to get more, but was much rejoiced at the sight of the army—her friends—as she called us. We found likewise a younger squaw at some distance shot and thrown into a ditch and half covered with mud. The old squaw said that she did not know the other woman. The General left her about 100 lb. of flour & 50 lbs of beef."[40]

Continental Army units from Pittsburgh wiped out Indian villages along the Allegheny River. Sullivan's retaliatory raids heralded death for the Iroquois Confederacy and weakened Chief Brant's power. A few years later, when the Iroquois Confederacy dissolved, Iroquois lands were divided up and doled out to Revolutionary War veterans and new settlers. Having won distinction as an Indian Fighter, Sullivan became a namesake for many counties of the Southwestern frontier. The Onondaga, Seneca, and Tuscarora stayed in New York; the Mohawk and Cayuga went to Canada; the Oneida migrated to Wisconsin.[41] Chief Brant went to England and became good friends with the Prince of Wales. After the war, Brant and those Iroquois Loyalists who had fought on England's side in the war received land grants in Canada.

In December 1779 Clinton boarded a British ship and sailed away from New York to personally pursue his campaign to subdue the South. Clinton left Lieutenant General Wilhelm, Baron von Knyphausen, a Hessian commander of German mercenary troops in the British service, in charge of New York City. The 6,000 regular troops left under the authority of Knyphausen were made up of Englishmen, Loyalists, and German mercenaries. Knyphausen doubled his force by arming inhabitants of the city and enlisting sailors stranded in New York harbor on icebound ships in the severe winter of 1779–80, the worst of the 18th century. Knyphausen's troops crossed the Hudson in the spring of 1780 and ransacked the village of Hackensack, New Jersey. More serious raids followed.

In May 1780, when Clinton, who had recently captured Charlestown, received reports that a French fleet might threaten New York he departed South Carolina. Confident that South Carolina and Georgia were firmly under British control, he left General Charles Cornwallis in command of the British Army in the South. Leaving only a few troops with Cornwallis, Clinton took "three-fourths of his army to surprise Washington in his encampment at Morristown in New Jersey."[42] Having learned that Washington's half-starved army at Morristown were reluctant to reenlist and therefore ripe for defecting to the British camp, Knyphausen seized the opportunity. In June he crossed New York Harbor from Staten Island to Elizabethtown, New Jersey, where they torched churches and other buildings. Mercy Warren tells the story of a New Jersey minister's wife, Mrs. James Caldwell: "This lady was sitting in her own house, with her little domestic circle around her, and her infant in her arms; unapprehensive of danger, shrouded by consciousness of her own innocence and virtue; when a British barbarian pointed his musket into the window of her room and instantly shot her through the lungs.... Mr. Caldwell returns to find his house burned and his wife murdered."[43]

Meanwhile, Clinton returned from his Charlestown Campaign to New York and reinforced Knyphausen's raids. The Springfield Expedition against Nathanael Greene was Clinton's last attack on Washington's main army in New Jersey. A historic marker erected by the State of New Jersey at Springfield describes the Battle of Springfield: "Here June 23, 1780, 1500 Americans, under Greene and Dayton, were attacked by 5000 British and Hessians under Clinton and Knyphausen en route to capture stores at Morristown. The British burned Springfield, but were defeated." A hero of the Springfield battle was Presbyterian minister and widower James Caldwell, the "fighting preacher" whose wife Knyphausen's men had murdered. Realizing that his company's muskets were out of wadding, Caldwell ran into the church and came out carrying an armload of *Watts Hymnals*. Trotting on horseback among the troops, the clergyman tossed the songbooks to the men and shouted, "Put *Watts* into them, boys."[44]

Clinton seemed reluctant to attempt further incursions in the North because he anticipated the arrival of a French fleet and army: "Besides ... he was preparing to shift the scene of action wholly to the south."[45] Hence, after their defeat at the Battle of Springfield, Clinton and his British Army left New Jersey, returned to New York City, and remained there, expecting a Franco-American alliance to attack New York at any time. After the Battle of Springfield, however, the northern states were fairly quiet for the remainder of 1780 and the first half of 1781.

Revolution in the South (Glen McCroskey).

7

Regulators and Wataugans

> The Regulators form the connecting link between the resistance to the Stamp Act and the movement of 1775.[1]
>
> —George Bancroft

By 1779 the commanders of the opposing armies in the North, General Sir Henry Clinton and General George Washington, were chiefly engaged in watching each other. The British were pretty much confined to New York. New England had become less involved in the war since British troops had moved elsewhere. Clinton and his second in command, General Charles Cornwallis, First Marquess, Second Earl Cornwallis, abandoned hope for reconciliation between Britain and America. Clinton gave up the British offensive in the North and concentrated on subduing the South. Looking South, he saw great wealth promising abundant spoils of war and valuable exports: tobacco, timber and rice. He aspired to occupy the whole country rather than continue European tactics of marching, besieging and capturing towns and cities. Savannah, Georgia, was already under British control when Clinton and Cornwallis anchored there in December 1779 and began honing their plan for the siege of Charlestown. To elucidate the critical situation in the South when Clinton arrived it is necessary to start the story a decade earlier with a look at the Regulator Movement (1766–1771), the Wataugans, the Cherokee and land speculator Judge Richard Henderson.

Regulators were poorly organized farm people of the Piedmont Carolinas who protested inadequate courts and the corrupt practices of Crown-appointed officials. They were the inland counterparts to the well-organized Sons of Liberty, who protested the Stamp Act and provoked the American Revolution on the Atlantic seaboard. Sectional differences—an unfair system of taxation—between piedmont and coastal Carolina led to virtual civil war between colonial militia and Regulators of the backcountry. One inland grievance was that steep mountainside land, which was less productive, was taxed at the same rate as the fertile farmland on the coast.

In South Carolina, the government, which was based in the wealthy coastal Charlestown area, failed to provide adequate funding for the court system and law enforcement in western (piedmont, interior, backcountry, upcountry) South Carolina. Therefore, in piedmont South Carolina, which had no courts of justice, inhabitants took the law into their own hands and punished offenders. "This mode of proceeding was called Regulation and its authors Regulators. Those who opposed them were called Scovilites, after their leader, Scovil, commissioned by the governor to suppress them."[2]

In North Carolina, farmers, supported by their womenfolk, of the Blue Ridge foothills began discussing their lack of money. They attributed their poverty to high taxes, corrupt sheriffs, and illegal fees. The discontent grew and spread. A large segment of North Carolina colonists known as Regulators protested the inequitable tax system and courts, which seemed to favor the coastal (Tidewater) inhabitants. Riotous Regulators also protested the abuse of power exercised by some, but not all, Crown-appointed officials of the provincial government. Even North Carolina's royal governor, William Tryon, reported in 1767 that county sheriffs embezzled more than half the taxes collected. At first the Regulators swore allegiance to the Crown; they wanted to reform the existing government, not do away with it. Regulators did not protest the organization of the government, only the corrupt practices of officers who ran it. In this sense, the Regulator movement was an insurrection, not a revolution.

It has been argued that the fervent religion of Regulators, the evangelical Christianity of frontier Protestants—Baptists, Presbyterians, Quakers, Moravians and others—"bonded the Regulators together and fueled their antiauthoritarian stance toward what they believed to be an unjust, essentially evil governmental structure. Women ... undoubtedly played essential roles as supportive and influential partners in the spiritual development of the Regulators as well as advocates of their cause."[3] Many Sandy Creek Baptist Church members became Regulators. This church was cofounded in 1755 by an evangelical Baptist minister at Liberty in Randolph County, North Carolina. Farm families—women, men and children—throughout the Piedmont traveled on horses, wagons and buggies as far as 40 miles to hear him preach. Regulator Quaker Herman Husband, a member of Sandy Creek Baptist Church, became the movement's chief spokesperson. He believed that the provincial government of Governor Tryon's administration abused the poor.

In 1768 an angry mob of Regulators demanded that the county sheriff publish tax lists, collection records, and fee tables. Tryon called out men from the westernmost counties to protect the Hillsborough Superior Court, near present-day Chapel Hill, from the enraged Regulators. Jonas Bedford, a former British lieutenant and veteran of the French and Indian War, was one of the frontiersmen who responded to Tryon's call. Tryon wrote that Jonas Bedford, a planter, had "marched with a body of men he had assembled from the North West settlements of the Province, and joined the Troops under my Command, on the march to protect the Supreme Court of Hillsborough from fresh insults. In testimony of so spirited an exertion I gave him the rank of captain of Militia and after the expiration of the Service his good conduct and loyalty induced me to put him in the Commission of the Peace for Tryon County, the western frontier county of the Province."[4]

Two years later, Judge Richard Henderson was on the bench of the North Carolina Superior Court at Hillsborough when there was a second Regulator uprising. An Orange County Regulator presented the judge with a petition demanding unprejudiced juries and a public accounting by sheriffs for the taxes they collected. The court deferred action on the petition until the following Monday. In an article datelined New Bern, the *New York Gazette* reported: "On Monday a very large number ... of people ... appeared in Hillsborough, armed with clubs, whips ... and many other offensive weapons, and at once beset the court house." The Regulators knocked down the deputy clerk, "ascended the bench, shook their whips over Judge Henderson [and] told him his turn was next." Henderson wrote, "I found myself under a necessity of attempting to soften and turn away the fury of these mad people, in the best manner in my power, and as such could well be, pacify their rage and at the same time preserve the little remaining dignity of the court." Soon, Regulators set fire to Henderson's plantation.[5]

In 1770, four years before Lexington and Bunker Hill, Quaker Regulator Herman Husband published a book, *Impartial Relation*, "full of sound maxims of political wisdom, and of the most scathing invectives against tyrants. It made a most profound impression. The spirit of resistance, which had now been thoroughly aroused, widened and increased, until the result was the battle of Alamance"[6] on May 16, 1771. The Regulator Movement spread, led by Rednap Howell, James Hunter, William Butler and their spokesman, Herman Husband. Tryon and his assembly repeatedly tried but failed to assuage Regulator grievances. As a last resort, he again called out several militia units and announced, "It is the Intention of Government to raise a Body of Men to suppress the Insurrections in the Western Counties." Tryon organized an expedition of 1,400 militiamen, mostly from the coastal part of the colony, and marched to the banks of Great Alamance Creek near present-day Burlington, North Carolina.

After setting up camp he received a petition from the 2,000 Regulators who were bivouacked several miles to the west. The petition asked Tryon to halt his march and hear their grievances. Tryon swiftly sent the rebels a letter offering terms. The governor said, "I lament the fatal necessity ... to require you ... to lay down your Arms, surrender up the outlawed Ringleaders, and Submit yourselves to the Laws of your Country.... By accepting these Terms in one Hour from the delivery of this dispatch you will prevent an effusion of Blood, as you are at this time in a State of War and Rebellion against your King, your Country, and your Laws."[7] The rebels rejected the terms and Tryon's forces continued their advance westward toward the enemy camp. The governor's final message cautioned the rebels to take care of themselves, as he would immediately give the signal for action. The Regulators replied, "Fire and be damned."

The Battle of Alamance lasted two hours. Tryon organized the militiamen in battle lines. The Regulators, having no battle plan, no officers, and little discipline, fought individually, every man for himself, crouching behind rocks and trees. Nine on each side were killed; the wounded numbered 61 militiamen plus an unknown number of Regulators. When the mob began to retreat, the militia cautiously followed. The militia hanged one Regulator to avenge the deaths of their fellow militiamen. On May 31, 1771, Tryon offered amnesty to all those concerned in the rebellion who would "lay down their arms, take the Oath of Allegiance [to the king] and promise to pay all Taxes that are now due or may hereafter become due." There were several exceptions. A few mob leaders were not offered amnesty. Fourteen prisoners were tried; 12 were found guilty; and six were hanged.[8]

The year after the Battle of Alamance the membership of Sandy Creek Church dropped from 600 to 16. Sandy Creek Baptists exited piedmont North Carolina, migrated, and created Sandy Creek Baptist churches in Western North Carolina, Tennessee Country and Georgia.[9] Westward expansion was greatly stimulated by the Regulator Movement. Many saw no hope of redress for their grievances and were eager to move farther west into various areas, including East Tennessee country. The Regulators moved their families overmountain and established the Watauga and Nolichucky settlements in what they thought was Virginia but was in reality Tennessee. These settlers wished to escape British rule as well as to establish clear title to their land.

The Wataugans, the first Tennesseans, were a people of diverse nationality living uneasily on Indian hunting grounds, beyond any organized government. Wataugans inhabited East Tennessee's four oldest main permanent settlements: Watauga, Nolichucky, the North-of-Holston Settlement and Carter's Valley. In 1771 Regulator James Robertson established the Watauga Settlement, the first permanent over-the-mountain settlement in what is now Tennessee. Located south of the Holston River, Sycamore Shoals (today Elizabethton) stood on the banks of the Watauga, a tributary of the South Holston. Robertson, now known as the father of Tennessee, moved his family—rugged women, men and children—over the Blue Ridge Mountains from Orange County, North Carolina, rather than sign an oath of allegiance to the king. He was a Scots-Irishman, tall and fair with blue eyes and dark hair, a quiet man and a born leader. His overmountain settlements would become a safe haven beckoning the revolutionary rebels who were fleeing the tyranny of British rule. Robertson's motto would be "We are the advance guard of civilization. Our way is across the continent."[10]

Early Tennessee historian John Haywood, who, along with J.M.G. Ramsey, is as close to a primary source as anyone Tennessee has, tells the story of Robertson's first trip to Holston country. He said it was "summer 1769"[11] when Robertson visited the "delightful country on the waters of the Holston to view the new settlements when they began to be formed on the Watauga. Here he found one Honeycutt living in a hut, who furnished him with food. He made a crop there the first year. On re-crossing the mountain he got lost for some time.... Fourteen days he wandered without eating.... He was accidentally met by two hunters (who helped him survive).... He reached home in safety and soon afterwards returned to Watauga with a few others and there settled."[12]

The Nolichucky Settlement stood on the Nolichucky River near Limestone, Tennessee, south of the Holston River. The settlement was considered to be one of the Watauga settlements and its inhabitants were Wataugans. Its first permanent settler in the Nolichucky Valley was 36-year-old Jacob Brown, who was of English ancestry. He and a group of Regulators from what is now Union County, South Carolina, set up a trading post and a blacksmith shop in 1771 on the Nolichucky River between present-day Erwin and Jonesborough, Tennessee. Brown paid the Cherokee a horse load of goods for a lease of land along the Nolichucky. "He then leased this land to settlers."[13]

The North Holston Settlement, located north of the South Holston River, was founded by Welshman Evan Shelby and was called Sapling Grove (present-day Bristol, Tennessee-Virginia). It was not a Watauga settlement, but its inhabitants bonded with the Wataugans. Shelby was a scout during the French and Indian War, and after that war he became a fur trader. He liked the triangle of wilderness made available by the Lochaber Treaty in 1770. He wrote home to his family in Maryland, telling his 19-year-old son, Isaac, and other sons to buy all the land certificates they could find. Shelby suspected that veterans of the French and Indian War might be entitled to purchase land there. Early deeds show that Marylander Evan Shelby and Isaac Baker "purchased the Sapling Grove tract from the executors of James Patton in 1768–1771 (Washington Co, VA DB2:96)."[14] The land was part of Virginia's Crown grant (granted by the governor and council of Virginia) of 120,000 acres to Colonel Patton in 1745.

In 1771 Shelby and his wife, Letitia Cox Shelby, moved their family to the Holston Valley, where they settled on an old Indian-Buffalo path at the site of a prehistoric Indian village called "Big Camp Meet," which Patton and Buchanan had renamed Sapling Grove. Here Shelby founded the North Holston Settlement by building Shelby's Fort on little more than 1½ acres on a hill overlooking Shallow Creek (modern-day Beaver Creek). Both the Holston and Watauga settlements received a "steady stream of emigrants."[15] Shelby's store ledger at Fort Shelby listed some of their distinguished customers: John Sevier, James Robertson and Daniel Boone. Shelby's Fort served as a blockhouse—a stockade, a trading post, a meeting place, and a way station—welcoming travelers on the Wilderness Road. At that time, before Boone bushwhacked a road to Kentucky, the Wilderness Road reached only from Big Lick (Roanoke, Virginia) to Long Island of the Holston (Kingsport, Tennessee).

The Carter's Valley Settlement was located on both sides of the Holston River just west of Long Island (Kingsport) and west of the Lochaber Line. It was clearly in Cherokee Territory. Carter's Valley Settlement was cofounded by two Englishmen from Virginia, trader-merchant John Carter and William Parker; Robert Lucas soon joined the partnership. The Carters and several other families settled Carter's Valley about the time the Watauga Settlement was founded. Although Carter's Settlement was not geographically connected to the Watauga Settlement, it was considered to be one of the Watauga settlements. The other three overmountain settlements were contiguous. John Carter traded at Shelby's Station at Sapling Grove in the North Holston Settlement before he opened his own trading post. Carter's store was once looted by Indians who were suspected but not proven to be Cherokee. Carter and the Cherokee had good rapport and the Indians liked to shop at his trading post, therefore their friendship was not damaged by the burglary. In 1775 the Cherokee ceded land in Carter's Valley to compensate Carter and his partners for their losses. During the Cherokee War of 1776 John Carter moved to, and became a prominent member of, the Watauga Settlement. As for the women, the following excerpt describes typical Wataugan women, the anonymous founding mothers of Tennessee, and their relationship to their children and their men:

> In the annals of all countries there is no age nor race that has given to the world more sterling valor than that displayed by the frontier woman of Tennessee. She shared with the men all the dangers of the wilderness, with all its toils.... She did not wait for the clearing and the building of the cabin and the planting of the crops. She went along and helped do these things.
>
> She rocked the cradle in the home—she swung the cradle in the field. She spun the flax and carded the wool and made the clothing for the family. She has gone to the aid of a sick neighbor and returned to find her own home in ashes. The frontier woman ... never lacked for courage nor opportunities to prove it.
>
> There was a peculiar trait which seemed to be born in the children of that day, or which mothers had taught them—to make no show of fear nor make alarm—much like the young of birds, which, at a call, seek the cover of the wing. It was a "hush" of caution rather than of fear. Once the men of Holston settlement were called to Shelby's station, an Indian raid being expected....
>
> About this time there was a ... remarkable example of the "hush" habit, in the Snodgrass settlement near Blountville. The Indians made their appearance in the neighborhood during the absence of the men of the homes. The women, being warned in time, took their children and sought refuge by digging out a place under a large haystack. Small babes were among them yet no sound disclosed their whereabouts. They instinctively fell into the hush that had previously marked the behavior of the others. On coming out they found moccasin tracks all about the place.
>
> The lofty regard and admiration for these women was almost idolatrous and is best told in the tributes paid them by the men of their times. The country's esteem was no more sought by these fearless and rugged frontier men than were the approval and praise of their own women. When the term of enlistment in their country's service was over, the men would hasten to their homes and lay what laurels they had won at the feet of those women, craving no richer reward than their approbation.[16]

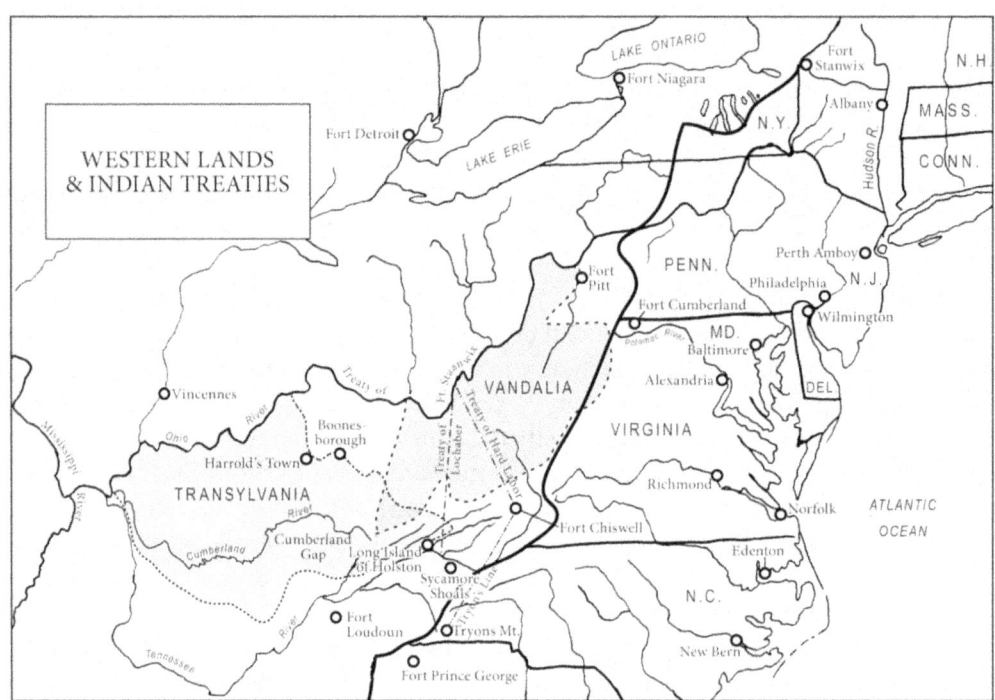

Boundary Lines: Tryon's Line; Fort Stanwix Hard Labor (Glen McCroskey).

Frederick Jackson Turner wrote, "Steadily the frontier of settlement advanced and carried with it individualism, democracy and nationalism."[17] Western expansion was greatly enhanced not only by the Regulator Movement, but Watauagans also were lured to the far western frontier by the Lochaber Treaty and by laws defining cabin and corn rights. The Lochaber Treaty agreement with Cherokee chiefs extended the Hard Labor Line westward and made more Indian territory available for settlement.

The Lochaber Treaty Line between the Cherokee Nation and Virginia created a pie-shaped wedge that pushed the Indian border farther into Indian territory. The treaty erased the Hard Labor Line and ceded a triangle of land already occupied by English colonists in the New River and Holston valleys. The Lochaber Line swung from its apex at Point Pleasant (today in West Virginia) to a point six miles east of Long Island of the Holston (Kingsport, Tennessee). The Lochaber Line drew hordes of settlers to the Holston Valley of Tennessee Country. The southern border of the Lochaber Line remained in limbo until the following year when Chief Little Carpenter agreed to make the South Holston River the southern boundary. The 1770 Lochaber Line was a "feeble barrier against the approaches of the emigrants, who came in greatly increased numbers to the West."[18]

The first Tennesseans believed they lived in Virginia until 1771, when Colonel John Donelson, a member of the House of Burgesses, surveyed the southern border of the line described by the 1770 Lochaber Treaty. Stanley J. Folmsbee, who annotated Ramsey's *Annals of Tennessee*, wrote:

In 1771, when the line was being surveyed by Col. John Donelson and some Cherokee chiefs, including Little Carpenter, it was discovered that some settlers had located between the 36° 30′ parallel and the

South fork of the Holston (presumable the Sapling Grove [Bristol] and Keywood settlements). Little Carpenter said he "pitied them" and therefore consented to having the boundary run from the intersection of the 36° 30′ parallel with the river along the course of the river to the point six miles east of Long Island. Thus the "north of the Holston" settlers were recognized as being outside of the Indian country.... [T]he [southern border of] the Lochaber line was also considered to be the North Carolina–Virginia boundary ... until 1779.[19]

Thus, due to the Little Carpenter's generosity in extending the southern boundary to the South Holston River, Shelby's North Holston Settlement was legitimized, while the three Watauga settlements were not. Carter Settlement was far west of the Lochaber Line, while the Watauga and Nolichucky river settlements were south of the Holston River.

When British Indian agent Alexander Cameron learned that Donelson's survey confirmed the South Holston River as the dividing line between North Carolina and Virginia he issued an ultimatum: The Watauga settlers must vacate the ancient Cherokee lands located south of the South Holston River. Living on the remote frontier, most of the Wataugans were honest folk who had moved west to cultivate land and improve their lives. Others were criminals who had fled to the inaccessible west to escape punishment. When the Wataugans realized that they were now living without laws and protection, they decided to govern themselves. In May 1772, soon after the Wataugans received Cameron's mandate, they organized the Watauga Association and drafted written articles based on Virginia law. The articles established a free and independent government to be administered by elected delegates: "The document, believed to be the first written compact for civil government west of the Alleghenies [Blue Ridge] has not been preserved."[20] To circumvent Cameron's decree that all inhabitants of the Watauga Settlement, corn rights or no, must immediately evacuate Indian country, James Robertson and John Bean represented the Watauga Association in successfully negotiating a 10-year lease (not purchase) of land from chiefs of the Cherokee Nation.

The Watauga frontiersmen lived fairly peacefully until 1774, when the events that precipitated Dunmore's War also drove the war whoops of the Shawnee to their doorstep. From thereon, and throughout the Revolution, Wataugans—regardless of whether they lived in Virginia, North Carolina or no-man's land—stuck together and acted as one. The North of Holston Settlement did not belong to the Watauga Association, but during the Revolution their histories were identical.

8

Pontiac's War, Boundaries and Treaties and Dunmore's War

> The Prosperity of the settlements of Kentucky and Tennessee had been greatly favored by the results of Lord Dunmore's War.... They were effectually relieved of all immediate peril from the Indians of the Northwest. The battle was thus of the greatest national importance. It was almost equivalent to the winning of the West.
> —George Elliott Howard[1]

Pontiac's War, the prelude to Dunmore's War, started festering in February 1763 at the end of the French and Indian War when the defeated French left America. Their American Indian allies were offered no part in the peacemaking process. Therefore they continued to attack the British colonists who were crossing the Indian border into Ohio Country. Pontiac's War erupted in the summer of 1763 when Ottawa chief Pontiac and Shawnee chief Cornstalk led attacks against British forts and settlements in Ohio Country. Fleeing the war zone, pioneers caravanned down the Great Pennsylvania Wagon Road and settled in the Carolinas. By July, American Indians held all British forts west of the Alleghenies except Detroit, Pitt, and Niagara. In August the British forces under Colonel Henry Bouquet broke Pontiac's siege of Fort Pitt at the Battle of Bushy Run. There, at the Forks of the Ohio, the narrow British victory over the Delaware, Shawnee, Mingo and Wyandot ended Pontiac's War and temporarily quelled Indian raids.

An imposing warrior at Bushy Run was Chief Cornstalk's sister, Nonhelema (Kate), who stood 6 feet, 6 inches. The whites called her "Grenadier Squaw" because Kate Cornstalk—like a British grenadier—was both fierce and tall. Nonhelema was leader of one of the Scioto River villages she and her brother founded when they migrated from western Virginia to the Ohio Valley. The Battle of Bushy Run convinced Nonhelema that "Shawnee survival depended on peace."[2] From that day on she would aid the colonists in conflicts with Ohio Country Indians.

In October, King George III imposed the Proclamation of 1763. It was a futile attempt to pacify Pontiac and improve Indian relations. The document established the Indian boundary and provided two superintendents of Indian affairs, Sir William Johnson for the North and Captain John Stuart for the South, to enforce it. The king's proclamation prohibited British settlements on lands west of the source of waters flowing into the Atlantic. In general, these lands lay west of the crest of the Blue Ridge chain of the Appalachian

Mountains. The edict also forbade provincial governors from granting land or issuing land warrants for these western territories. The proclamation, however, made exceptions for French and Indian War veterans. The king directed the governors to grant land "to every person having the rank of a field officer, 5,000 acres; to every captain, 3,000 acres; to every subaltern of staff officer, 2,000 acres; to every non-commissioned officer 200 acres and to every private 50 acres."[3]

The proclamation made by the distant king was disregarded everywhere by all classes of men, from land-hungry settlers and entrepreneurs to hunters and traders. Even George Washington considered it a guise, made merely to calm the apprehensions of the Indians against the advance of white settlements west of the Appalachians. The Indians were exasperated by the expanding encroachments, but the British colonists reasoned that they had fought and won the French and Indian War. By defeating the French and their Indian allies the pioneers had gained Ohio Country for colonial expansion. They now exerted their right of conquest

In contrast, North Carolina Crown governor William Tryon negotiated with the Cherokee Nation and agreed to move the proclamation boundary line westward for expansion of his colony. In 1767 Tryon powwowed with Cherokee chiefs, warriors and John Stuart, Esquire, his majesty's superintendent of Indian Affairs for the Southern Department. They agreed that Tryon's dividing line between the white settlements and Indian hunting grounds would run from the Spartanburg-Greenville area to Tryon Mountain in Polk County, North Carolina, and from there in a straight line to Fort Chiswell, Virginia. Tryon, working with the Cherokee Nation's assistant war chief, Ostenaco Outacite (Mankiller or "Judd's Friend"), laid a string of beads on a map showing the division between Cherokee country and the Province of North Carolina. During the next few years, three more boundary line treaties extended the Proclamation Line still farther west and impinged even more on Indian lands. The Stanwix Line encroached on the Mingo and the Shawnee of Ohio Country, and the Hard Labor and Lochaber lines claimed a chunk of the Cherokee Nation.

Though Tryon reached an agreement with the Cherokee on the Carolina frontier, the Ohio Country Indians bordering Dunmore's Virginia remained unappeased. For that reason, a deputation of the Six Nations of the Iroquois Confederacy, who inhabited the Mohawk Valley of New York, petitioned Sir William Johnson, the royal superintendent of Indian Affairs for the Northern Department of America. They requested that Johnson present a "formal remonstrance against the continued encroachments of the Whites upon their lands."[4] Johnson called a 12-day conference to meet on October 24, 1768, at Fort Stanwix, New York. Attending were the governor of New Jersey; representatives of other colonies; chiefs of the Six Nations; delegations from many other Iroquois-speaking tribes; and 3,200 Indians of 17 different tribes. When the Iroquois delegation agreed to open a large section in southwestern Pennsylvania and western Virginia for white settlements, Johnson gave them enough presents to fill 200 canoes. A few days later, an additional land cession was made—the Iroquois "give-away."[5] This addendum involved the Ohio Country, which was inhabited by the Shawnee and the Delaware (Lenape) Indians. But the tribes who lived there had no part in making the additional treaty to relinquish their land. The Iroquois claimed the land by right of conquest in the Beaver Wars, a series of wars between the Iroquois League and Ohio Country Indians.

The Treaty of Stanwix by which Johnson obtained a whopping portion of Ohio Country was an important step toward opening the western frontier for colonial settlement. The Shawnee, Delaware, Mingo and other Indians residing in Ohio Country maintained that the Iroquois, who did not live there, had no right to sell or trade Ohio land. They disputed the Iroquois claims to the land: "The Ohio Country tribes called the Treaty of Fort Stanwix illegal and refused to conform to its precepts."[6] When the Shawnee Nation disputed the treaty, the Iroquois threatened them with annihilation if they refused to accept it. Hence the Shawnee attempted to form a broad tribal alliance to defend their Ohio territory.

During the spring of 1772 Northwestern (Ohio Country) Indians attacked settlers in Kentucky along the southern banks of the Ohio. The settlers retaliated. Assaulting local Indians, they killed Bald Eagle, a Delaware chief who was hunting along the Monongahela River. They raided the salt-making village of Bulltown near the falls of the Little Kanawha River in present-day central West Virginia and killed many Indians in it. Bulltown was the namesake of Captain Bull, the Delaware chief who was the only son of the famous Teedyuscung, king of the Delawares. News of the Bulltown massacre spread like wildfire across the western frontier, spurring Chief Cornstalk to set fire to settlements in an attempt to drive out the whites. When Cornstalk, leading both Shawnee and the chiefless Delaware tribes, joined Mingo chief John Logan, the Indian effort to push settlers back across the Appalachians intensified.

Despite the danger on the frontier, Daniel and Rebecca Boone sold their North Carolina land on the Yadkin River in 1773, gathered a few neighbors, and set out for Kentucky. Before this time no white female and no pioneer family had seriously attempted to cross the Cumberland Mountains. Just before caravanning through the Cumberland Gap the little colony set up temporary camp in Powell Valley between Wallen Ridge and Powell Mountain, near where present-day Virginia, Tennessee, and Kentucky converge. There they were joined by 40 well-armed hunters.

Along the way Boone's 17-year-old son, James, and two Mendenhall brothers separated from the larger group to obtain flour from Captain William Russell at Castle's Woods (Castlewood), Virginia: "Captain Russell sent forward his oldest son Henry, a young man of 17, two Negroes named Charles and Adam, Isaac Crabtree, and a youth named Drake, with several horses loaded with farming tools."[7] When night overtook them they encamped within three miles of the main camp, where Daniel awaited them. On Wallen Ridge, Indians raided and killed James Boone, Henry Russell and most of their party. Virginians interpreted the massacre as "a harbinger of evil."[8] Nathan Boone recalled, "My brother, James Boone, was shot through his hips and rendered helpless. The affair was witnessed by a Negro who hid in the driftwood in the creek. He saw Big Jim, a man with very high cheekbones, an unusually broad face, and a peculiar chin, whom he easily recognized. This Indian was well known by the Boone family and spoke broken English.... Father was always inclined to believe that he was a Shawnee.... On the night of the murder, Big Jim approached my brother with a tomahawk. James implored him by name to spare him, but Jim paid no regard to these pleas."[9] Isaac Crabtree escaped the carnage and vowed "to kill any red-skin he could find."[10] When he reached the camp in Powell Valley and told the family of their son's death the Boones turned around and headed to nearby Castle's Woods. There they spent the winter in an abandoned Appalachian Mountain cabin on the Clinch River in Fincastle County, Virginia.

When Nobleman John Murray, fourth Earl of Dunmore, Viscount of Fincastle—"a red headed Scot with a large nose and fiery gaze"[11]—became the royal governor of Virginia in 1771 he was alerted not only to problems in New England but also to the Indian unrest on his own frontier in the Appalachians. Dunmore's Virginia was vast. In 1772 he lopped off a section of Botetourt County and created a new western frontier—his huge namesake, Fincastle County, whose east-west boundary ran from the New River to the Mississippi and included present-day Kentucky and much of the Old Northwest. Its southern boundary was the ill-defined North Carolina line. Dunmore established Fincastle's county seat as Lead Mines—a mining community on the New River near today's Wytheville—guarded by militia garrisoned at Fort Chiswell. Dunmore commissioned surveyor William Preston to be a member of Fincastle's first county court. The Scots-Irish Preston was the heir, nephew and adopted son of pioneer land-speculator-colonizer Colonel James Patton. The next year Preston became Fincastle County sheriff. Soon Dunmore appointed Preston to the important position of county lieutenant, the highest county official.

Dunmore, whose pay came from the Crown, was "financially independent of those he governed."[12] Land grants were the most powerful carrot the British government and Dunmore possessed to reward loyalty to the Crown. The stick that balanced the carrot was the governor's authority to dissolve colonial assemblies and remove from office some local officials, judges and justices of the peace. He could also suspend the House of Burgesses whenever he chose. Dunmore occasionally offered the carrot. At the request of prominent Tidewater men he directed Preston to dispatch several parties to lay out tracts, mostly in Ohio Country and the present state of Kentucky, "for colonial officers entitled to land grants for military services."[13] Among the recipients were George Washington, Patrick Henry, William Preston, William Byrd, Andrew Lewis, Evan Shelby, Arthur Campbell, and William Christian. Christian received a "land warrant ... for 3000 acres of land in Fincastle County for services as a captain in the Second Virginia Regiment."[14]

Dunmore's dilemma was that he had both personal and political interests regarding the settlement of lands in the Ohio Country. Personally, he was interested in land grants and speculating in western land where his family could settle. Politically, as governor, he sought to provide land to veterans of the French and Indian War as accorded by the King's Proclamation of 1763. Fear that the rebellion of the Sons of Liberty on New England's seaboard and the Regulators in the Carolina backcountry would spill over into coastal Virginia was a major source of Dunmore's distress.

Closer to home, however, was the Indian disharmony on the frontier. He was concerned with western expansion and protecting Virginians living on the frontier. Except for the killings near the Clinch River, Virginia's southwestern frontier where the Cherokee lived had been relatively quiet for almost a decade. But during that time the northwestern frontier of Ohio Country was steadily swamped with surveyors laying out grants for veterans of the French and Indian War and by individuals and land companies looking for choice acreage. The westward surge of people into these lands was an attempt to dislodge America's indigenous people from their ancestral lands. The Shawnee retaliated, attacking settlements all along the Indian border.

Dunmore's retaliatory Shawnee Expedition (Dunmore's War) marked the beginning of the breaking of boundary treaties signed to keep the seaboard settlers and the Indian people apart.[15] Dunmore's attempt to seize unoccupied Fort Pitt at the Forks of the Ohio to support Virginia's charter claim over that of Pennsylvania led to war with the Shawnees and Delawares. When he drew the Wataugans into his expedition in early 1774 they were living peaceably on Virginia's southwestern frontier in mutual respect with the Cherokee. In contrast, the Shawnee and other Indian nations of Ohio Country on the northwestern frontier, which Virginia claimed as part of their Northwest Territory, were disgruntled. What began as the Shawnee Expedition against northwestern tribes became the border conflict known as Dunmore's War.

Much of the information about Dunmore's War has been gleaned from letters preserved in Colonel William Preston's papers, now a part of the Lyman Draper Collection at the Wisconsin Historical Society. Preston accumulated a large and valuable collection of Virginia documents and letters. He was able to do so because he was Fincastle County's highest ranking county officer as well as its sheriff and county surveyor: "Practically all public business passed through his hands."[16] Preston also served as a member of Virginia's House of Burgesses. His wide-ranging network encompassed his tightly knit Scots-Irish clan, which included Patrick Henry, Andrew Lewis, William Christian, Arthur Campbell and Arthur's cousin William Campbell. The following abstracts of letters to Preston found in the Preston Papers voice the alarm of families fleeing their frontier homes at the onset of the Shawnee Expedition They also show the county lieutenant's role in coordinating militia defense and supplies during border warfare. Preston transmitted these communications to Governor Dunmore:

March 22, 1774	Capt. Daniel Smith from Castle's Woods writes to Col. William Preston at Smithfield that he has journeyed to Rye Cove: Settlers, alarmed by Indians, are fleeing Clinch Settlements, seeking safety in Holston Valley.
May 7, 1774	[Capt.] William Russell notes the evacuation of plantations on the Clinch River.
May 30, 1774	Captain Daniel Smith from Indian Creek reports the scarcity of powder for defense of the frontier, tells of his efforts to block pioneers from abandoning their settlements.
June 3, 1774	Abraham Hite Jr. from Hampshire reports that the Indian War has begun; inhabitants are fleeing; his brother and a party of surveyors are in danger.

In June 1774 Royal Governor Dunmore advised Fincastle County's Lieutenant Preston to alert the surveyors that war with the Indians had broken out. Preston in turn ordered Captain William Russell on the Clinch River to hire woodsmen to go to Kentucky, find the surveyors, and relay the message. Russell hired two long-hunters, Michael Stoner and Daniel Boone, to carry the warning.

Dunmore then organized volunteer militiamen to embark on a Shawnee Expedition, which became a border war between Virginia settlers and Indians of Ohio Country, especially the Shawnee. Ohio Country lay west of the Appalachian Mountains and north of the Ohio River. The only major encounter of the Shawnee Expedition, Dunmore's War, would be the Battle of Point Pleasant fought on the Indian border of Virginia (now West Virginia) and Ohio Country. Dunmore's War has been called the last colonial war in America. It is also known as the first war of the American Revolution.

Dunmore issued a circular letter to his county lieutenants asking them to raise a frontier militia for two purposes: to defend the colony and to crush a coalition of American Indian tribes led by the Shawnee chief Cornstalk (Keigh-tugh-qua). Dunmore orchestrated his Shawnee Expedition and obtained feedback from his county lieutenants, who were the highest ranking military officers in each county. In wartime the county lieutenant's rank was elevated to colonel. He often held other county offices. His job was like that of William

Preston, Fincastle County's lieutenant: organize militia throughout the county and find ways to pay them. The county lieutenant was responsible for corresponding with other county lieutenants, commissioning officers, and raising and provisioning troops. He also decided the location of forts and supervised measures of defense and offense. Colonel Preston kept his finger on the pulse of the frontier largely through correspondence. He issued orders, dispatched ammunition and provisions as needed, and acted as liaison between militia officers and the governor.

Governor Dunmore chose Scots-Irish colonel Andrew Lewis, the county lieutenant of Botetourt County, to organize the colony's militia for offense: an attack on the Shawnee. Lewis had an impressive military background, having fought as one of Washington's principal officers in the French and Indian War. He commanded the Big Sandy Expedition against the Shawnee and their northwestern Indian allies.

Dunmore appointed Botetourt County's militia lieutenant, Colonel William Christian—also a Scots-Irish veteran of the French and Indian War—to coordinate militia defense of the frontier during the expedition. Christian had achieved the rank of captain of a colonial militia at age fifteen. He had studied law under Patrick Henry, married Henry's sister, Anne, and was a member of the House of Burgesses when Dunmore selected him for service in the expedition. Dunmore directed Christian to "use every means possible to prevent inhabitants from leaving"[17] frontier settlements. He was also to build forts along the Clinch River. At a meeting between Christian and militia officers at Lead Mines, the Fincastle County seat, it was resolved that militia would accompany Christian to the Clinch River Valley and build palisaded forts (forts surrounded by a fence of closely placed stakes, pointed at the top) for the protection of Southwest Virginia. Colonels Christian and Preston and Major Arthur Campbell, who was responsible for protecting the Fincastle settlers, personally financed the militia as well as the building of the forts.

Christian chose two captains to build seven garrisoned multifamily forts along the Clinch in the inhabited part of Fincastle County's extreme western frontier. The stockades—built by local militia under captains Daniel Smith and William Russell and supervised by Colonel Christian—stretched westward from present-day Tazewell County to presend-day Scott County. They stood 12 to 25 miles apart except for the two at Castlewood, which were 4 miles apart. Moore's Fort was the largest and best known of the Clinch River forts. Repeatedly attacked by Indians, this two-gated fort housed as many as 200 people, sheltering about 20 pioneer families, militia guards and two dozen men patrolling as Indian spies. Daniel and Rebecca Boone stayed there for a while after their son James was killed. Boone commanded three of the four Lower Clinch River forts from 1774 to 1775. Nathan Boone told Lyman Draper, "I know very little about my father's military service in 1774 except that he raised a small company and started to march out on the Point Pleasant campaign. They traveled for a day or two, but he was overtaken with orders to return and take command of three forts on the Clinch. My father was commissioned captain by Governor Dunmore."[18] Selected items from the Preston Papers describe fort activity:

June 10, 1774	A circular letter from Governor Dunmore to county lieutenants suggests defense of the frontier, attacks on the enemy, and the erection of forts.
July 2, 1774	Col. Preston instructs Christian to order various militia captains, e.g., William Campbell, to draft men from their companies for frontier defense.

July 3, 1774	Dunmore writes from Williamsburg. Informs Preston of his plan to march into enemy country and erect forts at the mouths of the Wheeling and the Great Kanawha.
August 14, 1774	Lord Dunmore to Lord Dartmouth [secretary of state for the colonies]: "I wrote to your Lordship that I expected a War with the Indians, since that the Shawnees, Mingos and some of the Delawares, have fallen on our frontiers, killed, scalped and most cruelly murdered, a great many men, women and children.... I have ordered out a good many parties of our militia.... I hope in eight or ten days to march with a body of men over the Alleghany Mountains, and then down the Ohio to the mouth of the Scioto and if I can possible fall upon these lower towns undiscovered I think I shall be able to put an end to this most cruel war...."[19]
August 16, 1774	Captain William Russell writes from Fort Preston to Colonel Preston on the New River that "the volunteers are ready to march when relieved of duty at the forts; prefers to command a company on Clinch River rather than to go on the expedition...."
August 25, 1774	William Preston's letter to Major Arthur Campbell orders Captains Thompson and Daniel Smith to defend the frontier during the absence of the troops.

Preston was undoubtedly influenced by the frontier massacres of the French and Indian War in which his adoptive father, Colonel Patton, was killed at the Draper's Meadows Massacre when the home front was left unguarded during Braddock's Campaign in 1755:

October 4, 1774	Captain Daniel Smith from Elk Garden to Col. William Preston of Smithfield says that inhabitants on Clinch River, alarmed by late invasions of Indians, will "seek a place of safety unless assistance can be had."
October 13, 1774	Smith's letter from Castle's Woods reports that he and Daniel Boone had an "unsuccessful scout after Indians who attacked Blackmore's" Fort. He enclosed a petition from inhabitants of the Lower settlement to appoint Boone captain.

A network of forts in Holston Valley already existed to protect pioneers from Indian attack. Nine of these forts stood within the boundary of present-day Sullivan County, Tennessee, which was then part of Fincastle County in Southwest Virginia. Militiamen from these forts fought in Dunmore's War. The Clinch River forts were completed just in time. In September there was alarming news. Renowned Mingo chief Logan (Lahgahjute) was rampaging with warriors along the Holston and Clinch rivers. The Mingos, now known as the Iroquois of the Ohio, were mostly Seneca and Cayuga who had emigrated from the Mohawk Valley to Ohio Country. Logan divided his Ohio Mingo braves into small bands to strike simultaneously in widely separated settlements and spread dread and death among terrified frontier families. Logan, a half-breed who spoke good English, sought to avenge the April Yellow Creek Massacre of his family near present-day Wheeling, West Virginia.

Logan's mother belonged to the Cayuga Tribe. His French father had been captured, had been adopted into the Oneida tribe, and then had become a chief among the Susquehanna Indians. The name *Logan* came from James Logan, William Penn's secretary and a friend of the Iroquois. While remaining neutral in the French and Indian War, Chief Logan "took refuge in the peace-loving, Quaker atmosphere of Philadelphia."[20] He moved to Ohio and settled on Yellow Creek in 1772. Long known as a friend to the white man, Logan was once kind and gentle with women and children. Popular with frontiersman, he was admired for his honesty and respected as a skilled rifleman and a great hunter. Frontier folk were shocked to hear that white men had made nine Indians drunk and then killed them. Among those slain were members of Logan's family. There has been much controversy over who murdered Logan's relatives, although militia colonel Michael Cresap was blamed for the murders. Thomas Jefferson tells one version of the massacre in *Notes on the State of Virginia*. When Logan's sister was severely injured he retaliated by attacking settlers on the banks of the Monongahela River and Redstone Creek. Rampaging south of the Ohio, he killed 13 settlers in western Pennsylvania.

Captain John Connolly sent militiamen from Fort Dunmore (formerly Fort Pitt at the Forks of the Ohio) into Ohio Country to destroy Mingo villages and squelch the outbreak. Connolly was Dunmore's military commandant in the border country surrounding Pittsburgh, which Dunmore hoped to claim for Virginia. Chief Cornstalk joined Chief Logan's effort to drive the militia out of Ohio Country, and Dunmore prepared for war against the Mingo, Delaware and Shawnee.

Logan's raids soon forced settlers of Southwest Virginia and East Tennessee to move into forts. His Mingos took goods and livestock and assaulted settlers along the Holston. On the Reedy Creek border between the Holston and Watauga settlements a family was scalped and a little boy was tomahawked. Forts along the Clinch River, including Fort Blackmore and Moore's Fort under Boone's command, were attacked. Men were made to run the gauntlet. Several horses were stolen from Fort Shelby at Sapling Grove, as Logan's "Mingos did not intend to walk home."[21]

Near King's Mill Fort on Boozy Creek 12 miles west of Sapling Grove (Bristol) Indians murdered the John Roberts family except for a son who was captured. Before slaughtering the family, Logan made one of the captives write a note on parchment paper with ink made from water and gunpowder. The note, which is included in the Preston Papers, contains a handwritten copy of Logan's letter:

> Captain Cresap What did you kill my people on Yellow Creek for? The white people killed my kin, at Conestoga, a great while ago; and I thought nothing of that. But you killed my kin again, on Yellow Creek, and took my cousin prisoner. Then I thought I must kill, too; and I have been three times to war since; but the Indians are not angry—, only myself. Captain John Logan.[22]

Neighbors found Logan's note and the grisly corpses beside their log house in the cornfield. After burying the bodies, they took refuge for the next few weeks behind the gates of King's Mill Fort.

Major Arthur Campbell's duty was to provide safe passage for the steady flow of pioneers who began arriving in the Holston settlements. He is known as the "Guardian of the Wilderness Road," a leading figure in the "Taming of the West,"[23] and the Father of Washington County, Virginia. Red-haired, fair-skinned Campbell, whose ancestors had emigrated from Scotland to Ireland in the mid–1600s and to Pennsylvania in 1726, was born on the Virginia frontier. At fourteen Arthur joined a company of rangers stationed at Fort Jackson six miles southwest of Staunton. One day when he was away from the fort picking plums, Wyandotte Indians captured him. A Wyandotte chief adopted him and took him to Detroit, where Jesuits educated him. The Indians taught Arthur the value of silence, to talk little and to walk gracefully with erect posture. Striving to blend in with their culture, he dyed his red hair black.

During the French and Indian War, when he learned that the British were marching toward Lake Erie, Arthur Campbell made a daring escape. After walking 200 miles he found British troops who employed him as a guide. His knowledge of Indian ways and familiarity with the territory north of the Ohio proved valuable for his later work on the Virginia frontier. Receiving 2,000 acres for his services with the British during the French and Indian War, Arthur studied surveying and law at Augusta Academy. His frontier home,

Royal Oak, was near present-day Marion. He became a justice of the peace and a militia captain of Fincastle County and married his cousin Margaret, sister of William Campbell

In June 1774 Dunmore sent a circular letter urging Virginia's county lieutenants to prepare for war. As soon as the order reached Fincastle County, Preston relayed it to his militia majors and captains. Arthur Campbell was in the process of mustering militiamen to build forts and then march on the Shawnee Expedition when he learned that the Cherokees were wrought up over Isaac Crabtree's murder of Cherokee Billy. Crabtree had attempted to avenge the death of James Boone by shooting an innocent man, Cherokee Billy, during a racing contest between the Cherokee and the Wataugans. Savvy in Indian affairs, Campbell anticipated retaliatory Cherokee raids from the southwest as well as Shawnee attacks from the north. Guarding against the possibility of a Shawnee-Cherokee alliance, Campbell devised a plan to pacify the Cherokee. Writing to County Lieutenant Preston, Campbell said that settlers along the Watauga River planned to flee their cabins because they feared reprisal for the murder. To monitor Cherokee mood and look for signs of hostility, he alerted Evan Shelby, his second in command, whose Sapling Grove fort maintained a roster of 71 militiamen and was 45 miles west of Campbell's home.

Campbell requested Andrew Lewis, commander of the southwestern militia, to write a soothing letter to the Cherokee war chief Oconostota. Lewis had become acquainted with the chief when the Cherokee had requested that he construct a Virginia fort at Chota. Campbell himself wrote to Alexander Cameron, deputy commissioner of Indian affairs, asking his help in keeping peace with the Cherokee. Meanwhile Campbell sent spies and militia officers to apprise him of Indian sentiment and assess the mood of pioneers in the lower settlements. Complying with Campbell's peacemaking effort, Oconostota vowed that the Cherokee would not go to war unless Crabtree committed further provocations. Colonel Preston received and forwarded the following dispatches from Arthur Campbell and the Cherokee regarding Crabtree and Cherokee Billy:

June 1774	Campbell reports that settlers are "alarmed by killing of Cherokee 'Billey'… and are … in need of protection until matter can be made up with the chiefs": Crabtree is "suspected of the deed."
	Campbell sends two enclosures to be forwarded to Watauga settlers and to the Cherokee Nation. To Cameron he confirms the murder on the Watauga and the "ill conduct" of Crabtree.
	Campbell says that the Cherokee, although provoked by Crabtree, would avoid war and that Captain [Evan] Shelby would send "notice of any alarm."
July 1774	Oconostota's letter from Chota to Colonels Lewis and Preston expresses Cherokee desire for peace and preservation of respective boundary rights.
	Preston's "Letter to Oconostota the chief of the Warlike Nation of the Cherokee" acknowledges the chief's July 16 letter to Colonel Andrew Lewis and himself. He points out mutual advantages for Indians and Virginians to remain at peace and tells Oconostota about a "report that Cherokee parties have gone out to assist the Shawnee with whom the Virginians are at war." Preston informs Oconostota that the governor of Virginia is leading an expedition against the Shawnee and warns the Cherokee against being influenced by French traders.

While attempting to calm the Cherokee, Arthur Campbell also began to organize forces to join Lewis, who was assembling the Southwestern militia to move against the Shawnee. As the threat of war approached, some Wataugans fled to safety.

In August 1774 Pennsylvanian captain James Harrod (namesake of Harrodsburg, Kentucky) arrived at Arthur Campbell's Royal Oak. He was on his way to join Lewis in the

Shawnee Expedition. Harrod reported that northern Indians were on the warpath. In September Campbell received news of raids on Moore's Fort. Indian footprints were observed around other Clinch River forts.

Dunmore had ordered most of the available men to Point Pleasant. Campbell kept a small guard at Royal Oak and sent rangers 45 miles west to defend Shelby's Fort. He allocated other militiamen to augment Daniel Boone's forces at Fort Blackmore and Moore's Fort. By staying home and not marching with Lewis to attack the Shawnee, both Boone and Campbell played a vital role safeguarding the frontier settlements along the Great Road. Further correspondence between Arthur Campbell and William Preston ensued:

> September 1774 Campbell relays Oconostota's wish to "keep peace with the English. But if they would go to War he would have no hand in it." Campbell expresses general fear of a Cherokee war, mentions the offer of aid from Carolina, and notes "50 Catawba Indians desirous of being employed against the Shawnee.... Boone very diligent at Castle's Woods; in need of powder and flour."

In the spring of 1774 Dunmore had initiated a smaller offensive march. He authorized militia officer Angus McDonald to organize an advance march against Indian towns. McDonald assembled 400 militiamen under eight captains including "the Old Wagoner" Daniel Morgan and Michael Cresap. When four Indians and two militiamen were killed in a brief skirmish, the Indians seemed anxious to end hostilities. McDonald was suspicious. He believed that the peace gesture was a ploy to allow the Indian women and children time to escape an impending battle. McDonald burned five Mingo villages and trampled 70 acres of standing corn. Ravages upon the frontiers then began to increase rather than decrease. The retaliating northwestern Indians murdered pioneers on the western front of Virginia, Ohio and Pennsylvania. By August 1774 virtually all residents of Fincastle County were living inside forts.

In July Dunmore informed Lewis that repeated hostilities of various Indian nations and the universal alarm throughout the frontiers made it necessary for him to go in person to Fort Dunmore (the site of Fort Pitt):

> [I intend] to support that country for a barrier and give the Enemies a Blow that will Breake the Confederacy.... I ... Desire you to raise a respectable Boddy of Men and join me either at the mouth of the greate Kanaway [Point Pleasant] or Waiten [Wheeling] as is most convenient for you ... [and] the Indians having Spies on the Frontiers ... may Bring all the Force of the Shawnees against you in your march to the Kenewey ... so I would have you Consider in what Time you could ... meet me at eny place at Ohio in as Short time as you Can.... Forward the letter to Colo. Wm. Preston with the greatest Dispatch as I want his assistance as well as that of your Brother, Charles Lewis.... Prey be as explicit as you can as to the time and place I need not inform You how necessary Dispatch is.... I am Sir Your Most Obt. & very Hbl. Ser DUNMORE Winchester July 24th 1774.[24]

Andrew Lewis began raising militia regiments and volunteers for the Shawnee Expedition. Four regiments, three from Fincastle and one from Botetourt, were put on alert, ready to march. The Fincastle companies assembled under Captains Evan Shelby, William Russell, and William Herbert. Evan Shelby raised a company from the North Holston, Watauga, Nolichucky and Clinch River settlements. These overmountain men, wearing long, fringed hunting shirts of various colors, shot bags and powder horns strapped to their belts and rifles slung over their shoulders, marched to the banks of the New River, where they were joined by Herbert's New River group.

Colonel Christian, leading militiamen who had spent the summer building forts along the Clinch, also marched to the New River, where he took command of the companies that now merged to form the Fincastle Regiment. Christian then led the Fincastle Regiment to Camp Union (today's Lewisburg, West Virginia) at the Big Levels of the Greenbrier. There Christian's Fincastle Regiment joined militia from other counties. The combined force was under the overall command of Andrew Lewis who led his army, the southern wing, northward to the Kanawha Valley. There he expected to rendezvous with Dunmore's army, the northern wing, at the mouth of the Great Kanawha on the Ohio. Preston Papers from July through September 1774 describe the March to Point Pleasant:

August   Major James Robertson from Culbertson's reports "departure of John Draper [Mary Draper Ingles' brother] with about twenty men" and requests more men to join him; expresses difficulty in "making up his company for Shawnee expedition" and "requests provisions and ammunition."
Michael Woods from Rich Creek writes, "Men who have been drafted for the expedition refuse to serve; request that their petition for release shall not be countenanced."

September   Col. Wm. Christian: "Troops on the march for place of rendezvous." Lord Dunmore is at Fort Pitt [renamed Fort Dunmore at the Forks of the Ohio].
Christian notes the arrival and departure of troops for the Shawnee expedition: "Lord Dunmore with 700 men to be at the mouth of the Great Kanawha [Point Pleasant] some days after the 20th of Sept." Andrew Lewis, from Camp Union on the Great Levels to Preston, reports the expedition is on the march.
Lewis to Preston: "I received a letter from his Lordship ... dated ye 30th August ... which expressed his ... warmest wishes, that I would with all the troops from this quarter Join him at ye Mouth of the Little Kanaway [today's Parkersburg]. I wrote his Lordship that it was not in my Power to alter our rout..." Botetourt troops march "in a few hours" to the mouth of Elk Creek.

During the first week in September, Colonel Charles Lewis's troops from Augusta County and Arbuckle's company from Botetourt County detached with orders to herd cattle and drive 400 pack horses loaded with "flower, salt, & tools"[25] to the mouth of the Elk River (now Charleston, West Virginia). There they were to build a storehouse and canoes to float provisions down to the mouth of the Kanawha on the Ohio at Point Pleasant.

Andrew Lewis, who organized the march to Point Pleasant, ordered Christian to remain at Camp Union with 400 men, guard provisions, wait for reinforcements and then hurry to Point Pleasant. On September 12 Lewis began marching with the Botetourt Militia and one Company of the Fincastle Troops on a 25-day, 160-mile march to Point Pleasant. Lewis's army picked their way along riverbanks so steep that the men marched single file. Meanwhile, Governor Dunmore departed from the Potomac Valley, climbed the Blue Ridge, crossed the Alleghenies, descended into the Monongahela Valley, and marched to the Forks of the Ohio by the route that Braddock and Washington had bushwhacked during the French and Indian War.

On October 6 Lewis's 1,100 troops reached Point Pleasant on the Ohio at the mouth of the Great Kanawha. There, in a hollow tree, they found a letter allegedly left by Dunmore's scouts. Neither the contents of Dunmore's message nor Lewis's reply were revealed to the public, but Dunmore failed to show up for the Battle of Point Pleasant: "Many brave Men lost their lives. Yet I hope in its consequences, it will be a general Good to the Country, and this engagement will be long Remembered to the Memory & Honour of those who purchased the Victory by their deaths" (William Fleming).[26] The Indians watched. Alarmed to see Dunmore's northern wing approaching from the north and Lewis's wing advancing from the south toward their villages, the braves determined to attack Lewis's southern wing at Point Pleasant and prevent the union of their two columns.

Lewis's stout Scots-Irish Presbyterians from Fincastle County spent Sunday, October 9, in religious services at Point Pleasant. That night, as the militiamen were settling down in their tents, 1,000 painted warriors—mainly Shawnee reinforced by Mingo, Delaware, Wyandot and Ottawa—silently crossed the Ohio on rafts and "stood ready to assault the sleeping camp."[27] A West Virginia state historian and archivist described Virginia troop positions on the day before the Battle of Point Pleasant:

> An army composed of twenty-seven hundred men had been organized in two divisions, each, composed almost exclusively of frontiersmen west of the Blue Ridge and placed in the Ohio Valley. The Northern Division or right wing, comprising the Berkeley and the Frederick County Regiments, and the West Augusta Battalion, the whole numbering thirteen hundred men, and commanded by Lord Dunmore in person, lay at Port Gower, on the northwest bank of the Ohio, at the mouth of the Hockhocking river, now in Athens County, Ohio. The Southern Division or left wing composed of the Augusta and the Botetourt Regiments; and the companies of Shelby, Russell, and Herbert, of the Fincastle Battalion; together with Buford's Bedford Company riflemen, the whole commanded by General Andrew Lewis, lay at Camp Point Pleasant, at the mouth of the Great Kanawha River. Colonel Christian with companies of Campbell, Crockett and Floyd of the Fincastle Battalion, and Harrod's Kentucky Pioneers, together with a number of unorganized men from the counties of Augusta and Culpeper lay on the north or right bank of the Great Kanawha river, distant about 25 miles from its mouth. Captain Thomas Slaughter with the Dunmore Volunteers was at the mouth of Elk River—on the site of [Charleston] the capital city of West Virginia—and Captain Anthony Bledsoe, with his company of Fincastle troops was still at Camp Union, on the Big Levels of Greenbrier.[28]

Cornstalk's 1,200 struck Lewis's southern regiment at the confluence of the Kanawha and the Ohio rivers. The Battle of Point Pleasant—the only major battle of Dunmore's War—was a sunup to sundown pitched battle between the south wing of the Virginia militia led by Andrew Lewis and a confederation of Northwestern tribes under Shawnee chief Cornstalk. After significant losses on both sides, the Shawnee fled. Isaac Shelby's letter describing the Point Pleasant battle "may be considered as practically the official report of the battle."

Isaac Shelby, who would become the brain and muscle behind the overmountain march to the Battle of Kings Mountain as well as the first governor of Kentucky, wrote that an hour before sunrise on October 10 two men from Captain Russell's company discovered a large party of Indians about a mile from camp. One of Russell's men was killed. The other returned to camp and reported the surprise attack, which was confirmed within three minutes by two men from Captain Evan Shelby's company (James Robertson and Valentine Sevier). Colonel Andrew Lewis immediately ordered his brother, Colonel Charles Lewis, to take command of a division of 150 men from Augusta. Colonel William Fleming, the retired Scottish physician who led the Botetourt militia, was to take command of the second division consisting of 150 troops from Botetourt, Fincastle and Bedford. At sunrise Colonel Charles Lewis marched "to the Right some Distance up from the Ohio." He was only a short distance from camp when the front of his division was attacked by 1,000 Indians of the United Tribes: Shawnee, Delaware, Mingo, Taway (Ottawa) and several other nations. Colonel Lewis received a mortal wound, and his Augusta Division was forced to retreat from the "heavy fire of the enemy." Within a minute, the Indians attacked the front of Colonel Fleming's division on the Ohio. Fleming was wounded but before he returned to camp he calmly encouraged his soldiers to pursue victory. When Colonel Field's company reinforced Fleming's division, the Indians were no longer able to hold their ground. The retreating Indians killed Colonel Field around noon. Lewis assigned Captain Evan Shelby to take Field's command. "Extreemely hott" action continued as the Indians retreated, wrote Isaac Shelby, son of Evan Shelby: "The Bravest of their men made use of themselves, whilst others were throwing their dead into the Ohio and carrying off their wounded." Their line was about a mile and a quarter long. Firing continued from both sides until just before sunset. The enemy "had not the satisfaction of scalping any of our men" save one or two stragglers. "Many of their dead they scalped rather than we should have them but our troops scalped upwards of Twenty of those who were first killed; its Beyond a Doubt their Loss in Number exceeds ours, which is Considirable.... I am yr. truly Effectionate Friend & Humble Servt.... Isaac Shelby."[29]

Amid the rifle fire and war whoops of the battle, Cornstalk's booming voice could be heard encouraging his men: "Be strong. Be strong." He punished an act of cowardice in his army by cleaving the skull of one of his own men with his tomahawk.[30] When Colonel Charles Lewis was killed, Captain Evan Shelby became colonel and succeeded to the command of the regiment. His son Isaac was promoted to captain and took his father's place. The Preston Papers contain reports from participants in the battle:

October 13, 1774	Excerpted from Fleming's account of the Battle of Point Pleasant, written to his wife. "My D^ Nancy—I ... write you that you may be convinced I am yet amongst the living on Munday last ... the fire became general & very heavy. Colo. C. Lewis Receivd a mortal wound. I receivd three balls two through my left Arm, & one in my left breast, but I praise the Almighty, I did not fall and had strength with Assistance to reach my tent.... [I]t was a hard fought Battle lasted from 7 in the Morning to an hour by sun."
October 31, 1774	Preston's letter to Patrick Henry described the battle and enclosed "particulars of the action drawn up by Col. Andrew Lewis" and a list of the killed and wounded.

Estimates of casualties vary widely. Fifty-three to 87 of Lewis's men were killed at Point Pleasant, and eighty-nine to 160 were wounded. The number of Indian casualties is uncertain. Many were carried back to Indian country; some were thrown into the water. The father of Tecumseh—the famous future Shawnee leader of the Tecumseh Confederacy—was killed.

Anne Hennis Trotter Bailey immigrated to America and became the "Heroine of the Great Kanawha Valley." Nineteen-year-old Anne was an orphan when she left her birthplace of Liverpool and went to live with relatives in the Shenandoah Valley. When she was twenty-three she married Richard Trotter, a veteran of the French and Indian War. When Richard was killed at the Battle of Point Pleasant Anne Hennis Trotter vowed revenge on the Indians. Dressed as a militiaman with rifle in hand and attending military musters she became a familiar figure on the Virginia frontier. Anne urged the men to fight in defense of women and children against the Indians or to enlist in the Continental Army and fight the British. For eleven years she continued going from outpost to outpost as a scout and messenger. After the war she married John Bailey, "who had assisted in carrying Colonel Charles Lewis off the field" when he was fatally wounded at the Battle of Point Pleasant.[31] The Colonel Charles Lewis, Jr., Chapter DAR reinterred the bones of Anne Bailey in Monument Park, Point Pleasant.

While Andrew Lewis was marching to Point Pleasant, Dunmore raised a force of 1,200.

8. Pontiac's War, Boundaries and Treaties and Dunmore's War 119

McDonald's militia served as its nucleus, augmented by men from northwestern Virginia and Pittsburgh. At Fort Dunmore (formerly Fort Pitt) the governor conducted peace talks with all the Indian chiefs he could draw together. Cornstalk wanted to make peace but many of his tribesmen and allies did not. Dunmore then advanced toward the resistant tribes. During the march, "the short, sturdy Scotchman ... shared its hardships with the privates, marching on foot and carrying his own knapsack."[32]

Cornstalk's Shawnees were the terror of the English border. The Shawnees, said Dunmore, "would listen to no terms, and were resolved to prosecute their designs against the People of Virginia." White Eyes (Koquethagechton), a friendly Delaware chief indoctrinated by Moravian missionaries, restrained his tribe from the hostilities and helped Dunmore make peace. Dunmore officially reported that the chief "offered me the assistance of himself and his whole tribe.... I received great Service from the faithfulness, the firmness and remarkable understanding of White Eyes."[33]

The governor and 700 men floated down the Ohio in several large, flat-bottomed boats and 100 canoes. They joined 500 more who had marched by land driving beeves to Fort Fincastle (modern-day Wheeling, West Virginia), where they restocked supplies. Before September 13 Dunmore was moving his northern wing from Wheeling down the Ohio River, which was the Indian boundary line. At the mouth of the Hockhocking Dunmore built a military post, Fort Gower, garrisoned it and left his flotilla there while he filed upstream along the banks of the Hockhocking. He sent orders to Andrew Lewis to cross the Ohio immediately and join forces with him within sight of the Indian villages on the Pickaway Plains. On the day Dunmore began building Camp Charlotte, Lewis finished burying his dead at Point Pleasant and started marching toward the Scioto villages to meet Dunmore as ordered.

Dunmore built Camp Charlotte within eight miles of the Indian towns in the Scioto Valley, enclosing the 12-acre fort with a breastwork of trees and logs. On the center acre he erected a citadel encircled by a ditch and earthworks. Rising from the citadel was an elegant tent constructed for himself and his officers. The flag of England flew above the camp, which was named in honor of George III's wife, Queen Charlotte.

The northwestern Indians, having been repulsed at Point Pleasant, feared the combined forces of Dunmore and Lewis. Now desiring to make peace, they approached Dunmore immediately after the battle. Cornstalk's disheartened warriors, retreating from the battle at Point Pleasant, returned to the Scioto Valley to protect their settlements. Dunmore— aware of Lewis's victory—was not surprised on October 16 when the Shawnee chief sent emissaries to his tent with an offer to resume the peace talks. The governor promised to listen but stated that he would not withdraw from Indian country until satisfactory peace terms were agreed upon.

As Lewis neared the Scioto towns, Dunmore sent an express ordering him to halt and informing him that he, Dunmore, had almost concluded peace talks with the Shawnees. Having been fired upon on that very morning and finding no convenient place for his troops to camp, Lewis continued his march. Dunmore then ordered Lewis to encamp where he was. He invited Lewis and a few officers to come to Camp Charlotte. Instead Lewis took his whole army. Lewis's advancing army was eager to avenge their losses in battle, and they felt cheated to learn Dunmore was ready to sign a peace treaty with Cornstalk. They were disgruntled when the governor ordered Lewis to return to Point Pleasant. Frightened by the news of the approach of Lewis's army, the Shawnee ran away from the peace talks and hurried home to protect their villages. Fearing that war would break out anew, Dunmore rode from Camp Charlotte to intercept Lewis's army. He then personally ordered it to retreat to Point Pleasant, where they would continue constructing Fort Randolph. Fleming's Journal records the following: "My Lord informd us the Shawnise had agreed to all his Terms, and that as Our Presence could be of no service, but rather a hindrance to the peace being concluded he ordered the whole to return, which we did the next day. We reachd the Point the 28th."[34]

The chiefs returned to Camp Charlotte and the peace talks resumed. Dunmore met with Chief Cornstalk, who pled for peace in a voice that rivaled Patrick Henry's in its oratorical skill. By terms of the October 1774 Camp Charlotte Treaty the Shawnees acknowledged the Ohio River boundary and agreed from then on to restrict their hunting to the northwest side of the river. The treaty did not involve the Cherokee and did nothing to appease Logan's Mingos. The Shawnee agreed to return all prisoners, stolen property, slaves and horses. They would also honor white navigation rights on the Ohio. In return Dunmore gave "them every promise of protection and good treatment on our Side."[35] Both Chieftess Nonhelema and her brother, Chief Cornstalk, kept the Shawnee promise to honor the Camp Charlotte Treaty. They separated from the tribe and supported the American cause. Mingo chief Logan refused to meet with Dunmore and Cornstalk for the peace talks. Instead, he met with translator Simon Girty to write to Dunmore.

Simon Girty, a bright Scots-Irishman, had been captured when he was 14 years old by the French-allied Delaware Indians during the French and Indian War. He was then adopted into the Seneca tribe, one of the Six Nations of the Iroquois Confederacy. There he learned several Indian languages and customs. Once released, he became an interpreter. Later in the Revolution, he defected from the American army and pledged loyalty to the British Crown because he was disgusted by the way Americans treated Indians. Girty became a negotiator, scout and military leader for the British. He also became a "scapegoat for frontier atrocities."[36] Throughout his adult life Girty trod in two different worlds, American Indian and European. A wrong step on either side could have spelled his death. To American Indians Simon Girty was a trusted friend and translator. To Patriots of the American Revolution, he was a traitor who deserted to join the British.

Logan sent his now famous note to Dunmore. It is an eloquent Indian oration known as "Logan's Lament," translated by Simon Girty:

> I appeal to any white man to say, if ever he entered Logan's cabin hungry, and he gave him not meat; if ever he came cold and naked, and he clothed him not. During the course of the last long and bloody war, Logan remained idle in his cabin, an advocate for peace. Such was my love for the whites, that my countrymen pointed as they passed, and said, "Logan is the friend of white men." I had even thought to have lived with you, but for the injuries of one man. Col. Cresap, the last spring, in cold blood, and unprovoked, murdered all the relations of Logan, not sparing even my women and children. There runs not a drop of my blood in the veins of any living creature. This called on me for revenge. I have sought it: I have killed many: I have fully glutted my vengeance. For my country, I rejoice at the beams of peace. But do not harbour a thought that mine is the joy of fear. Logan never felt fear. He will not turn on his heel to save his life. Who is there to mourn for Logan? Not one.[37]

In response to Logan's Lament, Dunmore destroyed the Mingo towns.

Chief Cornstalk, after signing his "treaty with Lord Dunmore ... proved his desire to maintain peace by frequent visits to Fort Randolph [at Point Pleasant] to restore stolen horses, and to renew friendship with the whites."[38] Three years after signing the Camp Charlotte peace treaty Chief Cornstalk continued to visit Fort Randolph. Entering the fort under a flag of truce, he told the Americans that he could not maintain peace and that he could not dissuade his Shawnee tribesmen from joining the British in the Revolutionary War. Despite his white flag, Cornstalk, his son Elinipsico, Red Hawk and some other Shawnees were detained at the fort. "When a Virginia soldier was killed outside the fort, an angry mob ... murdered Chief Cornstalk and the other Shawnees."[39] In February 1778 Shawnee chief Blue Jacket led 102 warriors to avenge Cornstalk's murder. Daniel Boone was among the 27-man salt-making party that was captured at Blue Licks, Kentucky. Boone escaped in time to warn Patriots of the impending strike on Fort Randolph. Nonhelema, Cornstalk's 6-foot, 6-inch, peace-loving sister, also warned the fort's garrison of imminent attack. The brave "Grenadier Squaw" continued to support the Patriots even after her brother's assassination.

By spring Cornstalk's murder had set off a series of Shawnee, Mingo, and Wyandotte attacks on villages near Pittsburgh and settlements along the Kentucky and Clinch rivers. The Greenbrier River settlement was warned in time to reach refuge. Arthur Campbell, Evan Shelby and county lieutenants of the Western frontier prepared to send militia on expeditions to Kentucky to quell Indian attacks before they could spread eastward into Virginia and Tennessee Country.

Having acted as a guide, interpreter, and messenger warning of imminent Shawnee attacks, Nonhelema applied to Congress for a pension in 1785 to compensate for her service and loss of livestock. Instead of the requested 1,000-acre grant of land in Ohio "she was awarded a pension of daily rations for life and an annual allotment of a set of clothes and a blanket."[40] An award-winning female author, writing from anecdotal accounts, makes the ghost of Chief Cornstalk say, "My sister, the Grenadier Squaw, is taller than I..... [She c]an do more feats.... Her magic was always mightier than mine.... I was so proud of her. She makes women more than squaws. She was tall of body, taller of mind...."[41] The following inscription for Nonhelema ("Kate" "Grenadier Squaw") Cornstalk appears on an historic marker near Circleville, Ohio, in Pickaway County:

> Grenadier Squaw was chief of the largest Shawnee Indian village, located on the south bank of Scippo Creek, upon the Pickaway Plains in 1774. Born about 1720, Non-hel-e-ma, sister of Chief Cornstalk, was named "Grenadier Squaw" by white traders because of her imposing stature, regal bearing and unflinching courage. She spoke three languages, serving as peacemaker and interpreter between Indians and whites. Because of her friendship, she accepted Christianity. After the peace treaty in 1774, she was disowned by her people and became a homeless exile. Erected by Pickaway County Bicentennial Women's Organizations.

Other than Cornstalk there were many notable veterans of Point Pleasant. It is impressive that seven future Patriot generals of the Revolutionary War, five captains who would become regiment leaders, and two future first governors of states, Kentucky and Tennessee, fought in Dunmore's War. Having gained training and experience in 1774 in Dunmore's War, the veteran militiamen were of great benefit in organizing the forces from the southern colonies when the Continental Army was formed the next year. Scores of riflemen from the armies of Lewis and Dunmore participated in the Revolution. Andrew Lewis became a brigadier general and commanded colonial forces that drove Lord Dunmore from the Virginia colony. Colonel William Christian led Virginia's overmountain militia on the 1776

Cherokee Expedition. In 1779 Virginia governor Patrick Henry sent Evan Shelby on the Chickamauga Campaign to destroy Dragging Canoe's towns. In that same year surveyors determined that Shelby's Station was in North Carolina rather than Virginia. In 1787 North Carolina governor Richard Caswell appointed Evan Shelby brigadier general of the militia. Both Isaac Shelby and William Campbell (future heroes of Kings Mountain) served as captains in Dunmore's War. Both later became generals. However, Campbell did not fight at Point Pleasant. That is because Campbell's Company, rushing with Christian's regiment to reinforce Lewis's wing, did not reach Point Pleasant until midnight, after the decisive battle abated and the Indians retreated. One of Dunmore's captains, Daniel Morgan—later a brigadier general of the Continental Army and hero of Quebec (1775) and Cowpens (1781)—had led his renowned rifle corps to aid McDonald in Dunmore's War. "In fact, most of the men who were prominent in the West during the first decades of ... United States ... history were in the war of 1774, either upon the expedition or guarding the frontier."[42]

9

Transylvania, Great Bridge Battle and Kentucky County, Virginia

Even after their son was killed in Powell Valley and while they guarded Clinch River forts during Dunmore's War, Daniel and Rebecca Bryan Boone held onto their dream of planting a colony on the Kentucky River. Boone encouraged Judge Henderson and his Transylvania Company of Investors to contract with Indians for Kentucky land. This was the same justice who had sat on the North Carolina Superior Court during the Regulator insurrection, the same judge who would befriend former Regulator James Robertson at Watauga and make the big deal with the Cherokee at the Watauga Settlement. By trading and treating with the Cherokee Nation, Henderson soon would claim to all the lands between the Ohio, Kentucky and Cumberland rivers.

In January 1775, Fincastle County Militia major Arthur Campbell sent a dispatch to County Lieutenant William Preston. He reported "Colonel Henderson and Captain Hart" had returned from visiting the Cherokee, and Chief Little Carpenter had gone to New Bern, the capital of the colony of North Carolina. Preston relayed the dispatch to Lord Dunmore, royal governor of Virginia, notified him of Henderson's proposed purchase of Kentucky from the Cherokee, and told him and that the treaty would be held at Watauga. All were aware that the King's Proclamation of 1763 prohibited the purchase of land from the Indians by private persons in those areas reserved for the Indians.

In February six horse-drawn wagons, creaking noisily under a heavy load of tinkling bells and clanging pots—enough goods to stock a "half-dozen frontier stores"—crossed the North Carolina-Virginia line and entered the Great Appalachian Valley. Jolting along in one of the wagons was Judge Henderson "on his way to the Cherokee nation to buy an empire," which he would name Transylvania. Traveling with the judge was a partner, Captain Nathaniel Hart, whose daughter Susannah would marry Isaac Shelby, the future first governor of the State of Kentucky. Close by was Chief Attakullakulla of the Wolf Clan. He was a small, wizened ancient American Indian known as "the Little Carpenter." Having two slashes across each cheek and, like most Cherokee warriors, wearing a pair of heavy silver earrings that pulled his elongated earlobes down to his shoulders, he was the Cherokee peace chief as well as the Cherokee Nation's greatest diplomat. Accompanying Attakullakulla were a half-dozen Indian warriors and a clan matron said to be his wife, Nionne Ollie, of the Paint Clan. The diminutive chief and his savvy wife, having selected the treasures in Cross Creek (today's Fayetteville), North Carolina, were crucially interested in the valuable merchandise since they wanted to see that their people received fair exchange for the Cherokee land they planned to trade Henderson for the goods.¹ Henderson had vetted the trade to his North Carolina associates with whom he formed the nine-member Transylvania Land Company. He enlisted Daniel Boone to scout the said territory. The Cherokee Nation's war chief, Oconostota, had agreed to trade the vast amount of land between the Cumberland and Kentucky rivers.

The horses lumbered west down the Wilderness Road from Fort Chiswell on the New River to Wolf Hills (now Abingdon) and then 12 miles farther to Shelby's Fort at Sapling Grove in the North Holston Settlement. Crossing the South Holston River, Henderson and the Little Carpenter drove their wagons southwestward into the Watauga Settlement at Sycamore Shoals, the ancient Cherokee treaty ground on the banks of the Watauga River, a tributary of the Holston. Unloading the prizes and spreading the treasures for display in cabins at Fort Watauga, Henderson and the Little Carpenter prepared for the great conclave. The Indian nation would now decide whether or not to accept these goods in exchange for the vast Kentucky land that Henderson called Transylvania.

Leaving the precious wares at Sycamore Shoals, the Little Carpenter journeyed to his home village of Chota, the capital of the Cherokee Nation, on the Little Tennessee River 35 miles south of present-day Knoxville. He gathered his tribesmen and returned with them to make a deal with the Transylvania Land Company. Streams of Cherokees poured into Sycamore Shoals. Chieftains, old men, warriors, and women with babies strapped to their backs began setting up camp, building fires, and peeping into cabins to examine and admire the trade goods. The Wataugans supplied food but allowed no intoxicating beverages. They served mostly cornmeal and barbecued beef to the crowd. The Transylvania Company footed the bill.

Many chiefs powwowed with Henderson. Twelve hundred Indians spent several weeks at Sycamore Shoals before the final signing of the Transylvania Purchase Agreement. The Little Carpenter rose to speak. Contemporary journalist Felix Walker noted, "He was said to be about ninety years of age; a very small man and so lean and light-habited that I scarcely believe he would have exceeded more in weight than a pound for each year of his life."² The Little Carpenter said that he was now an old man who had been chief for half a century and that he had crossed the Big Water and dined with the Great White Father (His Majesty, the King of England) and British nobility. He concluded his oration by signing the Transylvania Purchase Treaty.

Dragging Canoe, the Little Carpenter's son, then stepped into the chief's circle. A tall warrior whose face was covered with smallpox scars, Dragging Canoe spoke fluently, delivering a moving, powerful and impassioned oration. He pointed out that the white man's "insatiable greed" had already caused Indian nations to "melt away like balls of snow before the sun" and said no doubt they would continue to drive the once-flourishing Indian nations westward. Dragging Canoe reminded the chiefs that the white man had broken earlier promises and settled beyond the mountain and would continue sweeping westward, forcing Indians to "seek retreat in some far distant wilderness and there to dwell but a short space of time before they would again behold the advancing banners of the same greedy host" intent on pushing the "whole Cherokee race into extinction."³

The chiefs heeded Little Carpenter's counsel and rejected his son's plea. On March 17, 1775, they signed the treaty that gave Henderson's group most of Kentucky and a generous slice of Middle Tennessee. Dragging Canoe, with outstretched arm pointing westward, warned that "a dark cloud hangs over that land" known as the Bloody Ground. Some say that the Cherokee word "Kentucky" in translation means "dark bloody road" ("ken" is "dark"; "tuck" is "bloody"; and "ky" is "road"). Dragging Canoe, disappointed that his plea to save Cherokee lands was ignored, began urging young braves to follow him on the warpath. His group of followers, made up mainly of young Cherokee mixed with a few Shawnee, became known to the whites as the Chickamauga band of Cherokee when they settled on Chickamauga Creek near present-day Chattanooga.

The Transylvania Purchase was the "biggest private or corporate land transaction in United States history" and involved the sale of 20 million acres of land between the Kentucky and Cumberland rivers to Henderson's Transylvania Company in return for 2,000 British pounds sterling and goods worth 8,000 pounds.[4]

March 21, 1775 From Williamsburg Dunmore instructed Preston to use "every means ... to defeat mischievous designs of Henderson and his associates." He ordered "copies of the enclosed proclamation to be distributed throughout the back country" and "also a paper addressed to the Cherokee to be forwarded to Little Carpenter" (Preston Papers).

The Transylvania Purchase deed was signed by "Oconistoto, the chief warrior and representative of the Cherokee Nation, and Attakullakulla [the Little Carpenter] and Savanooka [Chief Raven of Echota], otherwise Coronoh, appointed by the warriors and other head men to convey for the whole nation"[5] the land of Transylvania to Henderson's Land Company. Henderson further infuriated Dragging Canoe by pressing the Cherokees to sell him a right-of-way to his new land. With such a "Path Deed," a road to Kentucky, said Henderson, he would not need to walk over his red brothers' land to get there.

June 1775 Preston's letter to "Oconastota, Little Carpenter, Judge (Judd's) friend, and the other chiefs of the warlike nation of the Cherokee" encloses "a letter from Governor Dunmore relative to the recent sale (to Henderson) of lands on the Ohio below the Kentucky; states that the Cherokee have no claim to that land, that it belongs to the king by virtue of the treaties of Lancaster, Logstown and Fort Stanwix; hopes the affair will be settled in a friendly manner" [Preston Papers].

Even before signing the 1775 Transylvania Purchase Agreement, Henderson had hired pioneer trailblazer Daniel Boone to cut a trail to the new country. Daniel Boone's son Nathan stated that Richard Henderson's company "got most of their knowledge about the Kentucky country from my father... [as] he was employed by the company to gather the Indians for the treaty as well as to furnish the meets and bounds of the purchase ... (and) to mark the road to Kentucky."[6] Boone's Trace extended from Tennessee through extreme Southwestern Virginia and into Transylvania, Kentucky. It traveled from the Watauga Settlement (Elizabethton, Tennessee) to Cumberland Gap, through Warrior's Path for 50 miles and then bore west to Hazel Patch and the Kentucky River at the mouth of Otter Creek, where Boone built Fort Boonesborough.[7] When he began extending the Wilderness Road, he met his work crew of 30 woodsmen near Long Island of the Holston. Crew member Felix Walker, a 21-year-old axman-journalist, logged the following:

We rendezvoused at the Long Island in Holston. Colonel Daniel Boone was our leader and pilot. Never was a company of more cheerfull and ardent spirits set out to find a new country. We proceeded and traveled, cutting our way through a wilderness of near three hundred miles, until we arrived within about twelve miles of Kentneky River when, on the twenty-fifth of March, 1775, we were fired on by the Indians while asleep in our camp; Mr. Twitty and his negro man killed, myself badly wounded, the company despondent and discouraged. We continued there for twelve days. I was carried in a litter between two horses to the bank of the Kentucky River, where we stopped and made a station and called it Booneborough. I well recollect it was a "lick." A vast number of buffaloes moved off on our appearance. I saw some running, some loping and some walking quietly as if they had been driven. It was calculated there were near two hundred.

But let me not forget, nor never shall forget, the kindness, tenderness and sympathy shown me by Colonel Daniel Boone. He was my father, my physician, and my friend; attended me, as his own child.[8]

As soon as Daniel finished blazing Boone's trail, Henderson, unauthorized by any government, led settlers to "Kaintuckee." According to British law, Virginia law and North Carolina law, Henderson's purchase was illegal. Both North Carolina and Virginia denounced Henderson's plan immediately upon hearing about it. Colonel William Preston of Virginia pronounced the plan unfair. Governor Dunmore proclaimed the move illegal. North Carolina's Crown governor called Henderson and associates "an infamous company of Land Pyrates." House of Burgesses member George Washington, said, "There is something in the affair which I neither understand nor like."[9]

The purchase of Transylvania (Kentucky and Middle Tennessee) did not quench the settler's thirst for land. "Virginians" (the Cherokee called all southern frontiersmen Virginians) pushed upriver from the Carolinas and Georgia. From the north they caravanned down the Great Valley and turned westward through mountain gaps into Cherokee country, drawing ever closer to Cherokee towns. Oconostota, the old war chief, and the Little Carpenter, the old peace chief, were unable to keep the Cherokee Nation neutral in the war. The angry and impatient young Cherokees who became known as the Chickamaugas, led by Dragging Canoe, struck back at the overmountain frontiersmen. Backed by British supplies, Dragging Canoe's raids on the Indian border would keep many frontiersmen home guarding the home front rather than marching with their fellow militiamen against the British in battles on the seaboard.

The Creeks, who had no immediate cause to press the settlers, adopted a wait-and-see policy for the first half of the year 1776. The Choctaw were kept in a state of intoxication by bottles, kegs and barrels of rum sent to them by British traders from Pensacola and Mobile. John Stuart, the much beloved British superintendent of Indian affairs in the South, died in Pensacola in 1779. By the end of the war Patriots looked upon all southern Indians—Cherokee, Creek, Choctaw, Chickasaw, and Seminole alike—as defeated allies of the British. Whites thought that these conquered enemies should give up their land as spoils of war. By right of conquest, said North Carolinians, "We now own *all* Cherokee lands, but out of generosity we will allow the Cherokee to live on the land until we can provide a reservation for the tribe."[10]

While the Transylvania deal was being made on the frontier in March 1775, Virginia delegates to the Continental Congress convened at Richmond. It was a month before the Battle of Lexington, where farmers fired the shot heard round the world. The Virginia delegation met in response to the recommendation of the First Continental Congress that colonies put themselves in a "posture of defense."[11] Patrick Henry's "Give Me Liberty or Give Me Death" speech at the Virginia Convention so alarmed Lord Dunmore that he seized the gunpowder from the Williamsburg magazine. Then he ordered the marines from the schooner *Magdalene* to remove the 15 barrels of gunpowder from the magazine, load the powder onto horse-drawn wagons, and pack it onto a man-of-war. This left the local militia defenseless against Indian attack and slave uprisings.[12]

The alarmed citizens of Williamsburg appealed for relief. Responding to the call, militia colonel Patrick Henry, a member of the provincial Congress, called out the Virginia militia he had established earlier that month and quickly rallied 5,000 troops to retrieve the confiscated powder. Fincastle County dispatched militia, crack riflemen, to join Henry on his march. William Campbell's militia from the New River Valley advanced toward Williamsburg to join Henry. So did Evan Shelby's company from Sapling Grove and other Watauguans from points even farther west in the Holston and Tennessee valleys. Governor Dunmore vowed, "If an insult is offered to me or to those who have obeyed my orders, I will declare freedom to the slaves and lay the town to ashes." Dunmore, however, attempted to appease Henry's militiamen. He directed the receiver-general of the colony to pay Mr. Henry "in full for the powder that had been carried off, which he did."[13] Dunmore then fled, took refuge on a man-of-war in the York River, and denounced Henry as an outlaw. Fearing that Dunmore might abduct Martha, George Washington wrote, "I can hardly think that Lord Dunmore can act so low and unmanly a part as to think of seizing Mrs. Washington by way of revenge upon me, but it may be necessary to move both her and my personal papers to safety in Alexandria."[14]

In autumn 1775 Dunmore retreated from Williamsburg and sailed to the comparative safety of Norfolk. He put Norfolk under martial law, raided tidewater arsenals, confiscated private weapons, and shut down the local press. Dunmore and his pregnant wife and their children soon took refuge on the British frigate HMS *Fowey* off Yorktown. On November 7 Dunmore circulated his proclamation promising freedom to any able-bodied male slave who would run away from his Patriot master and swear loyalty to the British king. Dunmore, however, declared freedom only to those able-bodied indentured servants, black American or others, who were willing and able to bear arms and join His Majesty's troops. The emancipation did not include women, children, Dunmore's personal servants or the slaves of Loyalists.[15] He also suggested to Lord Dartmouth, the British secretary of state for the American Department, that Britain should entice Indians to fight against the rebels. The expedient of recruiting slaves became a British formal policy four years later when the commander of British forces in America, General Clinton, offered freedom and security to "every Negroe who shall desert the Rebel Standard." Many slaves as well as Creeks and Cherokee allied with the British.[16]

What could be more frightening to unarmed and defenseless colonists than a joint attack by slaves and hostile Indians armed by the British? There were 430,000 slaves (over half the population of South Carolina and one-third that of Virginia) who provided labor for the southern colonies and 50,000 slaves in the north. Many in the white community panicked when they heard the exaggerated notion that the king was "promising every Negro that would murder his Master and family that he should have his Master's plantation." A newspaper reported: "The monstrous absurdity that the governor can deprive the people of the necessary means of defense at a time when the colony is actually threatened with an insurrection of their slaves ... has worked up the passions of the people ... almost to a frenzy."[17] Dunmore's proclamation alienated not only Patriots but also many whites who otherwise would have been loyal to the British. As Dunmore anticipated, however, it also attracted black American men from Hampton Roads, Norfolk and Portsmouth. He needed these men to augment his dwindling army, which no longer received British troop reinforcement from Boston. If the deserters were caught by Patriots, however, their punishment was dire and drastic. Dunmore's five warships and six smaller ships in the Norfolk harbor comprised a floating town to which the blacks came in small boats or on foot and then swam out to freedom. Some joined the British fleet foraging along the James River. They were welcomed aboard, provided with weapons, and trained to use them. Their ragged shirts were replaced by new ones bearing the motto "Liberty to Slaves." To increase his fighting force Governor Dunmore outfitted two warships, both commanded by British regulars. He recruited white Loyalists to staff one ship and called them the Queen's Own Loyal Regiment. The other ship was manned by several hundred freed able-bodied Black males. He named its crew the Ethiopian Regiment.

In mid–November, Dunmore built Fort Murray, a small log fortress on the Norfolk end of a narrow causeway called "the Great Bridge." The governor guarded the bridge because it was a choke point between North Carolina and Virginia. Whoever controlled this strait controlled the exchange of supplies between northeastern North Carolina, southeastern Virginia and their shipping point at Norfolk. The Great Bridge of Virginia was a 150-foot wooden structure over the Elizabeth River 12 miles south of Norfolk. Located on the main road connecting Norfolk to North Carolina, the Great Bridge was the only feasible land connection between coastal North Carolina and Virginia. The main road was actually a rough path through marshes and swamps pieced together in places by rows of logs in washboard fashion. It was the route by which regional planters carried their products— shingles and barrel staves, pitch, tar, and timber—from forest and field on barges across the shallow Albemarle Sound. The goods were then transported overland through the marshes by ox-drawn carts to the deep Norfolk harbor in the Chesapeake Bay. Here the products were shipped to markets at home and abroad. All intercolonial traffic on the road had to cross the Great Bridge.

Patriot militiamen wearing hunting shirts poured into the Norfolk area from Maryland, North Carolina, and Virginia. Those from North Carolina were called "Leather Shirts." The Second Virginia Regiment shirts were purple. Culpeper minutemen were called "Shirtmen" and wore green linen canvas hunting shirts emblazoned with Patrick Henry's slogan: "Liberty or Death."[18] Their standard bearer carried the "Don't Tread on Me" flag with its coiled rattlesnake poised to strike. John Marshall, the future chief justice of the United States Supreme Court, was there with the regiment from Culpeper.

On December 2 the Patriots built a redoubt of several breastworks on the opposite end of the causeway from Dunmore's Fort Murray. A week later Dunmore ordered his troops—British regulars, Loyalists and armed freed slaves—to cross the causeway and attack the Patriot militia. The December 9, 1775, Battle of Great Bridge, the first Revolutionary War battle fought in Virginia, lasted half an hour. The struggle was disastrous for Dunmore, who lost 100 men. The Patriots were virtually unscathed.

Dunmore abandoned Norfolk and fled to his fleet in the harbor, where he commanded land and sea campaigns from the HMS *Otter*. His vessels raided Tidewater plantations for provisions and picked up more runaways. Patriots, now in control of Norfolk, refused to supply Dunmore's fleet with food or water. When Patriot sharpshooters began shooting at British ships Dunmore shot back, setting fires throughout the city. The Americans made no effort to control the flames because they wanted to eliminate Norfolk as a British base. Mary Webley of Norfolk, "while suckling her child ... had her Leg Broken by a Cannon Ball from the Liverpool Man of War." The fires lasted for three days. The Whig Patriot

Militia relied on women of coastal Virginia to nurse the sick and wounded and provide room and board for Whig soldiers. Margaret Rawlings nursed a soldier at her home for 16 days. Maria Carter Armistead boarded prisoners in her house at Williamsburg. By July 1776 the Continental hospital in Williamsburg depended on poorly paid, overworked and untrained women to act as nurses.[19]

After Dunmore left Norfolk on New Year's Day 1776, he sailed to nearby Gwynn Island in the Chesapeake Bay. The Great Bridge route was now free of redcoats and open for shipping food and supplies from eastern North Carolina and Tidewater Virginia to restock Washington's army in the North and support America's fight for independence. On the same New Year's Day that Dunmore left Norfolk, and more than two months after King George delivered his October speech to Parliament, a copy of the king's speech reached Boston by way of a London ship. The speech reaffirmed the monarch's unyielding policy, which refused to rescind the Intolerable Acts. George III had decreed the following: "The rebellious war now levied is become more general, and is manifestly carried on for the purpose of establishing an independent empire.... To put a speedy end to these disorders ... I have increased my naval establishment, and greatly augmented my land forces.... I have also the satisfaction to inform you, that I have received the most friendly offers of foreign assistance."[20] Outraged that the king would raise a huge enemy army and employ mercenaries, American soldiers who had besieged Boston since June 1775 burned the speech in public. George Washington proclaimed George III a tyrant, his ministry diabolical, and his state unjust.

In June 1776 Patrick Henry was elected as the first governor of the state of Virginia shortly before General Andrew Lewis defeated Dunmore, Virginia's last colonial governor, and his 100 vessels in a brisk engagement at Gwynn's Island. The *Virginia Gazette* of July 26, 1776, number 78, reported from Williamsburg;

> Capt. Denny has lately taken up before Gwyn's island 11 anchors and 10 cables, which were left by ... Dunmore's fugitive squadron. One of the anchors is ... supposed to have belonged to the *Otter*.... Lord Dunmore, in attempting to get possession of St. George's Island, in Maryland, was drove off with the loss of eleven men killed, and two tenders, which the Marylanders set fire to, after taking out what was valuable to them, and sending back to his lordship, by way of present, the ... black prisoners they had taken.—His fleet has since gone up Potowmack, to get water....

Failing to regain his power, Dunmore sailed for the West Indies, where he left the black Americans. The last royal governor of Virginia then sailed back to England.

Twenty-three-year-old George Rogers Clark was working as a Virginia surveyor-explorer, guiding settlers to that huge chunk of Kentucky Henderson had purchased. Clark noted that at first Judge Henderson and company ingratiated themselves to the Transylvania settlers. But when Henderson began to raise the price of their lands, many of them complained. Clark hurried to Transylvania after learning that opinions regarding the legality of Henderson's Transylvania claim varied. Encouraged by discontented Virginians and some Kentuckians, he conducted a general meeting at Harrodsburg in June 1776. He and another candidate, John Gabriel Jones, were elected as representatives of the people. They hoped to convince the Virginia assembly to declare Kentuckians citizens of Virginia.

Apprehensive that British-allied Indians would attack Kentucky, Clark and Jones lost no time in leaving for Virginia's capital at Williamsburg. Clark wrote, "We proceeded on our journey as far as Botetourt county, and there learned that we were too late, for the assembly had already risen."[21] Jones, having missed the spring session of the Virginia assembly, returned to Holston country to fight the Indians in the Cherokee War of 1776. Clark proceeded to Williamsburg and appealed to Governor Henry for 500 pounds of gunpowder for Kentuckians. When the fall session of Virginia's assembly opened, Clark and Jones were strongly opposed by Henderson and Arthur Campbell. "This caused it to be late in the session before we got a complete establishment of a new county by the name of Kentucky,"[22] said Clark. Finally, in December 1776, Dunmore's Fincastle County was dissolved and divided into three counties of Virginia: Montgomery, Washington and Kentucky.

10

Snow Campaign, Moore's Creek, Sullivan's Island and the Cherokee War

Early in the war the British hope of maintaining a Loyalist foothold in the South was smothered. Not only was it stifled in Virginia by the December 1775 Battle of Great Bridge and the fall of Lord Dunmore but also in the Carolinas by succeeding events: the Snow Campaign in South Carolina; the February 1776 Battle of Moore's Creek Bridge in North Carolina; and the June Battle of Sullivan's Island in South Carolina. Seeking to keep the frontier militia occupied on their home front and prevent them from fighting against British troops on the ocean, the British incited a group of disgruntled Cherokee. They furnished them with ammunition and triggered the Cherokee War of July 1776. These British-allied Indian attacks affected frontier families of all the southern colonies and soon backfired with a four-state retaliation against the Cherokee Nation.

The trouble in South Carolina began when the colony's Crown government confronted the newly formed provincial (rebel) government. In June 1775 the HMS *Scorpion* brought Lord William Campbell, the last royal governor of South Carolina, to Charlestown Harbor. His predecessor had dissolved the colonial assembly in January for sending delegates to the Continental Congress in Philadelphia. Governor Campbell's mission was to subdue the rising rebel government. Meanwhile, South Carolina's Patriot government, the extralegal South Carolina Provincial Congress, appointed a council of safety, which virtually took charge of the government. Confrontation between the popularly elected provincial government and the Crown-appointed government resulted in a war of factions.

The South Carolina Council of Safety anticipated the possible confiscation of munitions by the Crown, similar to the April confrontation at Concord and Dunmore's seizure of gunpowder at Williamsburg. Therefore, in July the council of safety ordered Major James Mayson to seize the gunpowder stored at Fort Charlotte, the South Carolina supply depot on the Savannah River. Mayson's seizure of powder was the first overt act by Patriots of the Revolutionary War in South Carolina. Scovilites, Loyalists militiamen who were organized by a man named Scovil and hired by the governor, recaptured the powder. Mayson was jailed and charged with robbing the king's fort. Within a few hours he posted bail and was released. Governor Campbell then fortified Fort Charlotte. Countering the royal governor's action, the Patriot Provisional Congress set up a fort at the village of Ninety Six and garrisoned it with 225 militiamen commanded by Major Mayson.

Patriots sought support from the Cherokee Nation. Meeting with the Cherokee at Fort

Congaree (now Columbia), the Patriots pledged to the chiefs that the new provincial government would send 1,000 pounds of lead and a similar amount of powder for their winter hunt. Soon the promised wagon train, loaded with ammunition, began wending its way toward Cherokee Country. Simultaneously, a separate band of Patriots decided to get even with Scovilites for capturing Major Mayson, although Patriot Mayson was now free and commanding Fort Ninety Six. These Patriots incarcerated Loyalist Scovilite Robert Cunningham and confined him to a Charlestown jail. Robert's brother, Captain Patrick Cunningham, evened the score. He intercepted the Patriot wagon train on its way to the Cherokee towns. Thus, the first incident between Loyalists and Patriots in South Carolina occurred in 1775 when Scovilite Loyalists intercepted the Patriots' caravan of ammunition on its way to placate the Indians. The wagon driver escaped and reported the robbery to Major Mayson at Fort Ninety Six. Mayson alerted his compatriot Major Andrew Williamson, who was assigned by the committee of safety to defend the district of Ninety Six. Williamson mustered Patriot forces to recapture the wagonloads of powder from the Scovilites. Upon learning that 1,900 Scovilites were marching toward the village of Ninety Six, Williamson sent 500 Patriot militiamen to reinforce Mayson's makeshift fort.

Loyalist Patrick Cunningham's larger force, armed with the hijacked weapons and ammunition, surrounded and cut off supplies to the Patriots at Fort Ninety Six. A fight broke out when the besieged Patriots left the fort and walked along the path to dip water from the spring. One Patriot was killed and several on both sides wounded. Thus, the first blood of the Revolutionary War in South Carolina was shed at Ninety Six. After the skirmish the Patriots dug a well inside the fort, reaching water at 40 feet. Neither side wanted war. Within two days hostilities were suspended. Patriots were allowed to go free on the promise that they would dismantle the fort and hand over their swivel guns for a period of three days. The first Revolutionary War skirmish south of New England then came to an end.

The encounter at Ninety Six ended in a truce, but soon was followed by an all-out campaign to round up Tories. Patriot major Andrew Williamson and his superior officer, Colonel Richard Richardson, marched through District Ninety Six and swept northward. They attempted to drive out upcountry Loyalists and oust the Crown (Tory) government of South Carolina. The North Carolina counties of Rowan, Mecklenburg, and Tryon sent 700 militiamen to ally with detachments in South Carolina. The combined Carolina forces continued to comb the piedmont and rout Loyalists. On December 22 snow began to fall, with 15 inches of accumulation over a 30-hour period, an unusually deep snow for that part of the South,[1] hence the name: Snow Campaign. Marching through snow on their way back to the Congaree many of Richardson's men suffered frostbite. By January 1776 the Patriots were in full control of the colony of South Carolina. The Snow Campaign's success was well received in neighboring colonies, especially by the ladies. In February the *South Carolina and American General Gazette* reported: "The young ladies of the best families of Mecklenburg County, North Carolina, have entered into a voluntary association that they will not receive the addresses of any young gentlemen of that place, except the brave volunteers who served in the expedition to South Carolina, and assisted in subduing the Scovellite insurgents."

Despite the Snow Campaign, the civil war of Patriots vs. Loyalists continued. The British government had hoped that Carolina Loyalists would help subdue the rebels, who had grown stronger during the Snow Campaign. The British believed that by working with

10. Snow Campaign, Moore's Creek, Sullivan's Island and Cherokee War

Loyalists in the South they could swing the pendulum of loyalty back toward the king. But their timing was off. The British strategy required 1600 Loyalists, most of whom were raw Scots Highlanders, to move overland from Cross Creek (Fayetteville), North Carolina, toward the coast, where they would join a British expedition that was supposed to arrive by sea. General Howe had sent his second in command, Sir Henry Clinton, with a fleet commanded by Commodore Sir Peter Parker to join the Highlanders. It was Clinton's first independent command, its purpose to establish a base in the South. Together the British troops, Loyalists and Highlanders were to conquer North Carolina and then advance southward to seize the port city of Charlestown. But Clinton's force arrived too late.

Unaware that the British expedition to reinforce them was delayed, the Loyalists started marching toward the sea, playing bagpipes and shouting, "King George and Broadswords!" The Patriots did not stand idly by. The whole Whig countryside rose en masse in response to Governor Caswell, the first governor of the State of North Carolina, when he called for a counterattack. Scarcely a man who was able to walk remained in the Neuse River region. Captain Ezekiel Slocumb, whose plantation house was on the Neuse, rallied his unit and began marching to Moore's Creek. Patriots at the creek anticipated the Highlanders' attack and partly dismantled the bridge by removing planks and then greased the stringers. The first shots of battle boomed when the Highlanders reached the bridge and charged into a barrage of bullets from 1,000 rebel rifles. Many kilted Loyalists slid off the slick planks or fell through the yawning gaps and drowned. "The company under Capt. Slocumb moved downstream during the battle of Moore's Creek Bridge, forded the creek, penetrated the swamp, and made a furious charge on the flank of the Loyalists. This action decided the fate of the day—the Loyalists broke and ran."[2]

Captain Ezekiel Slocumb would say later, "My wife was there!" This is the strange story of Ezekiel's wife, Mary Slocumb, her uncanny intuition and her strange midnight ride to find her husband at Moore's Creek. As a teenager the bright and lively Mary Hooks, an expert equestrian, married her 18-year-old stepbrother, Ezekiel Slocumb. The couple moved into his plantation house on the Neuse River. Through the primogeniture law, Ezekiel had inherited the house from his father, who had acquired it by coverture when he married Mary's widowed mother. Mary immediately assumed household duties, washing, cooking and quilting. She also often went fox hunting. Mary Slocumb took charge of the plantation when her husband joined a troop of light horse, scouting and rounding up Tories who threatened the neighborhood. In those perilous times, Mary laughingly said she had performed all the chores a man ever did except "mauling rails." So she went out one day and "split a few" logs simply to show that she could.

Just as Ezekiel said, Mary Slocumb was present at the February 1776 Battle of Moore's Creek Bridge. She would never forget her dream and her journey. Ellet's *Women of the Revolution* (chapter 24) lets Mary tell her own story as she told it to relatives and friends. The Patriot men of the Neuse area, said Mary, "left on Sunday morning. More than eighty went from this house with my husband":

> They got off in high spirits; every man stepping high and light. And I slept soundly that night. But I kept thinking where they had got to—how far. Where and how many of the regulars and Tories they would meet; and I could not keep myself from the study. I went to bed at the usual time, but still continued to study. As I lay—whether waking or sleeping I know not—I had a dream; yet it was not a dream. I saw distinctly a body wrapped in my husband's guard cloak—bloody—dead. The fire in the

room gave a little light; everything was still and quiet. My child was sleeping, but my woman was awakened by my crying out or jumping on the floor. If I ever felt fear it was at that moment. "I must go to him." I told the woman I could not sleep and that I would ride down the road. She appeared in great alarm; but I merely told her to lock the door after me, and look after the child. I saddled my mare ... and in one minute we were roaring down the road at full speed.... I was soon ten miles from home, and my mind became stronger every mile I rode. I should find my husband dead or dying—was as firmly my presentiment and conviction as any fact of my life. When day broke I was thirty miles from home. I was skimming over the ground through swamp country thinly settled, and very poor; but neither my own spirits nor my beautiful nag's failed in the least. We followed the well-marked trail of the troops. The sun must have been well up when I heard a sound like thunder, which I knew must be cannon. The battle was then fighting. So away we went again, faster than ever; and I soon found by the noise of guns that I was near the fight. I spoke to my mare and dashed on in the direction of the firing and the shouts. The blind path brought me to the Wilmington Road leading to Moore's Creek Bridge. A few hundred yards from the road, under a cluster of trees were lying perhaps 20 men. They were the wounded. I knew the spot; the very trees; and the position of the men I knew as if I had seen it a thousand times. I had seen it [in my dreams] all night! My whole sole [sic] was centered in one spot; for there, wrapped in his bloody guard-cloak was my husband's body! I remember uncovering his head and seeing a face clothed with gore from a dreadful wound across the temple. I put my hand on the bloody face; 'twas warm; and an *unknown voice* begged for water. A stream of water was nearby. I brought it; poured some in his mouth, washed his face; and behold it was Frank Cogdell. He soon revived and could speak. A puddle of blood was standing on the ground about his feet. I took his knife, cut away his trousers and stocking, and found the blood came from a shot hole in his leg. I could see nothing for dressing wounds except some heart-leaves. I gathered a handful and bound them tight to the holes; and the bleeding stopped. I then went to the others; and—Doctor! I dressed the wounds of many a brave fellow who did good fighting long after that day! While I was busy Caswell came up. He appeared very much surprised to see me; I interrupted by saying "Where is my husband?" "Where he ought to be, madam; in pursuit of the enemy." Just then I looked up, and my husband, as bloody as a butcher and muddy as a ditcher, stood before me. (It was his company that forded the creek, and penetrating the swamp, made the furious charge on the British left and rear, which decided the fate of the day). I would not tell my husband what brought me there, but I could see he was not displeased with me. In the middle of the night I again mounted my mare and started for home. Caswell and my husband wanted me to stay till next morning and they would send a party with me; but no! I wanted to see my child and I told them they could send no party who could keep up with me. What a happy ride I had back! I embrace my child as he ran to meet me!

"This fair equestrian, Mary Slocumb," said Ellet, "actually rode alone, in the night, through a wild unsettled country, a distance—going and returning—of a hundred and twenty-five miles in less than forty hours, and without any interval of rest!"

The February 17, 1776, Battle of Moore's Creek Bridge lasted only ten minutes, but it "changed forever the relationship between the Southern Colonies and Great Britain."[3] The defeat was a major setback for the Loyalist cause in the South. The royal governors, who were unable to rally Loyalist support, were driven out of office to seek refuge onboard warships. When Clinton's expedition arrived too late to reinforce the Loyalist Scots at Moore's Creek Bridge, Clinton delayed the expedition for a month to await reinforcement from Ireland by General Charles Cornwallis.

Alerted by the Battle of Moore's Creek Bridge, Patriot forces from Charlestown anticipated a British attack on their city and sent out calls requesting aid from the Carolinas and Georgia. Responding to the request, militia lieutenant Felix Walker rallied a platoon of East Tennessee country riflemen. Walker was clerk of court for the Watauga Association on the overmountain North Carolina frontier (this is the same journalist Felix Walker who had joined Daniel Boone's crew bushwhacking the trail to Kentucky). Walker's team of frontiersmen crossed the Blue Ridge and joined a South Carolina regiment marching toward Charlestown. They hoped to foil the plans of Major General Henry Clinton's forces and Commodore Sir Peter Parker's naval squadron that was sailing toward the South. Walker wrote, "The war of the Revolution commencing about this time, I considered it a favorable opportunity ... to distinguish myself as a young man and patriot in defense of my Country. I went to Mecklenburgh County, and ... by the recommendation of General Thomas Polk ... was appointed Lieutenant in Capt. Richardson's Company in the Rifle Regiment ... [and] was there furnished with money for the recruiting service. I returned to Watauga and ... recruited my full proportion of men and marched them to Charleston in May 1776, joined the Regiment, and was stationed on James Island."[4]

Patriots built fortresses at Sullivan's Island to defend Charlestown Harbor. Colonel William Thompson, known to his Rangers as "Old Danger," built a fort along the northeast end at the rear of Sullivan's Island to guard the Breach Inlet, a deceptively hazardous crossing filled with sinkholes and swirling currents. The Breach connected Sullivan's Island with Long Island (the Isle of Palms.) At the Breach, Thompson's advance guard, 750 militia sharpshooters, protected the rear of the fort against a possible amphibious landing.[5] Clinton's forces landed on Long Island, and he sent Cornwallis to camp nearby within sight of the Breach. Discovering that the Breach was seven feet deep at ebb tide instead of three, Clinton cancelled his planned amphibious attack.

To defend the entrance to Charlestown Harbor, Colonel William Moultrie, Thompson's cocommander, built a redoubt on the harbor end of Sullivan's Island. It was only a rough breastwork of spongy palmetto logs and sandbags.

Commodore Parker's flagship, the HMS *Bristol*, maneuvered across the strip of submerged sandbars known as the Charlestown Bar and sailed toward Charlestown Harbor. None other than William Campbell, the last royal governor of South Carolina, commanded the *Bristol*'s gun deck. On June 8, 1776, the Battle of Sullivan's Island began when the British fleet of nine ships shot 13-inch mortar bombs toward Moultrie's breastwork. Bomb after bomb whizzed across the beach and either bounced off or became buried in the spongy Palmetto logs, which smothered their explosions. Moultrie's cannons returned fire. The "magic" palmetto wall not only swallowed a nine-hour cannonade from 266 British guns, but it also provided cover for Patriots returning fire. The militia's 26 cannons bombarded and damaged every ship in the attacking fleet and almost wrecked the enemy flagship, HMS *Bristol*.

Firing with remarkable accuracy, Moultrie's American bombardiers blasted away at the *Bristol*. One round of American shot tore Sir Peter Parker's britches off, exposing his backside and wounding his leg. The intrepid British naval commander, dripping blood and unable to put one foot in front of the other, requested two soldiers to help him walk but refused to leave his post. Another officer, the *Bristol*'s brave captain, lost his arm, which was amputated during the battle.

(When the frigate HMS *Acteon* ran aground, its crew set her afire. "She blew up, and from the explosion issued a grand pillar of smoke, which soon expanded itself at the top and, to appearance, formed the figure of a palmetto tree."[6] The palmetto tree was subsequently incorporated into the seal of South Carolina and joined the crescent moon to become the South Carolina state flag.)

In the midst of battle a cannonball ripped through Fort Sullivan's flagpole, causing the

South Carolina banner to crash to the ground. Sergeant William Jasper jumped from behind the 10-foot-tall, 16-foot-wide redoubt, righted the broken pole and replanted it in the sand, risking his life to raise both the flag and the hopes of Americans. Only 10 militiamen were killed and 22 wounded. Hundreds of the British died on shipboard. Fort Sullivan was renamed Fort Moultrie.

Elizabeth Black's husband, Robert Black, was one of the few Patriot militiamen to be mortally wounded while fighting in Colonel William Moultrie's Second Regiment in the successful defense of Charlestown at Sullivan's Island. Black's death left Elizabeth and their six children destitute. Having no relatives or friends in the South who were able to assist her family financially, the indigent widow petitioned the South Carolina legislature for funds to help her and her children return to her relatives in Pennsylvania. The legislature granted Elizabeth Black "four hundred pounds to go there or to any other northern State in which she ... shall think the health of her family may be established."[7]

The Patriot victory at the Battle of Sullivan's Island happened just one month before the onset of the British-coordinated Cherokee War of July 1776 on the frontier. Wataugan Felix Walker, upon returning from Sullivan's Island to the East Tennessee frontier, wrote, "The war now becoming general through the American provinces, the British stimulating the Indians on the frontiers, the Cherokees breaking out and murdering the inhabitants of Watauga and Holston, where my property and interests lay, I was constrained to resign my commission, contrary to the wish of the commanding officer, and return home to engage against the Indians in the defense of my property and country. I was appointed to a command of company of Light Dragoons to range on the frontiers, was stationed at Nolachuckey for a year."[8]

In May 1776 the Virginia Convention received a petition from Wataugans who asked to be considered a part of Virginia. Rebuffed by Virginia, the Watauga Association drafted another petition. This time they asked the Provincial Council of North Carolina to annex them. Before the North Carolina Provincial Council received the request, however, the Cherokee War erupted on the frontier in the same month that the Second Continental Congress declared independence from Great Britain.

Abigail Adams's husband, John Adams, was a prominent delegate to the Continental Congress. Today's Supreme Court justice Ruth Ginsberg referred to Abigail's long ago March 1776 comments to John:

> I long to hear that you have declared an independency, and by the way in the new code of laws which I suppose it will be necessary for you to make, I desire you would remember the ladies and be more generous and favorable to them than your ancestors. Do not put such unlimited power into the hands of the husbands. Remember, all men would be tyrants if they could. If particular care and attention is not paid to the ladies, we are determined to foment a rebellion, and will not hold ourselves bound by any laws in which we have no voice or representation.[9]

Abigail Adams told her Massachusetts congressman husband to remember the ladies. "But he didn't,"[10] said Justice Ginsberg. At the time, John Adams and his fellow congressmen were busy directing a war and winning independence from England for all Americans. They would leave the battle for equal rights to be fought by women of other generations. It would be more than a century before women would march and, as Abigail foresaw, "foment a rebellion" to win the fight for women's suffrage.

North Carolina became the first colony to officially adopt an act recommending independence from England when, on April 12, 1776, the Fourth North Carolina Provincial Congress adopted the Halifax Resolves. This act authorized its delegates to cast their votes in favor of independence. Actions of the April provincial Congress marked a turning point in North Carolina's history. Until that time the war had been all about equal rights as British subjects. After April 1776 "independence was foremost in the minds of the people."[11] On May 15, 1776, the Halifax Resolves became the first document calling for independence to be approved by the Continental Congress.

The most significant and memorable action of the American Revolution was the achievement of the Second Continental Congress in July 1776 when its members drafted and adopted the Declaration of Independence. The document announced the separation of the 13 North American colonies from Great Britain and proclaimed "government is responsible to its people and must be ruled by the consent of the governed."[12] On July 2 Congress voted in favor of independence. The next day John Adams wrote to his wife, Abigail: "Yesterday the greatest question was decided which ever was debated in America, and a greater, perhaps, never was nor will be decided among men. A resolution was passed without one dissenting colony, 'that these United Colonies are, and of right ought to be, free and independent states, and as such they have, and of right ought to have, full power to make war, conclude peace, establish commerce and do all other acts and things which other States may rightfully do.'"

Fighting had been going on for a year when Continental Congress broadcast the Declaration of Independence, which was published on July 4. On that day the Second Continental Congress became the American government. By July 19 representatives from all 13 colonies had obtained authorization to approve the document, which was then written on parchment.[13] These independent 13 colonies then became the nucleus for the United States of America and the Declaration of Independence was read throughout the colonies. John Hancock, the presiding officer of the Second Continental Congress, was the first of 56 delegates to sign the document. Signing early, on July 4 instead of on August 2, 1776, when most of the other delegates signed, his lettering was so extra large that his name has become synonymous with the word "signature." He made the letters oversized so that "George the Third might read it without his spectacles." During the signing, someone said, "Now we must all hang together." "Yes," quipped Franklin, "or we shall all hang separately."[14]

When American soldiers in New York City heard the reading of the declaration, they tore down the statue of King George III that stood in Bowling Green Park at the end of Broadway in Lower Manhattan. More than 42,000 musket balls were made from its lead. The statue had been commissioned to commemorate the repeal of the Stamp Act. General Washington—ever the strict disciplinarian—understood the elation of his men but disapproved of their disorderly behavior.[15]

Mary Goddard published the declaration. At the time of the Revolution, newspapers published news and advertisements mainly on broadsides, large poster-sized pieces of paper. Mary Katherine Goddard, an educated woman whose mother was also highly educated, published the *Maryland Journal*, one of several newspapers started and owned by her brother. She proclaimed her support of the Revolution in print. In Baltimore, Miss Goddard published the news that a brigade of 1,000 men fired on the colony militia at Lexington, "killed 6 men and wounded 4 others." Mary Katherine Goddard was a postmistress, a store owner and a newspaper publisher in a "profession dominated by men." She is perhaps best known as the first to publish a copy of the Declaration of Independence that included all the names of the signers.[16]

While the attention of seaboard Patriots focused on declaring and winning independence from Britain, the eyes of the inland frontiersmen throughout the South were riveted on the American Indians and their alliance with the British. Frontier leaders of Virginia, the Carolinas, and Georgia anticipated border wars. They feared that the British superintendent of Southern Indian Affairs, John "Bushyhead" Stuart, and his assistant Indian agent, Alexander Cameron, would influence the Cherokees to aid British forces and Loyalists in their plan to gain control of the southern colonies. Uneasiness on the frontier was justified. The British government had instructed John Stuart to arm American Indians. Stuart sent to his Loyalist brother Henry loads of ammunition to be distributed among the Cherokee. Henry strapped bundles of lead and powder onto 60 pack horses and drove the caravan from Pensacola in the Florida Panhandle through the Great Smokies to Chota in Tennessee Country in April 1776.[17]

The coordinated American Indian-British scheme to subdue the rebellion in the South got under way when Stuart learned that Commodore Sir Peter Parker's British naval force was positioned off the coast of Charlestown ready to attack. The plan called for the British to attack colonists on the seaboard while American Indians struck the frontier. On July 1 Stuart and Cameron, both of whom were married to Cherokee women, smeared on war paint, dressed as Indians and marched with the Cherokee to assail settlers on the frontier of South Carolina. The news that the British had been repulsed two days earlier at Sullivan's Island did not stop the joint British-Indian plan to raid the frontier. The Cherokee Indians' "Beloved Woman," Warrior Nancy Ward (Nanyehi), would become an American Revolutionary War Patriot when she warned settlers of her cousin Dragging Canoe's impending Chickamauga attack.

Nancy Ward—daughter of Tame Doe of the Wolf Clan and niece of Peace Chief Attakullakulla—attained her status as "Beloved Woman" during the 1755 Battle of Taliwa, which was waged by the Cherokee Nation to drive the Creek out of Georgia. When Cherokee war chief Oconostota and his warriors headed south from the overmountain (upper town) village of Chota to fight at Taliwa his expedition included Peace Chief Attakullakulla (the Little Carpenter) commanding a group of 500 Cherokee. Nanyehi's husband, a Cherokee brave named Kingfisher, was mortally wounded in the battle. Taking up her dying husband's rifle and chanting a war song his teenaged wife, Nanyehi, led her fellow warriors to a memorable victory that drove the Creeks out of northern Georgia and earned her the title of Ghigau, "Beloved Woman." For this valiant feat she was given a swan's wing and a voting seat in the council of chiefs. The swan's wing symbolized a power so great that by waving it Beloved Woman could "deliver a wretch condemned by the council and already tied to the stake."[18] Later she helped free an Irish fur trader named Brian Ward and then married him. Thereafter she was known as Nancy Ward.

During the spring of 1776, Dragging Canoe went to Mobile, Alabama, to escort his white blood brother, British Indian agent Alexander Cameron, to Chota. Cameron, a deputy under the Little Carpenter's blood brother, John Stuart, advised Indian neutrality in the Revolutionary War because Indians would not be able to distinguish between Loyalists and Patriots. Cherokee peace chief Little Carpenter and his counterpart, War Chief Oconostota, followed Cameron's advice to remain neutral in the white man's war. But Dragging Canoe, the Little Carpenter's son, believed that the Revolutionary War offered an opportunity to regain the ancestral hunting grounds that had been signed away by the Transylvania Purchase. Neutrality was abandoned. The Cherokee War of 1776 was presaged by Dragging Canoe's band of Chickamaugas, which included some Shawnee, sounding the war whoop. The war eventually touched the sparsely settled Boonesborough when14-year-old Jemima Boone, daughter of Daniel and Rebecca Boone, along with two of Colonel Richard Calloway's daughters, were canoeing on the Kentucky River on July 14, 1776. They were captured by Hanging Maw, who was leading two Cherokee and three Shawnee warriors. A short time later a rescue party led by their fathers caught the Indians and returned the girls home safely.

"Dragging Canoe led the principal body of warriors from the Overhill Towns against the Watauga settlements."[19] A bloodbath in the Holston Valley was averted by Dragging Canoe's cousin, Nanyehi, (anglicized to Nancy Ward), then the ex-wife of Irish fur trader Brian Ward. Nancy's and Brian's daughter, Betsy Ward, married Joseph Martin of English ancestry. Nancy—like her son-in-law Martin, who became the Virginia ssuperintendant of Indian affairs—worked to make peace between American settlers and American Indians.

As Beloved Woman and a member of the council of chiefs, Nancy Ward was privy to Dragging Canoe's scheme for attacking Holston Valley settlements. She secretly revealed the plan to a captive fur trader, Isaac Thomas, and smuggled a horse to him. Thomas carried the warning to John Sevier, who was building Fort Lee at Limestone on the Nolichucky River. In return for the message, Nancy asked militia leaders Arthur Campbell and John Sevier to spare the Overhill (Upper) town of Hiawassee when they retaliated.

John Sevier, Indian fighter and future first governor of the state of Tennessee, had moved six miles west of Sapling Grove to the Keywood section of the North Holston Settlement in 1773.[20] He then moved to the Nolichucky Settlement. Sevier sent settlers from the Nolichucky River to the stronger fort on the Watauga at Sycamore Shoals. He then dispatched riders to alert Shelby's Fort in the North Holston Settlement, and Carter's Valley, west of Long Island. His letter to officers of Fincastle County, Virginia, was datelined Fort Lee, July 11, 1776: "Dear Gentleman: Isaac Thomas (and others) have this moment come in by making their escape from the Indians, and say six hundred Indians and whites were to start for this fort, and intend to drive the country up to New River before they return (signed) John Sevier."[21]

Nancy Ward's and John Sevier's warnings of the impending widespread attacks soon reached the Committee of Safety of Fincastle County and County Lieutenant William Preston. Wataugan women and children were evacuated to the east as far as Fort Chiswell on the New River in Virginia. Settlers on the Holston and Clinch also sought shelter. There were 11 forts within a few miles of Long Island of Holston: Evan Shelby's Fort, the largest, sheltered as many as 400 people.

While the Second Continental Congress were drafting and signing the Declaration of Independence in Philadelphia, Dragging Canoe's 700 warriors thundered east from Chota on the Great Indian War Path through Tennessee Country. Along the way they divided into groups. The Raven of Echota (Savanooka) split from Dragging Canoe's main group, crossed the Holston River and swooped down on the deserted settlement at Carter's Valley. The Raven's warriors then fanned out, set settlements afire and slaughtered livestock along the Lower Clinch River. Another detachment split off and demolished Sevier's abandoned Fort Lee on the Nolichucky. Old Abram (Ooskwha) also split from Dragging Canoe's group and led a large band of warriors toward Fort Watauga on the Watauga River. Dragging Canoe led the remaining and larger force to the Long Island Flats of the Holston River.

On July 21, 1776, Chief Old Abram of Chilhowee on the Little Tennessee River began his attack on Fort Watauga (Fort Caswell) with its 150 refugee men, women and children. On her way to safety at Fort Watauga, Lydia Bean had fled on horseback from her Boone's Creek cabin the preceding day. But she didn't make it to safety. Old Abram's warriors abducted Mrs. Bean and took her to a Cherokee camp on the Nolichucky and questioned her about the fort. Her captors said that she would not be killed there but would go to the Cherokee Overhill Towns. There she was sentenced to be executed for exaggerating the number of militiamen inside Fort Watauga. Lydia Bean was bound, taken to the top of a mound and strapped to a stake. Beloved Woman ("Ghigau," Nancy Ward) ran to the pyre, unbound Lydia, pulled her from the fire, and stamped out the embers. Exercising her power as Ghigau, Nancy waved her swan's wing and pardoned Mrs. Bean. This act of grace won for Nancy Ward the appellation "Pocahontas of the West."[22] She took Lydia Bean to the village of Chota, the Cherokee capital, a peace town where all, even criminals, were safe. There Lydia Bean taught Indian women to milk cows, make cheese and churn butter.

On the day after Mrs. Bean's kidnapping, several young women and girls, including Catherine Sherrill, the legendary "Bonnie Kate of Tennessee," were outside Fort Watauga's gate when "the bullets and arrows came like hail,"[23] said Catherine later. Indians sneaked up, blocking her way to the fort. But Bonnie Kate, who allegedly could "out-run, out-ride and out-shoot"[24] any man around, sprinted to the other side of the stockade, scaled the wall and grasped the hand that reached down to pull her to safety.

Meanwhile, inside the fort, where 150 women and children had taken refuge, the women who were boiling water for washing clothes formed a bucket brigade, passing pails of steaming wash water to Ann Robertson, James Robertson's youngest sister. Ann climbed to the top of the wall and poured bucket after bucket of boiling water onto the heads of the invading Indian braves.[25] The helping hand that had pulled Bonnie Kate to safety belonged to the fort commander, John Sevier, "Nolichucky Jack." Four years later, widower John Sevier took her hand again—this time in marriage. Bonnie Kate would become the first First Lady of the State of Tennessee.

Nancy Ward's warning to settlers through messenger Isaac Thomas gave them time to escape Dragging Canoe and take refuge at Eaton's Station on Island Road seven miles east of Long Island of Holston. They erected a breastwork and sent express riders to different stations to assemble an army to garrison Eaton Station. Soon 200 militia riflemen filed out of Eaton's Fort and marched down Island Road toward Long Island on the Holston, but when they reached the Island Flats the battle began. Cherokee warriors led by Dragging Canoe met the frontier militia at the Flats. The two forces, warriors and militiamen roughly equal in number, faced each other. The July 20, 1776, Battle of Long Island Flats was the first battle of the Revolutionary War west of the Blue Ridge. It was also the "first fought by the Overhill Cherokees in open battle formation"[26] in the British manner. The Indians began their attack with great gusto, with those in front hallooing, "Scalp the Unakas." The ensuing sharp engagement lasted three-quarters of an hour, until Dragging Canoe's thigh was broken. Seeing their leader wounded, the disheartened Cherokee disappeared and abandoned the battle. No militiamen were killed. Five were wounded but recovered. Forty warriors lost their lives.

The Battle of Long Island Flats alerted and united the frontier to resist British tyranny. Soon the Little Carpenter, Oconostota and Ostenaco Outacite realized there was nothing they could do to repossess the land or to stop Dragging Canoe and they resigned their positions. Old Tassel became the peace chief in the Little Carpenter's place; the Raven of Chota succeeded Oconostota and became the acting war chief and emperor.

Following the unsuccessful raids in Tennessee Country, Dragging Canoe's Chickamauga branch of the Cherokee Nation attacked Virginia forts along the Upper Clinch River. Their warriors spread out in small bands, burning cabins and killing and scalping settlers along the way. Their route went through what is now Sullivan County, Tennessee, and Southwest Virginia, through Wolf Hills (Abingdon) and near present-day Marion at the Seven Mile Ford home of Captain William Campbell.

As soon as the garrison at Eaton's Fort heard that Dragging Canoe was on the warpath, they had sent runners to warn settlements along the Holston. The hasty construction of Black's Fort in Wolf Hills began on the same day as the Battle of Long Island Flats. Charles Cummings, the "fighting parson," moved his precious books from his home to the fort.

A few days later a militia colonel who lived on the South Holston River about eight miles from Black's Fort went to the fort seeking information about the raids. Women, men and children huddled at the fort urged him to bring his family and neighbors to take refuge, which he did. Upon returning to tend his farm, he found his house and barn ablaze. Scouts who were sent in search of the arsonists found them resting by a campfire. Treading softly, a company of frontiersmen from the fort silently encircled the war-painted raiders. Eleven of the Indians were killed and their scalps hung on a pole and flown over Black's Fort as a trophy and a warning. Several days later a few settlers were attacked by Indians within earshot of the fort. Cummings, the "fighting parson"—who, along with the men of his congregation, always carried a gun, even to church—held the Indians at bay until help came from Black's Fort. One of the victims had fought at Long Island Flats a few days earlier.

Another victim of the Cherokee War of 1776 was Anne Armstrong when similar Cherokee raids occurred along the Carolina and Georgia frontiers. Warriors crossed the Blue Ridge and invaded unsuspecting Carolina settlements in Rowan County and near Gilbert Town and Spartanburg. They rampaged in the District of Ninety Six in South Carolina, where Anne Armstrong lived. The Indians stole all the Armstrong livestock, captured Anne's husband, John Armstrong, took him to a Cherokee town, and butchered him, leaving his widow and "his numerous family of small children … in distressing circumstances." Anne successfully petitioned the state legislature to vest to her and her children 500 acres of land purchased by her deceased husband.[27]

The *Virginia Gazette*, July 26, 1776, number 78, reported on the perilous situation on the frontier from Williamsburg:

> Advices from Charlestown, which arrived here by express, say, that the Cherokee Indians have committed several outrages; which seems to be only a part of the capital and favourite plan laid down by his *most excellent* and *clement* majesty, George the third, to lay waste the provinces, burn the habitations, and mix men women and children in one common carnage, by the hands of those merciless savages. It is hoped, however, that our frontier riflemen, joined to those of the Carolinas, will be able, before long, to strike some blows that may intimidate the numerous tribes of Indians from falling into the measures of the tyrant, and make a severe, lasting, and salutary example of the treacherous Cherokees…. By the same express, we learn that the army and squadron under Clinton and Parker have remained tolerably quiet since their late drubbing.

A fortnight before Dragging Canoe's carnage began, General Griffith Rutherford suggested that the North Carolina Council of Safety write to Virginia and South Carolina to propose a concerted movement of the four southern provinces—Georgia, the Carolinas and Virginia—against the Cherokee Nation. The president of the Province of South Carolina made a similar proposal. He wrote to North Carolina Revolutionary authorities suggesting simultaneous attacks on the Cherokee by the Carolinas and Virginia. General Charles Lee, commander of American forces in Charlestown, South Carolina, agreed, saying that the Cherokees should be treated as enemies at war because they were allied with the British. Similar communications sped from Charlestown to the president of the Virginia convention and to the Continental Congress. The proposed joint expedition was intended to be preemptive, but the Cherokee had pounced first.

As soon as Rutherford heard that the Virginia council had appointed Colonel William Christian in August to lead Virginia retaliatory forces, he wrote to Christian suggesting a joint march against the Cherokee. As it turned out, commanders from four southern colonies coordinated the Cherokee Expedition of 1776 not only to disrupt the British-Indian alliance but also to chastise the Cherokee Nation for its attacks on the backcountry. "Colonels Williamson and Rutherford, of the Carolinas, destroyed the Middle and Valley Towns. Colonel Christian, with an army of Virginians, burned the Overhill Towns. The Cherokee country was thus completely desolated."[28]

The capitulation of the Cherokee in December 1776 ended the first phase of the war in the South. Southern homes from Virginia to the Carolinas where Whig (Patriot) troops lodged for several months were also desolated. Whig congressman Henry Laurens of South Carolina found it "melancholy to see the abuse of so many good houses in [Charleston] which are now made barracks for the country militia who had come to defend the city from the anticipated British attack. Women undoubtedly were distraught to see soldiers "strip the paper-hangings (and) chop wood upon parlour floors."[29]

Following the Cherokee Expedition, the peace treaties signed at DeWitt's Corner (May 1777) and Long Island on the Holston (July 1777) forced the Cherokee to cede almost all of their remaining land in the Carolinas. The multistate Cherokee Expedition, with its widespread burning of Cherokee villages and cornfields in retaliation for the Cherokee War of 1776, forced the DeWitt's Corner Treaty. South Carolina and Georgia negotiated with Lower Town Cherokees at DeWitt's Corner south of Greenville, South Carolina. Via this May 20, 1777, treaty, the Indians "ceded their lands east of the Unicoi Mountains." This was most of their land east of the mountains, which was almost all their land in South Carolina. They also agreed to free prisoners, both white and black. "The states promised to provide trade goods and to keep whites east of the new boundary line. The hatchet was to be forever buried."[30]

As Christian's expeditionary forces approached the Cherokee Upper Towns, Dragging Canoe himself was nowhere to be found because the Cherokee chiefs were divided about what to do. The Raven of Echota (Chota) and other elders wanted to make peace. Dragging Canoe and Indian agent Cameron stood firm in their decision to abandon the Overhill Towns and withdraw to the Hiwassee. The elders prevailed. From the Upper Town, the new war chief, Raven, and the new peace chief, Old Tassel, sued for peace. They sent fur trader Nathaniel Gist (father of Sequoyah) to treat with Colonel Christian. The militia was at first suspicious of Gist but later accepted him as an ally.

Patrick Henry, the first governor of the state of Virginia, and Richard Caswell, the first governor of the state of North Carolina, appointed commissioners to represent the two states in negotiating with the Upper Town Cherokee chiefs. The commissioners and chiefs met at Long Island on Holston. Conspicuously absent from the powwow were chiefs Lying Fish and Dragging Canoe. At the convention, the Fourth of July was duly observed. "It was explained to the Indian that these festivities were in celebration of promised release from the tyrannical oppression of Great Britain." The meeting was filled with "Big Talks" and ceremony. The price of peace would be cession of a huge chunk of western North Carolina and all of upper East Tennessee. The treaty of Long Island on Holston was signed on July 20, 1777, exactly one year after the Battle of Long Island Flats. The delay occurred because Old Tassel had not expected to cede land; he had expected to make peace. Finally both the Raven and Old Tassel yielded, except for Long Island itself, their ancestral treaty ground. They would not give up Long Island except to Colonel Nathaniel Gist, who had purchased the land from the Cherokee in 1761. The Raven expressed hope that the treaty would draw the boundary line between the Indian and the whites "as a wall to the skies," so that no one could pass it.[31]

"The treaty was signed for the Cherokees by Oconostota, Attacullaculla, The Raven, Old Tassel, Abram of Chilhowie, Outacite of Hiwassee, and lesser known chiefs."[32] By signing, the aging National Cherokee war chief Oconostota and Peace Chief Attakullakulla (the Little Carpenter) agreed that the Cherokee Nation would remain neutral in the Revolutionary War. By the Treaty of Long Island on the Holston at Fort Henry (now Kingsport, Tennessee) the Upper Towns of the Cherokee Nation ceded all the land east of the Blue Ridge and north of the Nolichucky and brought peace to much of the South for a few years.

Dragging Canoe wanted no part of the Holston treaty his father—Peace Chief Attakullakulla, the Cherokee's greatest diplomat—and War Chief Oconostota had made. He formed a new band of Cherokee, taking with him 1,000 young Cherokee warriors. Calling his followers by the original name of the Cherokee, the "Real People" (Ani-Yunwiya) Dragging Canoe distinguished his new tribe of Cherokee from his father's Cherokee, whom he called "old men, Virginians, and rogues" because of their cession of lands during the Transylvania Purchase in 1775 as well as the Long Island on Holston Peace Treaty of 1777. Refusing to let go his land, Dragging Canoe scoffed, "Such treaties may be alright for men who are too old to hunt or fight. As for me, I have my young warriors about me. We will hold our land."[33]

Dragging Canoe and his Chickamauga warriors doggedly pursued his self-appointed mission, raiding white settlements. Indian fighter John Sevier and his Wataugans counterattacked, torching Cherokee towns. Censuring the Chickamauga incursions, Cherokee elders including war Chief Oconostota placed a 100-pound bounty on the heads of Dragging Canoe and Indian agent Alexander Cameron. The fugitive Dragging Canoe, still resisting the encroachment on Indian hunting grounds, was joined by many prominent chiefs. One was Old Tassel's nephew, a part Scots-Irish part Indian named Young Tassel (John Watts), who would succeed Dragging Canoe as leader of the Chickamaugas. Another was the Cherokee Nation's assistant war chief Ostenaco Outacite (Judd's Friend), who took his half-breed grandson, Richard Timberlake, with him. Spreading across Lookout Mountain, Dragging Canoe's renegades established eleven towns on Chickamauga Creek (today's Chattanooga, Tennessee). The newly organized tribe of Cherokee became known as the Chickamauga. The whites called Dragging Canoe and his followers Chickamaugans. At Sycamore Shoals on the Watauga, Dragging Canoe had said to Henderson, "You have bought a fair land, but you will find its settlement dark and bloody." To that end Dragging Canoe devoted his life.[34]

11

Northwest Territory, Chickamauga Expedition and Mid–Tennessee

The dark and bloody road to which Dragging Canoe pointed in 1775 ran through Tennessee Country. It also traversed Virginia's vast land, which encompassed both Kentucky and the Northwest Territory. The small state of Maryland would urge the Second Continental Congress to persuade the huge state of Virginia to relinquish its Northwest Territory.

America's founding fathers, delegates of the Second Continental Congress, were so busy directing the Revolutionary War that they had little time to debate and pass laws to legalize their actions. Finally, in 1777, Congress adopted America's first constitution, the 13 Articles of Confederation. The articles established the Confederation Congress, which was the legislative branch of government, created "a loose confederacy of states with Congress at its center," and legalized the powers that the Continental Congress had been exercising since 1775. Leaving most of the power with the state governments, the articles also created a weak central government: "There was no executive branch, no national judiciary, and each state, no matter its size, had a single vote."[1] Last, the articles lacked the power to raise either money or troops. Congress adopted these articles to secure union of the newly independent American states and to define and distribute power between the central government and member states, then submitted them to the 13 states for ratification. The states did not ratify them until 1781, when Virginia promised to relinquish her claims to the Northwest Territory.

The fundamental reason for the four-year delay in ratifying the Articles of Confederation was that Maryland refused to ratify until states owning uninhabited western land ceded their western territory to the new U.S. government. Virginia claimed not only Kentucky but also the entire Northwest, north of the Ohio River and west of Maryland and Pennsylvania. This territory embraced all or portions of six future states: Ohio, Indiana, Illinois, Michigan, Wisconsin and Minnesota. Overlapping Virginia's Northwest Territory were claims held by Massachusetts, Connecticut, and New York.

In 1777 an American Indian-British alliance attacked forts on Virginia's frontier (now West Virginia). The attacks alerted militia leader George Rogers Clark—who had helped make Kentucky a county of Virginia—to the need to increase protection for the citizens of his county. Representing Kentucky, Clark, a tall, muscular man with ruddy cheeks and auburn hair, rode horseback along the Wilderness Road from present-day Harrodsburg, Kentucky, to the Virginia capital at Williamsburg. There he petitioned Governor Henry for

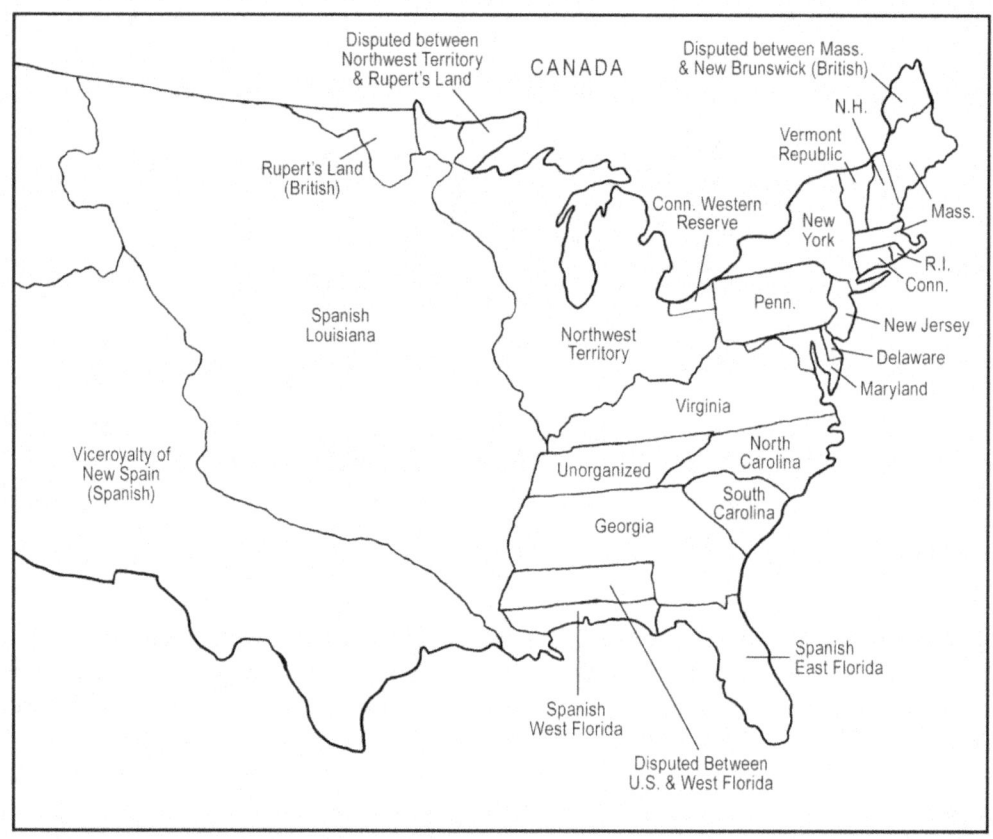

States and Territories of the USA, circa 1760 (Glen McCroskey).

permission to lead an expedition along the Ohio and Mississippi rivers to raid British outposts in the Northwest Territory. Clark reasoned that the best way to defend Kentucky, stop the scalping of colonists, and make the area northwest of the Ohio River safe for settlers was to raise local militiamen to cut off ammunition and supplies to Indian tribes. These weapons were coming to the Indians from three main British outposts: Kaskaskia, Cahokia and Vincennes. All of these villages were located within Virginia's Northwest Territory in today's Illinois and Indiana.

The Virginia governor gladly granted Clark both authority and aid to recruit men from counties west of the Alleghenies for the Vincennes Expedition against Colonel Henry Hamilton. The Irish-born Hamilton was one of five British lieutenant governors of the Province of Quebec, Canada. Governor Hamilton commanded Fort Detroit (Michigan), which was in the Quebec District. He was also a British superintendent of Indian affairs of the Province of Quebec. One reason for targeting Hamilton was that he encouraged scalping. Nicknamed "Hair Buyer General" for his policy of paying Britain's Indian allies for the scalps of settlers, Hamilton armed American Indians at Fort Detroit with 8,640 knives and sent them scouting for prisoners and scalps. On their return, he received the scalps and rewarded them for the trophies. Over a 10-month period in 1778, Hamilton reported to Quebec headquarters the receipt of 55 prisoners and 210 scalps.

11. Northwest Territory, Chickamauga Expedition and Mid-Tennessee

One of many grievances expressed by the American colonists was the "cruel" and "oppressive" act of Parliament in the King's Proclamation of 1763, which extended the Province of Quebec southwest so that it bordered on the western frontier of the 13 colonies, established an arbitrary government in the expanded country, and discouraged the settlement of British subjects there.[2] This meant that the king forbade British colonists to settle in the Northwest Territory. Clark attempted to rectify this grievance, penetrate the forbidden territory and open it up for settlement.

In late spring 1778 Clark organized a group of militia from Kentucky County, Virginia. Leading 175 expert riflemen and woodsmen, he floated 900 miles down the Ohio River from Fort Pitt, Pennsylvania, to Fort Massac at the mouth of the Tennessee. From there he marched overland 120 miles, storming a succession of British-held forts manned by Frenchmen along the Mississippi.[3] He attacked calmly and methodically. Although the French settlers inhabiting forts along the Mississippi had been under British rule since the French and Indian War, they had no great love for the British. Hence these Frenchmen made little attempt to defend the British outposts. They even supported Clark and his American militia.

On the Mississippi, at Fort Kaskaskia on July 4, Clark roused the sleeping French militia who were reluctantly serving under the British flag. Tumbling out of bed, they surrendered without firing a shot. Fort Cahokia followed suit, surrendering on July 9. Fort Sackville (Fort Vincennes) at the village of Vincennes (Indiana) capitulated about the same time to a detachment sent there by Clark. Impressed by Clark's Vincennes Expedition, American Indians promised to stop raiding settlements.

Quebec's governor Hamilton set out to regain his forts. Leading a mixed army of 1,000 British soldiers, French militia and Indian warriors, Hamilton swept down from Fort Detroit. In December 1778 he reclaimed Fort Sackville in the Vincennes Settlement. And there he hesitated. Awaiting warmer weather when he could more easily recoup the other forts, he allowed most of his command to return home for the winter. A fur trader from Vincennes warned Clark of Hamilton's plan to recapture the other forts when the ice and snow melted and the weather warmed. Clark promptly set out in the winter of 1778–79 to Vincennes to recapture the inadequately guarded Fort Sackville on the Wabash River.

Wading up to their armpits through sometimes icy waters across submerged lands along the riverbank, Clark's expedition stealthily moved through Illinois country on an 18-day journey. They sneaked up on the unsuspecting garrison at Vincennes' Fort Sackville. Inside the fort was Commander Henry "Hair Buyer" Hamilton, the lieutenant governor of Canada. Clark and his Kentucky militiamen began encircling the palisaded fort. Marching around and around the barricade, the flag-carrying men tricked Hamilton into thinking the fort was surrounded by a huge army. Falling for the ploy, Hamilton and his army filed out of the Sackville Fort and laid down their muskets. Hamilton was taken under guard from Vincennes to a Williamsburg, Virginia, jail. Remaining at Vincennes, George Rogers Clark represented the new United States in control of the Northwest Territory—Ohio-Indiana-Illinois country. Vincennes, then part of the Illinois Territory, would become the first capital of Indiana Territory. Today it is the oldest town in the state of Indiana.

By winning victories at British-held Kaskaskia, Cahokia, and Vincennes, Clark temporarily broke the British-Indian alliance and won the accolade "Conqueror of the Old Northwest." Although nothing can diminish Clark's heroic achievement in conquering the

Old Northwest in 1778–79, he could not hold onto it; he was continuously on the defensive in Detroit, Kentucky and Ohio Country. And yet—at the close of the Revolutionary War—Kentucky, Illinois, and much of the Territory of Ohio were in American hands while St. Louis was controlled by the Spanish.[4]

In the section of his journal entitled "A Prisoner of War, March 8 to June 16, 1779," Henry Hamilton, lieutenant governor of Canada, recorded his 1,200-mile journey from Vincennes, through Kentucky and along the Wilderness Road to Roanoke and then to Williamsburg. In Vincennes, Colonel George Rogers Clark put Hamilton and the other prisoners onto an oak boat at Fort Sackville on March 8, 1779, and rowed upstream against the current of the Ohio. A month into the journey Hamilton wrote, (April) "5th. Had a very fatiguing march, our guides lost themselves and misled us. One of our hunters killed a she bear about 3 years old, very fat, which was a great resource as we had not a morsel of flesh among us all at setting out—This Creature must have just quitted her winter habitation for tho so fat, she had nothing in her Stomach, or intestines— We got 30 miles this day."

April 6 saw them traveling on a Shawnee warpath used "to go against the Cherakees." Continuing on the path for 25 miles they reached Harrodsburg, a fort of 200 houses. Traveling on the Wilderness Road, they passed though Cumberland Gap, entering Powell's Valley on the 26th. On the 28th they crossed the Clinch River in sleet and hail: "I felt the gout flying about me and as it would have been dreadfull to have him fix while in such a country, I dismounted & walked the whole day in Moccassins which dissipated the humor and enabled me to keep up."

On April 30 the captives crossed the North Fork of the Holston, which, writes Hamilton, "being very rapid, I did not chose to trust my horse and rather than attempt it had a raft made & was ferryed over by two who could swim the raft being only large enough for one." The May 3 journal entry describes continuing on the Wilderness Road to Shelby's farm: "We breakfasted at Colonel Shelby's plantation (Bristol, Tennessee), where we were very frankly entertained—The Farm in extraordinary good order and condition, we were shown a black Stallion one of the first creatures of his sort I ever saw—at night we slept at a Captain Thompsons, where riches could not keep penury out of doors. we did not get our dinner till eleven at night."

On May 4 the prisoners continued east from the Washington Court House (Abingdon) on the Old Wilderness Road. Then (May) "5th. & 6th [we] Halted at Colonel Arthur Campbell's (Royal Oak, Marion, Virginia) where we repaired ourselves with sleep—Our Host was very civil to us, but from the difficulty of procuring Provisions in this part of the Country, some of the prisoners who were pressed with hunger and fatigue broke out into very injurious language, and even threatned to be revenged at a future day for the little attention payd to their necessities."

Having traveled the full length of the Wilderness Road, the captives crossed the Roanoke River seven times on the 11th. After a "disagreeable" stay at Richmond, they left that city on May 31. A fortnight later an officer intercepted them near Williamsburg with "a written order signed by Govr. Jefferson for William La Mothe Captain of the Volunteers of Detroit, and myself to be taken in irons and layd in Gaol at Williamsburgh.... We mounted with some difficulty being handcuffd, and I found a days journey of only 30 Miles tired my patience and wearyed my body exceedingly not having as yet repaired the uncom-

11. Northwest Territory, Chickamauga Expedition and Mid-Tennessee

mon fatigues of a March Route of 1200 miles from Fort Sackville, most part of the time but half fed, ill cloathed, menaced and reviled, but as Sancho says, This was spice cake and gilt gingerbread to what was to come—We lay I cannot say rested at James City Court house that night." On June 16 about sunset the prisoners reached Williamsburg: "I flung myself from my horse fatigued and mortifyed to be left a spectacle to a gazing crowd—(At last, an officer) conducted us to the Common prison (where) we were received by the jailer.... The opening and shutting doors and barrier, unbolting some Cells, and giving directions in an authoritative voice perhaps were designed to appall us poor Devils, and bring us to a due sense of our situation." Hamilton was held in jail for more than a year and was then taken to New York, exchanged for an American prisoner and arrived in London in June 1781.

While George Rogers Clark was breaking the British-Indian alliance in the Old Northwest, Evan Shelby and Joseph Martin confronted the British-allied Chickamaugas, who inhabited today's Chattanooga on the southwestern frontier. Although chiefs Oconostota and the Little Carpenter remained neutral in the white man's war, Dragging Canoe, the Cherokee exile who founded the Chickamaugas, and 1,000 warriors joined the British. Governor Patrick Henry appointed Joseph Martin as the first superintendent of Indian Affairs for the State of Virginia. Martin ousted British deputy superintendent Alexander Cameron, Dragging Canoe's blood brother. Martin's mission was to make peace with the Indians and prevent raids.

Early in 1779 Martin warned Governor Henry to expect a widespread Chickamauga attack on the frontier and encouraged him to launch a Chickamauga expedition to prevent it. Martin and Henry alerted Richard Caswell, governor of the new State of North Carolina. Virginia and North Carolina were to join forces under the overall command of Colonel Evan Shelby to invade Chickamauga villages.

One morning in the summer of 1779, while Shelby was gathering forces to assault the Chickamauga, Mrs. Jesse Evans sat weaving cloth in her cabin near the headwaters of the Clinch River. Her oldest daughter was folding, twisting and plaiting quills for her to weave into the clothing. The four younger children were playing and gathering vegetables in the garden. Her husband, Jesse, was away from home, working on the farm with hired men. No one saw ten Indians remove boards from the back of the garden fence. Springing forward, they scalped the children. Hearing the screams, Mrs. Evans ran toward the garden, saw the hopeless situation, sped back to the cabin and bolted the door in an attempt to save the life of her oldest daughter. When a warrior pushed his gun through a crevice in the door, Mrs. Evans—an athletic and fearless woman—seized the gun barrel so the Indian could not pry the door open and get his finger on the trigger. With amazing strength, she silently held onto the gun. And then she began to scream for her husband, who of course was not home, but the Indians feared that he would soon appear with militiamen. When the Indians left and Mrs. Evans decided to dash two miles to a neighbor's she passed by the sickening scene of her murdered children. Holding onto the gun and her daughter, she escaped the Indians and fled to the neighbor's house. When Jesse Evans returned home and looked for his family he saw the little ones lying in pools of blood in the garden. He found his wife and daughter at the neighbor's house. At daybreak neighbors went with him to bury the bodies of his slain children. Evans was approaching his springhouse when he was dumbfounded to see his four-year-old coming toward him through the semi-dark dawn with her partially detached scalp dangling before her eyes. "This poor, half-murdered little child lived, married and raised a large family."[5]

Meanwhile, Evan Shelby, under orders from Governor Henry, mustered 1,000 overmountain militiamen for the Chickamauga Campaign. Rendezvousing at Long Island of the Holston, they built boats and swept rapidly downriver. Caught off guard, the Chickamaugas, led by Chiefs Dragging Canoe and Big Fool, fled into the hills. Shelby captured a few stragglers and sent them into the mountains to call the chiefs to a conference. When the chiefs did not come, Shelby proceeded to burn 12 of Dragging Canoe's new towns and confiscate horses, cattle, deerskins and corn. Afterward Shelby's men destroyed the vessels that had carried them downstream. Instead of building boats that could be paddled and poled upstream, they returned home on foot. Indian agent Joseph Martin served as a battalion major on this expedition. This is not surprising since Martin represented the older Cherokee Nation of Oconostota and the Little Carpenter, who now considered Dragging Canoe and his Chickamauga to be deserters and traitors.

Later that year, when surveyors ran the North Carolina-Virginia line, Shelby's Station in the North Holston Settlement of Sapling Grove was determined to be in North Carolina rather than Virginia. Hence, Governor Caswell of North Carolina and not Governor Henry of Virginia would appoint Evan Shelby brigadier general of the militia for his service on the Chickamauga Expedition.

Because Shelby destroyed Chickamauga towns and warriors, his Chickamauga Expedition prevented the coalition of southern and northern Indians "Hair Buyer" Hamilton had envisioned. The fiery raids forced Dragging Canoe and his Chickamauga to take refuge along the 40-mile stretch at the foot of Chattanooga's Lookout Mountain. Here, below the swirling rapids of the Tennessee River called "the Sucks," they built five new Chickamauga towns—Nickajack, Running Water, Crowtown, Lookout Town and Long Island—at a point where Tennessee, Alabama and Georgia meet.[6]

When Dragging Canoe's tribe moved farther west, the western frontier surrounding Long Island of the Holston (Kingsport) was relatively free of Indian raids. Long Island's Fort Henry was garrisoned but never attacked, partly because it was protected by the newly established Sullivan County Militia under the command of Colonel Isaac Shelby, Evan Shelby's son. Other deterrents were Indian fighter Colonel John Sevier, militia commander of adjoining Washington County, North Carolina, and Arthur Campbell, who served just across the state line as county lieutenant of Washington County, Virginia. But its main protection was provided by its resident guard, Indian agent Joseph Martin.

The Cherokee had embraced Joseph Martin after his marriage to Betsy Ward, who was the daughter of Beloved Woman, Nancy Ward. As the first Indian agent for the new state of Virginia, Martin built a stone house on Long Island of Holston in 1777 where he could accommodate visiting Indians and store goods the Virginia government sent to them. Betsy's uncle, War Chief Oconostota (wearing glasses, which was unusual for Indians in those days) came to live with her and Martin at Long Island. Martin would keep his promise to place the chief into a canoe and paddle him to the Cherokee capital, Chota, for burial. Years later, at a Tennessee Valley Authority excavation site, the glasses confirmed Oconostota's burial canoe in the floor of Chota's Council House.

Back in 1776, when Virginia had refused to validate the Transylvania purchase of Kentucky from the Cherokee, Judge Henderson began to speculate in the Cumberland Valley.

11. Northwest Territory, Chickamauga Expedition and Mid-Tennessee 151

He hired Wataugan James Robertson and John Donelson to lead a Cumberland expedition to establish a settlement around the French Lick (Nashville, Tennessee). Exploring Middle Tennessee in the spring of 1779, Captain James Robertson, "Father of Middle Tennessee," and a small scouting group of frontiersmen traveled with packhorses from the Watauga Settlement in East Tennessee to the French Lick to establish corn rights. There on a bluff they planted corn to feed the settlers they planned to bring to Middle Tennessee later that year. Returning to Watauga, Robertson separated from the other explorers and detoured to Fort Kaskaskia, Illinois. There, he sought to purchase cabin rights from General George Rogers Clark, an agent for the state of Virginia. Robertson suspected that the French Lick most likely belonged to the state of Virginia, although he and his explorers had scouted Middle Tennessee under the patronage of Judge Richard Henderson's Transylvania Land Company. Henderson's purchase included the site of Nashville on the Cumberland River. Robertson was an agent for the Transylvania Land Company when he planned the settlement of the Cumberland Valley. As a safeguard, in addition to planting corn, Robertson wanted to buy Virginia cabin rights from Clark. It is believed that George Rogers Clark assured Robertson that French Lick (now in Middle Tennessee) was in North Carolina and that he therefore needed no favors from Virginia.

Upon returning to Watauga, Robertson gathered several hundred pioneers and headed west again. The winter was cold, the most severe within the memory of the oldest people, and the widespread snows were heavy and deep. Their route wound from the Holston Valley in Northeast Tennessee, through Southwest Virginia and the Cumberland Gap into Kentucky and then down into Middle Tennessee. There were no roads. When they arrived at the French Lick on Christmas Day 1779, the Cumberland River was a solid sheet of ice, and their horses and cattle walked across the frozen river to the bluff. There, on New Year's Day 1780, the newcomers began to build cabins and await the flatboats carrying immigrants guided by Colonel John Donelson, a riverboat captain.

At Watauga it had been decided that those women, children, and others who were not able to travel by land with Robertson would travel by water with Donelson, on the Holston, Tennessee, Ohio, and Cumberland rivers. Though delayed by the severe weather, Donelson kept a journal of his pioneer voyage to join Robertson in Middle Tennessee. Navigating his flatboat, the *Adventure*, Donelson led his flotilla. Three hundred people aboard 30 boats departed the Long Island of Holston boatyard at Fort Henry on December 22, 1779. Hard frosts and waterfalls lay ahead.[7] After only one day, blustery, cold, icy weather delayed their trip, and they camped at Reedy Creek until the weather moderated, resuming travel on February 20, 1780. Traveling with Donelson on the *Adventure* was his family, including his 13-year-old daughter, Rachael, the future wife of Andrew Jackson, seventh president of the United States.

Donelson's boats tossed like twigs on the treacherous white waters of Muscle Shoals. Floating, rowing and poling on hazardous rivers through Indian country paralleling the Chickamauga towns, the pioneers heard bullets whizzing overhead. Dragging Canoe's hostile Chickamaugas controlled the transportation through the big bend of the Tennessee River. Having traveled 1,000 miles by water, Donelson, in his journal entry for Monday, April 24, 1780, wrote, "This day we arrived at our journey's end, at the big salt lick, where we have the pleasure of finding Capt. Robertson and his company."

Judge Richard Henderson soon arrived at the settlement of French Lick (Nashville), which was situated in Washington County, North Carolina, 300 miles from the county seat at Jonesborough. By spring 300 people were living there.[8] Henderson wrote the "Cumberland Compact of Government." Similar to Robertson's Watauga Association, it would serve as a guide for land transactions and a representative government. The Cumberland Compact was discussed at a meeting of settlers. Amended and adopted on May 13, 1780, Henderson's compact named the place "Nashborough" in honor of his former clerk of court in Hillsborough, General Francis Nash, who was killed at the 1777 Battle of Germantown.

The resourceful Charlotte Reeves Robertson, wife of James Robertson, had walked with her Regulator husband across the Blue Ridge and worked shoulder to shoulder with him on the farm to found the Watauga Settlement. Of their 13 children, two of the boys were killed by Indians and another was scalped and left to die. Charlotte traveled with Donelson's flatboat flotilla to meet her husband, the Father of Middle Tennessee, at Fort Nashborough. The next year, in April 1781, Charlotte Robertson left the fort to warn the men, who were away farming or hunting, of an imminent Indian attack involving hand-to-hand combat. After she returned to the fort, she saw that Indians were now blocking the frontiersmen's return to the fort. Charlotte won her epithet, "Heroine of the Battle of the Bluff," when she unleashed the hounds. The howling dogs chased the attackers and created enough confusion to free the way to the fort for the men's safe return. Thus, Charlotte saved Fort Nashborough.[9]

The Cumberland Compact has since lost much of its historical impact because in 1783 North Carolina refused to recognize Henderson's 1775 Transylvania Purchase. Instead the state compensated him with a land grant of 200,000 aces in Powell Valley.[10] North Carolina then organized the Cumberland settlements to form Davidson County (named for General William Davidson), which included all 70 present-day counties of the state of Tennessee west of the Cumberland Plateau to the Mississippi River. The next year the name Fort Nashborough was changed to Nashville, North Carolina. Tennessee became the 16th state in 1796, with its centrally located village of Nashville as its capital.

12

Georgia Invades Florida, and the Savannah and Augusta Campaigns

While Virginia's George Rogers Clark attempted to break Indian-British alliances in the Northwest Territory, and North Carolina's Wataugans moved west past the Indian border to colonize Tennessee Country, the state of Georgia unsuccessfully invaded East Florida three times. Before that, Georgia had first penetrated the Florida border six years after the colony of Georgia was founded.

General James Edward Oglethorpe and a group of other philanthropists, acting as trustees (proprietors), obtained permission from King George II to found a new colony in the New World. The colony would be established to give the "the worthy poor" of England, as well as oppressed people throughout much of Europe, a new start.[1] The trustees named the colony Georgia in honor of the king. The king's purposes, for the most part, paralleled those of Oglethorpe. His Majesty wanted to provide employment for Britain's poor: to set them to work cutting timbers, planting crops of indigo, rice and wheat, and producing resources that could be sent back to England. He also expected the people of Georgia to defend the colonial frontier in the South. Georgia was to be a buffer colony between the Carolinas and Spanish Florida. From its inception, Oglethorpe's Georgia encouraged the trustees to send recruits with industrious wives. Myriad founding women came to Georgia as wives, mothers, daughters, spinsters and indentured servants. Among those especially known for their services and skills are Mary Musgrove and Jane Mary Camuse.

Mary Musgrove, interpreter and entrepreneur, was of mixed parentage. Her father was an English trader, her mother a Creek Indian. One of Mary's husbands was a trader named John Musgrove, whose name she took. Speaking both Creek and English, Mary helped maintain peace between the two nations and acted as a cultural bridge and interpreter for transactions between Englishman Oglethorpe and Chief Tomochichi, a Yamacraw Indian. Mary Musgrove was also the proprietress of a deerskin trading post.

In 1733, Italian-born Jane Mary Camuse, a skilled silk winder, came to Oglethorpe's Georgia as a servant with her husband and three children. Within three years the owners of the silk business left and Jane took over management of the company. The Georgia trustees hoped that silk would become the colony's chief cash industry. But Jane refused to teach apprentices and kept her knowledge of silk producing within her own family, thereby maintaining a powerful lever to negotiate for increased wages with the trustees.[2]

Georgia didn't quite provide all the treasures of the long-sought-after Silk Road, but some Georgians did produce wines and spices and Jane Camuse produced the silk that England heretofore had imported from foreign lands. The new colony not only supplied luxuries for England, but, as had been hoped, it also acted as a barrier protecting wealthy plantations in South Carolina by curbing Spanish and French incursions into the colonies.

In 1752, almost 20 years after founding Georgia, its trustees turned the colony back to the Crown. The king then appointed a governor. Colonists continued to prosper under the rule of Sir James Wright, Georgia's third and last Crown governor. Hence, they sent no delegates to the First Continental Congress, which met in the fall of 1774. But in January 1775 Georgia convened a provincial Congress in Savannah simply to consider the recommendation of the First Continental Congress to endorse the Articles of Association, which placed a ban on trade with Great Britain. Georgia's provincial Congress elected delegates, but none chose to attend. However, the battles of Lexington and Concord in April convinced many Georgians to switch loyalties and join the radical movement. St. John Parish, acting alone, sent a delegate, Lyman Hall, to the Second Continental Congress on its opening day, May 10, 1775. During that same month, the radical Sons of Liberty broke into a Savannah magazine, pilfered gunpowder and weaponry, and distributed arms and ammunition to the revolutionaries. That's when Georgia's burgeoning second provincial Congress belatedly elected delegates to the nation's Second Continental Congress and sent them to Philadelphia on July 4, 1775, seven weeks after its opening day. Georgia's provincial Congress then not only adopted the Continental Congress's "Association," the ban on trade with England (non-importation, non-exportation and non-consumption), but also established local committees of safety to enforce the boycott. Governor Wright was displeased that artisans and farmers—he called them "the wrong sort"—gained political power as members of local committees. He was even more concerned when Georgia's second provincial Congress established a standing council of safety and vested it with executive authority.

Immigrant Thomas Brown, son of a wealthy English merchant, was comfortably settled with his 70 indentured servants on the South Carolina side of the Savannah River when he, with Georgia's Governor Wright's encouragement, founded the settlement of Brownsborough near Augusta, Georgia. Brown vigorously objected to the Association, the ban on trade. He therefore formed a counter-association of "King's Friends," who openly denounced the ban on trade. Brown's refusal to honor the Association led the Whig activists known as the Sons of Liberty to seize Brown, scalp him, burn his feet, and drag him through the streets of Augusta.

Recovering from his scalping, Brown went to the backcountry around the village of Ninety Six, where he rallied Loyalists. He talked with South Carolina's royal governor, who advised him to wait for British troops before making a move against the Whigs. Biding his time but still recruiting, Thomas Brown went to Florida and received permission from Patrick Tonyn, east Florida's Tory governor, to enlist Florida Rangers. Brown's Ranger recruits would, in turn, enlist Indian allies, join Loyalists, and then team up with British troops who were expected to land on the Florida coast shortly.

In January 1776 British ships sailed into Georgia's Savannah River. Fearing that the troops intended to capture Savannah, the council of safety placed Governor Wright and his royal council under house arrest and put a conservative Whig, Lachlan McIntosh, an immigrant Scottish Highlander who was colonel of the Georgia Battalion, in charge of the defense of the city. The purpose of the warships, however, was not to capture Savannah but

12. Georgia Invades Florida, and the Savannah and Augusta Campaigns

to commandeer 11 merchant ships laden with rice. During the Battle of the Rice Boats in March 1776, after seizing two of the merchant ships (the rice boats), the British fleet rescued Governor Wright and his council, took them aboard the HMS *Scarborough* and sailed away, leaving Georgia without a governor.

The British attack on the rice boats prompted Georgia's third provincial Congress, which first met in Savannah in January 1776, to move to Augusta in March. There the Patriot (Whig) Congress established a government and elected a president who would also command the state militia. It was this congress that, belatedly, elected the then Conservative Whig George Walton and Radical Whig Button Gwinnett to join Lyman Hall as delegates to the Second Continental Congress, sending them to Philadelphia by July 1776 in time to sign the Declaration of Independence. The very next year Button Gwinnett called his political rival Lachlan McIntosh a Tory who was merely masquerading as a Conservative Whig. In the ensuing pistol duel, McIntosh, who was now a brigadier general of the Continental Army, shot and mortally wounded Gwinnett.

In 1776 Georgia's first Florida expedition of the Revolution had fizzled out when its military leader was recalled to the North. The second Florida expedition had fizzled out in the duel between militia leader Gwinnett and General McIntosh. In June 1778 Georgia would also botch its third and last Florida expedition of the Revolutionary War. In that fateful third expedition, acting under the direction of the Second Continental Congress, Georgia hoped to ally with South Carolina, occupy St. Augustine, conquer Florida and thereby end cattle-stealing incursions from Florida into their state. The raiders crossing the border into Georgia comprised Loyalist Thomas Brown's Florida Rangers and their allied nations of Creek and Seminole Indians.

When Georgia and South Carolina militiamen joined with Continental Line soldiers for the ill-fated third Florida expedition, there was woeful lack of military coordination. Inexperienced in military matters, Governor John Houstoun led the Georgia militia, and General Andrew Williamson led the South Carolina militia. They attempted to work with General Robert Howe, commander of the Continental Army in the South, who led the Continental Lines of both South Carolina and Georgia.

The third Florida expedition failed because the Continentals and the state militias could not work together. Moreover, the commodore of the Georgia navy refused to obey commands from either the Continental Line general or militia leaders since it was unclear whether the navy was allied with the Continental or the state military. During this third expedition, as General Howe moved with his Georgia and South Carolina Continental Army through the Okefenokee Swamp on the way to St. Augustine, he approached Fort Tonyn, on the St. Mary's River at the Georgia-Florida coastal border. Fort Tonyn, a refuge for fleeing Loyalists, was a base for Colonel Thomas Brown and his King's (Florida) Rangers. Brown and his Florida Ranger militiamen joined with American Indians to attack the Carolinas and Georgia. (Brown's bald head was a grim reminder that the Sons of Liberty had held his feet to the fire and scalped him in 1775 for denouncing the ban on trade.) Howe surprised Brown's Rangers while they were cooking by campfire at Fort Tonyn. When Brown and his mounted Rangers vamoosed, Howe hunkered down with his Continentals in the mosquito-infested swamp. For several weeks, the Continental general waited in vain for Governor Houstoun and his Georgia militia.

The retreating Brown and his Florida Rangers moved their camp to within 17 miles of Alligator Creek Bridge near St. Augustine. When Governor Houstoun finally arrived and found Fort Tonyn abandoned, he sent Georgia guerrilla colonel Elijah Clarke with a detachment of Patriot militiamen to reconnoiter the area. Clarke's men again flushed Brown's Rangers and chased them to Alligator Creek Bridge, where Major James Marc Prevost, the brother of General Augustine Prevost, was bivouacked. When the fleeing Brown and his Rangers loomed up at the bridge with Americans in hot pursuit, the British regulars were caught by surprise bathing in Alligator Creek. The dripping wet Regulars under Prevost and the escaping King's Rangers under Brown repelled Clarke. A historical marker erected in the town of Callahan, Florida, by the Jacksonville Chapter Sons of the American Revolution describes the skirmish at Alligator Creek:

> On June 30, 1778, a force of 300 American Cavalry commanded by Colonel Elijah Clarke, participating in General Robert Howe's invasion of Florida, attacked a column of British at [Alligator Creek Bridge] ... but were unable to penetrate the nearby entrenchments of 450 British Regulars and South Carolina Royalists under the command of Major James Marc Prevost. In this skirmish, Colonel Clarke was wounded and the Americans withdrew.... Casualties: Americans 13 British 9.

The Battle of Alligator Creek Bridge was the only major engagement in the failed Florida campaign to conquer British-held Florida during the American Revolution. From 1776 until 1778 Georgia Patriots accomplished little other than three feeble raids on Florida and patrolling the western frontier. The abundance of Tories (Loyalists and British troops) and the ambivalence of citizens who often switched sides accounted for the tenuous hold the Patriots maintained on Georgia.

By 1778 Major General Sir Henry Clinton, chief commander of British forces in North America had reached a stalemate in the North with Continental Army commander in chief George Washington. The commanders were mainly watching each other when Clinton departed New York, sailed south and used Georgia's strong Loyalist base as a springboard to launch his "Southern Strategy." First, Clinton sought to capture the vital ports of Savannah, Georgia and Charlestown, South Carolina.

To counter Clinton's strategy, the counsel of southern congressmen suggested replacing General Robert Howe as commander of American Forces in the South. The Continental Congress replaced Howe with Continental Army major general Benjamin Lincoln, who arrived in Charlestown on December 4. Lincoln found provisions as well as funds for restocking supplies direfully short. North Carolina sent 1,000 militiamen, but Virginia did not send troops because she underestimated the threat to the South. Unaware that the British were on the move and intent on occupying Savannah, Lincoln allowed Howe, the ex-commander of the Continental Army in the South, to retain command of that city. The Patriot situation in the South worsened.

General Clinton, conscious that Georgia harbored many Loyalists, depended on Loyalist support to bring the South back into the Royalist camp. Accordingly, he shipped Scottish colonel Archibald Campbell and 3,000 troops from New York to invade Georgia. Campbell's British army landed off Tybee Island in December 1778 and waded through swamps on their march to surround and seize Savannah. General Howe attempted to hold Savannah with a force of fewer than 1,200. When Campbell's 3,500 British regulars attacked, Howe ordered his small army to retreat.[3] During the withdrawal, British and German troops charged with fixed bayonets. The fleeing Howe and Colonel Samuel Elbert dismounted and swam across Yamacraw Creek. Many Patriots soldiers drowned in the rice swamps in their

12. Georgia Invades Florida, and the Savannah and Augusta Campaigns

headlong flight. On December 29, 1778, Campbell captured guns, stores and 500 prisoners and claimed the city of Savannah. Howe lost no time in warning Patriots to evacuate Augusta and Sunbury, the only two Georgia cities not under British control.

In 1779 Clinton's victorious British troops, stationed throughout Georgia, solicited the support of hundreds of backcountry Loyalists. Attempting to restore the state to British rule, Clinton planned to enlist southerners as allies, overrun the southern colonies, and then move against the North. He also expected British troops from Canada to invade the North and then, if things went well with the Clinton strategy, all Americans would once again be united under the Union Jack.

Archibald Campbell, having turned Savannah into a British stronghold, awaited reinforcement before advancing farther into the Georgia countryside. Support came with the Swiss-born general Augustine Prevost, a British Army veteran of the French and Indian War. Prevost led a group of Loyalists, including Thomas Brown's Rangers, to meet with Campbell in January 1779. Prevost and Campbell planned their campaign and then split. Prevost proceeded to Sunbury, a port on the Medway River that once rivaled Savannah in commercial importance but today is a ghost town south of Savannah. Leading 2,000 British and Indian forces, Prevost invaded Sunbury and captured its 200-man Patriot garrison, which, despite Howe's warning, had not evacuated. Prevost renamed the Sunbury fortress Fort George in honor of England's King George III. Meanwhile, Campbell led his Tory Highlanders, Florida Rangers and Loyalists to Augusta, a shipping center on the Savannah River. Along the way he freed 90 slaves and escorted them back to Savannah. Campbell took possession of Augusta on the last day of January. When the British occupied Augusta, 1,400 backcountry Loyalists flocked into that fallen city and joined the royal militia.[4]

Lincoln, the new Continental Army commander in the South, was unaware that Howe had actually lost Savannah to the British. Hence, Lincoln gathered an army of 3,500 regulars and militiamen. Determined to defend South Carolina and free Georgia of British control, the Continental commander began marching from Charlestown toward Savannah. On the road to Savannah, he was surprised to pick up the remnants of Howe's escaping American garrison and hear the bad news that Savannah had fallen to the British. He then took post on the east bank of the Savannah River 15 miles north of Savannah at the village of Purrysburg, near present-day Hardeeville. Staring across the River at Lincoln's Americans, Prevost occupied the west bank at the village of Ebenezer. His 5,000 Tory troops flanked the riverbank from Savannah to Augusta.[5]

Although the British took possession of Augusta on January 31, 1779, Campbell would hold the city for only 14 days. Patriots from the Georgia backcountry resisted the British takeover. Led by Lincoln, Americans reclaimed British-held Augusta via the battles of Beaufort (Port Royal Island), Kettle Creek and Brier Creek. When Prevost sent British Regulars to seize Port Royal Island (Beaufort) South Carolina, Lincoln sent General William Moultrie to stop them. This was the same Moultrie whose militia had built a palmetto redoubt and repulsed Clinton's naval attack at Sullivan's Island in 1776. Now, on February 3, 1779, Moultrie, leading militiamen and a few Continentals rolling three cannons—marched from Purrysburg to nearby Beaufort on the South Carolina coast. At the Battle of Beaufort (Port Royal Island) Moultrie repulsed the British advance, held Beaufort, and won an astonishing victory.[6]

Colonel James Boyd, recruiting under Archibald Campbell, set out from British-held

Savannah to enlist Loyalists throughout Georgia. Working from his base of operations near Spartanburg, South Carolina, Boyd attracted Loyalists from both Carolinas and started marching to Augusta, Georgia, to reinforce Campbell. On February 14 they were intercepted by Patriot militiamen under Colonels Andrew Pickens, John Dooly and Elijah Clarke. The Patriots caught Boyd at Kettle Creek, 50 miles northwest of Augusta. Boyd's horses were grazing while his troops were butchering cattle on a hillside above Kettle Creek when his sentries heard the accidental gunshot that warned them of Pickens' surprise attack. Presbyterian Andrew Pickens was known by his militia as the "Fighting Elder" and to the Cherokee as "Wizard Owl." In the ensuing battle, 200 South Carolinians fought under the command of Pickens, while 150 Georgians were led by Colonel John Dooly and Lieutenant Colonel Elijah Clarke. Boyd's 600 Loyalists spotted Pickens' advance guard and positioned themselves behind rocks and trees. The Patriots continued to advance. After a three-hour fight, Boyd was wounded and his recruits began to withdraw. Boyd and 20 Loyalists lay dead, and 22 were captured. Patriots Pickens, Dooly and Clarke lost a total of seven killed and 15 wounded.[7] Boyd's second in command, Colonel John Spurgeon of South Carolina, led 450 retreating Loyalists back to Savannah. The survivors organized two units: the North Carolina and South Carolina Royal Regiments of Loyalists.

Patriot victory at Kettle Creek, Georgia, on February 14, 1779, however small, was an important win for Americans in Georgia. It heralded the withdrawal of the British from Augusta and ensured that the upper state around Augusta was clearly in Patriot territory. The victory also slowed Loyalist recruitment in the South.

Tradition speculates that "War Woman," Nancy Ann Morgan Hart, as well as her husband, Lieutenant Benjamin Hart, served under Elijah Clarke in the Kettle Creek battle. It is said, "Of Georgia's back-country war there are few written records, but it gave rise to a treasure trove of legends."[8] So many Nancy Hart legends have grown up and been spread by oral history that schools, restaurants and even a Georgia county are named in her honor. Nancy Hart, a six-foot, muscular spy with light brown hair, sometimes tied together a vine raft and rowed across the Savannah River to gather information about British troops. She navigated back and delivered the intelligence to militia leader Elijah Clarke. Another time she dressed as a man, pretended to be crazy and marched into a British camp to gather facts, which she relayed to Colonel Clarke. Nancy lived in Georgia with her husband, Lieutenant Benjamin Hart, and their eight children. Benjamin served as a quartermaster and militiaman under Clarke.

There are many versions of the most famous Nancy Hart story. Some tell how her favorite tom turkey gobbler aided Elijah Clarke's men after the Kettle Creek battle. Elizabeth Ellet's version goes something like this. Some Tories barged into Nancy's house and demanded that she cook dinner for them. She replied, "I don't even have enough to feed my own family because some other Tories stole all my chickens and pigs." The Tories then shot the only bird she had, her pet turkey gobbler. "She stormed and swore awhile" before she plucked and singed it. While she cooked and the men drank liquor, Nancy sent her daughter Sukey outside to find the conch shell and blow a warning to the neighbors that Tories were in the neighborhood. While the men ate, Nancy edged toward the enemy guns that they had "stacked ... in view and within reach." She stealthily slid one, and then another, of the muskets through a crack in the log cabin. She again sent Sukey to play a tune on the conch shell to signal her father to come at once. When Nancy tried to sneak a third musket, "The whole party sprang to their feet." Nancy pointed the gun toward the Tories and warned that she "would kill the first man who approached her." When he made his move, she shot him dead and grabbed another musket. She shot the second man dead and demanded that the hostages surrender their "d—— Tory carcasses to a Whig woman." Upon arriving home, Benjamin wanted to shoot the devils but Nancy said that "shooting was too good for them." So Nancy and Benjamin Hart and their neighbors hanged them.[9]

Another treasured Georgia legend tells how Mammy Kate rescued Stephen Heard after the Battle of Kettle Creek. The slave Mammy Kate was "the biggest, the tallest, the most imposing"[10] black American woman in the state of Georgia. She was also known as "Aunt" Kate, an esteemed title reserved for only the most respected and beloved black women in the South. Mammy mounted her master's horse, Lightfoot, and trotted alongside her husband, Daddy Jack, 50 miles to British-held Augusta. She was determined to free her diminutive master, Steven Heard, a planter, patriot, soldier and future governor of the state of Georgia. Heard had served under colonels John Dooly, Andrew "Wizard Owl" Pickens and Elijah Clarke at Kettle Creek. After the Kettle Creek Battle, a band of roving Tory marauders captured Heard, sentenced him to hang for treason, and locked him in an Augusta prison. The clever Mammy Kate (Heard's surrogate mother) applied to the prison guard for a job as a laundress. Every day she walked through the prison, found the half-starved Heard, gave him food and then, with a basket placed on her head, collected dirty shirts and sheets and carried them away. On the next day she returned with the clean and ironed laundry. One evening the big woman put a bed sheet filled with laundry on the floor and beckoned Heard to climb in. Other prisoners piled on more laundry, tied the bundle at the top and lifted it onto Mammy Kate's head. Balancing her bundle, Mammy Kate found Daddy Jack, strapped the cocooned Steven Heard onto Lightfoot, and returned him to his plantation. Heard freed Mammy Kate, but she continued to work at his plantation until her death.

The American victory at Kettle Creek attracted North Carolinians and Virginians. The number of General Lincoln's Patriot forces swelled to 6,000. Lincoln then sent North Carolina militia general John Ashe up the east bank of the Savannah River to attack Augusta. When Colonel Archibald Campbell learned of Ashe's approach, he withdrew from Augusta. Campbell's coworker, General Augustine Prevost, consolidated their scattered British troops and deployed them down the west bank of the Savannah River toward a rendezvous point at Ebenezer.

Marching hot on the heels of the retreating British army were General Ashe leading Patriot militia of North Carolina, Colonel Samuel Elbert leading Georgia Continentals and militia, and Colonel Andrew Williamson leading South Carolina militia. On March 3, 1779, the chase along the Savannah River reversed. General Prevost dispatched his brother Lieutenant Colonel Marc Prevost from Savannah with 900 British troops to cross Brier Creek at its mouth on the Savannah, 50 miles above Ashe's camp. Marc planned to slip up on Ashe's rear guard and concealed this move by sending a battalion of Fraser Highlanders against Ashe's front. Prevost's encircling technique worked perfectly. By reversing course, the British Army caught Ashe's Patriots camping at Brier Creek surrounded by a deep swamp. Alerted by an express rider of an impending British attack, Ashe signaled the drummer to beat a call to arms. "General Ashe's affair at Brier Creek was nothing less than a total rout," said a contemporary, "Never was an army more completely surprised, and never were men more panic stricken."[11] Outnumbered and overpowered, Ashe and his North Carolina Patriots fled, breaking and running through the swamps, and some were lost or drowned trying to cross the Savannah River. Others were killed, drowned at other places or taken prisoner. Only 450 troops rejoined Lincoln's army. Nearly 600 of Ashe's men escaped. Of Prevost's Tory army, 5 were killed and 11 wounded.[12] Colonel Elbert and his Georgians bravely defended. Even while the British were clearly winning at Brier Creek, Elbert's men did not give up. Commemorating the valor of Georgia Patriots, a Georgia Historical Society marker at the Brier Creek Battle site reads, "So fiercely did these Georgians fight that the British had to bring up reserves. Asking no quarter, they fought until nearly every man was dead or wounded." Elbert, along with 11 officers and 162 noncommissioned officers and men, was taken prisoner by the British but released in time to take part in the Yorktown campaign. He later was promoted to the rank of brigadier general and served as governor of Georgia. "Ashe was tried by court martial and severely censured.... He was a patriot of the highest character but without military experience or instinct."[13] The upshot of the March 3, 1779, Battle of Brier Creek was that the Patriots suffered a costly and humiliating defeat. Lower Georgia remained in Tory hands. The Loyalist victory not only crushed Patriot morale but it also increased Loyalist recruits and reclaimed Savannah for the British. From this firm foothold, the British would spring an attack on Charlestown.

General Lincoln lacked the ammunition for an assault on Savannah, but, despite their defeat by the British at Brier Creek, American Patriots held Augusta and the backcountry. In April 1779 Lincoln marched from Charlestown to force the few remaining British out of Augusta, bolster Patriot support and cut off British supplies from inland Loyalists and their British-allied Indians. He left General William Moultrie to defend Charlestown. Moultrie scattered 1,000 men throughout the backcountry at Purrysburg and the Black Swamp and along the Savannah River on the South Carolina-Georgia border to guard South Carolina, especially Charlestown, against an influx of British troops from Savannah.

Prevost, realizing Moultrie's weakness, took advantage of Lincoln's absence from the port city. Marching out of his British stronghold in Savannah, Prevost crossed the Savannah River and pushed northward on an expedition to raid Charlestown. Guarding the border, Moultrie retreated but plagued him with rear guard skirmishes. Once Prevost reached Charlestown, however, he backed off because Lincoln had sent General Casimir Pulaski to reinforce the city. Pulaski, a Polish nobleman, was a Patriot cavalry general and military tactician. Realizing that the Patriots at Charlestown were more formidable than he had anticipated, Prevost aborted his attack and established a British base 18 miles south of Charlestown at Stono Ferry. This was a crucial crossing of the Stono River where plantation products were ferried to and from Charlestown. At Stono Ferry, Prevost could control navigation on the Stono River, continue Tory raids on Charlestown, and protect his path of retreat to Georgia.

On June 10 Prevost evacuated Stono Ferry and continued his retreat toward Georgia. He left Lieutenant Colonel John Maitland in command of the British rear guard at Stono Ferry. Maitland, a one-armed Highlander who had lost the limb in the French and Indian War, worked with his rear guard of Highlanders, Hessians and Loyalists to construct an abatis made of logs and sharpened sticks. Behind this barrier, he built three redoubts.[14]

There, on Johns Island near Stono Ferry on the Stono River, Maitland and his battalion of British and Hessians camped out on the beautiful plantation grounds of an ancient-looking brick mansion known as "Peaceful Retreat," its portico and side buildings flanked by live oak, aspen and sycamore trees and a river walk. The owner of the mansion was a refined, cultured and crippled Patriot named Robert Gibbs, who was confined to a wheelchair by the intense pain of gout that caused swelling and contraction of some joints of his hands and feet. His wife, Sarah Reeve Gibbs, managed his extensive estate and supervised their eight children as well as seven orphans of her sister plus two others. Of the many children under her care, the oldest was 15.

Mrs. Sarah Gibbs was alerted before dawn by an aged servant tapping on her door: "Mistress, the redcoats are all around the house." Sarah quickly put on a frock, silently awoke others in the household, dressed the children and gathered the family around her husband. The noise of his wheelchair rolling across the hall floor and the opening of the massive front door sounded like cannon to the Tories, who rushed in with pointed bayonets. Just as she planned, when the imposters saw the self-possessed, calm and quiet Mrs. Gibbs, her crippled husband and the passel of children unable to defend themselves, the enemy soldiers did not harm them. Nevertheless, the officers allowed the men total possession of the house and permission to pilfer whatever they wanted, including wine. Mrs. Gibbs, with aplomb and composure, sat at the head of her table while her servants served the food. Slightly taken aback by the royal treatment, the surprised soldiers showed her respect. As soon as news of the British encampment reached Charlestown, two boatloads of soldiers were sent to the Gibbs plantation. Sarah Gibbs, knowing there would be gunfire but having no access to horses, walked her family of children, and slaves pushing the wheelchair, to the next plantation, where she fell onto a bed chilled, exhausted and soaking wet.

When it was discovered that one little boy was missing the servants refused to risk their lives to find him. The Gibbs's 13-year-old daughter, Mary Anna Gibbs, ran along the path to her home at Peaceful Retreat. Ignoring the sentinel's refusal to grant her permission to enter, she rushed to the third story, lifted the child and ran. Shot flew thickly around, digging up the dirt along the path as she joined the rest of her family.[15] Young Mary Anna Gibbs earned the honorific title "heroine" that day when she rescued a boy cousin from the hands of the British. "Even the young girls had the spirit of heroism and patriotism which marked the women of the Revolution."[16]

On June 20, 1779, Lincoln attacked Prevost's rear guard at Stono Ferry. Lincoln hoped to trap the British between his American army coming from Charlestown and Moultrie's forces approaching from the South Carolina–Georgia border. But Moultrie, lacking boats to carry his troops across the river, failed to appear. Thus Prevost's rear guard under Maitland foiled Lincoln's poorly coordinated Patriot attack until all except 11 of the kilted Highlanders had fallen. The battle continued as the British fought from behind the abatis and redoubts. The American general Isaac Huger was hit by enemy fire. Twelve-year-old Andrew Jackson was wounded, and his brother Hugh was killed. Eventually the Americans withdrew. There were casualties on both sides: Moultrie suffered 153, Maitland 149. The Battle of Stono was a tactical success for the British, who retreated safely, island hopping to Savannah. But their strategic position was unchanged.

At Stono Ferry, Patriot Captain Richard Doggett sustained a mortal gunshot wound to his abdomen. As he lay dying under a tree he wrote a few lines to his father, Bushrod Doggett of Culpepper County, Virginia. In the note Richard acknowledged an illegitimate son. The message, as well as the captain's regimental clothes and epaulettes, were carried to Richard's parents by his "waiter" Ned, a young black man. Bushrod subsequently located his illegitimate 10-year-old grandson, took him into his home and sent him to school.[17]

After General Lincoln regained Augusta in the spring of 1779 he finally gathered enough military might to attack British-held Savannah in the fall. He then began working with Admiral Count Charles Henri d'Estaing. Lincoln and d'Estaing attempted to recapture Savannah from Colonel Campbell, who had seized that city the preceding year. D'Estaing's and Lincoln's Franco-American siege to retake Savannah from the British began in September when D'Estaing and his French army of 5,000 debarked at Beaulieu on the Vernon River, a saltwater tidal stream just south of Savannah. Patriot Count Casimir Pulaski and his cavalry met Admiral d'Estaing when he came ashore and led the French to within three miles of the city. The French were soon joined by Lincoln's Americans as well as black Haitian troops known as Chasseurs. The major assault against the British occurred on October 9, but Savannah's well-entrenched British garrison successfully defended. The Franco-American siege of Savannah lasted from September 16 until October 18, 1779. The Franco-American forces suffered 800 casualties, while the British sustained only 150.

The daring young sergeant William Jasper died at Savannah trying to repeat his heroic act of replanting the fallen flag during the 1776 Battle of Fort Moultrie at Charlestown. Another killed at the Siege of Savannah was Sally St. Clair, a French black American woman who disguised herself successfully as a soldier and managed to hide her sex from the army until her death. Legend has it that this South Carolina Creole girl was the fiancée of Sgt. Jasper. Another soldier killed on the Patriot side was General Pulaski of the cavalry, who charged on horseback into battle. Both the William Jasper monument and Pulaski Square stand in Savannah commemorating these Patriots.

Admiral d'Estaing and his French troops returned to their fleet on October 20, and the Americans recrossed the Savannah River. The Savannah Campaign of 1779 ended with the rejoicing British holding the city and singing a well known ditty:

> To Charleston with fear
> The rebels repair;
> D'Estaing scampers back to his boats, sir,
> Each blaming the other,
> Each cursing his brother,
> And—may they cut each other's throats, sir![18]

At the end of 1779, the British in the South held only Savannah, Georgia, and St. Augustine, Florida.

During parts of 1779 and 1780, three governments existed in Georgia. One Loyalist (Tory) government was in Lower Georgia; two Patriot (Whig) governments were in Upper Georgia. In Lower Georgia, the smaller portion of the divided state, Savannah was controlled by a Tory government under the last Crown-appointed governor of Georgia, Sir James Wright. Having fled Georgia during the Battle of the Rice Boats, Wright returned to Savannah on July 14, 1779, resumed his position as royal governor, and announced that Georgia, as the first (and only) of the 13 rebellious states to reestablish allegiance to the Crown, would enjoy the privilege of being exempt from taxation. Wright held onto his governorship as well as his 11 plantations and 523 slaves throughout most of the Revolutionary War.

12. Georgia Invades Florida, and the Savannah and Augusta Campaigns

In Upper Georgia at Augusta, two Patriot (Whig) rival governments vied for rule. One conservative, the other radical, they viciously attacked each other. In 1780 Colonel George Wells, governor pro tem, quarreled with Militia Major John Jackson, who was a Conservative. Because the Radical Whig Wells suspected that all Conservative Whigs were Loyalists at heart, he challenged Conservative Jackson to a duel. Jackson killed Wells. Thus two Radical Patriot leaders of Upper Georgia—Button Gwinnett and George Wells—were killed by Conservative Whigs.

13

Charlestown Campaign, Camden Battle and Fishing Creek

Soon after the British gained a stronghold in Georgia Sir Henry Clinton, the commander in chief of British forces in America, planned an expedition to conquer South Carolina. Clinton hoped not only to subdue the South but also to compensate for his 1776 defeat at the Battle of Sullivan's Island and his failure to establish a base in Charlestown at that time. Charlestown was the principal seaport in the South. Exporting rice, hides, indigo and cotton, and importing woolens and manufactured goods from England, the first settlers named the place Charlestown, or Charles Town. It would be renamed Charleston in 1783, when the town was rebuilt after the Revolutionary War. The British wanted possession of this important port.

Departing from Sandy Hook, New Jersey, for Charlestown on the day after Christmas 1779, Clinton and his second in command, Lord Charles Cornwallis, sailed southward conveying a British force of more than 7,500 soldiers and sailors over the Atlantic's stormy seas. Vessels capsized and sank on the hazardous ocean journey. Bold privateers seized transports. One ship of Hessian troops was "dismasted and driven across the ocean."[1] Most of the horses perished. At the rendezvous point at Tybee Bay between Tybee Island and the Savannah River, Clinton was joined by 1,500 Loyalist troops from Georgia. Needing even more troops, he ordered a brigade of 2,500 from New York. Clinton readied his entire Tory army of some 12,000 for attack and bore down upon the city of Charlestown.

The opulent city of Charlestown, at the confluence of the Ashley and Cooper rivers, with her 15,000 black and white inhabitants was garrisoned by fewer than 4,000 troops under the command of General Benjamin Lincoln. It was an insufficient number to defend the three-mile circumference of the city against Clinton's imminent attack.

Prudence Hall was one of the courageous women who pitched in to aid the Patriot cause. The Prudence Hall Chapter NSDAR in Arkansas is the namesake of Harriet Prudence (Patterson) Hall, "the petticoat courier." Its online chapter history states: "According to tradition, she delivered an important message to an American general after passing the British lines. Tradition also says that she nursed back to health an American man scalped by the Indians." Oral histories from many sources agree that Mrs. Hall's husband, John Hall, fought as a Patriot soldier in South Carolina. Prudence and two or three other women, under the pretense of visiting the apothecary, penetrated the enemy line into the city. Prudence smuggled a message sewn into her petticoat and delivered it to the American commander during the Siege of Charlestown.

13. Charlestown Campaign, Camden Battle and Fishing Creek

The Clinton-versus-Lincoln Charlestown Campaign comprised two parts: the Siege of Charlestown (February 10–May 12, 1780) and the Battle of Waxhaws (May 29, 1780). Remembering his failure to capture Charlestown by sea in 1776, Clinton took a different tack in 1780. This time he brought not only warships but also adequate British troops to surround and isolate the city, blockading it both by land and by sea. Redcoats completely encircled the city during the months of February and March 1780. The next month the additional 2,500 troops from New York disembarked at Charlestown Harbor. Lieutenant Colonel Banastre Tarleton marshaled the New York brigade to the outskirts of town. There, at Moncks Corner, he surprised and seized Patriot troops under the command of General Isaac Huger. Tarleton's victory at the Battle of Moncks Corner on April 14 severed all remaining Patriot lines of communication to Charlestown and isolated Lincoln's army inside the city.

But even when all hope of escape was crushed, Lincoln heeded the plea of citizens and refused to surrender. He declared, "From duty and Inclination I shall support the town to the last extremity." George Washington reflected, "The attempt to defend the town ought to have been relinquished." The bombardment continued. "Cannon balls by day and by night streaking through the air, crashing through houses" killed a child in his nurse's arms, a man and wife in bed, and a soldier embracing his terrified wife. Cannonades, mortars and howitzers belched forth the shot, setting the city ablaze. Piercing the smoke was the "incessant fire of cannon balls whizzing, shells hissing, and men groaning." At last, General Lincoln surrendered, but only when a "large majority of the inhabitants and of the militia petitioned to accede to the terms offered by the enemy."[2]

Forced to surrender to General Clinton on May 12, 1780, General Lincoln handed over the entire southern Continental Army of 5,000 as prisoners of war. Among those captured were 15 Virginia regiments, leaving that colony vulnerable to British attack. The regulars and sailors were shipped north until an exchange could be arranged. Militiamen were released on condition that they would not fight again as Patriots, but no restrictions were placed on officers who were exchanged. Lincoln was exchanged for a British officer and returned to the battlefield. Ironically, when the tide of war turned, Cornwallis's troops and Lincoln would meet again—this time at Yorktown.

Countless blacks went over to the British camp during the Charlestown siege. Due to crowded conditions many contracted smallpox and typhus, also called putrid or camp fever, a dreadful disease spread by body lice. They were left to "die in the woods where they remained unburied with infants drawing the breasts of their deceased mothers."[3] When Charlestown fell the British captured 2,000 blacks and shipped them to the West Indies market, and British officers divided up the spoils of war: 300,000 pounds of sterling and great quantities of silver plate.

Sergeant Robert Chambers, of the Virginia Continental Line, was taken prisoner of war twice and was twice exchanged, once at the Battle of Germantown in 1777 and again at Charlestown. His pension application chronicles the Siege of Charlestown: "We began our march on the 3rd day of November 1779 and we reached Charleston the 7th of April 1780[. T]he Siege began the 13th of the same and on the 12th of May the Commandant General Lincoln surrendered by capitulation to the enemy by articles solemnly agreed to[. W]e were to receive rations as a British soldier on duty [and] we were to have the Barracks for our residence and the liberty of the town but instead of complying with these articles they confined us on board prison ships where our distressed situation was too great to be expressed."[4]

In mid–May Cornwallis was on his way to reinforce British soldiers and Loyalists at the outpost of Camden when he received intelligence that Colonel Abraham Buford's 17th Virginia Regiment was nearby. Cornwallis, traveling with his slow-moving army, ordered Lieutenant Colonel Banastre Tarleton and his swift-moving cavalry to hunt down and destroy Buford and his army. Buford, leading the only remnant of the Continental Army in the South, was on his way to assist Lincoln at Charlestown when he learned of Lincoln's surrender. Buford then held his position and awaited orders from General Isaac Huger. Remembering the April Battle of Moncks Corner, where Tarleton had defeated him, Huger ordered Buford to get out of Tarleton's way and retreat to Hillsborough, North Carolina. (A portrait of Tarleton, "whose name became synonymous with ruthlessness," shows a beguilingly beautiful face and a manly, muscular body clad in green tunic, buff britches, and cavalry boots. His flamboyant headdress with swan's feathers became known as the Tarleton Helmet. His mercantile, rather than land-owning, background might explain his social pretentiousness.[5] "Tarleton boasted of having butchered more men and lain with more women than anybody else in the army." Waving a hand with two missing fingers, he frequently shouted, "These gave I for King and Country!")[6]

On May 29, 1780, Tarleton caught up with the withdrawing Buford at Waxsaws, a piedmont region on the North Carolina-South Carolina border, and demanded his surrender. Buford refused, voicing a standard Revolutionary War reply: "Sir, I reject your proposals, and shall defend myself to the last extremity." Buford's infantry then held their fire too long against Tarleton's fast approaching cavalry. After firing only one volley, Buford's men were attacked by the slashing sabers of Tarleton's dragoons.

The exact sequence of the ensuing confrontation at the Battle of Waxhaws has long been controversial. Some accounts describe Buford's American soldiers flinging up a flag of truce and holding up their arms in surrender. Simultaneously, someone shot Tarleton's horse out from under him. Believing that their commander had been deceptively fired at by an enemy who was faking a flag of truce, Tarleton's men proceeded to slaughter Americans. True to Tarleton's "take no prisoners policy," they killed even those with hands held high, waving white flags in surrender, and begging for quarter—but they received no quarter. The merciless massacre of Buford's army at the Battle of Waxhaws earned Banastre Tarleton the monikers "Ban the Butcher" and "Bloody Ban Tarleton." These dreadful epithets would strike fear even into the hearts of the tough Overmountain men marching to Battle of Kings Mountain in October. The term "Tarleton Quarters," meaning no quarter at all, comes from Tarleton's cutting down Patriots who were surrendering under a white flags of truce at Waxhaws.

Tarleton's massacre of Buford's troops ended the Charlestown Campaign of 1780. There 13-year-old Andrew Jackson, a Scots-Irish future president of the United States who lived in Waxhaws, watched his mother, Elizabeth Hutchinson Jackson, nurse patriots who were wounded by Bloody Ban. Years later President "Old Hickory" Jackson recalled having seen Tarleton through child's eyes from 100 yards away. "I could have shot him," he said.[7] Instead Jackson was captured by Tarleton's henchman: "I was in one skirmish ... and there they caught me, along with my brother Robert.... A lieutenant of Tarleton's Light Dragoons tried to make me clean his boots and cut my arm with his saber when I refused. After that they kept me in Jail at Camden about two months, starved me nearly to death and gave me the small-pox."

While they were prisoners both Andrew and Robert contracted smallpox. Their widowed mother, Elizabeth, whose husband had died three weeks before their son Andrew was born, arranged for her sons' release on account of, said Jackson, "our extreme youth and illness.... When I left there (the prison) ... I was a skeleton not quite six feet long and a little over six inches thick!"[8] Robert died of smallpox. Elizabeth died of cholera while nursing soldiers. Before the Revolutionary War ended, Andrew Jackson was an orphan.

Escaping capture at Charlestown, several key partisan (guerrilla) groups maintained a Patriot military presence in the South. Their hit-and-run techniques kept the South Carolina state government alive. Partisans were local militia groups who frequently plowed by day and fought by night. These guerrillas annoyed and delayed Cornwallis's army by breaking enemy communications as well as their spirit. Partisan leaders Thomas "Gamecock" Sumter, Francis "Swamp Fox" Marion and Andrew "Wizard Owl" Pickens played key roles in the South during 1780 and 1781.

Back when guerrilla leader Thomas "Gamecock" Sumter, son of a Wales immigrant, was a teenager, he had palled around with future Virginia Indian agent Joseph Martin, and future North Carolina militia leader Benjamin Cleveland. They were a terrible threesome, gambling on cockfights and horse races. In May 1762 Sumter voyaged to London with Henry Timberlake and Cherokee chief Ostenaco Outacite ("Judd's Friend") to act as interpreter when the chief met the newly crowned George III. At the end of the French and Indian War Sumter was languishing in a Staunton, Virginia, debtor's prison when Joseph Martin came through town and gave him a tomahawk and 20 guineas, one or both of which helped him escape. Sumter became a surveyor and a successful country-store owner at Eutaw Springs on the Santee River. He was a veteran of the Snow Campaign, the Battle of Sullivan's Island and the Cherokee Expedition of 1776. Sumter married the widow Mary Jameson, a cripple eleven years his senior, and moved into her plantation home at Santee. Their son, Thomas Jr., was born when Mary was 45.

As soon as Sumter, retired from the military, heard that "Bloody Ban" Tarleton was coming their way, he put on his old uniform and rode out to battle. Tarleton dispatched a Tory captain to capture Sumter. Upon arriving at the Sumter plantation, the captain learned that Sumter was away from home. The captain then cruelly lifted the crippled Mary in her chair and made her watch the burning of her plantation home in May 1780. That's when Sumter stuck a fighting cock's feather into his hat and flew into the war full force. Like an iron-willed gamecock that never gave up, he earned his epithet "the fighting gamecock" by organizing South Carolina backcountry Patriots for guerrilla warfare.

In July 1780 Sumter set out to capture Captain Christian Huck. Lieutenant Colonel Francis Lord Rawdon, headquartered at Camden, had sent Huck to establish a British base at Rocky Mount. Huck's dragoons and Loyalist militia destroyed Patriot militia camps in Chester and York counties and abducted black American slaves. His foraging parties stole wheat, corn, cattle and horses to take back to Rocky Mount. Local Whig frontiersmen from the Catawba River and Broad River whose wheat fields had been destroyed and whose women had been violated formed a partisan militia brigade. They chose Colonel "Gamecock" Thomas Sumter as their commander.[9]

On July 11, 1780, Captain Huck's army tramped through the wheat fields of the Bratton plantation and burst into the home of Martha Robertson Bratton.[10] They were looking for her husband, Colonel William Bratton, who served in Sumter's brigade. One of the soldiers held a reaping hook to Martha's throat when she refused to reveal her husband's whereabouts. Half-choking, she defiantly hissed that she would stay true to his Patriot duty even if he perished in Sumter's army. Another Tory soldier intervened, grabbed the hook and saved Martha's life. Huck then forced her to cook dinner for his men. Resisting the impulse to poison the food, she put dinner on the table. The men then slept next door at Williamson's plantation while their horses grazed on Williamson's oat fields on the South Fork of Fishing Creek in present-day York County.

Finding Huck sleeping at Williamson's, Sumter's militia, including Colonel Bratton, sprang a surprise attack, killing Huck and 35 enemy soldiers. The fighting spilled over to the Bratton plantation house. Martha Bratton hid her young children in the fireplace to protect them from stray bullets. Afterward she cared for the wounded on both sides in her home. The Gamecock and his Patriots sustained only one casualty. Huck's Defeat—Sumter's backcountry militia victory—was one of the first Patriot successes after the fall of Charlestown and helped boost the morale of the people of South Carolina. After Huck's Defeat, Cornwallis dubbed Sumter his greatest plague. (Sumter was 97 when he died, outliving all other generals of the American Revolution.) Working under General Sumter's command were guerrilla militia leaders General William Davidson and Colonel William Richardson Davies of North Carolina and Colonel Elijah Clarke of Georgia.

Some time after Huck's Defeat, Martha Bratton again survived the wrath of the Tories. While her husband was again away from home fighting in Sumter's army, Martha took charge of the supply of gunpowder hidden on their North Carolina property. Knowing that the British were fast approaching to seize the powder, Martha didn't have time to move it. So she spread a path of powder a safe distance from where the bulk of the ammunition was stored. As the British drew near, she lit the path and it exploded. Hearing the explosion the Tories were angry when she told them she had destroyed the powder, but they did not kill her.

While Thomas Sumter was annoying the British in the upcountry (backcountry) west of the Santee, Francis "Swamp Fox" Marion covered the coastal area east of the Santee. Shortly before Clinton captured Charlestown, Marion had jumped out of a two-story window there and broke his ankle. He was carried from the city to recuperate in the country, hence he was not present in the city when Charlestown fell to the British. The diminutive and crafty Marion, a lieutenant colonel in the Continental Army, then organized a band of militia partisans known as "Marion's Brigade" to engage in guerrilla warfare against the British invaders. He annoyed the enemy throughout the low country of the Carolinas. "As for this damned old fox, the devil himself could not catch him," exclaimed Tarleton after pursuing Marion through the swamps for several hours and then giving up the chase. Thus, Francis Marion became known as the "Swamp Fox."[11]

The grandson of Huguenot (French Protestant) immigrants, the elusive Francis Marion and his faithful black servant Oscar sometimes hid in the Great White Marsh of North Carolina or in the Little Pee Dee Swamp of South Carolina. Combing the woods and wetlands along the Pee Dee and Santee rivers, they attracted partisan troops to join their band of guerrillas. Marion established a base in the swamp, and by directing hit-and-run attacks he effectively intercepted dispatches, interrupted communications, and cut off British supply lines in the South.

In October 1780 Governor John Rutledge, South Carolina's first governor under the new state's constitution, would commission both guerrilla leaders, Francis Marion and Thomas Sumter, as brigadier generals of the South Carolina militia. Marion became a folk hero as well as namesake for several towns and countless children. After the war, Francis "Swamp Fox" Marion advocated leniency towards Loyalists. (Probably because he was practically penniless after the war, Marion, age 54, married a wealthy shrew—his ill-tempered, 49-year-old cousin Mary Esther Videau. It was the first marriage for both, and marriage did not improve her temper. Rumor has it that whenever he rode up to their home Marion threw his hat through an open window. If it came sailing back, he rode on.)

Following the Siege of Charlestown, South Carolinians were subdued and Georgians were overrun by the British. But the partisan spirit of Marion and Sumter of South Carolina and Elijah Clarke of Georgia was unconquerable. Mercy Warren wrote that Clinton vainly flattered himself that he had conquered one wealthy colony. So he returned to New York and left Cornwallis in charge of the Southern Department. Cornwallis "turned his attention to the commercial regulations and the civil government of the newly conquered province."[12] He maintained his stronghold at Charlestown, but partisan bands made the British position in outlying South Carolina tenuous. Cornwallis immediately detached a strong force under Rawdon to subjugate and guard the frontiers. Rawdon urged the country to submit to royal authority, but many paroled soldiers who had been captured at Charlestown decamped from the British and joined Sumter on the borders of the Carolinas. Within two months of the subjugation of Charlestown, the opposition in the South stabilized.

Aside from his walleye, corpulence and rolling gait, Lieutenant General Lord Cornwallis exuded composure, elegance and an "air of authority." The most aristocratic of the British commanders in America, he was unpretentious and averse to pomp and fanfare. He disliked the war in America, voted against the Stamp Act, and eschewed the Declaratory Act, which allowed Parliament absolute authority over America. But he put personal preferences aside. Above all, he was a top-notch general who was committed to the king and did his job well. Known for his personal austerity and integrity, Lord Cornwallis had resigned his command and rushed home in December 1778 to the bedside of his dying wife. Afterward he resumed his command in America. He never remarried and was never rumored to have a love affair. He devoted his life to professional military service and traveled with his unit of the 32nd Regiment throughout his career, often equipping his men at his own expense. Although "Cornwallis' army was notorious for its bad behavior," instead of punishing his officers and men for their plundering and crimes against both men and women, he indulged them in order to maintain good will and unity. Despite his humane image, two of his favorite officers, Banastre Tarleton and Lord Francis Rawdon, "were advocates of brutal repression." Like Tarleton, Rawdon condoned butchery and rape.[13]

Taking command of 8,000 British forces in the South, Cornwallis, Lieutenant Colonel Banastre Tarleton and Major Patrick Ferguson set out to recruit southern Loyalists. The dashing cavalryman Tarleton was a brutal officer who outraged women and offered no quarter. Ferguson, on the contrary, was a courteous, affable and fearless soldier as well as the best pistol and rifle marksman in the British army.[14] Marching with Tarleton and his 2,500 notorious Green Dragoons, Cornwallis personally covered the coastal region from the northeast side of the Santee to the village of Camden. Major Patrick Ferguson was promoted to brevet lieutenant colonel and assigned to cover the Piedmont and the western frontier.

The Patriots at Ramsour's Mill wedged the first major crack in Cornwallis's confidence as he swept through coastal Carolina. His plan to push into North Carolina when the weather turned cool was foiled by one of his own men.

Contrary to orders, the impulsive Lt. Colonel John Moore mustered 1,300 Loyalist militiamen at Ramsour's Mill.[15] There, in Lincoln County, North Carolina (a division of Old Tryon County), Moore organized and drilled militiamen in preparation for joining Cornwallis's anticipated march north from South Carolina. Cornwallis had specifically ordered Moore not to fight but to wait for backup. Moore was to gather provisions and harvest corn to feed the king's forces that would arrive in the area in September. He was not supposed to assemble and train troops. When General Griffith Rutherford heard that Loyalists were congregating at Ramsour's Mill, he sent Colonel Francis Lock to raise Patriot militiamen from Rowan, Burke and Lincoln counties to rout Moore and his Loyalists.

In mid–June 1780, when the two militia armies of small farmers clashed, both sides were dressed in civilian clothing. The Loyalists stuck green twigs in their hats to distinguish themselves from the Patriots, who wore white slips of paper tucked under their hatbands. Exchanging fire in a fight that ended in hand-to-hand combat, they clubbed one another with muskets, making green twigs and white tags swirl like June bugs on a hot day. There is no official record of losses. Lock's Patriots, however, defeated Moore's Loyalists, the King's Friends, at Ramsour's Mill. This Patriot victory put a small but effective damper on the booming British campaign in the Carolinas. Moore was "threatened with court martial for disobedience of orders in raising the Loyalists at Ramsour's Mill before the time appointed by Lord Cornwallis, but it was at length deemed impolitic to bring him to trial."[16]

After the British captured Charlestown, General Washington replaced the defeated Benjamin Lincoln, who remained a prisoner of war until he could be exchanged for a British officer. Lincoln's successor, General Horatio Gates, was the same Gates who had received undue credit for the Patriot victory at Saratoga, credit that rightfully belonged to Benedict Arnold and Daniel Morgan. Gates took command of the Continental Army in the South in July 1780. In the wake of the Siege of Charlestown, his command numbered only 1,200 ill-equipped American regulars severely debilitated from hunger, plus an unknown number of militia.

Gates increased the numbers in his Southern Department before he led the Continental Line regulars and untrained colonial militia in an attempt to track down and crush Cornwallis. Meanwhile, Cornwallis moved his army inland from Charlestown to reinforce British and Loyalists at Camden, 35 miles northeast of Columbia, South Carolina. Cornwallis's 2,000 troops comprising 800 British regulars and 1,200 Loyalists soon were outnumbered by Gates' army of 3,100. Gates' American forces included 1,400 Continental soldiers, mainly from Maryland and Delaware,[17] plus the remnant of Lincoln's Southern Army and 1,700 militiamen from Virginia and North Carolina.

One of Gates' many mistakes occurred when, against well-informed advice, he took his starving Patriot army from Hillsborough, North Carolina, to Camden, South Carolina, not by the friendly route through Salisbury and Charlotte, the hornet's nest of Patriot support, but by a shorter, though treacherous, route. He marched through forage-depleted wilderness and swamp and belligerent enemy territory flooded with Loyalist banditti. He pushed his underfed men to march 18 hours a day, feeding them an inadequate ration of molasses, cornmeal and under-cooked meat that caused dysentery in a great number of his troops.

13. Charlestown Campaign, Camden Battle and Fishing Creek

In the August 16, 1780, battle at the British stronghold of Camden between the opposing armies Gates made still another error. He mobilized American militia riflemen who were accustomed to fighting Indian style, shooting from behind rock and tree, and placed them face to face with bayonet-carrying British regulars who were trained to fight toe to toe. The American militia fled. Cornwallis then surrounded and decimated the Continentals. British losses numbered 324; American losses were 2,000—two-thirds of Gates' total command. Mortally wounded was Johann DeKalb, a Bavarian-born peasant who earned his military commission and title of "baron" in the French army and was commanding the American Continentals.

Horatio Gates led the retreat of his surviving army on the fastest horse in the country, traveling 70 miles from Camden to Charlotte before resting. The terror-stricken Gates raced on horseback 180 miles before reporting his defeat to Congress and thus became the laughingstock of Washington's staff. "He ran away from his whole army," chuckled Alexander Hamilton.[18] The disastrous debacle at the Battle of Camden ruined the career of the inept Gates, and the Continental Congress authorized Washington to replace him.

The Camden fiasco was one of the worst whippings ever inflicted upon an American army. General Griffith Rutherford, who fought bravely under Gates at Camden, was shot in the leg, stabbed in the head by a saber and taken prisoner by Cornwallis. He was exchanged the following summer. Colonel Charles McDowell succeeded Rutherford as the militia leader of western North Carolina. The remnants of the Patriot army, the few survivors of the Battle of Camden, rendezvoused at Charlotte Town, a small community of 20 houses, where officers divided them into units. The troops then began their long march to Salisbury, the oldest town in western North Carolina, carrying the wounded on litters, wagons and horseback. Three hundred allied Catawba Indians accompanied the dispirited Americans.

A Catawba warrior named General New River led Catawba women and children into exile with a neighboring Virginia tribe before Cornwallis's excited troops rampaged into their reservation after the victory at Camden. General New River and his wife, Sally New River, returned home to find villages destroyed and livestock devoured. General New River then served with other Catawba warriors under Colonel William R. Davie, leader of one of General Sumter's guerrilla forces. Sally New River, the shrewd, bilingual and beautiful queen of the Catawbas, was born to a white trader and a Catawba woman whose father was the famous Catawba chief King Haigler. There are myriad myths to demonstrate Sally New River's remarkable wisdom. Her husband, aided by her charm and wit, became a Catawba chief. He had appointed himself General New River after winning tribal acclaim for killing a Shawnee chief and refused to be called by any other name.

Another fabled idol of the Camden battle was Peter Francisco, the "Giant of Virginia." Often exaggerated, and sometimes true, stories about this giant were once as well known as those of Daniel Boone or Davy Crockett. This "Hercules of the Revolution" fought in almost all major Revolutionary War battles. A commemorative U.S. stamp bears the caption "Peter Francisco Fighter Extraordinary" and shows his legendary feat of shouldering an eleven-hundred–pound cannon at the Battle of Camden.

Among the 800 wounded Americans that Cornwallis took prisoner when he defeated Gates at the Battle of Camden was militiaman Nicholas C. Christenbury of Mecklenburg County. While Christenbury was in captivity, his wife, Anne, stated that she found it "exceedingly inconvenient to ... pay Her Taxes for the present Year together with the charge of Five small Children," and she was granted the requested tax relief. Her husband was later released and returned home.[19]

Two days after General Horatio Gates' disastrous defeat at Camden, Thomas "Gamecock" Sumter and his army were camping at Fishing Creek. This is their story. Before his defeat, and confident that he would win, Gates had issued orders to guerrilla leaders to block all paths to and from Camden. He sent Francis "Swamp Fox" Marion to destroy boats, block the waterway, and prevent the British from floating downriver and escaping after the Camden battle. He ordered Thomas "Carolina Gamecock" Sumter to barricade the road from Charlestown and intercept Cornwallis's reinforcements on their way to Camden before the battle. He was to maintain that roadblock after the battle to stop what Gates mistakenly considered the soon-to-be-conquered British soldiers from fleeing Camden and seeking refuge in Charlestown.

Before the battle Sumter captured 300 British soldiers and 40 loaded supply wagons that were making their way to replenish General Cornwallis's camp at Camden. Sumter was still guarding his prisoners and the Charlestown Road when he learned that Gates had suffered catastrophic defeat. Knowing that triumphant and exuberant British soldiers would pour out of Camden and trample him, Sumter moved his army and prisoners out of the way. After two days of hasty retreat, en route to Charlotte Sumter and his weary band tethered their tired horses and encamped on the banks of Fishing Creek, 30 miles northwest of Camden.

As the exhausted Sumter sat beside Fishing Creek under the hot August sun in the shade of a wagon, he was half finished shaving when he abruptly stopped. Looming on the horizon were Banastre Tarleton's 160 fast-approaching British dragoons. "Bloody Ban" easily won the ensuing August 18 Battle of Fishing Creek. Sumter's surprised men dispersed so quickly that some—including the Gamecock himself—cut horses loose and rode bareback through the thicket while others fled on foot. Taking Sumter completely by surprise, Tarleton killed 150 Patriots, captured 300, and freed 100 British prisoners. Only 16 British were killed. The Tories declared Tarleton a national hero. After Sumter's defeat by Tarleton at Fishing Creek, Marion's Brigade became the major partisan force fighting the British. Sumter escaped and soon rallied another large guerrilla force.

14

Militiamen Cross the Blue Ridge and Face Ferguson in Tryon County

Overmountain North Carolina militia colonel Isaac Shelby said that following the fall of Charlestown in May 1780, the annihilation of Gates' army at Camden, and the defeat of Sumter at Fishing Creek in August, the southern states were all but crushed. Militia units throughout the country were forced to flee the enemy.

One such refugee was militia captain Richard Richardson, husband of Dorcas Richardson. The British took Richard prisoner during the Siege of Charlestown and incarcerated him at a military station on Johns Island just south of the port city of Charlestown. Richardson escaped. Fleeing the British, who offered a bounty for his arrest, he returned to his plantation home on the Santee River near the confluence of the Congaree and Wateree. There he hid out in the dense woods and dark thickets of the Santee Swamp. The low rise in the swamp where he camped out was known to the locals as Johns Island.

By this time, "Bloody Ban" Tarleton had turned Richardson's plantation into a station for a regiment of British cavalry and restricted Dorcas and her children to a small area of the house. Although the provisions came from her own plantation, she and her children were allowed barely enough food to survive. However, she managed to smuggle a small portion of daily rations, by way of a faithful servant, to her husband in the swamp. At times she personally delivered the food, taking her small daughter with her. One day a Tory officer asked the child if she had seen her father recently. When the little girl answered that she had, her mother grew pale but kept silent. In answer to the officer's next question of where she had seen him the youngster answered, "On Johns Island." Her mother's apprehension mounted. But the officer, knowing that it was unlikely that the child had traveled as far south as the military prison on Johns Island near Charlestown, decided that the child was dreaming. Mrs. Richardson relaxed when he said, "Pshaw, that was a long time ago." During the time they were occupying her home, Tarleton's soldiers often tried to intimidate Dorcas. Showing her their swords dripping with blood from her slaughtered cattle, they told her they would do worse to her husband when they found him.

Richard Richardson managed to leave the swamp and join the forces of guerrilla general Francis Marion. There he resisted appeals of the British to pledge an oath of allegiance, receive pardon and join the British Army. When peace came and Richardson, now promoted to colonel, returned to his plantation, its mansion and buildings were still standing. But everything movable had been plundered or destroyed. In much-reduced circumstances but enjoying tranquility with his heroically devoted Dorcas, "he cheerfully resumed the occupations of a planter."[1]

After the fall of Charlestown, when Major (brevet colonel) Ferguson's victorious British began moving northward through the Carolina frontier, the Patriot militia mobilized. Colonel Charles McDowell was the overall commander of the militia of western North Carolina, part of which was overmountain Tennessee Country. McDowell's overmountain militia, though separated from his piedmont command by high mountains and dense forests, empathized with and aided their fellow Patriots on the east side of the Blue Ridge in what was once Tryon County.

Tryon County was at one time a refuge for pioneers fleeing war-torn Pennsylvania after Pontiac's War; they rolled their covered wagons down the Carolina Road and rumbled west toward the relative safety of the foothills. Before these settlers began cutting trees, building cabins and planting corn in piedmont Carolina, these red clay foothills of the Blue Ridge were a common hunting ground between two Indian nations, the Catawba and the Cherokee. The Broad River defined the boundary between the two.

In 1760 and 1762 the peace-loving Catawba Nation negotiated treaties with the Crown governors of both Carolinas to establish the 15-square mile Catawba Reservation covering both sides of the Catawba River. In 1767 North Carolina governor William Tryon negotiated with the war-loving Cherokee to draw a boundary line to separate settlers from Cherokee hunting grounds and keep Indians away from settlements. Tryon's Line began at today's Greenville, South Carolina, and then shot in a straight path from Tryon Mountain, North Carolina, to Fort Chiswell (near present-day Wytheville), Virginia.

Two years later Tryon lopped his namesake county off the western part of Mecklenburg County. He described his county as "a tract of forty five miles in breadth due north and south and eighty miles due east and west." It was 80 miles from the Catawba River to the "western frontier line which was run last year between the Cherokee hunting grounds and this province."[2] Tryon County then became North Carolina's western frontier. The Iroquoian-speaking Cherokee towns lay in the Blue Ridge Mountains west of Tryon County. The Siouan-speaking Catawba bordered Tryon County on the east.

From 1769 until 1772 Tryon County, North Carolina, covered all or parts of 14 present-day Carolina counties. In 1772 the original Tryon County became "Old Tryon County" when a survey divided the two Carolinas. The new line renamed the area now covered by seven of the 14 counties of the original Tryon County and assigned them to

Old Tryon County (courtesy of Miles Philbeck, editor, Bulletin of the Genealogical Society Old Tryon County).

South Carolina. The territory covered by the remaining seven counties, those in North Carolina, retained the name Tryon County.

In 1779, the Whig (Patriot) North Carolina General Assembly abolished Tryon County, erasing the name of the former royal governor. The assembly renamed and divided Tryon County into two counties: Lincoln to the east and Rutherford to the west. Rutherford then joined Burke County, North Carolina, on the north and the future Spartanburg, South Carolina, on the south. When the governments of Lincoln and Rutherford counties were organized, Patriots accepted the name change. But Tories, like Ferguson, and Loyalists (Tories living in America) refused to recognize the authority of the rebel provincial Congress and persisted in calling the area "Tryon County."

The western frontier of Carolina during the Revolutionary War comprised Old Tryon County, Burke County and overmountain Washington and Sullivan counties in Tennessee Country, where the Watauganss lived. Many Watauganss had fled Tryon's royal government during the Regulator Movement of 1766–1771. Located on the border of the Cherokee Nation, these frontier counties were linked politically, geographically and culturally. They worked together to repulse British incursion into western North Carolina. Except for an occasional Indian raid and the British-instigated Cherokee War of 1776, settlers of the Carolina frontier were not much affected by the Revolutionary War until Charlestown fell to the British in May 1780. Having won Charlestown, Cornwallis assigned Tarleton to subdue the coastal Carolinas as far west as Camden. There he would recruit soldiers for his army and obtain pledges of allegiance to the Crown. Cornwallis marched with Tarleton and put Ferguson in command of the western flank of the British Army on the southern frontier.

Ferguson swelled his army by recruiting Loyalists in the upcountry. His watch covered more than 100 miles from the Wateree River to the Saluda. Establishing headquarters in the village of Ninety Six, Ferguson worked with Scovilite captain Robert Cunningham, the Loyalist leader of the district of Ninety Six on the southwestern fringe of Tryon County, North Carolina. Ninety Six, 60 miles south of today's Greenville, South Carolina, was a frontier outpost mistakenly believed to be 96 miles (but actually more like 75 miles) from the important Cherokee Indian trading village of Keowee in the foothills of the Blue Ridge Mountains. At Ninety Six, traders from Charlestown exchanged firearms and beads for fur and pelts brought from Keowee by Indians traveling over the ancient trail known as the Cherokee Path.

Ferguson, with a provincial militia corps of 200 men, fortified Ninety Six—a dozen houses, a courthouse, and a jail—and turned it into a British fort. At Fort Ninety Six he imprisoned Patriots, recruited and organized a Loyalist militia and attempted to restore British rule to the upcountry. Leaving Ninety Six, Ferguson proceeded 16 miles north and confiscated the plantation of Colonel James Williams, a veteran of the 1755 Snow Campaign and the 1776 Cherokee Expedition. There Ferguson made camp on the Little River, a tributary of the Saluda.

A likable and personable man, Ferguson mingled easily with the people and exacted many oaths of allegiance to the king. He recruited and drilled Loyalists for the king's army. "No one could have been better qualified" for the job than the distinguished Ferguson. A born commander, he was experienced in war and military discipline. His personal magnetism influenced many people of upcountry South Carolina to fully recognize British authority.[3] Ferguson promised, "We come not to make war on women and children but to relieve their distress."[4] Loyalists under the leadership of the Cunningham brothers flocked to his camp and his army increased.

From his camp at Williams' plantation, Ferguson moved into the Fair Forest Settlement in Spartanburg County in northwestern South Carolina. Still recruiting and training Loyalists, he turned his horses loose to graze and trample grain fields and sent out foraging parties to slaughter Patriots' cattle to feed his army. Ferguson attracted Loyalists at least as far north as the newly formed Rutherford County, North Carolina, which he still called Tryon County. Typical of the unwavering Loyalists who joined his campaign was Rutherford County judge Jonas Bedford. In his "memorial," the British government equivalent of what was called a "pension application" by the U.S. government, Bedford declared, "I have been sworn as an Officer and Magistrate under my lawful Sovereign. I never will turn my back to my King's cause and perjure myself. I shall remain a loyal Honest Subject during my Life to my King and Country."

Colonel McDowell of Quaker Meadows (Morganton, North Carolina), the overall commander of the Patriot militia in western North Carolina, was the Patriot counterpart of the Tory Scottish Highlander Patrick Ferguson. Mustering the frontier militia to face Ferguson, McDowell established his main camp on a tributary of the Tyger River called Fair Forest Creek in the Ninety Six District of South Carolina (present-day Spartanburg County). Three consecutive night fights between Ferguson's Loyalists and McDowell's Patriots camping at Cedar Spring occurred near the site of a cedar tree for which Cedar Spring was named. The lovely spring, two miles east of Fair Forest Creek, was 50 feet in circumference and three feet deep and bubbled up from three fountain sources.

In the first night confrontation, the First Battle of Cedar Spring, Ferguson's Loyalists attacked a small detachment of Patriots commanded by Colonel John Thomas, Jr., who was encamped at Cedar Spring. The heroine of this battle was Colonel Thomas's mother, Jane Thomas, whose home was in the Fair Forest Settlement. Jane rode on horseback 65 miles to visit her husband, who was imprisoned by Ferguson at Ninety Six. While there she overheard a conversation between Loyalist women: The Tories intended to surprise the Rebels at Cedar Spring the next night. Jane galloped back home to warn her son, Colonel Thomas, of an imminent enemy attack. The Thomas group stayed wide awake, awaiting the Tory attack. Thus, by light of campfire, his Whigs—warned by Jane Thomas—repulsed the Tories.

Two more minor Fair Forest night fights ensued. The Patriots won all three. News of these encounters prompted Ferguson to hasten his move to join his advance detachment in the Fair Forest area. Ferguson's advance northward convinced Colonel McDowell that he intended to invade North Carolina.

Militia commander Colonel Charles McDowell watched apprehensively as Ferguson moved northward from South Carolina. Having been decimated at Charlestown, the Continental Army in the South was practically nonexistent. Only scattered groups of militia remained to stop Ferguson. Leading 3,000 Loyalists,[5] Ferguson was now near the North Carolina border. To defend the western frontier of the Carolinas, McDowell gathered as many Patriots as he could find in the sparsely inhabited settlements of Old Tryon County. He also dispatched a messenger to rally overmountain North Carolina (Tennessee) militia colonels under his command. The messenger alerted Isaac Shelby from Sullivan County (the Holston and Carters Valley settlements) and John Sevier of Washington County (the

14. Militiamen Cross the Blue Ridge and Face Ferguson in Tryon County

Watauga-Nolichucky settlements) to the alarming news of Ferguson's advance toward the Blue Ridge. McDowell ordered Shelby and Sevier to begin mustering overmountain militiamen immediately.

Isaac Shelby, a veteran of Dunmore's War, was surveying in Kentucky when he received McDowell's summons. Returning to the Holston Valley he led 200 Sullivan County militiamen southeastward across the Blue Ridge range of the Appalachians to join forces with McDowell, who had moved his camp to Cherokee Ford, a strategic crossing on the Broad River. The Broad was the next river west of the Catawba River.

John Sevier held back part of his Watauga regiment to assist him in guarding the frontier. (Widower John Sevier would marry Catherine Sherrill, "Bonnie Kate," in August 1780, making her the stepmother of his ten young children and the future mother of eight more.) Under the leadership of his second in command, Major Charles Robertson, a former Regulator, he sent 200 Washington County, North Carolina, militiamen to join McDowell. Sevier and Robertson often alternated leading Wataugans over the Blue Ridge; while one crossed the mountain, the other guarded the home front.

Patriot Colonel Shelby and Major Robertson and their militia under the overall command of Colonel McDowell gathered at Cherokee Ford, where they were joined by Colonel Andrew Hampton and his Rutherford County militia. Georgia militia colonel Elijah Clarke, who was tough enough to survive both smallpox and mumps during the war, found it risky to remain at Augusta on the border of British-controlled Georgia. He moved his Patriot comrades to South Carolina, where they joined "Fighting Gamecock" Sumter on the Catawba.

All summer long militia Colonels Sumter and McDowell worked together to stop Ferguson. At Pacolet River near Spartanburg McDowell, Shelby, Robertson and Clarke continued to block the advance of the British. In late July 1780 McDowell detached 600 light cavalrymen guided by Shelby to track and attack Ferguson's Loyalist troops at Thicketty Fort. Colonel Isaac Shelby's "Gallant Six Hundred" militia was made up of mounted riflemen, including Colonel Shelby's overmountain men from Sullivan County, North Carolina; Colonel Sevier's overmountain volunteers from Washington County, North Carolina, led by Major Robertson; Colonel Andrew Hampton's militia from Rutherford County in Old Tryon County; and Colonel Elijah Clarke's militia from Georgia. Thicketty Fort, originally called Fort Anderson, was an outpost situated on Thicketty Creek, a tributary of the Broad River.

On July 30 Shelby's Gallant 600 galloped to Thicketty Fort, located 10 miles from Cowpens and held by a Loyalist garrison. It was 20 miles from McDowell's main camp. Shelby sent a captain to surprise the fort's garrison commander. Carrying a flag, the captain approached the fort and demanded its surrender. Shelby's 600 then captured Thicketty Fort without firing a shot. Shelby's men returned to McDowell's camp loaded with the spoils of conquest: one British sergeant major, 93 Loyalists, 250 firearms loaded with bullets and buckshot, and other munitions of war.[6]

The spoils of war from Thicketty Fort were significant since the British used the fort as a base for plundering the countryside, stealing clothing, bread, meat, salt and even the bed covers of settlers. Before Shelby's 600 arrived, Miss Jane McJunkin defended her rights by chasing and attacking a Tory from Thicketty Fort who was carrying off her quilt. Their struggle caused the man to slip on mud in her yard. Jane then snatched back her quilt while the thief's Loyalist companions laughed to see him bested by a Whig girl. Soon afterward, on a nearby farm, Miss Nancy Jackson kicked a Tory down the stairs as he descended with an armload of loot. But tough as she was, Nancy fled when he threatened to get even by sending Hessian soldiers to her house the next day.

In early August, shortly after Shelby's 600 captured Thicketty Fort, McDowell's Patriot militia numbered 1,000 compared to Ferguson's 1,500 Loyalists. As Ferguson advanced, recruiting more Loyalists, his command swelled to 2,000, with an additional small squadron of horse. Ferguson pitched his main camp a few miles south of Wofford's Iron Works near Cedar Spring in the Fair Forest section of present-day Spartanburg.

McDowell and his army encamped 25 miles above Cedar Spring at Cherokee Ford. He detached Colonels Shelby, Clarke, Joseph McDowell, and William Graham with 600 cavalry to keep an eye on Ferguson's camp. They were to cut off as many of his foraging parties as possible.

At Wofford's Iron Works, in the Second Battle of Cedar Spring, in the dim light of dawn on August 1 Ferguson's foraging party of 600 Loyalists confronted the Shelby-Clarke detachment of 600 Patriots. The sharp conflict lasted half an hour. Clarke was nicked by a saber cut across his neck. When "Ferguson came up with his whole force ... the Americans withdrew, carrying off the field of battle twenty prisoners, with two British officers.... The American loss was ten or twelve killed and wounded."[7] Shelby recalled that the Americans killed twice that number of Tories and took 50 prisoners. Clarke was captured but freed 10 days later.

A diversion occurred at Hanging Rock when Cornwallis moved out of South Carolina and sent Ferguson throughout western Carolina to recruit Loyalists to rendezvous with him at Charlotte. Cornwallis left 25-year-old Lord Francis Rawdon in command of the backcountry. Rawdon, who was as young and brutal as Tarleton, reinforced the strategic British post at Hanging Rock, a boulder overhanging a creek in South Carolina on the road to Charlotte in Mecklenburg County, North Carolina. Rawdon said, "My object ... was to retard the progress of Gates till Lord Cornwallis should collect force from other parts of the Province."[8] At Hanging Rock, Rawdon's garrison would face Sumter's partisans.

Major William Richardson Davie commanded Sumter's guerrilla unit of mounted militia from Mecklenburg County. Davie, future father of the University of North Carolina and Andrew Jackson's boyhood hero, worked under Generals Sumter and William Davidson. A number of pubescent boys participated in the Battle of Hanging Rock. Andrew Jackson's 16-year-old brother was there, and so was 13-year-old Andrew, running errands and delivering messages for Davie, whom he greatly admired and respected. Recalling the battle, Andrew Jackson, future Indian fighter and president of the United States, said that his own personal style was modeled after William Richardson Davie.

On July 30 Davie led 40 dragoons (mounted soldiers armed with short sabers) and 40 mounted rifleman in a successful preliminary run on the Tory garrison's houses near Hanging Rock Fort. They took 60 horses and 100 stand of arms. The larger, four-hour battle occurred on August 6 (partway through the struggle Sumter's men looted enemy camps and drank too much rum). There were serious losses on both sides. It was not a complete American victory but it gave the Patriots hope.

A week earlier eighteen-year-old Esther Gaston had nursed the wounded following Sumter's unsuccessful guerrilla attack on the British base at the Battle of Rocky Mount. Now, she and her sister Martha mounted horses and rode to the Waxhaw Presbyterian

14. Militiamen Cross the Blue Ridge and Face Ferguson in Tryon County 179

Church, which served as a hospital for the wounded soldiers from the Battle of Hanging Rock. Working there as nurses, the sisters tended their younger brother and a cousin. This is the same log church where Andrew Jackson was baptized and in whose graveyard Jackson's mother, Elizabeth, as well as General William Davie are buried.

Describing the Hanging Rock battle, General Thomas "Gamecock" Sumter wrote, "We have got a great victory; but it will scarcely ever be heard of, as we are only a handful of raw militia; but if we had been commanded by a continental officer, it would have been sounded loud to our honor."[9]

One of the Loyalists who fought against Sumter's rebels in the backcountry was Beaks Musgrove, under the leadership of Robert Cunningham and Colonel Ferguson. One day Beaks dropped by his home at Musgrove Mill near Spartanburg for a quick change of clothes. Leaning his sword beside the doorpost, he found his pretty sister Mary standing at the hearth and stirring stew over the open fire. Unexpectedly, Patrick "Paddy" Carr—a Patriot captain who served under Colonel Elijah Clarke of Georgia and was searching for Beaks—burst through the cabin door. Grabbing Beaks' sword from beside the door, Paddy thrust it toward him and demanded, "Are you Beaks Musgrove?" "I am sir," replied Beaks. Mary Musgrove, aware of the drawn sword, feared for her brother's life. Throwing herself between the sword point and her brother, she asked, "Are you Paddy Carr?" The intruder replied, "I am." Mary said, "I am Mary Musgrove, Mr. Carr, and you must not kill my brother." Mary was happy when her brother pledged to join the Patriots and thereby save his life, but in his heart he was still a Tory.[10] The Musgrove home, land and gristmill soon became the site of a British encampment. On that battlefield site today stands a monument to Mary Musgrove.

At the time Sumter's guerrillas were attacking the British at Hanging Rock, McDowell took advantage of the diversion and attacked the British at Musgrove Mill. McDowell, who changed campsites frequently, was based at Smith Ford on the Broad River when he heard that only 500 Tories remained on guard 40 miles away at Musgrove Mill. McDowell sent Colonels Elijah Clarke and Isaac Shelby with parties of 200 mounted men each to surprise the sparsely guarded post there (McDowell, an armchair commander, preferred to send rather than to lead men into battle).[11]

South Carolina's Colonel James Williams, commanding 200 men, joined Clarke and Shelby. The joint force, known as Shelby's 600, set out in the cool of the night when travel was easier for horses and darkness kept the movement of men secret. They hoped to intercept Ferguson's treasure-filled military chest along the way. Riding at a gallop without a single stop, the nightriders crossed Gilkey and Thicketty creeks and the Pacolet River. Stealthily they passed within three miles of Ferguson's main camp at Fairforest Shoal and cautiously advanced another 12 miles to within a mile of Musgrove Mill and sent out scouts to observe the enemy camp. At daybreak the Patriot scouts exchanged rifle fire with a patrol party from Musgrove Mill. The Tories and Loyalists retreated. At that moment a neighboring farmer alerted the Patriots that the enemy had been reinforced during the night with several hundred British Regulars.

The Shelby-Clarke-Williams detachment—Shelby's 600—was now trapped between Ferguson's main camp on one side and his reinforced Musgrove Mill garrison on the other side. Having no choice but to fight, the 600 Patriots quickly tethered their horses and improvised a breastwork of logs and brush. It stretched in a semicircle across the road 300 yards in length. Shelby commanded the right, Clarke the left, and Williams the center. Twenty horsemen were on each flank. Captain Shadrack Inman, at his own suggestion, sallied forth with 25 mounted men to tempt the enemy. Like matadors, Inman's men advanced and retreated, luring the bayonet-wielding Tory infantry into following them toward the concealed Patriots crouched behind the breastwork. The ploy worked splendidly. Marching to the beat of the drum and the call of the bugle and shouting "Huzza for King George!" the Loyalists opened heavy fire, overshooting the barricade and their hidden opponents.[12] The Whig men, as was customary in those days, held their fire until they could see the whites of the enemy's eyes or count the buttons on their coats. Then, springing from behind the barricade, the frontier riflemen, whooping and yipping Indian yells, rushed the enemy. The surprise attack won a Patriot victory at the Battle of Musgrove Mill on August 18, 1780. Coming after a series of British victories, this stunning success was a needed and timely triumph for American Patriots.

The main fight of The Battle of Musgrove Mill was at the breastwork. It "lasted only 15 minutes when the enemy were obliged to retreat, and were pursued two miles." This was a short but bloody battle, fought amid thick smoke with small arms alone. The iconic Shelby, who had fought in Dunmore's War and would lead the Overmountain Men to the Battle of Kings Mountain, later described it as "the hardest and best fought action he ever was in." He attributed its success to the courage and persistence of "the great number of (militia) officers who were with him as volunteers."[13] Inman, who had lured the enemy into the trap, was among the six or seven Americans killed. The number of the enemy killed and wounded was larger. Two hundred British regulars were take prisoners.

The Patriots were ready to push on toward Ninety Six when McDowell forwarded an express message from North Carolina governor Caswell informing them of the defeat of the American army under Gates at Camden. The message advised McDowell to get out of the way of the victorious enemy, who likely would attempt to cut up the small corps of the American army. McDowell temporarily disbanded his force, and he and Shelby headed north toward the mountains.

On the 29th of August 1780, Cornwallis hovered around Charlotte, North Carolina, the "hornet's nest" of rebel resistance. From there he sent a message to Henry Clinton in New York: "Ferguson is to move into Tryon County with some militia."[14] Ferguson—hot on the heels of McDowell, Shelby and Clarke—moved into North Carolina, and his detachments spread out. Plundering whatever they needed for food or fancy, they searched for Whig leaders and administered the oath of loyalty to the Crown.

One of Ferguson's marauding parties of 23 soldiers approached Grahams Fort, a large, weather boarded log house in what is now Cleveland County, North Carolina, near Kings Mountain. It was a place of refuge for older people, women and children, accompanied by three men bearing arms: the vigilant Colonel Graham; another fearless man; and a brave 19-year-old youth named William Twitty. It was the strongest house in the neighborhood but not strong enough to defend against the Tory raiders demanding surrender and firing volleys. One Tory, John Burke, stuck his gun between the logs of the cabin wall and aimed at young William, but Susan Twitty, William's fearless sister, yanked her brother out of harm's way just in time. The bullet penetrated the opposite wall. Looking out the window and seeing the Tory reload his musket, 17-year-old Susan cried, "Brother William, now's your chance—shoot the rascal." Twitty's rifle cracked and Burke lay dead. Susan dashed out the door amid a shower of bullets and brought back the Tory's gun and ammunition as trophies. The Tories soon retreated.[15]

Other Tory foraging parties including Colonel Patrick Ferguson himself penetrated into extreme western Burke County (now McDowell) to the very foot of the Blue Ridge. Ferguson was not only marauding but he was also searching for notable Whig leaders, including Captains Thomas Hemphill and Thomas Lytle, who had driven their cattle into Black Mountain coves rather than allow them to become boiled beef to feed Ferguson's army. Ferguson told Burke County citizens that the rebel cause was all but crushed, and that he came to offer Hemphill and Lytle pardon for their rebellious activity if they would sign an oath of allegiance to King George III.

Mrs. Thomas Lytle, though she supported the Patriot cause, was in a flurry the minute she heard that the Tory colonel intended to visit her home. He was rumored to be a prominent British officer as well as a gentleman. Living on the frontier and having few visitors or social occasions to look forward to, Mrs. Lytle decided to dress up. The attractive young housewife put on her finest petticoat and gown, painted her face with powder and rouge, donned her beaver hat, which had cost many Continental dollars, and awaited her guest. When Colonel Ferguson and his squadron arrived at her door, she greeted him graciously, curtsied and invited him to dismount. He declined, saying that he was hurrying through the countryside and needed to talk with her husband. When she told him her husband was away from home, Ferguson replied, "Madame, do you know where he is?" She replied, " I really do not; I only know that he is out with his friends whom you call Rebels.... All I know is that he will never prove a traitor to his country." The colonel said, "Well, madam, I have discharged my duty; I felt anxious to save captain Lytle, because I learn that he is both brave and honorable. If he persists in rebellion, and comes to harm, his blood be upon his own head." Ferguson added, "Mrs. Lytle, I admire you as the handsomest woman I have seen in North Carolina—I even half-way admire your zeal in a bad cause." He then bowed to her and rode off, leading his troops. A soldier in the rear turned back, took off his "old slouched hat, made her a low bow, and with his left hand lifted the splendid beaver from her head, replacing it with his wretched apology. With mock gravity he observed, 'Mrs. Lytle, I can not leave so handsome a lady without something by which to remember you.' As he rode off, she hallooed after him, 'You'll bite the dust for that, you villain!'" Dressing up was fun, and she had won a compliment, but she long mourned the loss of her beautiful beaver hat.[16]

Making further excursions into Burke County, marauders met Mrs. Davidson. When this Patriot lady complained to Ferguson that one of his soldiers had eaten her chicken, the British commander displayed his famous sense of justice. He "immediately punished (the culprit) and gave the good lady a dollar in compensation for her loss."[17]

After the Battle of Musgrove Mill, while Ferguson canvassed Tryon County and the Shelby-McDowell forces turned their horses toward the mountains, Clarke rode south to his wife and home in Augusta, Georgia. Back in 1774, when Clarke and his wife, Hannah Harrington, moved their growing family to Georgia from Anson County, North Carolina, he was an impoverished, rough and rowdy illiterate. Five years later, when Savannah fell and the British overran Georgia, Clarke—now a militia lieutenant colonel in the state minutemen—refused to accept British rule. He and 100 Georgians fled over the Blue Ridge to the remote overmountain Watauga and Holston settlements in the autumn of 1779. When the Wataugans learned of the atrocities perpetrated by the Loyalists in Georgia, many sympathetic frontiersmen and former Regulators returned with Clarke's band to Georgia to retaliate. Clarke's corps lured the enemy from their British camp into an ambush and won the skirmish in Georgia. Thus began a lasting friendship between Georgians and overmountain folk. Colonel Elijah Clarke became one of Georgia's most renowned war heroes and one of Thomas Brown's most annoying enemies.

When Clarke returned to Georgia after the late August Battle at Musgrove Mill, Lieutenant Colonel Thomas Brown, Clarke's nemesis at Alligator Creek Bridge, was in command of Augusta on the South Carolina-Georgia line. Clarke enlisted several hundred men to aid the Patriot cause. His recruits were former Loyalists who had recently sworn an oath of allegiance to the king. These men, however, now decided to renege on their Tory oath, join Clarke, and switch to the Whig side. Clarke and his newly converted Patriots stormed Augusta on September 14, 1780, attacking Thomas Brown, his Florida Rangers, and his Indian allies. Lieutenant Colonel John Harris Cruger led a group of New York Loyalists from Fort Ninety Six to Augusta to reinforce Brown. When Brown, Cruger, British troops, Loyalists, Rangers, and Indians all began chasing Clarke, he retreated—but not fast enough. Brown's Tories overtook many of Clarke's recruits and hanged 13 of them as traitors.

Elijah Clarke failed in his attempt to seize Augusta, but he escaped capture and fled toward Watauga. He did, however, not escape the wrath of the British. Ferguson pursued not only Georgia's Clarke but he also hunted down North Carolina Colonels McDowell, Shelby and Sevier.

15

Watauga, Kings Mountain and the Journey Home

> If all else fails, I will retreat up the valley of Virginia, plant my flag on the Blue Ridge, rally around the Scots-Irish of that region and make my last stand for liberty amongst a people who will never submit to British tyranny whilst there is a man left to draw a trigger.
> —George Washington, Valley Forge[1]

Both Clinton and Cornwallis agreed that "the battle of Kings' Mountain was the turning point" of the Revolutionary War.[2] After losing the August 1780 Battle of Musgrove Mill in South Carolina, Major Ferguson moved northward. Seeking to subdue Patriot leaders, secure pledges of loyalty to the crown and recruit volunteers for his army, he was on his way to rendezvous with Cornwallis in Charlotte, North Carolina. The joint forces of Cornwallis, Tarleton and Ferguson hoped to march through Flour Gap of the Blue Ridge into Virginia and seize the Chiswell Lead Mines on the New River. Along the way, Ferguson continued to monitor the movements of McDowell, Sevier, and Shelby from North Carolina, Sumter and Williams from South Carolina, and Clarke and John Twiggs from Georgia, all of whom had annoyed him in South Carolina.

After winning the battle at Musgrove Mill, McDowell, the commander of the Western North Carolina Patriot Militia, and some of the colonels under his command began wending their way home toward the mountains. Isaac Shelby and his crack-shot riflemen retreated through Gilbert Town, in the newly formed Rutherford County, to the overmountain land of the Western Waters. McDowell pitched camp 20 miles north of Gilbert Town (Rutherfordton) at Bedford Hill on Cane Creek. Ferguson pursued. Deviating from his path eastward to Charlotte, he followed his prey northward to Gilbert Town. Early in September Ferguson arrived at the small village, with its well-built and comfortable log houses. By that time his forces numbered 1,000 men, and most of them had muskets. Ferguson asked his recruits to affix hunting knives to their barrels, turning them into bayonets. One of his men, Lieutenant Anthony Allaire, wrote in his diary on September 7, 1780: "Major Ferguson with about fifty American volunteers and three hundred militia got into motion and marched to Gilbert Town in order to surprise the rebels that we heard were there. Captain DePeyster and I remained on the ground we took in the morning with the remainder of the American volunteers and militia."[3]

Ferguson sent a detachment of Loyalists from Gilbert Town to rout McDowell from his campsite on Bedford Hill. McDowell, however, had advance notice of the enemy plan.

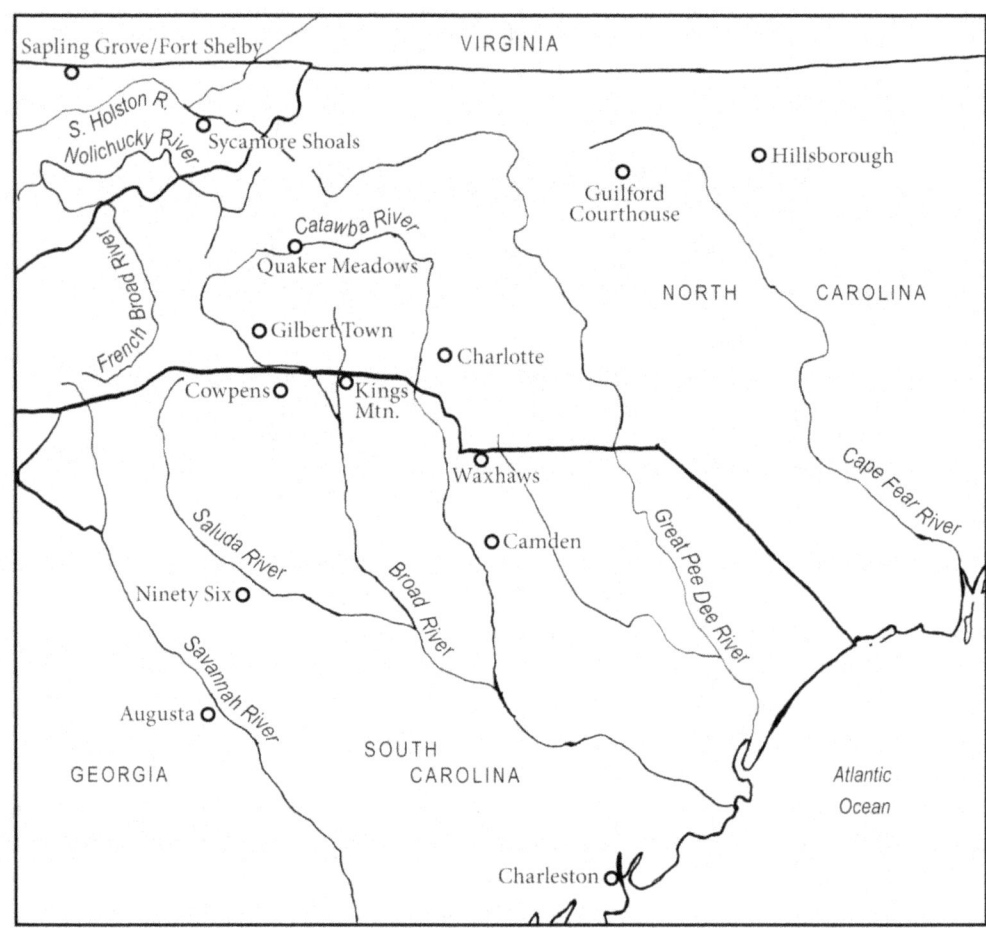

The Southern Campaign of the American Revolution (Glen McCroskey).

Laying an ambush and armed with long rifles, the Patriots hunkered down and waited for the Brown Bess muskets of the Loyalists. As the Loyalists approached, McDowell's riflemen fired a salvo. The Loyalists recoiled, recovered, and then beat back the Patriots. The skirmish was indecisive. Both armies withdrew. Taking a few prisoners, Ferguson's men returned to their camp in Gilbert Town. The fleeing McDowell and his Patriots attempted to distance themselves from Ferguson. Hurriedly bypassing McDowell's home at Quaker Meadows (Morganton, North Carolina), they began their long trek to safety across the Blue Ridge to the banks of the Watauga River at Sycamore Shoals. The Watauga Settlement in Washington County, North Carolina, adjoined the Holston Settlement of the newly formed Sullivan County, North Carolina, home of Colonel Isaac Shelby.

The overmountain folk felt great empathy for McDowell's men hiding out in their midst. An overmountain colonel noted that in early August 1780, Cornwallis had ordered British Indian agents to "excite the Indians to invade American settlements west of the mountains; and, if practicable, to proceed as far as the Chiswell Lead Mines, and destroy the works and stores at that place." The exiled militia commanded by Charles and Joseph McDowell took refuge in a settlement on the Watauga River with their "Whig brethren...."

Their tale was a doleful one, and tended to excite the resentment of the western militia, who of late had become inured to danger by fighting the Indians, and who had an utter detestation of the tyranny of the British Government."[4] "The refugee Whigs received a hearty welcome from their hospitable but plain countrymen on Watauga and Nolichucky. The door of every cabin was thrown open."[5]

Shelby and McDowell resolved to recross the mountain and "beard the lion in his den" when the weather turned cool and crops were harvested. Ferguson did not, however, wait until cool weather to strike again. He found a messenger familiar with mountain trails. He paroled Samuel Phillips, who had been captured, possibly at Musgrove Mill, and sent him over the mountain with a verbal message to officers of the western waters of Watauga, Nolichucky and Holston. Ferguson referred to the overmountain area as the land of the western waters because its rivers and streams originated west of the crest of the Blue Ridge and flowed west to the Gulf, instead of east to the Atlantic.

Phillips arrived in the village of Sapling Grove in the North Holston Settlement and delivered the message to overmountain men directly to his cousin Colonel Isaac Shelby: "If they did not desist from their opposition to the British arms he would march his army over the mountains, hang their leaders, and lay waste with fire and sword." Phillips also revealed to Shelby the position, strength, and plans of the enemy.

Ferguson had intended for the message to frighten the frontiersmen, end their resistance and win their oath of allegiance to King George III, but Shelby's reaction surprised him. Instead of intimidating these western waters frontiersmen, the message goaded them into action. Shelby quickly reacted much more aggressively than Ferguson had anticipated. Shelby recalled, "Philips came directly to me with this intelligence.... I went fifty or sixty miles to see Colonel Sevier, (militia) commander of Washington County, North Carolina, to inform him." When Shelby arrived at Sevier's home on the Nolichucky River near Jonesborough, an event redolent with barbecue, horse racing and mountain music was in full swing. The celebration honored Colonel Sevier's marriage to his second wife, Catherine Sherrill, "Bonnie Kate of Tennessee," whose life he had saved in 1776 at Watauga Fort. Shelby alerted Sevier of the impending danger, and they spent two days planning their defense. Shelby reported, "After some consultation, we determined to march with all the men we could raise, and attempt to surprise Ferguson."[6]

Together Shelby and Sevier planned the Overmountain March. Their strategy involved rallying militia forces for a surprise attack. They figured that if their scheme failed to stop Ferguson and if the British actually invaded their counties they could escape hanging by floating down the Holston, Tennessee, Ohio, and Mississippi rivers and hiding out in the Spanish territory of Louisiana.

Shelby and Sevier resolved to raise riflemen to stop Ferguson, as they had to prevent him from pursuing them across the mountain. They chose Sycamore Shoals (Elizabethton, Tennessee) on the Watauga River, a tributary of the Holston, as the point of rendezvous for the Overmountain Men to begin their march. The handsome Sevier—five-feet nine, muscular, fair-haired, blue-eyed, friendly and persuasive—rallied border men without difficulty. He rode to nearby Sycamore Shoals and revealed the plan to his regional commander, Colonel Charles McDowell, and to Colonel Andrew Hampton, commander of the Patriot militia of Rutherford County. Both agreed to join the Overmountain March. Having fled from Ferguson at Bedford Hill on Cane Creek, these exiled colonels were still living with their band of 160 refugee militiamen encamped in crude huts and lean-tos on the banks of the Watauga.

Shelby—tall, dark, lean, and determined, with penetrating eyes, intellectual force and unfaltering courage—contacted Colonel William Campbell, a militia regiment commander in neighboring Washington County, Virginia. Shelby twice sent his brother, Captain Moses Shelby, with letters to Campbell. "I wrote to Col. Campbell [who] declined to meet us," said Shelby in his *Pamphlet to the Public*. Campbell wanted to maintain a defensive position to protect the Lead Mines. Shelby and Sevier, on the other hand, favored the offensive. They considered it necessary to preempt Ferguson and catch him before he joined forces with Cornwallis.

Shelby was disappointed to hear William Campbell's negative reply to the first letter. The "Cherokee towns were not more than eighty or one hundred miles from the frontiers of my County," wrote Shelby. "[W]e received information that these Indians were preparing a formidable attack upon us in the course of a few weeks; I was, therefore unwilling that we should take away the whole disposable force of our Counties at such a time; and without the aid of the militia under Col. Campbell's command, I feared that we could not otherwise have a sufficient force to meet Ferguson. I therefore wrote a second letter to Col. Campbell, and sent the same messenger back with it immediately to whom I communicated at large our view and intentions." In his pamphlet Shelby said that in response to the second letter "Campbell wrote me that he would meet us at the time and place appointed on the 25th day of September, 1780 at Watauga."

Shelby and Sevier contacted Colonel Benjamin Cleveland of Wilkes County in the North Carolina foothills, requesting him to raise all the troops he could. The Overmountain Men would meet him at Quaker Meadows on the east side of the mountain. Seeking public money to outfit his men for the journey, Sevier appealed to John Adair, Sullivan County entry-taker and state officer for the sale of North Carolina lands. Adair replied: "Colonel Sevier, I have no authority by law to make that disposition of this money; it belongs to the impoverished treasury of North Carolina, and I dare not appropriate a cent of it to any purpose; but, if the country is over-run by the British, our liberty is gone. Let the money go, too. Take it. If the enemy, by its use, is driven from the country, I can trust that country to justify and vindicate my conduct—so take it."[7] After organizing the rendezvous at Sycamore Shoals, Shelby and Sevier met with their recruited officers to share their scheme for the overmountain march into Tryon County to catch Ferguson. When the colonels told their militia captains about Ferguson's threat to use the halter and the torch (hanging and burning) they were outraged and ready to carry out the colonels' plan.

Wataugan women supported their men of Holston Valley—mostly Presbyterian, Patriotic and Scots-Irish—who were ever ready at a moment's notice to turn out for military service. But the men responded only *if* their wives, sisters and daughters could plant, sow and harvest, even in the busiest crop season. The Wataugan womenfolk not only farmed they also worked needles and looms, busily mending and weaving clothing for the journey. Gristmills ground meal for Johnny cakes and corn mush for the march. Mary Patton, a pioneer gunpowder manufacturer living on Powder Creek near Sycamore Shoals, performed the physically strenuous task of supplying 500 pounds of the black powder to the Overmountain Men. Lead for shot was mined in Bumpass Cove (now Unicoi, Tennessee), a small community in Washington County. The cove was situated in the Blue Ridge Mountains near John Sevier's home on the Nolichucky.

15. Watauga, Kings Mountain and the Journey Home

Many mustering sites were scattered from Marion to Abingdon, Virginia, and from Sapling Grove to Jonesborough and Limestone in overmountain North Carolina—Tennessee Country. Militiamen from every knob and hollow of East Tennessee and Southwest Virginia mustered throughout the mountains. One gathering ground was in Abingdon. Another was the Pemberton Oak on the outskirts of Sapling Grove (Bristol). One was with Isaac Shelby at Fort Shelby and another with Sevier on the Nolichucky.

These mountain men, as tough as laurel burls, as resilient as hickory sticks, lived by the rifle, targeting bear or stalking deer for food. They had learned their marksmanship by shooting varmints and studied soldiering by fighting Indians in Dunmore's War and in border wars on the western frontier. These backwoodsmen volunteers, some accompanied by their wives and families, some walking and some mounted, traveled along various paths through the Wilderness, or along the Old Wilderness Road, to rendezvous at Sycamore Shoals on September 25, 1780. "Colonel Campbell went to the place of rendezvous by way of Colonel Shelby's [at Sapling Grove] while his men, who had assembled at the first creek below Abingdon, marched down a nearer way—by the Watauga road."[8] Colonel John Sevier's son on the Nolichucky—hearing that their home was threatened by fire and their father was doomed to hang—wanted to meet at Sycamore Shoals and march across the mountain to catch Ferguson. "Here Mr. Sevier," said his new wife, Kate, pointing to her stepson, not yet sixteen, "is another of your boys who wants to go with his father and brother Joseph to the war; but we have no horse for him, and, poor fellow, it is too great a distance for him to walk."[9] Horses were scarce, but James Sevier, mounted or not, went on the expedition.

In September Colonel Arthur Campbell, the county lieutenant of Washington County, Virginia, was in Richmond being briefed by Governor Thomas Jefferson about the massive defeat of General Gates at Camden during the preceding month. When Arthur returned home and received Isaac Shelby's message informing him of Ferguson's threat, he rallied militiamen and personally escorted one-half the men under his command to rendezvous at Sycamore Shoals with Shelby and Sevier. Colonel William Campbell's regiment of 200 Virginia militiamen had already arrived at Fort Watauga when, much to everyone's surprise and delight, his cousin Arthur Campbell appeared with 200 more Virginians and placed them under William's command. Arthur then returned to Royal Oaks to guard the frontier near the lead mines.

Half the volunteers living on the Indian border needed to man the forts against Indian attack. The remainder, the younger men, enrolled for the march. The colonels and militia assembled on September 25 at Sycamore Shoals. Isaac Shelby's pamphlet states the following:

> When assembled our forces were as follows: Col. William Campbell with four hundred men from Washington County, Virginia; Col. John Sevier with two hundred and forty men from Washington County, North Carolina; Col. Charles McDowell with one hundred and sixty men from the counties of Burke and Rutherford, who had fled before the enemy of the Western waters; and two hundred and forty men from Sullivan County, North Carolina, under my command. On the next day we crossed the mountains, and, on the 30th were joined by the Col. Benjamin Cleveland with three hundred and fifty men from the Counties of Wilkes and Surry, North Carolina.

This group of Overmountain Men, says Griffin's *History of Old Tryon County*, was "in many respects the most remarkable army ever assembled in America. They were all volunteers ... had no government behind them ... had not been requested to take part in the war. They were genuine patriots.... Before they left Sycamore Shoals they had religious service, conducted by that great educator and divine, the Reverend Samuel Doak."

Scots-Irish, Princeton-educated Presbyterian minister Samuel Doak was a corpulent, sandy-haired, blue-eyed circuit rider of medium height. Like other frontiersmen, he often wore short breeches and long stockings. With his Calvinistic doctrine and powerful voice he became a proponent for religion and education in the West. Walking through Maryland and Virginia, driving before him a horse whose packs were laden with books, Doak settled near Jonesborough, the oldest town in Tennessee. There, with the help of neighbors, he erected three log cabins: his home, Salem Church, and a schoolhouse that later became Washington College. Thus, in 1777 Doak established the first church and the first school in Tennessee. He founded Tusculum College, which still operates in Greeneville, Tennessee, as a private, liberal arts, Judeo-Christian college.

The Reverend Samuel Doak delivered his most famous sermon at Sycamore Shoals. His stertorous voice rang out: "Taxation without representation and the quartering of soldiers in the homes of our people without their consent are evidence that the Crown of England would take from its American Subjects the last vestige of Freedom." The Reverend revved up the worshipers with these words: "The enemy is marching hither to destroy your homes. Brave men, you are not unacquainted with battle.... You have wrested these beautiful valleys of the Holston and Watauga from the savage hand. Will you tarry now until the other enemy carries fire and sword to your very doors?" In his closing prayer, Doak, drawing inspiration from Judges 7:20, invoked, "Help us as good soldiers to wield 'a sword for the Lord and for Gideon.'"[10] This chant resonated with the Overmountain Men. "A sword for the Lord and for Gideon" became one of their battle cries as they marched toward the Blue Ridge.

Refugee Colonel McDowell, the over-all militia commander of Western North Carolina, who had been camping with his countrymen on the banks of the Watauga ever since their encounter with Ferguson's men at Bedford Hill, was the first to hurry back southeast over the mountain. His mission was to give confidence to the people, keep track of Ferguson's whereabouts, and speed up the march of Colonel Cleveland and the militiamen of Wilkes and Surry.

The Overmountain Men alternately chanted the battle cries "A sword of the Lord and of Gideon," "Catch Ferguson" and "Remember Bufort" as they began the first lap of their long journey, marching from Sycamore Shoals to Roan Mountain. Undoubtedly many were thinking of their farms or "The Girl I Left Behind," a popular Irish folk song of the period. Most of them carried a blanket, a short pouch, a knapsack, a Deckard rifle and a tomahawk. Fringe and tassels partially waterproofed their hunting shirts by collecting moisture so that dewdrops and raindrops dripped to the ground. Leather leggings (gaiters) protected against briars and snakes and proved useful for riding horseback on the trail. A frontiersman rarely appeared without a hat or a scarf on his head. His hat had a rounded crown and three corners made by tying the brim against the crown. The brim could be let down and used as a sunscreen. That part of the brim on the right or left—depending on whether a rifleman was right- or left-handed—was tied up to facilitate shooting.

Not knowing where they would catch Ferguson, these 1,040 Overmountain Men would walk more than 200 miles before they found him. Crossing the Watauga and Big Doe rivers, they followed streams to the "shelving rock" near Roan Mountain's looming height of almost

6,300 feet. The shelf-like rock projected from the hillside with a shallow cave underneath that provided a dry spot to store supplies and powder. Across from the rock was a meadow with a stream running near it where they spent the night. Each man carried a cup, a skillet, and means to build a fire but no tents or food, except for a little parched corn mixed with maple sugar in their saddle bags. Many, but not all, had horses. A blacksmith shod their horses while they slaughtered and cooked beeves for food on the mountain crossing. The remaining cattle, being unlikely to survive the mountain journey, were herded back to Sycamore Shoals, perhaps by young boys following the camp. On the rest of the journey the men camped on Tory farms, butchered and roasted the enemy's livestock, and raided cornfields and pumpkin patches.

Leaving the village of Roan Mountain, the frontiersmen climbed Roan Mountain itself, with its 10 miles of grassy balds, to a particular bald, where they drilled in "shoe-mouth" deep snow, parading and firing their rifles upon the command of their respective colonels. During the drill, two of Sevier's men, James Crawford and Samuel Chambers, deserted. It was correctly suspected that they were going to tell Ferguson about the march of the Overmountain Men. These two were eventually captured and condemned to hang, but Sevier intervened. Crawford went on to fight bravely for the Patriot cause at Guilford Courthouse. It was decided Chambers was merely an immature youth, "easily misled."[11] After the drill, traveling to Gilbert Town, the volunteers crossed the mountain at a gap between Yellow Mountain and Roan Mountain. They then proceeded down the other side (the southeastern slope) of Roan Mountain to Spruce Pine. (In the distance was Brown Mountain, famous for its ghostly Brown Mountain Lights believed by the frontiersmen to be spirits of Cherokee and Catawba warriors slain long before in battle.)

There were two main routes down the east side of the Blue Ridge. The Overmountain Men did not know that Ferguson was south of Gilbert Town tracking guerrilla leader Elijah Clarke, who had escaped from Thomas Brown in Augusta, Georgia. Afraid that Ferguson might be on his way up the mountain and that they might miss him, the militiamen split. Campbell's Virginians took the Turkey Cove route down the mountain, while the North Carolinians chose the North Cove route. Eventually the two groups converged in Old Tryon County.

On September 27, in a ravine on the east side of the mountain, they met up with Colonel Benjamin Cleveland in command of 400 men. On the fifth night, the men camped around fires and ate fresh meat at the home of Colonel McDowell in Quaker Meadows. Here, Campbell, Sevier, Shelby, McDowell and Cleveland were joined by other North Carolina units: Major Joseph Winston and Captain William Lenoir, with their Surry County militia; and Major William Chronicle with his Lincoln County men.

The Patriot militiamen camped at Bedford Hill, where McDowell and a Ferguson detachment had skirmished earlier. In conference the officers agreed that they were all of equal rank, had gathered without orders or authorization, and their combined volunteer army of 1,500 men had been recruited from two states, North Carolina and Virginia. They expected to be joined by 1,000 more soldiers from North Carolina, South Carolina, and Georgia. South Carolina militiamen were under the leadership of Colonels William Hill, James Williams, William Lacey, James Hawthorne, Frederick Hambright, and William Graham. The South Carolinians were encamped not far away in the community of Sunshine, situated between Bedford Hill and Gilbert Town. Thirty Georgia militiamen under the command of Major William Candler, a guerrilla fighter who had served under Elijah Clarke, were expected to join the group at Cowpens.

Senior militia officer Charles McDowell suggested that because there would be troops from several states no one person had a clear mandate to command the whole army. The commanding officers agreed and worked together drafting a letter requesting that Gates send such an officer. They envisioned either Continental Army general Daniel Morgan or partisan militia General William Davidson. They also requisitioned supplies, especially ammunition. The letter—signed by McDowell, Cleveland, Shelby, Sevier, Hampton, Campbell, and Winston—promised that McDowell would wait for Gates' answer. McDowell, a true Patriot working for the good of his country, generously volunteered to carry the letter to General Horatio Gates. Gates, despite his defeat at Camden, was still acting as the American commander in the South. Washington had appointed Nathanael Greene to replace Gates, but Greene would not assume command until December 2, 1780.

Before McDowell returned with Gates' answer, however, Shelby stressed the urgency of acting quickly. As the Overmountain Men were now less than 20 miles north of Gilbert Town, where they believed the British leader was posted, Shelby wanted to "catch Ferguson" before he moved, and certainly before he was reinforced by Banastre "Bloody Ban" Tarleton. It was rumored that Ferguson might get away, that he might be heading to the South Carolina stronghold at Fort Ninety Six. Shelby's pamphlet recounted the following:

> We met in the evening and consulted ... [and] resolved to send to Head-Quarters for a general officer to command us and that in the meantime, we should meet in council every day to determine on the measures to be pursued.... *I was not satisfied with this course, as I thought it calculated to produce delay, when expedition and dispatch were all important to us.* We were then within sixteen or eighteen miles of Gilbert Town, where we supposed Ferguson to be. I suggested ... that we were all North Carolinians except Col. Campbell, who was from Virginia ... [and] that he commanded the largest regiment; and that if they concurred with me, we would, until a general officer should arrive from Head-Quarters, appoint him to command us, and march immediately against the enemy.... I made this proposition to silence the expectations of Col. McDowell to command us—he being the commanding officer of the district we were then in.... He was a brave and patriotic man, but we considered him too far advanced in life, and too inactive for the command.... In this way, and upon my suggestion, was Col. Campbell raised to the command, and not on account of any superior military talents or experience he was supposed to possess....

The colonels were to meet in council every night to decide the next day's action; Campbell's job was to execute these plans. The logic of Shelby's proposal was recognized and agreed upon by the other officers, and William Campbell took command. Shelby, the youngest colonel present, knew that his own superior, Colonel McDowell, would never accept him or any other North Carolina junior officer as commander. Better, he thought, to choose someone from out of state.

Since McDowell was the commanding officer of the district and superior to both Sevier and Shelby, he was the logical choice to lead this group. His junior officers, however, doubted his ability to lead in battle and bring harmony to this disparate group. When Shelby nominated Colonel William Campbell, he gave each man a chance to withdraw from the campaign. Not a single man got up to leave. "A murmur of applause arose from the men, who seemed proud of each other." Shelby then instructed the Overmountain Men, to fight Indian style in the upcoming battle:

15. Watauga, Kings Mountain and the Journey Home

I am heartily glad to see you, as a man, resolved to meet and fight your country's foes. When we encounter them, don't wait for the word of command. Let each of you be your own officer and do the best you can, taking every care of yourselves, and availing yourselves of every advantage that chance may throw your way. If in the woods, shelter yourselves and give them Indian play. Advance from tree to tree pressing the enemy, killing and disabling all you can. Your officers will shrink from no danger. They will be constantly with you, and the moment the enemy gives way, be on the alert and strictly obey orders."[12]

While Overmountain Men camped at Bedford Hill 18 miles north of Gilbert Town and the colonels were planning their course of action, Ferguson was already on the move. Back on September 7, when Ferguson arrived in Rutherford County, he drove off the Patriot militia and set up headquarters at Gilbert Town. He sent a detachment to Cane Creek to fight McDowell on September 14 and sent prisoner Samuel Phillips over the Blue Ridge to threaten Shelby. He then began canvassing Burke County northeast of Gilbert Town for recruits. He learned on the 24th that Patriot Elijah Clarke had surprised Tory Thomas Brown in Augusta and held him at bay for five days until Loyalist militia from Ninety Six drove Clarke off. Ferguson expected Clarke to head for safety across the Blue Ridge in the Watauga area. Hence, he evacuated Gilbert Town and combed the area in an attempt to arrest Clarke. Ferguson's Loyalists captured one of Clarke's Patriots and learned that Clarke had escaped along the foot of the mountain at the Indian border. Ferguson, in pursuit of Clarke, foraged through the countryside, killing cattle for food and plundering Patriot farms. While making camp at Denard's Ford on the Broad River south of Gilbert Town, Ferguson learned from Crawford and Chambers, the deserters from Roan Mountain, that the Patriot army had crossed the mountain and were rapidly approaching.

Ferguson relayed the news of the advancing "backwater" men to Cornwallis. But General Cornwallis did not receive his plea and did not send Tarleton to support him until the day after the Battle of Kings Mountain. Simultaneously Ferguson sent a dispatch to the Loyalist commander of Ninety Six requesting reinforcement. He then spread the rumor that he was going to Ninety Six when he actually was en route to Charlotte via Kings Mountain to meet Cornwallis. He also immediately circulated a recruiting notice to the people of North Carolina: "Gentlemen, Unless you wish to be eat up by an inundation of barbarians, who have begun by murdering an unarmed son before the aged father ... in short if you wish or deserve to live, and bear the name of men, grasp arms and run to camp" to avoid being "pinioned, robbed and murdered" by "the Back Water men [who] have crossed the mountains" with that "set of mongrels ... McDowell, Shelby and Cleveland ... at their head so that you know what you have to depend upon." Because he refused to recognize the validity of the illegal rebel assembly that had abolished Tryon County in 1779, Ferguson datelined his circular "Denard's Ford, Broad River, Tryon County, Oct. 1st, 1780," and signed it "Pat Ferguson, Major 71st Regiment."[13]

The Overmountain Men pursuing Ferguson left Bedford Hill for Gilbert Town on October 4, crossing and recrossing Cane Creek. According to Tory lieutenant Allaire's diary, Cane Creek was so crooked that it had to be crossed 19 times within four miles. Shelby's pamphlet says:

> On the morning after the appointment of Col. Campbell we proceeded towards Gilbert Town, but found that Ferguson ... had left. It was determined to pursue him unremittingly, with as many of our troops as could be well armed and well mounted [910 men were selected] ... leaving the weak horses and footmen to follow on as fast as they could. We were joined at Cowpens, on the 6th, by Col. James

Williams, of South Carolina, and several field officers, with about four hundred men. Learning from him the situation and distance of the enemy, we traveled all that night, and the next day, through heavy rains.

Continuing their march, militiamen from Virginia, Tennessee Country, North Carolina, and South Carolina converged at Cowpens. There they encamped with additional regiments from South Carolina and Georgia. A favorite password among them was "Buford," because Bloody Ban Tarleton only four months earlier had offered no quarter when he massacred Colonel Abraham Buford's command at Waxhaws. From Cowpens part of the army proceeded toward Kings Mountain. About 1,500 men "were left at The Cowpens and did not reach the battle site."[14] The number of Patriot militiamen engaged at Kings Mountain was 1,840, including footmen. The general officer that McDowell's hand-carried letter requested never came. Time was too short. Colonels Campbell, Sevier and Cleveland noted the weary condition of both men and horses and decided to halt and refresh. But Shelby drove the expedition forward with bulldog determination, declaring with an oath, "'I will not stop until night, if I follow Ferguson into Cornwallis' lines.' Without replying, the other colonels returned to their respective commands and continued their march."[15] As they marched they tried to keep their guns and powder dry in the heavy rain.

Scout Enoch Gilmer, posing as a Tory, was sent ahead to spy and gather information about Ferguson. Gilmer, an accomplished actor who could cry and laugh at the same time, visited farmhouses and learned that only a few miles ahead, on Kings Mountain, was Ferguson, wearing a checked shirt that made him an easy target. From the combined volunteer army of 1,790 a select party of 900 men advanced toward Kings Mountain. Riding through drizzling rain on the cold night of October 6 they wrapped shirts around their rifles to keep them dry. Gilmer guided the Americans. When it was safe to ford the Broad River, he began to sing the agreed-upon signal: the Irish folk song "Barney O'Lynn." Another Patriot scout, Joseph Kerr, also went ahead to gather information about Ferguson's position and strength. Because he was crippled and therefore not suspected of being a spy, Kerr was able to get into Ferguson's camp.

When they crossed the Broad River 18 miles from Cowpens and 15 miles from Kings Mountain the men wanted to rest, but Shelby rode on and the men followed. Shelby's pamphlet describes the Ferguson camp: "The next day, through heavy rains, we came up with them about three o'clock in the afternoon of Saturday, the 7th of October. They were encamped on an eminence called King's Mountain.... Our plan was to surround the mountain and attack the enemy on all sides."

About 16 miles long, Kings Mountain lies in both Carolinas; but the battle would take place in South Carolina one and one-half miles from the North Carolina line. Floating as stealthily as Indians, the rebel "cloud of cavalry" approached Kings Mountain on October 7, the wet ground from a soaking rain the night before muffling both sound and dust. Colonel Frederick Hambright helped forge the way up the mountain with his band of 60 Lincoln County soldiers known as the South Fork Boys, who were familiar with the terrain.[16] William Campbell, commander of the day and without any previous war experience, was leading these soldiers to victory at Kings Mountain. He did so under the guidance of many experienced officers, not the least of whom was Shelby, who kept the men moving. Shelby, "stiff as iron ... dauntless ... went right onward and upward like a man who had but one thing to do, and but one thought—to do it."[17]

Leaving their horses at the foot of the ridge, the Patriot militia under Colonels Shelby, Campbell, Sevier, McDowell, Hambright, Cleveland, Lacey and Williams completely enveloped Ferguson and his Loyalist camp on the elliptically shaped flat summit. The Kings Mountain summit was a 700-yard-long, 70 to 120-yard-wide ridge rising abruptly 100 feet above the surrounding ravines.

Twenty-nine-year-old Colonel Isaac Shelby later wrote to his father, General Evan Shelby: "The Mountain was high and exceedingly steep, so that their situation gave them greatly the advantage; indeed it was almost equal to storming a battery.... They repelled us three times with charged bayonets; but being determined to conquer or die, we came up a fourth time, and fairly got possession of the top of the eminence."[18] Shelby wrote that Ferguson had chosen high ground at Kings Mountain to make his stand: "But his position which he thought impregnable was really a disadvantage to him. The summit was bare, whilst the sides of the mountain were covered with trees. Ferguson's men were drawn up in close column on the summit, and thus presented fair marks for the mountaineers, who approached them under cover of trees."[19]

The American militiamen stealthily emerged at the top of Kings Mountain. Obeying Colonel William Campbell's order to "shout like h—l, and fight like devils," their blood-curdling war whoops echoed throughout the heavily wooded mountain as they began firing rifles from behind rock and tree. Captain Abraham DePeyster, a New Yorker, second in command to Ferguson, muttered, "There are the same yelling devils that were at Musgrove Mill."[20] Breathing puffs of gun smoke and watching the glint of approaching bayonets, Patriots heard the piercing trill of one of Ferguson's silver whistles beckoning his red-coated Loyalists to commence their death charge.

The resulting battle was unique. It was "the single significant clash in which rifles alone were pitted directly against musket-and-bayonet." Time after time, whenever a cluster of Patriot militiamen came into sight, Ferguson's Loyalist militia charged, their Brown Bess muskets fixed with long knives to simulate bayonets. But the frontier riflemen, fighting Indian style, simply retreated, taking cover behind rock and tree, firing their rifles all the time at Ferguson's "closely packed platoons." The return musket fire of the Loyalists proved futile. Owing to the mountain's steep slope, said one Whig soldier, "they overshot us altogether, scarce touching a man, except those on horseback."[21]

Wounded in the thigh, Patriot colonel Hambright ignored the blood running into his boot. Remaining on his horse, he exclaimed in a German accent, "Huzza, my prave poys, fight on a few minutes more, and the battle will be over!" Simultaneously, Tory colonel Ferguson hollered to his Loyalists, "Huzza, brave boys, the day is our own!" The flaming mountain was thick with smoke and reverberated with the continuous roar of gunshots. Sevier later said to Shelby, "I perfectly recollect on seeing you at the close of the action. They had burnt off your hair, for it was much burnt on one side."[22]

Captain William Lenoir, wearing his hair in a queue, also got a quick haircut at Kings Mountain. Years after the battle, then General Lenoir, writing from his home, Fort Defiance, beside the Yadkin River, reminisced about the reason for his short hair: "I received a slight wound in my side and another in my left arm, and after that a bullet went through my hair about where it was tied and my clothes were cut in several places." From that time on, the general, careful not to mess with Providence, always wore his hair "clipped to the length where the bullet had sheared it."[23]

Draper hyperbolized the amazing marksmanship of Kings Mountain men: "The fatality of the sharpshooters at Kings Mountain almost surpassed belief. Rifleman took off rifleman with such exactness, that they killed each other when taking sight, so instantaneous that their eyes remained, after they were dead, one shut and the other open—in the usual manner of marksmen when leveling at their object." When the Loyalists found themselves surrounded on all sides, they flung out flags of truce, white handkerchiefs tied to their guns. "Few Americans understood the signal and the few that did chose not to know what it meant; so that, even after submission, the slaughter continued." Everywhere the beaten Tory soldiers were crying, "Quarters! Quarters!" The frontiersmen, whose rallying call was "Buford," gave them Tarleton quarters, the same quarters Bloody Ban had given to Buford's massacred men at Waxhaws. Among the shouting leaders who were trying to stop the killing was Isaac Shelby. One witness saw "the intrepid" Shelby "rush his horse within fifteen paces of (enemy) lines" [exclaiming], 'D—m you, if you want quarters, throw down your arms!' Some would call this an imprudent act; but it showed the daring bravery of the man."[24]

In his pension papers, Private Joseph Starnes described his role in the Battle of Kings Mountain:

> I lived within 3 miles of Colonel Wm. Campbell.... When I went to Kings Mountain ... I was a mounted volunteer ... under Colonel Campbell.... Colo. Cleveland of North Carolina Militia commanded the right wing; and Colo. [Sevier] of the North Carolina Militia from over the mountains commanded the left wing of the army. Colo. Campbell of the Virginia Troops marched up in front. We surprised and took their picket guard—without a noise—then a man named Philip Giever, a messmate of mine, who stood next to me on the Left side, shot a man who came off from the British Guard into the wood; this made the enemy's guard retreat to the main body—we advanced on them before they could form and gave them a fire and before we could load again the British formed and charged on us and we retreated across a little hollow and loaded and then advanced on them and kept up such a constant fire for 40 or 50 minutes that they never made us retreat again—but we advanced upon them 'till the end of the battle. I understood that the principal part of the force of the enemy were Tories. I saw Ferguson of the British army lying dead— 'twas said he had 7 bullets shot through him.[25]

Riflemen riddled Major Ferguson's body, flinging him off his white charger, his body taking many lead bullets. Some attribute his killing to Wataugan Robert Young's rifle, "Sweet Lips." Captain Abraham de Peyster, who became the British commanding officer upon Ferguson's death, presented his sword of surrender to Colonel Isaac Shelby's brother, Major Evan Shelby. "Three long, loud, spontaneous shouts" arose from the throats of the victors.[26]

Ferguson's bullet-shattered corpse, clad elegantly under his checked hunting shirt, was carried by Tories to a spring on the southern slope of the mountain, propped up against a rock and covered with blankets. Looking down at the lifeless body, Colonel Shelby exclaimed, "Colonel, the fatal blow is struck—we've Burgoyned you?"[27] History has answered Shelby's question. Like the 1776 American victory won by the Continental Army at the Battle of Saratoga, the turning point of the Revolutionary War in the North, the Battle of Kings Mountain won by militia of the southwestern frontier was the turning point of the war in the South. Jefferson called it "a turn of the tide of success" leading to victory at Yorktown and American independence.

Isaac Shelby claimed the largest of the fallen British chieftain's famous silver whistles as a trophy. Many officers picked various other souvenirs: six china dinner plates, a cup and saucer, Ferguson's silken sash, his smaller silver whistles, de Peyster's sword. There were other spoils of war. Loyalist Jonas Bedford, who escaped, reported that he personally lost his chest, clothing, and many papers, accounts, certificates, and vouchers on the mountain. The baggage wagons and many supplies were thrown into campfires and burned. Only a few Loyalists escaped capture by putting pieces of white paper in their hats to disguise themselves as Patriots. The October 7 entry in Allaire's diary accounts for Ferguson's entire command: "Maj. Ferguson had eight hundred men.... Capt. Depeyster ... thought it necessary to surrender to save the lives of the brave men who were left.... We lost in action Maj. Ferguson ... [and] eighteen men killed on the spot.... Capt. Ryerson and thirty-two privates wounded. Lieut. McGinnis ... killed.... Taken prisoners, two captains, four Lieutenants, three ensigns, and one surgeon, and fifty-four sergeants ... [and] of the militia, one hundred were killed ... wounded ninety; taken prisoners, about six hundred."[28]

Although reports were contradictory and unreliable, more Patriot officers were killed or mortally wounded than privates. The ratio for Campbell's Virginians was 13 to one: "The disparity of losses between the leaders and privates is a striking proof how fearlessly the (militia) officers exposed themselves in rallying the regiment when broken, and leading on their men by their valor and heroic examples to victory." One Patriot officer killed at the Battle of Kings Mountain was Nathaniel Gist (father of Sequoya, who developed the Cherokee alphabet) while fighting as a militiaman in William Campbell's Virginia regiment. A Loyalist surgeon from New Jersey attended wounded Whigs and Tories alike on the battlefield while his compatriots buried Ferguson and the other Tory dead. Two women Loyalist camp followers at Kings Mountain were "Virginia Sal" and "Virginia Paul." In May 2003 the *Gazette* (a British publication) reported that a radar scan showed two bodies buried at Ferguson's gravesite. This study supports the traditional story that Ferguson's courtesan-cook—red-haired Virginia Sal—was shot, wrapped in a beef rawhide, and buried with him in the same grave at Kings Mountain. Another female cook, Virginia Paul, was taken with prisoners of war to Burke County Courthouse. Afterward, she was allowed to join the army of Cornwallis.

"The groans of the wounded on the mountain," said a Patriot soldier, "were truly affecting—begging piteously for a little water; but in the hurry, confusion and exhaustion of the Whigs these cries, when emanating from the Tories, were little heeded."[29] Loyalists returning from foraging, oblivious that their comrades had hung white rags on their guns signifying surrender, shot and mortally wounded Patriot colonel James Williams. Campbell, perhaps thinking that the advance guard of Tarleton's army had fired the shots, ordered Williams' command to return fire on the Tories. One hundred Loyalists who had already surrendered were killed in the confusion. The South Carolina Provincial Congress awarded Williams a postmortem commission of brigadier general. His estate furnished 150 gallons of whiskey for the militia.

Shelby noted that the Overmountain volunteers neither expected nor received compensation for their services, except certificates of little value. Shelby received a liquidation certificate that bought six yards of broadcloth, but one coat cut from it was given to the person who delivered the cloth to him in Kentucky. Shelby said he was glad to get the remainder of the cloth. "It is often assumed that the North Carolina grants in Washington County were for service in the Revolutionary War. There were no grants for Revolutionary service in Washington County; all land grants here were purchased."[30] The American Revolution was a political revolution. It was not a war waged to win territory but was fought for independence. Fighting for ideology, these militiamen would not compromise their stance. The Battle of Kings Mountain was a mighty blow struck by American patriots against British forces. Clinton said it was the first "Link of a Chain of Evils" that finally ended in the total loss of America.

There were no newspapers on the western frontier of piedmont North Carolina during the Revolutionary War. The news of the day reached the Carolina backcountry in the form of ballads written to the tune of popular songs, delivered to a local press, printed on broadsides, oversized sheets of paper, and distributed to the people. A broadside ballad titled "Ferguson's Defeat, 1780" mentions Colonel Williams as well as Ferguson. Some ballads of the period were set to tunes such as "Pop Goes the Weasel":

> We laid old Ferguson dead on the ground. Four hundred
>   and fifty dead Tories lay round—
> Making a large escort, if not quite so wise,
> To guide him to his chosen abode in the skies.
> Brave Colonel Williams, and twenty-five more,
> Of our brave heroes lay rolled in their gore;
> With sorrow their dead bodies we laid in the clay,
> In hopes that to heaven their souls took their way.[31]

Born in Aberdeenshire, Scotland, Patrick Ferguson, the British hero of Kings Mountain, joined the military when he was fourteen. In 1759, at the age of fifteen, the small-framed boy entered service with the Royal North Dragoons. His mother's brother, a major general, told Ferguson's mother, "You must no longer look upon him as your son. He is the son of Mars, and will be unworthy of his father if he does not give proofs of contempt of pain and danger."[32] Ferguson's incredible marksmanship astonished military dignitaries. During an exhibition, it was said, "he would check his horse, let the reins fall upon the animal's neck, draw a pistol from his holster, toss it aloft, catch it as it fell, aim, and shoot the head off a bird on an adjacent fence."[33] King George III attended this demonstration.

Ferguson and his green-jacketed rifle corps arrived in North America in spring 1777. His legendary sense of morality and fairness shone through when he refrained from shooting George Washington at Brandywine because the idea of shooting someone in the back disgusted him, but Ferguson did not regret his chivalry. Moments later he sustained a shattering wound to his right elbow that required multiple surgical procedures over a period of eight months in Philadelphia. The wound left him crippled for life. His detractors called him the "one-armed devil." Others called him "Bulldog." After resuming active duty, but still unable to use his right arm, Ferguson fought under Cornwallis in upper South Carolina in 1780. At Kings Mountain, said historian Draper, "Ferguson's conduct in the battle ... was that of a hero ... but he trusted too much to the bayonet against an enemy as nimble as the antelope."

Ferguson is renowned for developing the first successful breech-loading rifle. Loaded in the middle near the gunstock, it required no ramrod and could be loaded from a crouched position. It fired at a remarkable speed for its day: six shots per minute. Far superior to the standard Brown Bess musket, it was considered the finest military firearm used in the American Revolutionary War, but only about 100 were available for use at that time. Ferguson commanded a special experimental breech rifle unit at Brandywine in 1777. It is unknown whether any Ferguson rifles were used at Kings Mountain. There his battalion fought with Brown Bess muskets and bayonets.

Reports vary regarding the number of dead at Kings Mountain because successful operations were characteristically exaggerated in those times. After the battle the Patriot army hastened to pick up. They left quickly, fearing that Cornwallis would send fresh dragoons under "Bloody Ban" Tarleton to resume the fighting. Patriots hurriedly rigged up litters suspended between teams of horses to transport the wounded. Seven hundred captured Loyalists formed lines as the army slowly began to move on Sunday morning, October 8. Colonel Campbell took charge of burying the dead. He left Patriot private Joseph Starnes "to care for the wounded for two months." Starnes "got home just about Christmas."[34] Ellen McDowell and her daughter Jane, having heard the firing of 1,800 rifles and muskets from their home, joined their neighbors from the surrounding countryside, rushed to the battlefield, and spent several days nursing the wounded.

General George Washington learned about the Battle of Kings Mountain when Colonel John Sevier dispatched a runner, a giant of a man, to carry the news of victory to the Continental Congress assembled at Philadelphia. The messenger was militiaman Joseph Greer of the Watauga Settlement at Sycamore Shoals. Knowledgeable about Indians and experienced as a woodsman, Greer—a young Scotsman standing 6 feet 7 inches tall—armed himself with compass and rifle and set out on horseback for the long and perilous journey north. Swimming cold streams and hiding out in hollow logs to escape Indians, Greer made his way to the congressional headquarters in Philadelphia but was refused admittance by the doorkeeper. Towering over the guard, Greer pushed him aside and startled the assembly. When he strode down the aisle and delivered his report Washington commented, "With soldiers like him, no wonder the frontiersmen won."[35]

Militiamen on the overmountain journey home had difficulty guarding the long string of hundreds of Loyalist prisoners trying to escape over narrow paths and rutted roads. Some captives fled into the surrounding forest. Three hours into the trip, Patriot Colonel Williams died. Along the way, various Whigs took the wounded into their homes until they recovered enough to resume the long march home. The hungry army had last eaten a hearty meal at Cowpens on Friday. It was not until Sunday night, returning home, that they again ate, after raiding a farm, roasting beeves and digging sweet potatoes. On Wednesday they found a pumpkin patch.

On Sunday, October 15, nine miles northeast of Gilbert Town, the men returning from battle spotted the Biggerstaff farm. Above the hand-hewn log house smoke billowed from large red brick chimneys made of the iron-rich red clay of the piedmont. It was the plantation house of Loyalist captain Aaron Biggerstaff, who had been killed at Kings Mountain. Aaron's widow, Martha, looked out her window and saw the rebel army milling around her yard. The next morning, after a sleepless night, she found nine corpses twisting on ropes from the big oak tree in her now deserted yard. Jonas Bedford was not among them, although his wife, Mercy, living on a nearby plantation, heard that he was. Together with an old farm hand, Widow Biggerstaff cut down the dangling Tories. Aided by neighbors, she dug a two-foot–deep trench in the red clay earth and buried the bodies.

Historians disagree on events at the Biggerstaff farm. Some say the soldiers were too drunk to remember the details. The inability of many of the officers to maintain discipline allowed some soldiers to plunder the countryside. Weary and hungry, the Overmountain militia grew tired of guarding the long line of prisoners and simply wanted to do away with them. Somehow a court trial was decided upon. Acting on the North Carolina law stating that it was legal for two magistrates to summon a jury and hold a trial, a court-martial was ordered and witnesses were selected. A jury composed of field officers and captains convicted 36 Tories of "breaking open houses, killing the men, and turning the women and children out of doors, and burning the houses."[36] The convicts were condemned to hang on a huge oak tree—the "Gallows Tree." By torchlight, ropes were gathered and nooses were tied. "The hangings began ... three at a time," until nine were hanged. No one really remembers what stopped the hangings.[37]

Another account states that Isaac Shelby formed a court from the North Carolina magistrates present within his ranks and tried the prisoners under North Carolina law, not by court-martial. Draper reports that the hangings stopped and the Overmountain Men resumed their march when one of the reprieved prisoners, grateful to Shelby for sparing his life, murmured to him, "You have saved my life, and I will tell you a secret. Tarleton will be here in the morning—a woman brought the news."[38] Mercy Warren, looking South from her farm in New England and having lost a son on the frontier, had only a dim notion of what frontier folk were like. In regard to the executioins at the Biggerstaff Farm, she wrote the following: "This summary infliction was imposed by order of some of those fierce and uncivilized chieftains, who had spent most of their lives in the mountains ... amidst the slaughter of wild animals, which was necessary to their daily subsistence." Her concept was that justice practiced by backwoodsmen was more primitive than allowed by polite society.[39]

The Patriot army began marching toward Quaker Meadows to put the Catawba River between them and Tarleton. The army scattered; the prisoners were taken to Hillsborough, North Carolina. Tarleton, however, was not on the way. He was retreating with Cornwallis to Winnsboro. When the victorious Patriot militiamen returned home from Kings Mountain they learned that a British-instigated Cherokee attack on the frontier was imminent. Dragging Canoe and his Chickamaugas were again threatening settlements of the Holston and Watauga valleys. Wataugan John Sevier of Washington County, North Carolina, and Arthur Campbell of Washington County, Virginia, decided to carry the war to Indian towns rather than wait for the tomahawks and war clubs to come crashing through their cabin doors. Hence, Sevier gathered a band of militiamen from the Nolichucky Settlement. They crossed the French Broad River at the ford near the mouth of Boyd's Creek in present-day Sevier County. From their encampment on Boyd's Creek, the militia sallied forth, encountered an ambush, and exchanged fire with the Chickamauga warriors. Sevier's December 16, 1780, victory at the Battle of Boyd's Creek was "one of the best fought battles in the border war of Tennessee,"[40] declared early Tennessee historian Ramsey. After the Battle of Boyd's Creek, Arthur Campbell and his Virginia militia joined Sevier for more attacks against hostile Indian towns.

Private Joseph Starnes, having served at Kings Mountain under Colonel William Campbell and tended the wounded afterward, returned home just before Christmas. He immediately joined Arthur Campbell's expedition in the Cherokee War of 1780. Starnes explained: "I stood as a Minute Man and served very often whenever the Indians or Tories troubled us. I kept a good horse and thought myself bound to protect the frontier—and we did so, although many lives were lost." In addition to protecting the frontier, Starnes sought to avenge the murder of his father and relatives. Recalling those murders Starnes recounted that as a young Virginia militiaman he drove packhorses for the relief of settlers

15. Watauga, Kings Mountain and the Journey Home

at Boonesborough in 1778. He arrived there just after Daniel Boone had defended the fort against Indian attack. ("The horses were branded with '1778,'" wrote the 77-year-old Starnes when applying for his pension. "That's why I remembered it.") The next year, on his way home after carrying supplies to Fort Boonesborough, Starnes watched helplessly as Indians killed three members of his family. He said the family was "fired on by about 25 or 30 Indians and my father ... my uncle ... and brother-in-law were shot and I made my escape, although they ran me for upwards of a mile and kept firing on me but I made my escape in the cain [sic] and other undergrowth." Starnes joined Colonel Arthur Campbell's militia to "seek satisfaction" for the murders. His pension application notes that he "was with Col. Arthur Campbell of the militia, against the Cherokee Nation ... burnt their towns ... ate Christmas dinner on the Tennessee and then went over to the Valley and 'Hiwassy' towns ... burnt Cherokee towns and beat them well."

Many Overmountain Men like Starnes joined Arthur Campbell and Sevier in guarding the Indian border against Dragging Canoe. Other Kings Mountain veterans asked Colonel Isaac Shelby to recommend them to serve in General Daniel Morgan's militia under General Nathanael Greene in the North Carolina piedmont.

16

Cornwallis Reverses Course and Confronts Greene in the South

After demolishing Gates at Camden and defeating Sumter at Fishing Creek, Cornwallis moved into North Carolina expecting to rendezvous with Ferguson at Charlotte. When Cornwallis received Ferguson's distress signal from Kings Mountain, he sent Tarleton to reinforce him. But it was too late. Tarleton returned to the British camp in Charlotte, bringing the news of Ferguson's defeat and death on October 7, 1780. He also relayed to Cornwallis the rumor that Americans planned to reclaim the British strongholds at Camden and Ninety Six.

The stunning news from Kings Mountain stopped Cornwallis in his tracks, and he promptly abandoned his foothold in North Carolina. Temporarily dispensing with his plot to cross the Blue Ridge and launch his Virginia Campaign, Cornwallis retraced his steps to a defensive position in Winnsboro, South Carolina, 35 miles north of Columbia. The Patriot victory at Kings Mountain forced him to return to piedmont South Carolina in order to bolster his British bases at Camden and Ninety Six and delayed his recruit-and-subdue strategy in the South. All along the way from Charlotte to Winnsboro guerrillas under Sumter doggedly nipped and annoyed Cornwallis's rear guard and made off with supply wagons and rations. South Carolina governor John Rutledge had encouraged partisan leaders to defend the backcountry and harry Cornwallis until General Nathanael Greene could arrive in the state, replace the inept Gates, and weld together a new Continental Army. Partisans created a hornet's nest of resistance around Charlotte.

Quick-moving partisan forces were made up of citizen soldiers under the command of three well-known guerrilla (partisan) bands: Francis "Swamp Fox" Marion, Thomas "Gamecock" Sumter, and Andrew "Wizard Owl" Pickens. These leaders aided Greene's southern plan by keeping up pressure on Cornwallis in dozens of skirmishes around British forts in South Carolina, from Charlestown in the low country to Winnsboro and Charlotte in the upper piedmont. An eyewitness account of Cornwallis's encounter with the "hornet's nest" of partisan resistance in Charlotte is recorded in the pension application of Mecklenburg militiaman and guerrilla captain William Holland:

> Colonel Davie stationed his forces on the Waxsaw Creek and maintained for sometime (about two months) a partisan warfare with the British, when the enemy marched out and drove us from this encampment and marched into Charlotte where they encamped. General William L Davidson [under Thomas Sumter] had made a stand on Rocky River about ten miles from Charlotte, and Col. Davie and his forces were with him. Occasional and frequent skirmishes with the foraging parties occurred

until Cornwallis was compelled to leave this place and proceeded to Winnsboro in Fairfield District of South Carolina, where subsistence could be more easily procured. They were pursued to the crossing of the Catawba River by Col Davies' forces. The British remained at their camp near Winnsboro about 3 months.[1]

Cornwallis, acting on the rumor that Americans were planning to attack British bases in the South, sent Tarleton to stop Sumter from advancing toward Ninety Six. Patriot Mary Dillard, the wife of Captain James Dillard, was riding horseback through the woods of her farm near the Blackstock Plantation on the Tyger River just east of Spartanburg when she spotted "Tarleton's line of march." Galloping to Blackstock's "by a nearer route," she told Sumter of Tarleton's approach.[2] Alerted by Mary Dillard's courageous ride, the "Gamecock" took cover and braced for the attack. Near dark on November 20, 1780, in the ensuing Battle of Blackstock Plantation, Sumter, whose militia far outnumbered Tarleton's regulars, repulsed Tarleton, killing 50 British regulars and losing only three Patriots. "Bloody Ban" Tarleton withdrew for the first time. Sumter's Blackstock Farm victory, though small, helped balance the score for his humiliating defeat at Fishing Creek. The victorious "Fighting Gamecock," however, was hit by a musket ball beneath his left shoulder. By torchlight, the wounded Sumter, swinging on a raw bull's hide litter attached to two poles slung between two horses, was quietly carried to a farmhouse, where a doctor dug out the shot. Fording the Tyger, Pacolet and Broad rivers, the party then made their way to a guerrilla camp in South Carolina.

Court records of Washington County, North Carolina (now Tennessee), name at least two militiamen who fought alongside General Sumter at Blackstock's and then returned home across the Blue Ridge. The record states, "Jordan Roach made oath that he was in company with Solomon Massengill in South Carolina … at Blackstock under command of General Sumpter and that … Massengill had his right ear cut off by a Brittish Dragoon, and the same is ordered to be recorded." It was important to verify the reason for Mr. Massengill's missing ear because ear cropping as punishment for certain criminal offenses was common on the frontier. "Any newcomer in town, minus one or both ears, was immediately an object of suspicion."[3]

Cornwallis's change of plans due to Ferguson's loss at Kings Mountain and his delay at Blackstock's Plantation allowed time for General Greene to take command in December and begin rebuilding the Continental Army in the South. Rhode Islander Nathanael Greene, Washington's friend and most treasured military subordinate, was good-natured, hard-working, and self-educated. Back in his youth, he was always reading and studying, except when he rose to his burly height of five-feet-ten, looked around with his unforgettable blue eyes, one of them cloudy from a smallpox inoculation, and resumed his manual work. With his massive shoulders and muscular arms he lifted anchors and chains at his father's iron foundry, and in the family fields he plowed and loaded heavy sacks of grain. Greene's well-to-do father owned a gristmill, a sawmill, an iron foundry, a general store, a home, a farm, and even a luxurious sedan chair. The patriarch was a pious Quaker, understanding and kind but opposed to schooling and literary accomplishment.

Crippled by a childhood accident, Greene walked stiff-legged. When one of his dance partners accused him of dancing stiffly, he replied, "Very true, but you see I dance strong."[4] The limp, however, disqualified him as a candidate for officer's training. Undeterred, he bought a musket from a British deserter in Boston. When Greene enlisted in his local county militia, he was banished from the Quaker community, but he drilled as a private in the militia for eight months and became a "fighting Quaker." Miraculously zooming up the military ladder, he emerged as a full commander of the Rhode Island Regiment and head of the Rhode Island Army of Observation. The next year, in June 1775, he became a brigadier general. He met George Washington in July.

Commanding the Continental First Division in the American Revolutionary War, Greene helped Washington save the remnant of his army as it retreated from Chadds Ford after the Battle of Brandywine. In 1778 when Washington appointed Greene as quartermaster general of the Continental Line, Greene was disappointed. He grumbled that nobody had ever heard of a quartermaster making history. However, he soon became Washington's second in command. Washington described him as "a man of abilities, bravery and coolness. He has a comprehensive knowledge of our affairs and is a man of fortitude and resources." Henry Knox, Continental Army artillery commander, said of him, "He came to us the rawest, the most untutored being I ever met with." But within a year he "was equal in military knowledge to any general officer in the army and very superior to most of them."[5]

Nathanael Greene was nominated by Washington and confirmed by Congress to replace Horatio Gates as commander of the Southern Army following Gates' colossal loss of American lives at Camden. This made Greene second in command of the entire American army. Greene, however, could not assume command in the South immediately because he was serving as commander of West Point after the traitor Benedict Arnold defected to the British. Prior to Greene's departing for the South, Washington—having insufficient knowledge about the enemy forces and their resources in the southern campaign—said, "I can give you no particular instructions but must leave you to govern yourself entirely."[6]

Greene desperately needed funding for his southern campaign. Mary Digges Lee of Maryland met the challenge. Although no major Revolutionary War battles occurred in Maryland, the well-trained Maryland Continentals served in both the northern and the southern campaigns. In the North, Marylanders served in Washington's main army in New York, Pennsylvania and New Jersey. In the South, Marylanders participated in most of Nathanael Green's campaigns. Maryland's first lady at the time, Mary Digges Lee, inspired women to collect money and supplies including 260 linen shirts for Continental Line troops. George Washington's letter of 11 October 1780 to Mary Digges Lee thanked her for the "patriotic exertions of the ladies of Maryland in favor of the army." "Respecting the disposal of the Gratuity ... the Money which ha[d] been ... collected" was used to purchase shirts and black socks "for the use of Troops in the Southern Army."

In early December 1780, two months after the Battle of Kings Mountain, Greene arrived in Charlotte, North Carolina, where Gates had moved the southern headquarters of his ruined army. Greene handed Gates official notice of his removal from command. The next day, with complete composure, Gates handed over command to his successor. The former foundry worker Greene then welded together the remnant of Patriot troops following the carnage at Camden and forged an iron-willed army for the South.

Greene's efforts to rebuild the American army were reinforced by southern militia adopting the modus operandi of partisan bands. Cornwallis found their guerrilla hit-and-run tactics more troublesome than an enemy army that withdrew when threatened. When Greene took command of the southern army, the Patriot magazines at Charlotte, North Carolina, were almost empty and only a three-day supply of food was left. The British occupied Georgia and controlled the port city of Charlestown, South Carolina. Cornwallis, headquartered 65 miles south of Charlotte at Winnsboro, had robbed Whigs of food and fodder in order to feed his Tory soldiers and livestock. Greene realized that the poorly equipped remnant of Gates' American force in the South was not strong enough to compete with Cornwallis's main British force. The American army numbered only 1,500 troops and over half of those were militia.[7] That's why Greene broke a long-standing military tradition of never dividing a weaker army when confronting a stronger one. He split his weaker American army into two wings. Separating and spreading out would make it easier to forage for adequate food and would also avoid giving the impression that his army was retreating. If Cornwallis decided to pursue one of these wings, Greene's other wing could strike the British base at Charlestown or Ninety Six. To escape British pursuit Greene depended on the swift mobility of his flying camp to outdistance Cornwallis's slow-moving British infantry. Intending to gain enough strength to confront Cornwallis, Greene took command of the east wing and marched southeast from Charlotte toward Cheraw Hill, South Carolina, on the Pee Dee River. He assigned the command of the west wing—the frontier—to Brigadier General Daniel Morgan, "the Old Waggoner."

Back when he was a young man, New Jersey-born Daniel Morgan loved to fight and drink and play cards and could barely read and write. Six feet tall and weighing 200 pounds, he had emigrated to Virginia and worked as a teamster hauling freight and supplies for General Edward Braddock's unsuccessful campaign at the Forks of the Ohio in the French and Indian War. In 1756, Daniel had a run-in with a British officer in which the officer hit Morgan with his sword. The feisty young teamster struck back. The British Army court-martialed Morgan and sent him to be flogged with a cat-o'-nine tails. But instead of delivering the sentenced 500 lashes, the whip cracked only 499 times. A drummer boy—rolling the drum with each stroke—miscounted. Afterward, Morgan always said that the British owed him one more lash. In the early 1760s, he drove a team of horses carrying wagonloads of supplies for the British Army to the newly constructed Fort Chiswell, Virginia, which guarded the lead mines, a vital source of ammunition.

When the French and Indian War ended in 1763 Morgan bought a house in Winchester, Virginia, and set up housekeeping with his sweetheart, Abigail Curry. They married ten years later after having two daughters. Abigail improved Morgan's reading and writing skills, polished his manners and knocked the edge off his tendency to fight impulsively and to drink hard. When Daniel was furloughed for a year in 1779 due to painful sciatica Abigail treated him with herbal potions, compassion and cold baths.

Morgan, "the Old Wagoner," joined the American Army at the beginning of the Revolutionary War. Serving as captain of a rifle company called "Daniel Morgan's Independent Rifle Company," he led a unit of sharpshooters who surrounded and strangled the British in the Siege of Boston. Benedict Arnold and Morgan fought jointly in the December 1775 Battle of Quebec. When Arnold was wounded, Morgan and 375 riflemen were taken prisoner. Morgan was paroled in late 1776 and exchanged in January 1777. Both Arnold and Morgan fought fiercely and victoriously against Burgoyne in the decisive 1777 Battle of Saratoga. Credit for the win, however, was given to American general Horatio Gates, who subsequently lost his command after Cornwallis defeated him at Camden. (Morgan would finally garner his long-overdue glory at Cowpens.) In December 1780 Greene instructed Morgan to use guerrilla tactics—harass, torment, vex—and deter Tarleton. He was to engage the enemy either offensively or defensively west of the Catawba River. Morgan's mission also was to forage for food, fill the empty magazines and lift the morale of backcountry people.

When General Cornwallis learned of General Greene's almost unprecedented plan to divide the Patriot army, he had no choice but to split his Tory army in order to track both Greene and Morgan. Cornwallis personally pursued Greene and assigned his cavalry officer, Lt. Colonel Banastre Tarleton, to hunt down Morgan. The Tory Tarleton was well qualified for the job. Born into the British gentry, he attended Oxford University and became an officer of dragoons at age 21, soon volunteering for service in America. There he commanded the British Legion, a Loyalist regiment of mounted infantry, green-jacketed dragoons known for their brutality.

At Charlotte, the Patriot Morgan began assembling his west wing, a flying camp of horse and foot designed for rapid movement. This mobile corps of cavalry and light infantry consisted of 320 Maryland and Delaware Continentals under Lt. Colonel John Eager Howard and a detachment of 200 Virginia militiamen under Major Francis Triplett. Morgan's main reserve was a regiment of 100 Light Dragoons led by Lt. Colonel William Washington (at Cowpens one of these dragoons, an unnamed black soldier, would fire a pistol and save the life of Colonel Washington).

Morgan's 600 soldiers left Charlotte on December 21 traveling west. They crossed the Broad River on Christmas Eve and camped at Grindall's Fort on the left bank of the Pacolet River near Cowpens, South Carolina. on Christmas Day. When Morgan learned that Tarleton's forces outnumbered his, he called for reinforcements. Over the next few days and weeks Morgan's flying army wing expanded, with soldiers pouring in from many directions. Two companies joined Colonel Washington's cavalry battalion. Militiamen formerly under the command of General Thomas Sumter responded. More militia reported from Mecklenburg County, North Carolina, under the command of Brigadier General William Davidson. Morgan awaited further reinforcements from South Carolina guerrilla commander Andrew "Wizard Owl" Pickens and his mounted militia, who were racing to Cowpens.

At Cowpens, Morgan's flying army multiplied, attracting soldiers from six states. Two-thirds of the army were militia, bolstered by a hard corps of Continentals plus some state troops. Continentals, the national army of the United States, were the precursors of the United States Army. Each state was required to recruit and provide uniforms for the national force. State troops were organized and financed by the states for defending the boundary of the state. Morgan's troops numbered 300 Continentals and 700 militiamen. Some of the militia had camped at Cowpens three months earlier on their way to fight at Kings Mountain. Overmountain militiamen esteemed Daniel Morgan, who had won fame at Saratoga. After the Battle of Kings Mountain some of the veterans had asked Colonel Isaac Shelby to recommend them to join General Morgan, which he did.

Tarleton's mission was to corner Morgan and push him back east across the Broad River where Cornwallis could trap him. Early in January 1781 Tarleton began marching with his green-jacketed Legion Cavalry, the 16th Light Infantry, plus a battalion of Fraser Highlanders pulling a three-pounder cannon. They headed in the direction of Ninety Six in pursuit of Morgan. To reinforce Tarleton, Cornwallis sent troops and 18 royal artillerymen rolling two light cannons. On January 12, Tarleton's scouts spotted Morgan at Grindal Shoal on the Pacolet River between Spartanburg and the Broad River.

Elizabeth Ellet tells the story of Mrs. Potter and Mrs. Beckham, who lived at Grindal Shoal. Mrs. Potter's house and hut were visited by the famous "Bloody Bill Cunningham" and his party of 250 men. These Tories encamped in her cornfields, allowed their horses to feed in the fields, and tore down her fences to build bonfires to roast corn. Cunningham's men robbed the neighborhood looms of cloth, ripped open bedding, scattered the feathers and used the ticking as tent covers. On their way to Cowpens to face Morgan, Tarleton's soldiers burned the thatched roof of a crudely built hut where Mrs. Potter and her children were living while their house was occupied by a critically ill and contagious relative suffering with smallpox. After setting fire to the straw, the Loyalists approached Mrs. Potter but were unable to free her wedding ring, which had been confined behind her knuckle for 40 years. Though swearing to amputate her finger to steal the ring, they finally marched on to the home of Mrs. Beckham.

The first time Mrs. Beckham saw the renowned Tarleton was when he ordered his green-jacketed dragoons to catch her chickens for supper. She politely prepared and served the meal. On the next morning Tarleton's soldiers pillaged her bedding and ordered her house to be burned, but she protested and he recalled the order.

Tarleton resumed his pursuit of Morgan. On January 15 Morgan was encamped at Burr's Mill on Thicketty Creek. He was writing to Greene, telling him just how low supplies were, when he was informed that Tarleton's forces numbered 1,200 British regulars. At the same time, a courier was galloping cross country to deliver Greene's warning: Colonel Tarleton is "on his way to pay you a visit. I doubt not that he will have a decent reception and a proper dismission."[8] The "Old Waggoner" quickly broke camp and got moving while his men were chewing their half-cooked breakfast. "Wizard Owl" Pickens was en route to reinforce him. To ensure that Pickens could easily find him, Morgan took his stand at Hannah's Cowpens, a pasture well known to Patriots since it had marked the place of rendezvous for militiamen on their way to the Battle of Kings Mountain three months earlier. On the road to Cowpens, Morgan's heavily loaded wagons wore deep ruts in the muddy, rain-soaked clay roadway, over which Tarleton's British regiments traveled in pursuit. Despite ruts in the road and briars on the banks of Thicketty Creek, "Bloody Ban" Tarleton traveled light and fast, leaving his own wagons and baggage behind. Tarleton was now outnumbered, but he remained confident in his belief that he led the best troops in the British Army (plus some Loyalists) against Morgan's army, which was made up mainly of militia supported by a few Continentals.

Near Spartanburg, Morgan found a female spy to keep him apprised of Tarleton's approach. Catherine Moore Barry, a scout for the Patriot militia, was thoroughly familiar with the people and woodland paths surrounding her home, Walnut Grove Plantation. Married to militia captain Andrew Barry, Catherine—an excellent horsewoman—rounded up militiamen to fight under Morgan. As a spy and a messenger, she warned Morgan when Tarleton and the British were approaching Cowpens.

Expecting Tarleton to attack, Morgan's army encamped on the meadows of Cowpens with its overlooking knoll. All night long the Old Waggoner—half crippled with chronic sciatica and arthritis—moved among the militia, helping them fix their swords [bayonets], and joking with them. Repeatedly he said, "Hold up your heads, boys—three fires and you are free!" to go home, to be blessed by old folks and kissed by girls.

Morgan's ability to establish rapport with his militia was remarkably crucial for the success of the upcoming battle. These expert riflemen were accustomed to fighting Indian Style, shielded behind trees. He instilled into them the courage to stand in line, unshielded, face the enemy and fire before instinctively running for cover.

Before dawn on the bitter winter morning of January 17, 1781, pickets began shouting that Tarleton was only five miles away. Morgan bellowed to his men to get up, eat a hearty breakfast, and roll their wagons to the rear. On the wooded slopes, he began strategically posting his troops in three lines—each 150 yards behind the other on a slope—to face Tarleton. Their horses, saddled, bridled, and raring to go, waited restlessly among the pines. Morgan cautioned his men to be patient: "Let the enemy get within killing distance.... Fire at the men with epaulets."[9]

On the battlefield the "Old Wagoner," who preferred homespun clothing to an officer's uniform, confidently and competently commanded both Continental Army regulars and militia. The militia riflemen considered him one of their own, "a backwoodsman [who] had the speech and manners of the frontier."[10] An experienced Indian fighter, Morgan was well acquainted with the ways, strengths, and marksmanship of the militia. He encouraged his troops at Cowpens, showing them the scars from the 499 lashes the British had given him when he was fighting as a British colonist against the French and the northern Indians. Morgan was preparing to lure Tarleton into an "elaborate and brilliantly conceived trap."[11]

Tarleton's army, intent on a surprise attack, quickly paraded to Morgan's campsite in a blur of color. Marching to the mournfully chilling wail of bagpipes, the plaid-kilted Highlanders set the pace for the red-and-green–coated legionaries, green-jacketed dragoons, and red-and-white–coated infantry and cavalry going to battle. Royal artillerists pushed and pulled two three-pounder cannons. Tarleton, unaware that Morgan's troops were waiting for him, marched forward surrounded by a cacophony of sound—the roll of drums, the shrill pitch of fifes, and the British hallo. They "raised a prodigious yell and came running as if they intended to eat us up," said Morgan. With its awesome array of color, "it was the most beautiful line I ever saw," according to an American cavalryman.

Morgan waited to intercept Tarleton in a preemptive strike and cantered along the lines shouting the often-used Revolutionary War slogan "Don't fire until you see the whites of their eyes." Every officer echoed his words: "Don't fire." General Morgan finally gave the command, shouting, "They've given you the British hallo, now give them the Indian hallo!"[12] The first line of expert rebel riflemen yelled out blood-curdling yips and war whoops. A split second later they opened fire. Morgan's front-line militia riflemen were agile enough to run, load, and shoot more rapidly than the Continentals. These skirmishers were led by Major John Cunningham of Georgia and Major Joseph McDowell, the brother of Colonel Charles McDowell of Quaker Meadows. After firing two or three shots these gutsy skirmishers immediately fell back, as planned, to reload behind the next line, which was 150 yards behind. On the second line the Georgia and Carolina militia under Pickens fired two volleys at the advancing Tories and then reloaded. As Morgan had anticipated, Tarleton mistook this falling back as a frightened militia retreat and kept on rapidly advancing, galloping headlong toward the mouths of the guns of the regular troops of the Continental Army on the third row. Howard's 600 Delaware and Maryland Continentals and Virginia militia made up the third row. William Washington's 125 cavalrymen, Morgan's main reserve, were posted hidden from view behind the crest of the northernmost ridge.

Even as Morgan's sharpshooters struck down red coats, green jackets and epaulets, the

16. Cornwallis Reverses Course and Confronts Greene in the South

experienced but startled British horsemen still thundered forward. Tarleton's 71st Highlander Bagpipers added to the dissonance as his dragoons charged the American lines. The Continentals on the third line fired. William Washington's reserve cavalry courageously and fiercely repelled and routed the charge of Tarleton's dragoons (an achievement for which Congress would award Colonel Washington a silver medal). The battle lasted an hour. In Morgan's positioning of his troops with militia in front, Continentals behind and cavalry in reserve—one of the most brilliant battle tactics of the war—his Patriots crushed the British and won the Battle of Cowpens. Tarleton's troops sustained 600 casualties. One hundred ten of his Tories were killed; 800 were taken prisoner. Patriots suffered 12 killed and 61 wounded. Morgan's surprising victory at Cowpens was a tactical masterpiece still marveled at today.

After the battle, Morgan was "so elated he picked up his nine-year-old drummer boy and kissed him on both cheeks." A few days later he wrote to his friend William Snickers: "You remember that I was so desirous to have a stroke at Tarleton—my wishes are gratified and [we] have given him a devil of a whipping."[13] "Morgan outgeneraled Tarleton," said a Tarleton lieutenant at Cowpens.[14] "The British suffered a reverse almost as serious as that of Kings Mountain three months earlier."[15] Both battles encouraged the Americans, disheartened the British and eased the way to Yorktown. The death of Ferguson had moved Cornwallis from Charlotte to Winnsboro. The defeat of Tarleton at Cowpens on January 17 caused Cornwallis to give up his fight for the backcountry.

Upon hearing the news of Tarleton's defeat at Cowpens, Cornwallis pressed down on the hilt of his sword so hard that he broke it in two, swearing that he would find Morgan and free Tarleton's captured men no matter the cost. Tarleton and 54 of his cavalry, who had escaped capture at Cowpens, joined Cornwallis's camp on a branch of the Broad River 40 miles north of Cowpens. Major General Alexander Leslie arrived at the Cornwallis camp with reinforcements from Camden. Cornwallis had called Leslie to fill the void when Ferguson was killed at Kings Mountain. Leslie then abandoned the Virginia campaign in the Chesapeake to join Cornwallis in Carolina. Cornwallis pursued Morgan. Thus began the January 18–February 15, 1781, "Race to the Dan." But Cornwallis took the wrong road at least twice and never caught up with Morgan. Cornwallis often lost his way as he marched hesitantly across the unfamiliar and hostile North Carolina countryside where Patriots swarmed like hornets and Loyalist support was lethargic.

The victorious Morgan hurried to rejoin Greene. The two Patriot wings were separated by 140 miles and Cornwallis stood between the two. Morgan's 600 men crossed the swollen Broad River. Stopping for two days at Gilbert Town, Morgan set up a temporary hospital and dispatched a letter to Greene telling him of his Cowpens victory. He left Gilbert Town on the 20th and crossed the swollen Catawba River, meeting Greene north of the Catawba River on the 30th. Unfortunately, Morgan's painful sciatica forced him to request a leave of absence. Upon meeting Greene, Morgan suggested that the command of his army be turned over to three partisan militia leaders: General William Lee Davidson, Colonel Andrew Pickens, whose rank would be raised to general after his performance at Cowpens, and General Thomas Sumter.

Greene knew that Cornwallis would have to ford the Catawba River to continue his pursuit. He therefore commissioned militia partisan General Davidson and his detachment of guerrillas to impede the crossing. Delaying Cornwallis's advance would buy time for

Greene's army, herding its 600 British captives from Cowpens, to row across the Dan River to Virginia. Many Catawba Valley farmers comprised Davidson's small detachment of 300 Patriots. These partisans needed to anticipate where Cornwallis would cross the Catawba so that they could annoy him, as guerrillas do, and prevent his catching up with Morgan's slow-moving troops and their long string of prisoners. Davidson opted to set up camp less than a mile from the Cowan's crossing of the Catawba River. There, on the Mecklenburg (east) side of Cowan's Ford, the detachment awaited the arrival of Cornwallis's much larger army, which was approaching from the Lincoln County (west) side of the Ford.

The following eyewitness version of the crossing was told by Robert Henry, a teenager who was attending school in Lincoln County near Cowan's Crossing. Cornwallis was encamped nearby when news came to Henry's schoolmaster that Tarleton was ranging through the county "catching Whig boys to make musicians of them in the British army." The schoolmaster hurriedly dismissed the students and sent them home. The schoolboy Henry, however, procured a gun and ammunition and went to the ford, where its 30 Patriot guards welcomed him. Each guard picked a stand from which to fire at the British when they crossed the ford. At sundown a Patriot from across the river hooted like an owl, signaling that all was quiet in the enemy camp. The guards at Cowan's Ford then lay down and slept cradling their guns. At dawn on February 1, 1781, they were awakened by a battle cry: "The British! The British!"

The water of the flooded Catawba was shoulder deep as Cornwallis crossed Cowan's Ford west to east, from the Lincoln County side to the Mecklenburg County side at Cowan's Ford. Cornwallis's horse was shot from under him but it kept going until it reached the other bank and fell dead. Strong currents swept General Leslie's horse downstream. Brigadier General Charles O'Hara (Cornwallis's second in command) and his horse rolled 40 yards.[16]

Each American guard ran to his station. Some fired at the Redcoats who were splashing on horseback through the waist-deep water, and the swirling current carried the bodies away. As the British emerged from the river, Colonel William Polk, Davidson's infantry commander, shouted, "Fire away, boys, help is at hand!" A lively exchange of fire dropped bodies on both sides. "Davidson was killed by the first gun that was fired on the British side on that occasion, for they did not fire a gun whilst in the river ... [and] an utter silence prevailed—not a gun firing on either side: Silence was first broken by the report of the gun that killed Davidson."[17] Polk, unable to fight Cornwallis on equal terms, marched Davidson's army away from danger. Davidson's Patriot militia, however, had accomplished their mission. They delayed Cornwallis's crossing, thus proving once again the value of part-time citizen soldiers (militiamen) to the Continental Army. The delay allowed time for Greene to maintain his lead in the race to the Dan.

Greene, exhausted by his arduous retreat across the Carolinas, anxiously awaited the arrival of Davidson's small body of militia. Sometime after midnight on February 2 Greene heard that General Davidson had died at Cowan's Ford. Riding on with a heavy heart, Greene dismounted and checked into Elizabeth Steele's Tavern, the principal hotel in Salisbury. Seeing his weary friend unaccompanied and dejected, Dr. Reed inquired about his health. The landlady, widow Elizabeth Steele, overheard Greene's melancholy reply: "Yes—fatigued—hungry—alone, and penniless!" Just as Greene took his seat at the well-spread table, Mrs. Steele entered the room, closed the door and drew from her apron two small bags of hard-earned money. "Take these," said she, "for you will want them and I can do without them." Touched and cheered by her words of encouragement, Greene accepted and thanked her for her offer. "His spirits were cheered and lightened by this touching proof of woman's devotion to the cause of her country." He did not remain long in Salisbury, but before he left, Greene autographed a memento for Mrs. Steele. He lifted a portrait of George III off the tavern wall and wrote in chalk on the picture's back, "O, George, hide they face and mourn." The general then replaced the portrait, face turned to the wall. The Steele family has preserved the portrait until this day.[18]

When Cornwallis learned that Greene had already crossed the Catawba River, he lightened his own army's load and increased its speed. He discarded all the wagons, supplies, baggage and tents, including his own. Cornwallis's force, now light and agile, was also hungry and cold. To escape Cornwallis, Greene and his army continued racing northward through North Carolina to cross the Dan River into Virginia where they hoped to find more troops and ammunition. The east wing of Greene's army consisted of the mere fragment of the Continental Army that had survived Lincoln's surrender at Charlestown and Gates' defeat by Cornwallis at Camden. It was ill prepared to fight, and Cornwallis hoped to attack the weakened American army before Greene could rebuild it. Cornwallis and Tarleton were hot on their heels when Greene and Morgan, carrying the wounded from Cowpens, escaped by commandeering all available boats and ferrying the troops across the swollen Yadkin River. Overnight, a late winter thaw and pouring rain had raised the river level two feet. The pursuing British had no boats, and the high water forced them to detour 35 miles upstream to cross the Yadkin at a shallow ford just west of the Moravian Settlement at Salem. A historical marker at Trading Ford on the Yadkin reads, "General Nathanael Greene, in his masterly retreat from the British Army under Lord Cornwallis, crossed the Yadkin at Trading Ford ... February 2–3, 1781. A sudden rise in the river prevented the passage of the British and permitted the American Army to escape and prepare for the Battle of Guilford Court House."

Having detoured upstream on the banks of the raging Yadkin, Cornwallis resumed the chase. But partway through his pursuit he turned back to recruit more Loyalists and restock supplies. Meanwhile, Greene reached the Virginia border, where he commandeered boats along the Dan River to prevent the British from crossing. Greene crossed the Dan in mid–February 1781 in Halifax County, Virginia, where his army took refuge, recuperated, found reinforcements and obtained supplies. Patrick Henry rallied 300 volunteers to join Greene. Henry's plantation, Leatherwood, at the mouth of the Dan supplied "167 bushels of corn for (Greene's) army and forage for twenty-eight horses."[19] In March, as soon as his militia reinforcement arrived, the refreshed Greene recrossed the Dan and reversed the vigorous pursuit, chasing Cornwallis all the way to Guilford Courthouse (Greensboro), North Carolina. Ten years later, General Ortho Williams wrote the following: "The retreat of the southern army to the Dan River, though now forgotten, was, in my estimation, one if the most masterly and fortunate maneuvers of our beloved Greene."

Back in mid–January 1781 Greene had sent a request to the "famous Colonel William Campbell ... to bring, without loss of time, a thousand good volunteers from over the mountains."[20] By March, Campbell and Colonel William Preston, despite trouble at home from Indian attacks, gathered 400 Overmountain Riflemen, led them over the Blue Ridge, and delivered them to Greene near Guilford Courthouse and Wetzel's (Whitesell's) Mill.

Greene then dispatched light infantry—riflemen under colonels Campbell and Preston, William Washington, Henry "Light Horse Harry" Lee, and Ortho Williams—to guard Wetzel's Mill. They were to keep Cornwallis's forces away until Greene's wagons could load enough flour to feed the American troops.

Cornwallis also sent detachments to Wetzel's Mill. Using the whimsical weather to their advantage, Cornwallis's advance parties, under cover of a thick fog, cut off Greene's light infantry from their main body. The ensuing Battle at Wetzel's Mill on March 6, 1781, was a preliminary skirmish between two detachments of riflemen: Cornwallis's Jaegers, who were an elite corps of Hessian riflemen, and Greene's advance guard of crack-shot marksmen. While Greene's men loaded the meal onto provision wagons, the British and American advance columns met each other 200 yards below the mill on Reedy Creek. Enshrouded by fog, Cornwallis's approaching Jaegers exchanged fire with Campbell's frontier riflemen.

The Americans narrowly accomplished their purpose of procuring food before retreating through the haze of mist and the stench of gun smoke. The aging and corpulent Colonel William Preston, collector and custodian of the Preston Papers, was unhorsed as he forded the millstream over slippery rocks. With assistance he remounted and ascended the steep, brushy north bank. Greene and Cornwallis offered discordant accounts of the Wetzell's Mill skirmish. Greene reported, "The enemy were handsomely opposed and suffered considerably."[21] Cornwallis wrote, "At Wetzell's mill, on the Reedy fork, where they made a stand, the back mountain men and some militia suffered considerably, with little loss on our side."[22]

Immediately following the skirmish at Wetzel's Mill, Greene prepared for the upcoming March 15, 1781, Battle of Guilford Courthouse, North Carolina. It was not the traditional stand-up fight that Cornwallis preferred; it was Greene's premeditated series of fights and deliberate withdrawals involving 4,400 American troops (1,700 Continentals and 2,700 militiamen) using both small arms and hand-to-hand combat against Cornwallis's smaller force of Redcoats and Hessians. Greene organized his troops into three lines. Along the Salisbury Wagon Road the first line, the North Carolina militia, was positioned behind rail fences and extended into the woods on either side. Militia also made up the second line. The third line contained Continentals. After several hours of battle, Greene, a renowned military strategist, withdrew and thus allowed Cornwallis to win a Pyrrhic victory for the British. By withdrawing, Greene avoided the type of disastrous defeat that Gates had suffered at Camden. Greene sustained light casualties, 79 killed and 185 wounded. He left Cornwallis's army heavily crippled, 93 killed and 413 wounded. The number of British casualties equaled almost a third of Cornwallis's army. "I never saw such fighting since God made me. The Americans fought like demons," said General Charles Cornwallis.[23]

The militiamen of the western waters fought ferociously under Greene. When he sounded the retreat and drums echoed the command to withdraw, the fearless mountaineers ignored the signal and simply moved back into the woods. Approaching stealthily and fighting Indian style, they unplugged their powder horns, loaded their rifles and fired with deadly accuracy. They inflicted casualties in what Cornwallis called "the bloodiest Battle of the War." The bravery of these overmountain men prompted Greene to say, "The back country people are bold and daring in their make, but the people of the seaboard are sickly and indifferent militia."[24] The battle at Guilford Courthouse wore down Cornwallis's British

Army and rescued North Carolina from Tory hands. It helped break British control of the Carolinas and freed Greene to conquer the South. He lost battles but won the campaign.

While the men of their church congregation fought the British at Guilford Courthouse, two groups of women, one in Buffalo and the other in Alamance, earnestly prayed for their families and their country. Many others offered silent prayers.[25] Elizabeth Forbes, the widow of militia officer Patriot Arthur Forbes, who was mortally wounded in the Battle of Guilford County, successfully submitted a petition to the North Carolina State Legislature for the distressed condition of her "helpless family of Small children," the appeal supported by a letter from a county official. The state granted Elizabeth Forbes "twenty five barrels of Corn out of the Specifick Tax for the County of Guilford for the year 1782, and the like Quantity out of the Tax for 1783."[26]

The Battle of Guilford Courthouse delayed but did not deter Cornwallis's determination to invade Virginia. Leaving Guilford Courthouse, he led his army down the Cape Fear River to Wilmington. From there he advanced northward and resumed his attempt to subdue Virginia, cut off supplies to the Carolinas, and strengthen his grip on the southern states. He had left colonels in control of the three major British strongholds in South Carolina. Lord Francis Rawdon, the acting chief commander, was posted at Camden. Nisbet Balfour took charge of Charlestown. John Cruger commanded Star Fort at Ninety Six. These three, plus Thomas Brown of Augusta, Georgia, were the enemy commandants who confronted Greene. Their mission was to quell Patriot resistance in the South, recruit Loyalists and restore American allegiance to the King.

Greene's strategy to regain the South hinged on attacking these British outposts, rather than chasing Cornwallis to the Chesapeake. Systematically, Greene began attacking British strongholds, rounding up Tories, and driving them to the main British fortification at Charlestown in order to confine them to one place. He dispatched three detachments of partisan militiamen to cut the arteries and interrupt supplies connecting these vital outposts. General Francis "Swamp Fox" Marion and Colonel "Light Horse Harry" Lee, together with 600 overmountain troops under Sevier and Shelby,[27] were to sever the artery between Charlestown and Camden; General Thomas "Carolina Gamecock" Sumter was to disrupt supplies between Camden and Ninety Six; and Colonel Andrew "Wizard Owl" Pickens would break the line of communication between Ninety Six and Augusta.

The 22-year-old Rawdon, British chief commander in the South, now faced some of the most formidable guerrilla leaders in the country. Marion, Sumter, and Pickens began attacking British posts throughout South Carolina and interrupting their vital lines of communication. Rawdon detached Loyalist lieutenant colonel John Watson with 400 troops to protect the artery between Camden and Charlestown. But Francis Marion outfoxed Watson's patrol and besieged Fort Watson, the main fort between Charlestown and Camden. Guarded by 114 Tories and Loyalists, Fort Watson stood on the 30-foot– high Santee Indian mound at Wright's Bluff. The Swamp Fox and Light Horse Harry Lee, working in the dark of night, cut logs in the forest and built a tower 40 feet high. It rose above, and looked down into, the garrisoned fort. At dawn, aiming their rifles downward and picking off enemy troops, the Patriot partisans soon persuaded the Tories inside Fort Watson to surrender. The seizing of Fort Watson on April 23, 1781, broke supply routes between Charlestown and Camden, provided needed ammunition for the Patriots, and led to the May 10 evacuation of Camden, which the British would never occupy again. Partisan Thomas "Carolina Gamecock" Sumter and three regiments of state troops patrolled the country between Camden and Ninety Six. Sumter assailed the British post at Orangeburg on the North Edisto River. The fort's garrison of 60 Loyalist militiamen and 12 regulars surrendered with little resistance on May 11, 1781. Meanwhile, "Wizard Owl" Pickens intercepted supplies between Ninety Six and Augusta. One enemy of the guerrillas in District Ninety Six was Bill Cunningham and his "Bloody Scouts."

A 15-year-old spy, Laodicea (Dicey) Langston, an expert horsewoman and skilled rifle shooter, lived in District Ninety Six, the westernmost district of South Carolina. There, Whig-Tory rivalry viciously divided neighbors and families. Dicey, her invalid father and her brothers, all of whom were guerrillas, lived in a mixed neighborhood of Tories and Whigs. Surrounded by Loyalists, many of whom were her relatives, Dicey overheard tidbits of information to pass on to her Patriot brothers. Her extraordinary Patriotism to the American cause and her remarkable disregard for personal danger became legendary when she repeatedly rebuffed the threats to her life made by Loyalists led by Bill Cunningham, a cousin of Scovilites Richard and Patrick Cunningham, who had gained notoriety in the Snow Expedition. By 1781 Bill headed a particularly violent band of Loyalists known as the "Bloody Scouts," who massacred Patriots throughout the Ninety Six District.

One of Dicey's brothers was encamped with his fellow Patriot soldiers at the Elder Settlement at Little Eden in the Ninety Six District when Dicey discovered that Bill Cunningham planned to attack her brother's military camp. She needed to alert her brother! The Tyger River was swollen on that dark night when Dicey Langston decided it would be safer to go silently on foot, rather than on horseback, through the woods, so she had to wade across the river to find her brother. The swift currents of the Tyger concealed treacherous deep spots, forcing her to lose her footing and swim in places. Swirled around by the furious current for which the Tyger was named, she lost her sense of direction in the dark. Frightened and cold, she continued traveling 27 miles and finally reached her brother's military camp, delivered the warning and urged him to alert the neighborhood. Thus, when Cunningham's Bloody Scouts reached their campsite, Dicey's brother and his colleagues had vanished.

The Tories suspected Dicey of spying and warning the rebels of impending Loyalist raids. They admonished her father to keep a close check on her and held him responsible for her espionage, blaming the father for instilling his Patriotic principles into his daughters as well as his son. One day Cunningham's bloody band went to the Langston homes to massacre the men of the family. Angry because the sons were absent, one of the scouts leveled a gun at the feeble, elderly Mr. Langston. Dicey shrieked and sprang between the rifle and her father. The scout ordered her to move. Refusing, Dicey put her arms around her father's neck and declared, "My own body shall first receive the bullet aimed at his heart." Langston was spared and the "Bloody Scouts" left their house. The next time Cunningham's band came back, Dicey refused to give them the information they desired from the Whig neighborhood. The soldier ordered her to disclose the secrets or "die in her tracks." Dicey opened the bodice of her dress and pointed to the place on her bosom where she would receive the bullet. An officer threw up his hands and saved the courageous girl's life.[28] Both Dicey and her guerrilla brothers continued working for the Patriot cause.

Greene, having dispatched three bands of guerrillas to disrupt communications, personally began marching to confront Lord Rawdon at Camden. When Rawdon learned that

Greene was marching to Camden, he pulled reinforcements from Colonel Watson and his 400 troops who were patrolling the route between Camden and Georgetown. Greene set up camp in the woods on Hobkirk's Hill, two miles from his intended attack target at Camden. His camp was made up of North Carolina militia, two Virginia regiments, two Maryland regiments, and Delaware Continentals. He also expected reinforcement from Thomas "Gamecock" Sumter. When a drummer deserted Greene's camp that night and informed Rawdon of the weakness of Greene's army and the anticipated arrival of reinforcements the next day, Rawdon attacked Greene preemptively on Hobkirk's Hill before the Gamecock appeared.

Moving 840 infantry, 60 cavalry, and two six-pounder cannons through thick woods, Rawdon reached the Patriot picket line undetected. When the Tory invaders were discovered, however, the Delaware Continentals delayed Rawdon's troops long enough for Greene to position his army. A 90-foot-wide clearing—part of the Great Road from Camden to Waxhaw—separated the armies of Greene and Rawdon.

On April 25, 1781, the Battle of Hobkirk's Hill (the Second Battle of Camden) opened with gusto. Artillery from both sides spat grapeshot from cannons. Rawdon's British broke through the center of the American line, pushed up Hobkirk's Hill, and forced Greene to retreat. Rawdon's men gave chase. Losses were heavy, 300 on each side. Greene recovered his artillery and baggage, rallied his men, and crossed the Wateree River above Camden, keeping most of his remaining army intact. He had failed to drive Rawdon's Tories out of Camden, but the sum of Tory losses at Watson's Fort and Hobkirk's Hill influenced the British decision to leave Camden two weeks later. On their way out of the abandoned village, the British destroyed buildings, stores, and homes. Greene advanced west-southwest to besiege Cruger's British stronghold at Ninety Six.

Rawdon returned to Camden and assembled a reinforcement of 500 men. He and Watson then crossed the Wateree in pursuit of Greene on his way to Ninety Six. Unable to catch up with Greene, Rawdon proceeded down the Santee to assist the British troops garrisoned at Fort Motte, who were besieged by Francis "Swamp Fox" Marion. Tories had confiscated Fort Motte, Patriot Rebecca Motte's home, and converted it to a reservoir for British convoys between Charlestown and Camden. On May 12, 1781, supporting the American cause, Rebecca Motte gave to a Patriot soldier a quiver of arrows imported from India and attached to balls of blazing rosin and brimstone to be shot onto the shingled roof of her own home. Her courageous act smoked out 165 Tories who then surrendered Fort Motte to the Swamp Fox. After the inferno at Fort Motte, other forts capitulated. The post at Nelson's Ferry submitted two days later. Fort Granby (Cayce) surrendered 352 Tories. At Georgetown, Rawdon faced Marion and then retreated to Moncks Corner, 33 miles from Charlestown. Soon Greene had confined enough Tories to Charlestown to recover northeastern South Carolina. Only Ninety Six and Augusta were still held by the British.

When Cornwallis converted the old trading post of Ninety Six into a British base, he had placed Cruger in command. Under Cruger, the Loyalists and slaves from surrounding plantations began building a star-shaped fort at Ninety Six. A year later, from May 22 to June 18, 1781, Nathanael Greene—often assisted by Light Horse Harry Lee—besieged the Star Fort for twenty-eight days, but he never took the fort. True to his famous attack-and-retreat strategy for wearing down the enemy, he halted the siege when he heard that British reinforcements under Rawdon were on the way.

Elizabeth Ellet's research revealed no reason to doubt the often-told story of the heroic teenager Emily Geiger. Near the Broad River, while Greene was retreating from Rawdon's Star Fort at Ninety Six, he needed to send a message to General Sumter on the Wateree River. The country between the two rivers was teeming with "blood-thirsty Tories." No man was willing to undertake Greene's hazardous mission. When 15-year-old Emily Geiger volunteered, the surprised Greene was happy to give the girl the message, both verbally and in writing. On the second day of her trip, riding sidesaddle on horseback, Emily was intercepted by Lord Rawdon's scouts and locked up until a Tory matron could search her. Left alone and not wishing to be caught spying, Miss Geiger chewed and swallowed the message bit by bit. The searcher was unable to find any message on her. Emily was released. She continued to Sumter's camp by a circuitous route and delivered the message verbally. Soon afterward Sumter joined Greene's main army at Orangeburg.[29] A month later the British gave up control of the interior backcountry, abandoned Star Fort, and moved to the coast.

While Greene besieged the Star Fort at Ninety Six, Loyalist Thomas Brown commanded the British base at Augusta. In mid–May partisan colonels Andrew "Wizard Owl" Pickens and Elijah Clarke teamed up with Light Horse Harry Lee and began strangling the British stronghold at Augusta. They took outlying posts and cut off supplies. Lee then engineered the construction of a wooded tower similar to the one he and Sumter had built at Fort Watson. Pointing cannon down into Fort Cornwallis, the primary fortification of Augusta, these partisans forced the British to capitulate.

One of the Patriot partisans killed at Augusta was Artillery Captain William Martin, who had served with distinction at the sieges of Savannah and Charlestown. Just before his death William had placed his cannon on one of the towers constructed by Pickens. Martin was one of seven brothers his mother, Elizabeth Martin, had sent to battle exclaiming fervently, "Thank God, they are the children of the Republic." A British officer vented his hatred of the Whigs by riding to the Williams home and asking Elizabeth if she had a son in the army at Augusta. When she replied that she had the monster gleefully told her, "Then I saw his brains blown out in the field of battle." Careful not to show her shock and suffering, the mother said, "He could not have died for a nobler cause!" During the siege, two of Elizabeth's daughters-in-law, Grace and Rachel Martin, had disguised themselves in their husbands' clothes and waylaid a courier and his guards in the middle of night. Pointing pistols at the courier, they demanded his dispatches and then paroled the men and sent them on their way. The gutsy women then sent the messages to General Greene.[30]

Surrendering at Augusta to Pickens and Clarke on June 5, 1781, at Fort Cornwallis were the fort commander, Loyalist colonel Thomas Brown, his King's Rangers and 300 Tories. The captive Brown, on the way to Savannah where he would be paroled, required an escort to protect him from the people whose kinsmen he had sent to the gallows or tortured and whose homes he had burned. By August the Whig (Patriot) government was restored to Augusta.

Shortly after Rawdon's hollow victory at Hobkirk's Hill and his withdrawal from Camden, he boarded a ship and sailed away due to ill health. Rawdon, the British commander in chief in the South, left Lieutenant Colonel Alexander Stewart, his field commander, in charge. By midsummer Greene had gained control of virtually all of South Carolina. The retreating British forces united at Orangeburg under Steward and began marching toward refuge at Charlestown. On the way the Tories encamped at Eutaw Springs, South Carolina, 32 miles east of Orangeburg.

Greene, persistent in his effort to overtake enemy outposts, confronted Stewart at the September 8, 1781, Battle of Eutaw Springs. Working with Greene were detachments from great leaders of the South: Otho Holland Williams, John Eager Howard, Jethro Sumner, Andrew Pickens, Henry Lee, William Washington, Francis Marion, Wade Hampton, and other partisans, plus troops from the Maryland, Delaware, and North Carolina lines. The disparate units were a hodge-podge, ragtag bunch of 2,000 ill-clad, ill-shod men in loincloths. These barefoot Patriots left bloody tracks on the banks of the Santee when they sprang a surprise attack on Stewart's 2,300 well-equipped troops at Eutaw Springs.[31] (Wounded by a bayonet, Lieutenant Colonel William Washington of Virginia was among the 60 prisoners captured in the cavalry charge at Eutaw Springs. He was sent to Charlestown for surgery, and there he met nurse Jane Elliot, his future wife. Their marriage took place in spring 1782. William, a second cousin of George Washington, then began farming the plantation of his wife's family at Sandy Hill, South Carolina.)[32]

Unable to dislodge the British from their stone house stronghold at Eutaw Springs, Greene withdrew. But his army accomplished its purpose, which was to support General George Washington's elaborate scheme to surround the British at Yorktown. By blocking the British at Eutaw Springs, the Patriots interrupted the flow of reinforcements from the Tory stronghold at Charlestown to Cornwallis in Virginia. Once again Greene won a strategic victory but failed to win military victory. Although he lost Hobkirk's Hill and Eutaw Springs to Rawdon and Stewart, the Pyrrhic victories of the British in those battles and numerous others forced Stewart to move to Charlestown and stay put there until the end of the war. Deliberately and methodically Greene was accomplishing his goal: severing communications and confining the retreating Loyalists and the British to the Charlestown peninsula.

Seeking reinforcements from overmountain riflemen, Greene wrote to militia commander Shelby "in the back parts of North Carolina":

> Dear Sir: ... [W]e had an action with the British Army (at Eutaw Springs) on the 8th in which we were victorious. We took 500 prisoners in and killed and wounded a much greater number. We also took 1000 statn of arms, and have driven the enemy near the gates of Charleston ... [and] a large French fleet ... has arrived in the Chessepeak bay, with a considerable number of land forces; all of which are to be employed against Lord Cornwllis who it is suspected will endeavor to make good his retreat through North Carolina to Charleston.... If you can intercept his lordship it will put a finishing stroke to the war in the Southern states.[33]

By the end of 1781 Greene's army, strengthened by militia and partisans, had captured all the interior parts of the Carolinas, but the British retained the coastal bases of Charlestown, Savannah and Wilmington.

While Greene managed the war in South Carolina and Georgia, Patriot militiamen of North Carolina made plans to attack the Tory stronghold at Elizabethtown, where a great number of Loyalist Highlander Scots lived. Sally Salter, a volunteer Patriot spy, aided the colonels in planning the invasion. An unsuspecting sentry rowed Sally across the Cape Fear River to the Tory camp. Selling eggs from her basket, she gathered bits of information that helped with the planning of the path of the march to battle. North Carolina Highway Historical Marker I-11 in Elizabethtown, North Carolina, describes the Battle of Elizabethtown: "Whigs broke Tory power in Bladen Co., August 1781 driving them into a Tory Hole 50 yards N."

The September 13, 1781, Battle of Lindley's Mill, North Carolina, closed the Revolutionary War in North Carolina. Trouble began when Loyalist colonel David Fanning and 600 Tory soldiers barged into the North Carolina state capital of Hillsborough. Arousing sleeping villagers from their beds, he confiscated supplies, captured 200 soldiers, nabbed Patriot governor Thomas Burke and arrested several other military and civil officials. Patriot general John Butler and his 300 militiamen lined up on a hilltop where they watched Fanning's Tories wend their way toward Wilmington. When Fanning crossed Cane Creek near Lindley's Mill, the Patriots descended the hill and fought but failed to rescue the governor. Fanning's Tories safely delivered the governor and their other prisoners to Wilmington. It was the last stroke the Loyalists made in North Carolina. A North Carolina historical marker at Lindley's Mill on the road from Greensboro to Chapel Hill in Alamance County reads as follows: "In a battle September 13, 1781… Butler's Whigs failed to rescue Governor Burke from Fanning's Tories."

On the western frontier, a renewed British-allied Indian uprising in late February and into March kept Colonel John Sevier and other overmountain men occupied in the Cherokee Border War of 1781. The uprising kept them away from the anticipated battle between Cornwallis and Greene that would occur at Guilford Courthouse in March. The raids were instigated by Cornwallis, as evidenced by a letter datelined Wynnesborough, December 29, 1780, in which Cornwallis informed his commander in chief, Sir Henry Clinton, "When the Back-mountain men came down to attack Major Ferguson, I directed Lt. Colonel [Thomas] Brown to encourage the Indians to attack the settlements of Watag, Holstein, Caentuck and Nolachuckie…. A large body of the mountaineers were soon obliged to oppose the incursions of the Indians."[34]

At this time, Georgia's Loyalist colonel Thomas Brown, Elijah Clarke's archenemy, was superintendent of Indian Affairs in the South. His territory involved the Cherokee, Creek, Catawba and other nations of the eastern division. His counterpart, Alexander Cameron, advocated for the Choctaw, Chickasaw and Indian nations in the western division. Obeying Cornwallis's orders, Brown had war talks with the Raven of Chota. As the acting Cherokee War Chief in Oconostota's place, the Raven immediately threw his war belt into the ring and agreed to go to war.

Colonel John "Nolichucky Jack" Sevier suspected that the perpetrators of these attacks on the frontier came from the Cherokee Middle Towns. In March he mustered 130 men at Greasy Cove—so-named because bear fat was rendered there—on the Nolichucky River in what is now Unicoi County, Tennessee. Sevier's militia, piloted by fur trader Isaac Thomas, marched through the Cherokee Middle Towns. Sevier's expedition killed warriors, captured prisoners, burned six villages, and confiscated 200 horses. They then proceeded through the Great Smoky Mountains to the Cherokee settlements on the Tuckaseegee River, a tributary of the Little Tennessee. Taking the town of "Tuckasejah" by surprise, Sevier's men slew 50 warriors, captured 50 women and children, burned 20 towns, and destroyed all the granaries of corn they could find—harsh measures, but ones that prevented more massacres of pioneers on the frontier. After three years Sevier delivered 10 of the prisoners to the state of Virginia's Indian agent, Colonel Joseph Martin, who returned them to their own nation.

The British instigators accomplished their goal: They made it necessary for a substantial number of militiamen from North Carolina and Southwest Virginia to guard the frontier against Indian attack during the Revolutionary War. Thus, the border wars kept many frontiersmen from fighting in southern wars against the British farther east. Throughout the War in the South when Wataugans and Southwestern Virginians were torn from the frontier to fight the British the Indians had ample opportunity to raid the sparsely guarded settlements. The December-January 1780–81 Cherokee Expedition of colonels John Sevier and Arthur Campbell, however, had quickly quelled the Cherokee on the western frontier of the Holston, French Broad, and Tennessee rivers.

In July 1781, six months after the Cherokee Expedition ended, General Nathanael Greene appointed commissioners to arrange an exchange of prisoners and a peace agreement—the Second Treaty of Long Island on the Holston—with the Cherokee. Indian agent Joseph Martin picked up the commission papers from Greene in piedmont North Carolina. On his way home, Martin delivered the papers to Virginia colonels William Preston and William Christian.

At Long Island on the Holston in Tennessee Country, Greene's appointed commissioners met with Cherokee chiefs. At the meeting, John "Nolichucky Jack" Sevier assured the Indians, "I have never hated the Cherokee, but have had to fight them for the safety of my people." Cherokee Nation chieftain Beloved Woman (Ghi Ghu, Nancy Ward, Nanyehi), in an unprecedented move by an Indian woman to speak in negotiation with white men, said, "You know that women are always looked upon as nothing; but we are your mothers; you are our sons. Our cry is all for peace; let it continue. This peace must last forever. Let your women's sons be ours; our sons be yours. Let your women hear our words." Commissioner Christian replied, "We have listened well to your talk.... No man can hear it without being moved by it. Such words and thought show the world that human nature is the same everywhere. Our women shall hear your words.... We are descendants of the same women. We will not quarrel with you, because you are our mothers. We will not meddle with your people if they will be still and quiet at home and let us live in peace." So moved were the assembled group by the persuasive words of Nancy Ward—"the Pocahontas of the West"—that the resulting 1781 Treaty of Long Island on the Holston was one of the few treaties in which whites made no request for more Indian lands.[35]

In 1777 the Cherokee had let go large areas of land via the First Treaty of Long Island of the Holston. The 1777 treaty, however, did not cede the Great Island itself but reserved it for the use of the Cherokee and Nathaniel Gist. "The Raven ... in behalf of the Indians ... desired that Col. Gist might sit down upon it when he pleased, as it belonged to him and them to hold good talks on."[36] Gist had purchased the land in 1776 from the Cherokee about the time of the birth of his son Sequoyah, whose mother, Wut-teh, was the daughter of a Cherokee chief. The Cherokee honored the Gist purchase, but the colony of Virginia deemed the purchase illegal. The Second Treaty of Long Island of Holston, the one commissioned by Greene in 1781, made peace and confirmed the cessions of 1777; but the Cherokee still honored the Gist purchase and did not release Long Island. The Cherokee finally ceded the island to the United States in 1806.

Back in 1780 when Washington had transferred General Nathanael (Nat) Greene to the South Nat feared for the safety of his wife and their five small children,[37] so he asked her not to join him even though she wanted to be by his side. His frequent letters to her during that year showed affectionate respect for her judgment and confided his hopes and plans. He needed to feel her support and sympathy in all his endeavors and throughout his troubled campaigns. Catharine Littlefield Greene rejoined the general after he concluded his campaigns of 1781

Always happy and playful, Catharine Littlefield had grown up with relatives 12 miles from Providence, Rhode Island, overlooking the Narragansett Bay. Of medium height, the brown-haired and gray-eyed Kate often visited her family at Block Island. There the fun loving, coquettish Caty met Nathanael Greene. Both Caty and Nat relished riding and dancing, which his Quaker father considered frivolous and idle. Although the lovely Miss Littlefield did not enjoy studying, she occasionally read books and her mind was remarkably retentive and perceptive. She was an intelligent listener and an animated, fluent, and even brilliant conversationalist. Unaware that she would become the wife of a soldier, Catharine Littlefield married Nathanael Greene in July 1774 when she was 21. They moved into a house on the bank of a small stream at Coventry, Rhode Island. News of the battles of Lexington and Concord called Nathanael Greene to Boston.

When the army at Boston was inoculated for smallpox, Caty converted her house into a hospital. At Valley Forge she shared her husband's cramped quarters. Her sunny attitude lit up the gloom of those dark hours of the Revolution. The war separated them for one year in 1780 when Nat was rebuilding and commanding the Southern Continental Army. Two years after Caty rejoined Nat in 1781, they moved to Mulberry Grove, a Savannah River plantation presented to them by the State of Georgia. In 1786 General Greene's brilliant career ended with his sudden death at age 44. Moving north and then returning, Caty and their children considered the South their home and continued to live at Mulberry Grove.

In 1792 Mrs. Greene took a law student into her home to live while he pursued his studies. Recognizing his mechanical genius when he constructed a tambour frame for her children, she introduced him to Phineas Miller. The young student, Eli Whitney, was interested in Miller's idea that cotton could be cultivated as a staple if the cotton fiber could be mechanically removed from its seed. When Eli expressed interest in inventing such a machine, Mr. Miller negotiated to finance the invention and split the profits of the finished product. Catherine allowed Whitney to set up shop in a basement room at Mulberry Grove. Laboring day after day in his room, into which no one was admitted, he made the necessary tools. By spring, Eli Whitney had invented the cotton gin. In 1796 widow Catharine Greene married her friend, and Whitney's financier, Phineas Miller.

17

British and American Strategy in the Virginia Campaign

After the Battle at Guilford Courthouse, Major General Nathanael Greene, commander of the Continental Army in the South, had pursued Major General Charles Cornwallis, British commander in the South. Partway through the chase Greene abruptly reversed course, marched south, captured all the interior posts in the Carolinas, confined the retreating British to Charlestown, and achieved a peace treaty with the Cherokee.

Concomitantly, Lord Cornwallis, perhaps the most capable British general in the war, proceeded to Wilmington on the North Carolina coast. In April, he resumed his long-term strategy to march to Virginia. His plan to enter the Old Dominion had been delayed for six months by the defeat and death of Ferguson at Kings Mountain. Britain's campaign strategy to subdue Virginia had already begun on a small scale in December 1780. That's when General Henry Clinton, commander in chief of British forces in America, sent Benedict Arnold, who had recently turned traitor, into Virginia. Arnold's mission was to stop Virginia from supplying salt, ammunition and gunpowder to Greene's Patriot army in the Carolinas.

When the Connecticut-born Arnold fought as a Patriot officer in the Canada Campaign he was hailed as "the American Hannibal" and was called the "Hero of Saratoga" for winning the battle that brought French aid to America. But the turncoat Arnold was now a Loyalist, fighting on the British side against the very Franco-American alliance he had helped forge. In December 1780, as a new brigadier general in the British Army, Arnold sailed from New York through a violent gale that separated his fleet and scattered the vessels. Having weathered the storm, his expeditionary force arrived at Hampton Roads in the Chesapeake Bay. Sailing up the James River, Arnold docked at Westover Plantation and marched 25 miles north to Richmond.

Richmond was inadequately prepared to counter Arnold's attack for at least two reasons. One was that Major General Benjamin Lincoln had surrendered the entire Continental Army in the South, including 15 Virginia regiments, to Clinton and Cornwallis at Charlestown only a few months earlier. Another was that Governor Thomas Jefferson was reluctant to strengthen Virginia's military. Arnold, therefore, was virtually unopposed when he raided that capital city on January 5. He overpowered the city's weak defense and set buildings ablaze, burning Richmond's cash crop. Torching a trail, he burned tobacco warehouses and buildings, filling the air with the smell of tobacco from Richmond to Petersburg. His tornadic raids along the James River severely hurt Virginia's Patriot support for the war. In mid–January 1781 Arnold recruited additional Loyalist support, occupied Portsmouth, and built several redoubts around the town.

Governor Jefferson, having fled Richmond on January 5, appealed to General Washington for aid. When Washington received the request he was at his headquarters on the Hudson meeting with French general Jean Baptiste Donatien de Vimeur, Comte de Rochambeau. Washington and Rochambeau were planning a Franco-American attack on Clinton's Army garrisoned in New York. Washington responded to Jefferson's plea by sending a 23-year-old French nobleman, Major General Marie-Joseph-Paul-Yves-Roch-Gilbert du Motier, Marquis de Lafayette, to oppose Arnold. Lafayette launched America's counter-strategy for the Virginia Campaign in the spring of 1781.

French aid played a vital role in foiling Britain's Virginia Campaign and winning American victory in the Revolution. A prominent figure in securing that aid was Lafayette. In 1773 at the age of 16 the orphaned and rich Lafayette, tall, muscular and plump, with reddish hair, a freckled face and a candid demeanor, married 14-year-old Adrienne. He and his bride had the hearty approval of her wealthy parents. Friends, guests and family followed them to their wedding chamber. When they fell into bed the bride's father discretely pulled the curtains around the four-poster.[1] A few short years later, however, Lafayette would rouse to the voice of America calling.

The call came in 1776 when the Second Continental Congress sent a small delegation to Paris seeking aid for the American cause. Envoy Silas Deane temporarily chaired the committee pending the arrival of diplomat Benjamin Franklin. Deane's job entailed recruiting French noblemen to join the American military as volunteers. In exchange, he offered each a high commission in the Continental Army. One of those noblemen contacted by Silas Deane was 19-year-old Marquis de Lafayette. The French foreign minister, however, vetoed Deane's request for funds and troops because France was not yet ready for another war so soon after surrendering its entire American territory to Britain in the Seven Years' War, which Americans called the French and Indian War.

But Lafayette, flaunting the French minister's veto, was determined to cross the Atlantic. The young nobleman purchased his own ship and stocked it with munitions, supplies, a captain and a crew. The delighted Deane instantly promised to recommend Lafayette for a commission in the American army. Setting sail in April 1777, Lafayette had never fought in battle. Hence, during his 59-day transatlantic voyage, and ever after, he studied military tactics and embraced the American pursuit of liberty. His favorite reading was Caesar's *Gallic Wars*. Debarking in Charlestown, South Carolina, in June, Lafayette learned to love Low Country food. And he loved America. He championed democracy and defended the personal rights of man. The young marquis traveled to Philadelphia and convinced the Congress of his patriotism and his willingness to serve in the Continental Army as a volunteer, without pay. Congress commissioned Lafayette major general of the Continental Army in July 1777. He was the youngest man ever to be commissioned major general in the American army. He was wounded at Brandywine and wintered at Valley Forge, where he formed a life-long friendship with Washington.

With boyish zest and his French propensity to hug people, the "starry-eyed" Lafayette was modest, affable and ambitious. While the reserved and childless Washington saw the admiring Lafayette as a surrogate son, Jefferson saw him as always "panting for glory" with an almost "canine appetite for popularity and fame."[2] In early 1781 when Washington, Lafayette's father figure, gave him the massive assignment to capture Benedict Arnold, Lafayette was well acquainted with his onetime friend Arnold. That friendship had ended in September 1780 when Arnold's treachery was revealed. A story of that intrigue follows.

Back in May 1779 Benedict Arnold, a clever Continental Army brigadier general, had approached General Clinton with a proposal to betray the American rebel cause. The idea of a high-level defection appealed to Clinton, but Arnold demanded a higher price than Clinton was willing to pay. Clinton suspected that Arnold might not be in a position to provide intelligence useful enough to be worth his asking price. Negotiations therefore ceased but then resumed the next year. Arnold kept in contact with Clinton through a British spy, Major John André, who was Clinton's chief of intelligence

Throughout the long siege of Charlestown, from February through May 1780, André spied on citizens and military personnel trapped inside the city. Dressed in homespun clothes and disguised as a cattle driver delivering beef to Charlestown inhabitants, the espionage chief frequently stayed at the home of a Charlestown citizen. André began gathering intelligence at dawn. Exiting the city at dusk he rowed across the surrounding salt marshes and delivered his scoop to General Clinton at the British encampment. As an undercover agent, André traveled to and fro between Charlestown and New York and became the confidant of Benedict Arnold.

In June 1781 Washington, unaware of Arnold's planned treachery, put Arnold in command of the strategically placed West Point, the gateway to the Hudson and America's strongest military post. Arnold's access to West Point enticed Clinton to pay Arnold's price for defecting and joining the British army. In September 1780 Lafayette paid a social visit to Arnold. As the two crossed the Hudson on their way to West Point, Lafayette told Arnold the news: Clinton's intelligence chief, Major John André, was caught dressed in civilian clothes with compromising papers hidden in his boot. André was taken to headquarters for questioning. Any British officer who appeared in civilian dress behind enemy lines was assumed to be a spy. The news so distressed Arnold that he dashed to shore, telling Lafayette to go to the fort at West Point and start breakfast with Mrs. Arnold without him and he would join them later. The 38-year-old Arnold's second wife, a well-born and beautiful 18-year-old Loyalist, Peggy Shippen Arnold, had been André's paramour. Having introduced the spy André to the would-be traitor Arnold, she acted as the André-Arnold go-between for Arnold's defection from his command at West Point. Peggy had aided and abetted her husband's decision to betray America.

Arnold never showed up to meet his wife and Lafayette for breakfast. "Struck with astonishment and terror in the agitation and agonies of a mad man, he (Arnold) called for a horse, mounted instantly and rode down a craggy steep, never before explored on horseback. He took a barge ... and soon found himself safe beneath the guns of the Vulture sloop of war ... and ... got safe to New York ... where he received ten thousand pounds of sterling in cash ... and a commission under the crown of Great Britain."[3]

With his crippled leg from Saratoga, his bruised ego from having been passed over for promotion and then denied seniority when he finally achieved the rank of major general in the American army, and his inherent itch for money—Arnold fled. He ran because he was a turncoat, a traitor. He had bargained to surrender the strategic Hudson Valley fortresses of Stony Point and West Point to Clinton. In return, André had slipped him today's equivalent of three million dollars. Arnold then gave André "written descriptions of the forts, their armaments and stores, the strength of the garrisons, copies of their orders in case of attack, and copies of the proceedings of a council of war recently held at West Point."[4] It was these papers that were found in André's boot. When Arnold's treachery was revealed, Clinton refused Washington's offer to exchange prisoner-of-war André for Arnold. The brave, artistic, handsome, charismatic, cunning, multilingual and beloved British spy was tried before a tribunal of American generals—and hanged.

The next year Washington assigned Lafayette to capture Arnold in Virginia. Washington requested Lafayette to reassemble his troops and place himself under the command of General Greene. Greene then instructed Lafayette to join Baron von Steuben, military commander of Continental and state militia forces in Virginia. Lafayette and Steuben together were to launch a Virginia campaign to stop Arnold. In the spring of 1781 Lafayette marched south from Philadelphia with a land force of 1,200 New England and New Jersey troops. Arriving in Annapolis, Maryland, Lafayette expected to be reinforced by an equal number of Frenchmen. The French troops were to be sent by Rochambeau aboard French ships from the French base at Newport, Rhode Island. The combined Franco-American troops would then be transported by French ships from Annapolis to Yorktown. Hence Lafayette confidently left his army garrisoned at Annapolis awaiting transport while he went to Virginia to further strengthen his army. Lafayette and a few officers boarded a sloop and then a barge in the Chesapeake Bay and arrived at Yorktown, Virginia, on March 14. There he began his campaign against the British.

Attracting additional Patriot soldiers in Virginia to augment the 1,200 men waiting in Annapolis, Lafayette often paid for their shoes and clothing out of his own pocket.

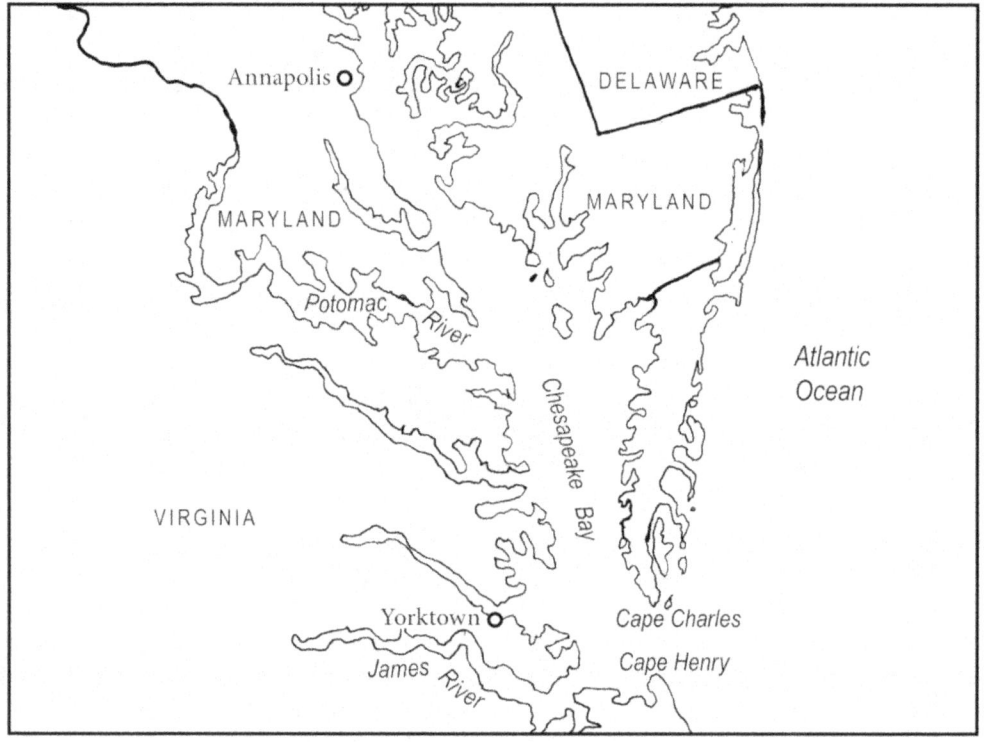

Chesapeake Bay, Virginia Capes (Glen McCroskey).

When he and his new recruits joined Steuben's larger force of militia in Williamsburg, he learned that the French ships had not arrived in Annapolis to embark his troops. The Rhode Island French fleet failed to reach Annapolis because it was intercepted by the British at the First Battle of the Capes. That battle occurred on March 16, 1781, when a superior number of British warships arrived in the Chesapeake ahead of the smaller French fleet sailing on the Atlantic from Newport. The British ships formed a barricade stretching from Cape Charles to Cape Henry, blocking the entrance to the Chesapeake Bay. When the French ships approached the barrier, fire was exchanged, and casualties occurred on both sides. The French fleet, unable to sail up the Chesapeake Bay to Annapolis and transport Lafayette's troops, returned to Newport. The British then connected with Arnold and gained control of the bay area. The disappointed Lafayette returned to Annapolis to take command of his stranded 1,200 men, march them to Virginia, and resume his pursuit of Arnold.

Arnold's Tory force in Virginia was too small to carry on an intensive campaign. Clinton therefore sent reinforcements numbering 3,000 troops, under the leadership of Major General William Phillips, commander of British forces in Virginia. Ironically, this was the same Phillips who had commanded the battery that killed Lafayette's father in the Seven Years' War when Lafayette was two years old. The Virginia Campaign fortuitously offered Lafayette a chance to avenge the death of his father.

On April 18 Phillips and Arnold launched a major British campaign in Virginia. Sailing up the James River, they destroyed warehouses and shipyards along the way as well as those at City Point, 12 miles from Petersburg. Steuben's resistance at the Battle of Petersburg, however feeble, delayed Phillips long enough to allow Lafayette time to become entrenched in Richmond. Lafayette then guarded that capital city against a burning similar to the one that Arnold had ignited several months earlier. On April 30 Phillips' army destroyed hogsheads of tobacco at Manchester across from Richmond. From Richmond, Lafayette, outnumbered and powerless, watched the destruction without interfering.

General Phillips died of "fever" at Petersburg on the morning of May 13. He had "conducted one of the British army's most successful campaigns in the American Revolution." To his credit and for the welfare of citizens of Petersburg and Chesterfield County, one of his standing orders to his army was that "private property and the persons of individuals not taken in arms are to be under the protection of the troops." By this decree Phillips saved the city of Petersburg from destruction. Though an enemy, he won the respect of Virginians. A Hessian Jaeger under his command called Phillips "the most pleasant, unselfish and courteous man in the world."[5] For one week—from the time on May 13 when Phillips died at Petersburg until Cornwallis arrived one week later—Arnold was commander of British forces in the Virginia Campaign.

The following excerpts from Ellet's *Women of the American Revolution* recount that on his march from Wilmington to Halifax, Virginia, Cornwallis encamped for several days in North Carolina on the Neuse River in what is now Wayne County. Cornwallis headquartered at Springbank while Tarleton went to a plantation Cornwallis named Pleasant Green. It was the home of Mrs. Mary Slocumb, Lieutenant Ezekiel Slocumb's wife. Mary Slocumb was the same fearless horsewoman who had made a midnight dash to look for her husband and nurse the wounded at Moore's Creek Bridge five years earlier. The charming Mary, known for her expressive blue eyes and caustic wit, was sitting with her child and a relative on the piazza of her ancient-looking mansion when a splendidly dressed officer, Banastre Tarleton, rode up. He was accompanied by two aides and a guard of 20 troopers. Raising his cap and bowing to his horse's neck, he addressed the lady:

"Have I the pleasure of seeing the mistress of this house and plantation?"

"It belongs to my husband."

"Is he home?"

"He is not."

"Is he a rebel?"

"No, sir. He is in the army of his country, and fighting against our invaders; therefore not a rebel."

"I fear, madam," said the officer, "we differ in opinion. A friend to his country will be the friend of the king, our master."

"Only slaves acknowledge a master in this country," replied the lady.

Tarleton ordered one of his aides to pitch tents for 1,000 British dragoons in an orchard and field near the house. The other was to detach a quarter guard and station a small unit of soldiers to scout each road for Lieutenant Slocumb and troops under Colonel William Washington. Next, with a low bow, Tarleton added, "Madam, the service of his Majesty requires the temporary occupation of your property; and if it would not be too great an inconvenience, I will take up my quarters in your house."

"We are your prisoners," answered Mrs. Slocumb.

For her uninvited houseguests Mary prepared a good dinner of several meats, fowl, greens, pickles, stewed fruit, and abundant and varied desserts. Savoring the peach brandy from Lieutenant Slocumb's own orchard, an Irish captain said, "When we conquer this country, is it not to be divided out among us." Mrs. Slocumb interposed. "Allow me to observe and prophesy," said she, "the only land in these United States which will ever remain in possession of a British officer, will measure but six feet by two."

After more repartee, and harboring an apprehension that her husband would return home and be captured, Mary struck Tarleton with another shaft of her wit when she said to him, "You would not of course, be surprised at a call from Lee or your old friend Colonel Washington, who, although a perfect gentleman, it is said shook your hand [pointing to the scar left by Washington's saber] very rudely when you last met." She was referring to the Cowpens Battle, where Colonel William Washington's American cavalry had crushed the British cavalry of Tarleton's green-jacketed dragoons.

Warned by Big George, a faithful plantation slave, the mounted Lt. Slocumb, who was returning home, jumped fences and evaded Tarleton's reconnaissance scouts after a brief encounter. Meanwhile, Mary Slocumb continued to preside at her table with dignity. Her lofty spirit gave her slender body a majesty that commanded respect from all the Tory officers and protected her from insolent familiarity. Tarleton issued strict orders that no ransacking of her house or plantation would be tolerated, but he couldn't save even one feather of her poultry or one four-footed farm animal from his hungry soldiers. The Slocumb's little son amused several Tory officers who undoubtedly missed their own children back home. They perched him on their prancing chargers and watched him clap his little hands in glee as he pretended to be a dragoon.

When the British Army broke camp, Tarleton departed with Cornwallis and continued toward Halifax. But before he left, the so-called Bloody Ban Tarleton continued to belie his dreadful reputation by ordering a sergeant to stand at the door to protect Mrs. Slocumb, a lady who "inspired them all with the most profound respect."[6]

General Clinton was appalled at the presence in Virginia of Cornwallis, his second in command. He wrote, "My wonder at this move of Cornwallis will never cease."[7] From the beginning Cornwallis and Clinton had disagreed on Virginia's role in the overall strategy of the war. Cornwallis urged Clinton to abandon New York and seize Virginia. This move, he maintained, would win the war because Virginia was central to the line of communication between North and South. Cornwallis's scheme would destroy arsenals and the stores of food in Virginia, cut the lines of supply and communication, and thereby force surrender. Clinton, however, refused to endorse Cornwallis's plan. Deeming the Virginia Campaign pointless, Clinton preferred Cornwallis had stayed in the Carolinas and sent part of his troops to reinforce his own army, which was defending New York. Hence, Clinton—Cornwallis's superior officer—kept the bulk of the British Army in New York to foil a possible French-American invasion.

Before Cornwallis took command of British troops in Virginia, Clinton had restricted Phillips and Arnold to raids along the rivers. Cornwallis, however, believed that occupying the entire colony of Virginia was key to winning the war. Thus he committed all his energy to that end. He communicated with Lord Germaine, the secretary of state for the Colonies in North America. Germaine encouraged Cornwallis to invade Virginia and discouraged Clinton from withdrawing troops from the Chesapeake.

Cornwallis's strategy to subdue the South by conquering Virginia depended on raising vigorous Loyalist support, but this expectation never materialized. Loyalist support simply was not there. After the fall of Charlestown, the perseverance of the Partisans in the South brought more and more Patriots to the American side. At the time of the Battle of Guilford Courthouse, Cornwallis had even struggled to find guides in the North Carolina hornet's nest of Patriots. Rawdon informed him that Loyalist support in South Carolina had collapsed. Despite the lack of Loyalist support, Lord Germaine, viewing the situation from London, believed that the bold military moves and steadfast ability of Cornwallis could crush the rebel cause.

Germaine's hope was bolstered by a weak Continental Congress crippled by a tremendous financial burden and having no power of taxation. Without money to supply adequate food, clothing and salaries to an American army, Congress issued paper money backed by nothing but hope. States also printed money. As the value of the dollar fell, inflation soared. An ordinary horse cost $20,000. By 1781 Continental paper money was worthless. A starving American army, signs of a collapsing American economy, runaway inflation, and a deflated dollar whose worth had dropped to 1/40 of its former value gave rise to the expression "not worth a Continental."[8]

Upon entering Virginia in May 1781, General Cornwallis, General Alexander Leslie and Colonel Tarleton took advantage of Virginia's abundant supply of fine horses. Cornwallis found mounts for 600 light dragoons and doubled his cavalry by mounting 800 infantrymen. His army from the Carolinas was supplemented by Loyalists from Virginia and reinforcements from New York. Cornwallis joined Arnold in Petersburg on May 20. With their combined forces numbering 7,200 they attempted to outwit and outmaneuver Lafayette, whose army numbered 3,250. Arnold returned to New York. Cornwallis took command of all the British forces in Virginia and moved up the James River in an attempt to trap Lafayette. Lafayette's letter to Washington from Richmond on May 24th, 1781, states:

> Should they [General Wayne and his Pennsylvanians] have arrived in time enough to support me in the reception of Lord Cornwallis' first stroke, I should still have thought it well enough; but from an answer of General Wayne, received this day, and dated the 19th, I am afraid that at this moment they have hardly left Yorktown. Public stores and private property being removed from Richmond, this place is a less important object. I don't believe it would be prudent to expose the troops for the sake of a few houses, most of which are empty.... Were I anyways equal to the enemy, I should be extremely happy in my present command, but I am not strong enough even to get beaten.

Nathanael Greene, the Continental Army commander in the South, had assigned the relatively inexperienced Lafayette to command the Patriot army in Virginia. Hence Lafayette was now pitted against Cornwallis, a seasoned campaigner commanding an army twice the size of Lafayette's. Forced to play the part of "a terrier baiting a bull,"[9] Lafayette found the role to be both thrilling and challenging. Regardless of the odds, he was careful to keep himself between Cornwallis and Philadelphia, home of the Second Continental Congress, which was the brain, director, and treasurer of the new U.S. government.

Approaching from Petersburg, Cornwallis reached Westover Plantation 25 miles southeast of Richmond. There he learned that Lafayette had left the state capital at Richmond and moved north and that Governor Jefferson had evacuated Richmond and escaped with the Virginia government to Charlottesville. He also knew that Steuben was at Point of Fork (Columbia) guarding the Virginia State Arsenal, which supplied arms, gunpowder and lead shot to the Continental Army. This left the south and west of the state free for Cornwallis to overrun. Cornwallis also learned that General "Mad Anthony" Wayne was only a few days' march away. Cornwallis scrambled to strike both the assembly and the arsenal before Wayne joined Lafayette. He sent Tarleton to attack the government at Charlottesville and General John Graves Simcoe to strike Steuben's arsenal at Point of Fork.

Cornwallis's swift cavalry officer Banastre Tarleton rushed to break up the Virginia legislature meeting at Charlottesville. Uniformed in a tight-fitting short green jacket and white buckskin breeches, galloping with his customary zeal, Tarleton and his Green Dragoons—Loyalist horse soldiers composed mostly of New Yorkers and Pennsylvanians—covered 70 miles in 24 hours. Arriving at Charlottesville on June 4, Tarleton targeted the legislature and captured seven assembly members, including Daniel Boone. Jefferson, watching through a spyglass, saw Tarleton's dragoons approach his home at Monticello. The author of the Declaration of Independence had narrowly escaped. The Tory soldiers spent 18 hours at Monticello, but under orders from Tarleton they disturbed nothing. The dragoons "preserved everything with sacred care," said Jefferson.[10]

On June 5, Simcoe, renowned commander of the Queen's Rangers, who never lost a battle, attacked the arsenal at Point of Fork. There, on the James River near Charlottesville, Simcoe destroyed arms, powder, and supplies. His invincible Queen's Rangers worked freely without interference because Steuben abandoned the depot as soon as he received word that Simcoe was coming. Following their lightning raid to the west, Cornwallis, Tarleton, and Simcoe's detachments rendezvoused at Elk Hill and camped there until June 13. Elk Hill was Jefferson's small James River Plantation 35 miles southeast of Charlottesville on the road to Richmond. Unlike Tarleton, who was ordered to spare Monticello, Cornwallis laid total waste to Elk Hill. Afterward, he successively occupied Richmond and Williamsburg. Without enough troops to resist, Lafayette and Wayne followed along, watching Cornwallis's whirlwind wreckage.

Lafayette had united with Wayne's detachment of 600 Pennsylvania Line troops on June 10. He was further strengthened two days later by 600 overmountain militiamen commanded by William Campbell, a southwest Virginia brigadier general of the militia. Two months later 36-year-old Campbell complained of a "pain in his breast" and died suddenly. In a general order Lafayette characterized Campbell as an officer whose glory "acquired in the affairs of Kings Mountain and Guilford Courthouse will do his memory everlasting honor" as a defender of liberty in the American cause.[11]

Lafayette's militia soon dwindled as many men returned home to tend their farms. Steuben, however, arrived at Lafayette's camp, 20 miles northwest of Richmond, on June 19, bringing Lafayette's American Army total to 2,000 regulars and 3,200 militiamen.[12] Reinforced though still outnumbered, Lafayette shadowed Cornwallis, watching the British general halt his westward movement, encamp at Richmond on June 18, and leave Richmond two days later. Turning toward Williamsburg, Cornwallis intended to occupy that city until Clinton sent further orders. This was not easy, because communication between Clinton and Cornwallis frequently exploded in argument. Enmity between the petulant, paranoid Clinton and the courtly, self-controlled Cornwallis became apparent when Clinton blamed Cornwallis for failing to annihilate Washington at Trenton. Tension mounted when Clinton began to suspect that Cornwallis, who was in line to succeed him as commander in chief of British forces in America, was undermining him among the officers. Cornwallis then requested the home government to assign him to "any theater of action where Clinton was not in command."[13] The slow communication further aggravated the ongoing controversy between Clinton in the North and Cornwallis in the South. Problems, misunderstandings and miscommunications were exacerbated when Clinton's long-standing fear—that the Americans would cut off New York by land and the French would block communications by sea—was confirmed by an intercepted letter. Washington's May 31 secret letter to Lafayette revealed that Washington and Rochambeau agreed that a Franco-American "attempt upon New York with its present Garrison ... was deemed preferable to a Southern Operation."

Clinton then had validation for his belief that the inevitable British versus Franco-American showdown would explode in New York. The Clinton-Cornwallis controversy peaked when Clinton requested Cornwallis to reinforce the northern army in New York immediately. He was to send 2,000 troops, if they were not otherwise engaged, from Virginia's southern army. Clinton's order was based on "an overestimation of Cornwallis' strength and an underestimation of Lafayette's command." Clinton mistakenly believed Lafayette's American army was makeshift, made up of light infantry and an unarmed mob of militia. Cornwallis, remembering the militiamen at Musgrove Mill, Kings Mountain, Cowpens and Guilford Courthouse, replied: "I will not say much in praise of the militia of the southern colonies, but the list of British officers and soldiers killed and wounded by them since last June proves but too fatally that they are not wholly contemptible." Cornwallis was further irritated when Clinton directed him to order the commanding officer at Portsmouth "to dispatch a runner once a week ... whether he has anything material to say or not."[14] However, Cornwallis never forgot that Clinton was in command; he always loyally obeyed his commander in chief.

On June 28 Clinton's letter to Cornwallis reiterated his request for the reinforcement he called for in his letters of the 8th, 11th, 15th, and 19th. Cornwallis indeed was already on his way from Richmond to Portsmouth to ship the requested troops to New York. He intended to cross the James River to the southern shore and then march to Portsmouth. From there he planned to send troops aboard ship to Clinton in New York. But at Green Spring Lafayette would interfere with Cornwallis's crossing the James.

On July 4 Cornwallis and the Royal army, marching from Williamsburg, encamped on the north bank of the James River. A narrow inlet separated the campsite from Jamestown. Cornwallis prepared to cross the shallow inlet at Green Spring Plantation. He placed his troops in a wooded area and sent his baggage and Simcoe's unbeatable Queen's Rangers across the river to stand guard in front to cover their crossing. Cornwallis then told Tarleton to spread the word that his entire British Army had already crossed the river and that the men remaining on the bank (the Queen's Rangers) were merely part of the rear guard. Knowing that his army would be especially vulnerable as it crossed, Cornwallis assigned Tarleton to protect the rear of the British line during the march.

On July 5 Lafayette, misled by Tarleton's misinformation, sent Wayne and a corps of 800 to Green Spring Plantation. Lafayette assigned Wayne to reconnoiter the Cornwallis position. Arriving at the plantation, Lafayette spotted Wayne moving south through a narrow, swampy causeway from Green Spring and encountering British sentries. The Frenchman then realized the fallacy of Tarleton's report. Wayne was marching into the entire bulk of Cornwallis's forces, not just the rear guard. It was too late to warn Wayne, and without enough time to escape there was nothing Wayne could do but bravely engage the enemy. Lafayette quickly called additional troops to reinforce Wayne.

When Cornwallis's large main army began crossing the James River at the ford leading over to Jamestown Island, "Mad Anthony" Wayne's small reconnaissance party charged full force, valiantly surprising Britain's advancing main army. The Battle of Green Spring followed. Wayne's attack was short, giving most of his troops a chance to retreat in orderly fashion to Green Spring Plantation. Cornwallis soon gave up the pursuit due to darkness. This was the largest infantry engagement to occur on Virginia soil during the Revolutionary War. Wayne, falling into Cornwallis's trap, was beaten, sustaining 139 casualties. After the battle, Cornwallis moved on to Portsmouth as planned. He could have quashed Lafayette on the spot, but he did not press his advantage because he was under Clinton's orders to send troops to New York immediately.

Accounts vary as to the losses, but two days later Lafayette reported the Green Spring Battle to General Greene: "From all accounts, the enemy's loss is great. We had none killed, but many wounded. Wayne's detachment suffered most. Many horses were killed, which rendered it impossible to move the field pieces. But it is enough for the glory of General Wayne, and the officers and men under his command, to have attacked the whole British army, with only a reconnoitering party, and to have obliged them to retreat over the river."[15] Historical Marker V-39 at Green Spring, Virginia describes the battle:

> [L]ate in the afternoon of 6 July 1781, Gen. Charles Cornwallis and cavalry commander Col. Banastre Tarleton with 5,000 British and Hessian troops clashed with 800 American troops commanded by Brig. Gen. "Mad" Anthony Wayne and the Marquis de Lafayette, believing that the main British force was across the James River, and that he was attacking Cornwallis' rear, Wayne soon realized that he was facing far superior numbers. He startled the advancing British forces by charging them, exchanging volley, and then withdrawing his troops from encirclement and certain defeat. Dusk prevented Cornwallis from pursuing the Americans.

17. British and American Strategy in the Virginia Campaign

In Lafayette's July 9, 1781, letter to his wife, Adrienne, he said, "This devil Cornwallis is much wiser than the other generals with whom I have dealt. He inspires me with a sincere fear, and his name has greatly troubled my sleep. This campaign is a good school for me. God grant that the public does not pay for my lessons."

When Lafayette realized that Cornwallis was shipping forces to the North, he figured that the focus of the war was shifting to New York. He therefore requested transfer to the North where the action would be. But Washington, his adoptive father and namesake of Lafayette's son, told him to stay in Virginia because the new plan of operation was to expel the enemy from the Southern states.

18

The Virginia Campaign and the American Victory at Yorktown

> The British never clearly understood what they were up against—a revolutionary struggle involving widespread support in the population.... Hence they continually underestimated the staying power of the rebels and overestimated the strength of the loyalists. ...And in the end, Independence came to mean more to the Americans than re-conquest did to the British.[1]
> —Gordon S. Wood, *The American Revolution*

Clinton soon rescinded Cornwallis's orders. The Clinton-Cornwallis confusion arose partly because the British had no idea where the French fleet would land next. After Cornwallis left Green Spring, Clinton directed him not to proceed to New York but to recall his embarked troops and secure a harbor in the Chesapeake Bay deep enough for battleships. Upon receiving conflicting orders from Clinton, first telling him to go to Portsmouth and then to Point Comfort at the mouth of Hampton Roads or to Yorktown, Cornwallis boarded British naval ships at Portsmouth and moved his army to Yorktown, a small tobacco dock and the major seaport of Williamsburg. There he began constructing defense lines on the York River at Gloucester Point, a spit of land across from Yorktown that juts into the channel and narrows the river.

In light of the upcoming siege of Yorktown, the enormous significance of the American victory over the British in the Battle of Saratoga four years earlier must be reiterated. Most important, it helped Benjamin Franklin convince France that the American cause was worthy of an open military alliance with America. France became the first foreign power to provide aid to the rebelling colonies: "The colonies could not survive without French supplies."[2] The Saratoga victory brought not only France but also Spain and the Dutch Republic to assist the cause of the hard-pressed colonists. After Saratoga, the American military situation remained tenuous even though France and Spain sent equipment, funds, and military experts to assist the colonies. Without the power of taxation, Congress found it practically impossible to raise sufficient money to operate a government and finance a war.

In 1780 French minister Charles Gravier, Count de Vergennes, won the trust of King Louis XVI and became "the virtual first minister of the French government and the chief supporter of aiding the Americans." The bespectacled scientist Benjamin Franklin, America's greatest diplomat—wearing a fur hat and leather coat symbolizing the freedom of the American wilderness and the possibility of a hard-working American laborer pulling him-

18. The Virginia Campaign and the American Victory at Yorktown

self up by his bootstraps—won the adoration of the French people. He also won the confidence of Vergennes and persuaded him to continue supporting the American cause.[3]

When Vergennes perceived that the anti–French, anti–Catholic sentiment that existed in the colonies during the French and Indian War had subsided, he concluded that French soldiers would now be welcomed on American soil. Vergennes then deployed a convoy carrying a French expeditionary force to America. The French transport, under the command of Admiral Charles d'Arsac de Ternay, departed the harbor of Brest, France, in May 1780. Its troops, under the command of General Rochambeau, began disembarking at Newport in July. There they established a military base and awaited French naval reinforcement, which would not arrive for many months. In the interim, the French force from Newport, lacking adequate naval support, was blockaded by British ships of the line under Admiral Thomas Graves in the previously described First Battle of the Chesapeake Bay Capes. A similar British blockade at Brest, France, prevented a second convoy from reinforcing Rochambeau's army at Newport.

The French force and financial aid were crucial for victory at Yorktown. Thus Washington greeted Rochambeau with great joy. Technically both Admiral Ternay and the expeditionary force commander, General Rochambeau, would be under the command of General Washington. In reality, however, the short, thickset Rochambeau, with a scar over one eye and a mild limp, would "do exactly as he pleased," at least at first. Alexander Hamilton, future secretary of the U.S. Department of Treasury, and Lafayette, who had recently returned from his leave of absence to France, acted as interpreters for Rochambeau and Washington. At his reunion with Lafayette, Washington's "eyes filled with tears of joy, a certain proof of truly paternal love," said the boyish Lafayette, beaming with excitement. "Washington lost no time in lobbying Lafayette for a Franco-American invasion of New York."[4]

Washington proposed a combined attack against Clinton in New York City for mid–August. But Rochambeau disagreed with the plan. Washington eventually saw the Frenchman's point and agreed that any successful attack against the British must have French naval support. Rochambeau sent his son to ask Vergennes for more aid. Rochambeau hoped that additional French troops would arrive the next spring.

Washington's Continentals were frequently poorly equipped, unpaid and unclothed. Even so, the Pennsylvania and New Jersey Continental lines did not desert—they mutinied. Washington stopped the string of mutinies and prevented defection of his cold and hungry troops. He sent 600 men to quell the last insurrection and arrested and executed the instigators of the January Pompton Mutiny at Federal Hill, New Jersey. In April 1781 Washington wrote in secret code to South Carolinian John Laurens, special minister to France, urging him to solicit funds: "You may rely on it as a fact, that we cannot transport the provisions from the States in which they are Assessed to the Army, because we cannot pay the Teamsters ... that our Troops are approaching fast to nakedness and that we have nothing to cloath them with. That our Hospitals are without medicines, and our Sick without Nutriment.... [I]t may be declared in a word, that we are at the end of our tether, and that now or never our deliverance must come."[5] The deliverance Washington sought began to materialize in the form of a military coalition with Rochambeau's soldiers encamped at Newport. In May, Rochambeau's son returned with good and bad news. The needed money was granted, but the request for an additional unit of infantry was denied. The fledgling Continental Army, with its few merchant ships and privateers, was weak. All hope now hinged on a French fleet. It was the vital component for victory over the British crown.

The American naval force, with a maximum of 27 ships in commission, could not compete with the British Royal Navy, which grew from 270 ships at the beginning to 480 by the end of the war.[6] The daring and successful raids by Continental navy commander John Paul Jones with his small fleet and even his intrepid attitude ("I have not yet begun to fight") were no match for the renowned sea power of the British.

French sea power was launched when naval commander Francois-Joseph Paul, Comte de Grasse, sailed out of Brest, plowing towards the West Indies. Grasse was accompanied by a small squadron under Admiral Jacques-Melchior, Comte de Barras. The handsome 59-year-old Count de Grasse had remained a bachelor until he was 42 because he had taken a vow of celibacy when he entered the naval service of the Knights of Malta, the most important of all the Christian military orders. At the Azores, Grasse met briefly with Count de Barras and directed him to sail immediately to Newport. Arriving there in May 1781, Barras took command of the French naval convoy, the commander of which, Chevalier de Ternay, had died at Newport in 1780. Barras brought news to Rochambeau and Washington that Grasse and his powerful fleet, fighting for the sugar trade, were at war with the British in the West Indies. In June Grasse captured the Island of Tobago and attained the rank of admiral[7] (Tobago exported cotton and indigo at that time because ants had destroyed its sugar crop in 1775). Simultaneously, 49-year-old Washington and 55-year-old Rochambeau planned a joint Franco-American military operation to attack British-occupied New York City.

The secret of French success in North America was their base at Newport. With a small fleet in the harbor, commanded by Admiral de Barras, it was a key naval position, garrisoned for 11 months by 5,000 regulars under General Rochambeau. The French garrison was reinforced from time to time by American militia. Unlike allied American-French armies, which could not move overland toward their objective of New York without being reconnoitered by spies who were everywhere, Barras's small French fleet could move clandestinely, escaping the espionage network. Another reason for French success was reduced competition. Britain's concomitant war with the Netherlands and Spain kept her ships close to British shores, far away from the American coast.

Neither Washington, headquartered on the Hudson, nor Rochambeau, headquartered at Newport, knew that Cornwallis was in Virginia until letters from Lafayette in June disclosed his whereabouts. Having learned of Grasse's powerful fleet in the West Indies, Lafayette wrote to Washington on July 30, 1781: "Should a French fleet now come in Hampton Roads, the British army will, I think, be ours." On August 2 Lafayette reported to Washington that Cornwallis had begun fortifying Yorktown. Lafayette urgently persuaded Admiral de Grasse to join the Virginia campaign. Grasse, whose job was to protect the French interest in the West Indies, reluctantly agreed to come to the Virginia coast, but for only a few weeks.

Aboard his flagship, *Ville de Paris*, Grasse weighed anchor in August and set sail for the Chesapeake Bay. His fleet numbered 26 ships of the line carrying regiments of infantry and artillerymen and 100 dragoons. Barras still commanded the French squadron of eight ships of the line at Newport.

On 14 August Rochambeau notified Washington that Grasse was not sailing to New York but to the Chesapeake Bay. The two commanders in chief, Washington and Rocham-

18. The Virginia Campaign and the American Victory at Yorktown 233

beau, quickly shifted strategy. Washington found the need to change plans disappointing because the task of marching thousands of American troops overland from Hudson Heights, New York, to Yorktown, Virginia, was daunting. Besides, with more troops and French aid the time would be ripe to attack Clinton at New York. Even more difficult would be keeping

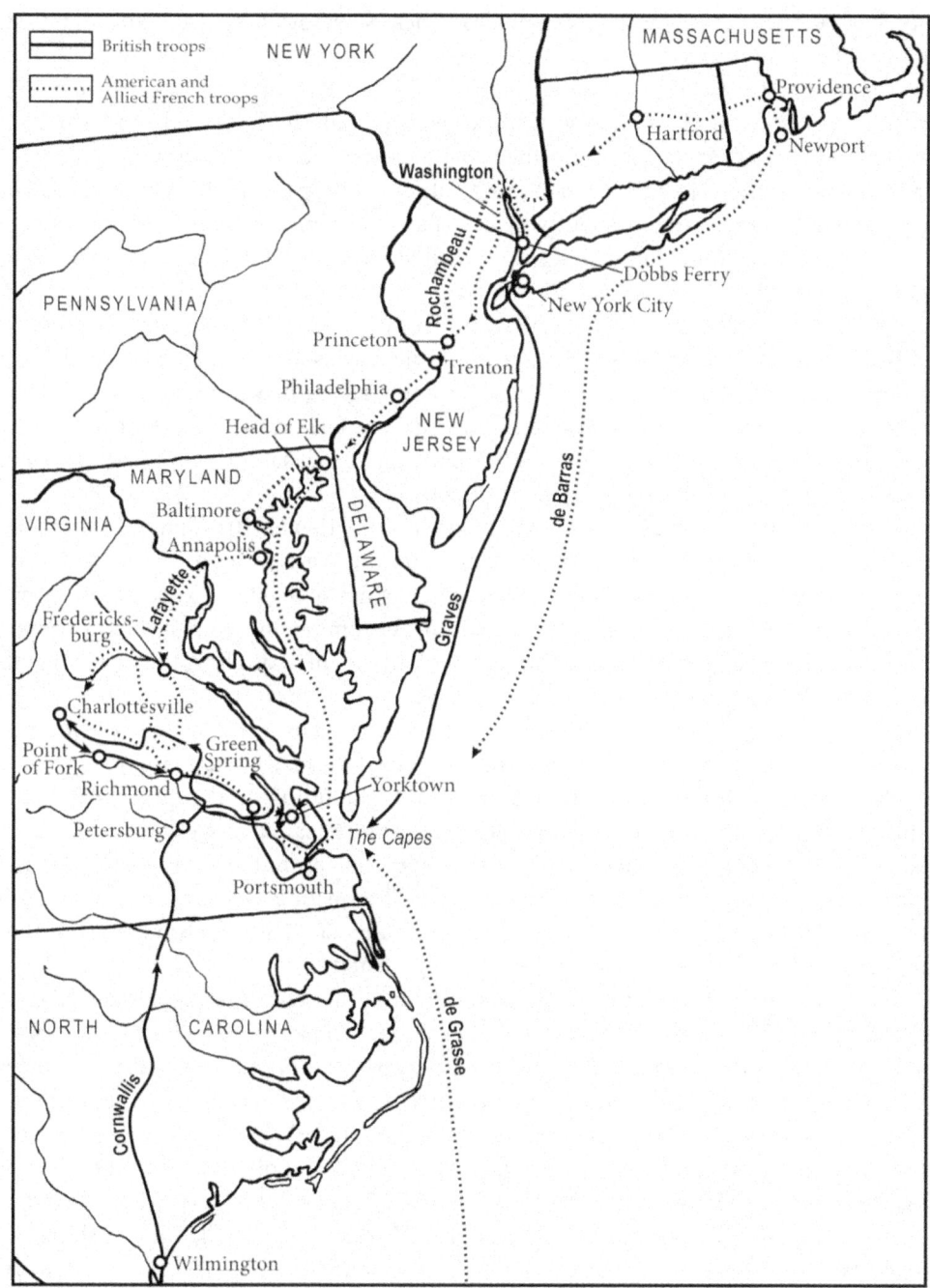

Virginia Campaign of 1781: American, French and British Routes to Yorktown (Glen McCroskey).

the movement of thousands of troops secret from Clinton and thereby preventing his deploying troops from New York to reinforce Cornwallis at Yorktown. Washington and Rochambeau managed to keep the move hush-hush. To convince Clinton that they were still preparing to attack New York City they concocted numerous ploys, including leaving a major general with 2,000 troops in New York as a decoy.[8] Secrecy worked. Even Washington's army believed they were preparing to attack New York City; and Clinton was still convinced he was the target.

Meanwhile, Cornwallis, starved of supplies, dug in at Yorktown and converted it to a naval and military base. He would stay at Yorktown and make his last stand there. Ironically, it was just 20 miles from Jamestown, where British expansion in America had started 175 years earlier. Cornwallis idled for two months, futilely waiting for reinforcement from Clinton while the American enemy silently gathered around him. Lafayette changed his tactic from annoying Cornwallis to blocking any possible retreat of British and Loyalists troops toward North Carolina.

On August 25 Admiral de Barras departed Newport with eight ships to join Grasse in the Chesapeake. On August 29 the billowing sails of Grasse's 28 ships appeared on the horizon. The next day he sailed into Lynnhaven Bay at Virginia Beach near the mouth of the Chesapeake Bay, captured the British lookout ship, and ferried the bulk of his fleet, 3,000 French troops, to shore. His ships then began returning to sea, sailing between Capes Henry and Charles, to block Graves' entrance into the bay.[9]

Admiral Sir George Rodney, the most senior and experienced British naval commander in North America, sent Admiral Samuel Hood from the West Indies to reinforce Admiral Thomas Graves at Sandy Hook. Hood set sail with 14 ships of the line. Expecting the French to attack New York and confident that he could outnumber the French, Hood dropped anchor at Sandy Hook on August 28. Rodney had miscalculated. The number was insufficient and the battle would not occur in New York.

On September 1 a fleet of 19 ships under the command of Admirals Graves and Hood weighed anchor from Sandy Hook intending to intercept Barras's French supply ships before Grasse's larger French fleet reached the Chesapeake. "Standing on the quarterdeck of his 98-gun flagship *London*, all Graves had to do was rapidly scan a long glass over the forest of tall masts to recognize at once that this was not de Barras, but de Grasse with the main French body. The supreme moment was at hand."[10] The ensuing Second Battle of the Capes would bear out Washington's prediction in his December 20, 1780, letter to Franklin: Naval superiority was the "pivot upon which everything turned."

On September 5, 1781, off the coast of Virginia at the mouth of the Chesapeake Bay, the British fleet of Rear Admiral Graves fought Admiral Grasse's French fleet in the Second Battle of the Capes. While their ships of the line were aligning their broadsides, Barras's French squadron arrived from Newport and joined de Grasse's fleet. Grasse's superior fleet of 30 French ships and 1,700 guns then outnumbered Graves' 25 English ships of the line. When the British navy got their signals mixed, the French fleet outmaneuvered the British. Grasse formed an additional line of battle of French ships along the Maryland coast outside Cape Charles on the Chesapeake Bay and set fire to HMS *Terrible*.[11] The leading ships from both fleets fired deadly volleys of cannonballs. The maritime duel lasted more that two hours, with ship damage and casualties on both sides.

Grasse's French victory over Graves' British in the Chesapeake, the Second Battle of the Capes, was the most significant naval battle of the Revolution. "Before it, the creation of the United States of America was possible; after it, it was certain."[12] Graves and his badly battered British returned to New York, leaving the Chesapeake Bay under the undisputed control of the French. Caught between Grasse at sea and Lafayette on land, Cornwallis was bottlenecked on the Yorktown peninsula. Until that time Cornwallis had been fairly relaxed, expecting relief forces from Clinton. Grasse remained on the coast of the Chesapeake, blocking Cornwallis's exit and preventing the Royal Navy from reinforcing or rescuing the British Army trapped at Yorktown. Thus, Grasse commanded the French fleet that defeated the British fleet off the Virginia Capes and made possible the Franco-American capture of Cornwallis at Yorktown.

Both Cornwallis and Clinton agreed in retrospect that Britain could have won the war if Admiral Rodney had personally commanded the British at the Chesapeake Bay battle. Instead, Rodney was commissioned to cut off American supplies by continuing the British conquest of the tiny but wealthy Dutch-owned Caribbean island of St. Eustatius. In 1780 Britain had declared war on the Netherlands to cripple the St. Eustatius port, seize the valuable cargo from the heavy-laden merchantmen anchored in the harbor, and suppress Dutch trade with France and America. Thus, Britain's effort to increase the Crown treasury via the Anglo-Dutch War competed with her will to win the Revolution in America.

Washington's officers reported that when their commander in chief heard that Admiral de Grasse had arrived in the Chesapeake with 3,000 troops plus siege artillery he "lost all reserve, waved his hat in the air and hugged Rochambeau. And no wonder, for triumph was at hand."[13] That was because Grasse, according to his sailors, ordinarily stood six feet two but on days of battle he stood six feet six.

In mid–August, the first American forces had crossed the Hudson River to begin their 450-mile move to Yorktown. Within the next two days additional American infantry, plus French artillery and infantry, were marching in the largest troop movement of the war. Only a few officers knew their destination. In the last days of August, the Continental and French forces entered New Jersey by separate routes. Dispersal allowed them to forage for food without depleting all the area's resources. By the first few days in September, when the troops paraded before the Continental Congress in Philadelphia, everyone knew they were heading to Yorktown to engage Cornwallis's army.

On September 6–8, 1781, the allied armies of Washington and Rochambeau camped near Elkton, Maryland, where Washington paid his disgruntled soldiers' wages with hard currency borrowed from Rochambeau. Washington left Head of Elk and stopped briefly in Baltimore. On September 9—accompanied by a small escort, an aide-de-camp and his ever-present valet, William "Billy" Lee—Washington rode horseback nonstop for 60 miles to visit Mount Vernon. Washington, who, according to Jefferson, was "the best horseman of his age, and the most graceful figure that could be seen on horseback," was going home for the first time in six years. Rochambeau and his staff arrived the next day. On the 13th the two commanders left Mount Vernon and reached Williamsburg the next day, ahead of their combined armies. On September 18 Rochambeau and Washington visited Admiral de Grasse on his flagship. When Grasse embraced and kissed him on both cheeks, "Washington was less amused than Knox and his officers who roared with unrestricted laughter."[14] Much to the amusement of the guests, the six-foot, two-inch de Grasse kept calling the equally tall Washington "mon petit general." Pressed for time because Grasse needed to return to the West Indies, the commanders were ready for the siege to begin on September 18, but their troops were still en route. Between September 19 and 23, however, all elements of Washington's Army gathered at Williamsburg and then set out for Yorktown.

Petite and feminine Deborah Sampson, masquerading as a male named Robert Shurtliff, marched with her detachment to Yorktown. As will be shown later, she kept her female identity a secret and won a pension after the war. Sara Osborne, the wife of a commissary sergeant, usually walked with the baggage wagons as commanded or occasionally rode in a wagon or, rarely, on a horse as she traveled with Washington's army south from New York to Yorktown. An estimated 50 women marched with the 2,525 enlisted men. At Yorktown Sara set up camp behind the American tents, where she assisted other women in washing, mending clothes and cooking for the soldiers. Maria Cronkite, a New York Regiment fifer's wife, also worked as a washerwoman for officers and accompanied her husband until he was discharged. While in the service, she gave birth to several children.[15] The 50-year-old Martha Washington and her fast friend 25-year-old Lucy Knox, trembling and gripped with fear, consoled each other at Mt. Vernon waiting for the daily express with news of the September 28–October 19, 1781, siege of Yorktown

During the joint three-week-long siege, the Franco-American allies surrounded Cornwallis's 10 redoubts, cutting off his British army by sea and by land. Grasse's fleet, with 40 ships of the line, continued to block the entrance to the Chesapeake Bay for its entire length between Maryland and Virginia. Cornwallis and the British were encamped on a peninsula at Yorktown completely surrounded by allied troops (9,000 American and 8,000 French) across the York River at Gloucester. Confronting Cornwallis on the east were Washington's Continentals. Blocking him on the west were the French units under Rochambeau. Cornwallis was trapped! The French excelled in the European-style siege. Washington and Rochambeau scouted together, but Washington deferred to the French expertise on sieges and took a secondary position, putting the French general in command of the siege of Yorktown.

The French-American alliance captured two redoubts on October 14. The British counterattack failed. On the morning of October 19, Cornwallis—short on food, outnumbered and outgunned—sent out a white flag, surrendering 7,000 men. At 11:00 A.M. the articles of surrender were signed. Cornwallis, pleading failing health, did not attend the surrender ceremony. He had experienced two bouts of malaria during the southern campaign. Therefore, his illness at Yorktown was probably genuine. Instead, General Charles O'Hara presented the sheathed sword of surrender to General Rochambeau, in recognition that the French had won the war. But Rochambeau—to emphasize to the British that they had dealt with more than the French army—directed O'Hara to present the weapon to General George Washington. Lafayette ordered the American band to play "Yankee Doodle" to emphasize America's part in the war. Washington refused to accept the sword from a Cornwallis deputy. He directed O'Hara to present it to General Benjamin Lincoln, who had been captured by Clinton and Cornwallis at Charlestown. Consequently, O'Hara presented Cornwallis's sword to Lincoln and effectively ended the major fighting of the American Revolution. The British soldiers flung their weapons onto a stockpile, trying to smash them. "It wasn't the well-dressed French army who were the true victors of the day, but the weather-beaten, half-clad American troops." Still, Washington knew that "the Yorktown victory had depended on the French skill at sieges, backed up by French naval supremacy."[16] Cornwallis could not attend the dinner Washington threw that night for American, French and British generals. But the next day, when Cornwallis made a courtesy call on Washington, the two developed a rapport based on mutual respect. Together they toured Yorktown on horseback to oversee the demolition of defenses.

General Cornwallis subsequently sailed as a prisoner of war to New York, where he was exchanged for American ambassador Henry Laurens, who had been imprisoned in the Tower of London for more than a year. In the spring of 1782 King George III recalled Sir Henry Clinton, commander in chief of the British Army in America, and replaced him with Sir Guy Carleton, ex-governor of Quebec. Carleton then "directed all military affairs of Canada, New York and wherever else England claimed in the United States."[17]

General Washington resigned his military commission in 1783. Returning to private life, Washington intended never again to serve in public office, but he was not allowed to stay long at Mt. Vernon. After presiding over the Constitutional Convention, he was twice elected unanimously by the electoral college America's first president (1789–1797). He performed magnificently. As Ron Chernow observed, "Washington had forged the executive branch of the federal government, appointed outstanding department heads, and set a benchmark for fairness, efficiency and integrity that future administrations would aspire to match." He guaranteed the survival of the Constitution. "He had taken the new national charter and converted it into a viable, elastic document." His "catalogue of accomplishments was simply breathtaking."[18]

Upon his return to England Clinton—and not his second-in-command, General Charles Cornwallis—was blamed for the British loss at Yorktown. Clinton spent the rest of his life believing he had been made a scapegoat. He became obsessed with vindicating himself and blaming Cornwallis for the defeat.[19] Clinton's two-volume tirade criticizing Cornwallis fantasizes that Cornwallis confessed that he himself was responsible for the British defeat at Yorktown. Clinton returned to Parliament in 1790. In contrast, Lord Cornwallis continued his military career and became governor of India in 1786 and governor-general of Ireland in 1797.

When news reached 10 Downing Street that Cornwallis had surrendered at Yorktown, Lord Frederick North, the prime minister, exclaimed, "Oh God, It's all over!"[20] Cornwallis's defeat ended the North administration. Lord North resigned his office as British prime minister.

Lafayette wrote to Andrienne about Yorktown:

> The end of this campaign is truly brilliant for the allied troops. There was a rare coordination in our movements, and I would be finicky indeed if I were not pleased with the end of my campaign in Virginia. You must have been informed of all the toil the superiority and talents of Lord Cornwallis gave me and of the advantage that we gained in recovering lost ground, until at length we had Lord Cornwallis in the position we needed in order to capture him. It was then that everyone pounced on him.[21]

For his heroic service at Yorktown, General Rochambeau was awarded one of the captured British cannon surrendered by Cornwallis. Comte de Rochambeau—cheered and admired by the officers and men of the American army—then embarked for France.

Andrew Jackson O'Shaughnessy's *The Men Who Lost America*[22] names ten men as subjects of his book: King George III, who was declared a tyrant in the Declaration of Independence; Prime Minister Lord North, who triggered the war by his Coercive Acts, which punished the people of Massachusetts for the Boston Tea Party; the brothers General Sir William Howe and Admiral Lord Richard Howe, who missed the opportunity to defeat the Continental Army in 1776; John Burgoyne, who surrendered at Saratoga; Lord George Germaine, secretary of state for America, who directed the war from Britain; Sir Henry Clinton, commander of the British Army in America, who was accused of inactivity during the second half of the war; Lord Cornwallis, who surrendered at Yorktown; Admiral Sir George Rodney, who failed to prevent the French from entrapping Cornwallis at Yorktown; and John Montague, Earl of Sandwich, first lord of the Admiralty, who was faulted for the failures of the Royal Navy. What motivated these men was a desire to quell insurgency and defend "liberty and the rule of law which they believed could be safeguarded only by upholding the supreme authority of Parliament." The greatest obstacle these well-meaning Brits failed to hurdle was the overwhelming popularity of the revolutionary movement. Between 1774 and 1776 the revolutionaries took control of government, "including the assemblies, councils, court system and local authorities as well as the press." American Patriots ousted royal governors and gained control of the militia.

Not only did France enter the war, but British fighting forces also were diverted after 1778 when both the British Army and the Royal Navy were engaged in protecting their widespread global holdings, which helped finance the war. In America there was a steady stream of victory and defeat by both the British and the Americans, so that each side kept on believing total victory was possible for their country. Even the defeat of the British at Yorktown in 1781 failed to deter the king's determination to continue the war, which continued for two more years after Yorktown, the last major battle of the war.

19

The Last Pockets of Revolution and the Treaty of Paris

As tremendous as it was, the victory at Yorktown did not mean that the Americans had totally won the Revolutionary War. Neither did the British defeat at Yorktown spell complete loss of America for the British. After the Yorktown battle, Admiral de Grasse withdrew French naval resistance, 40 battleships, and sailed back to the West Indies. Without further French financial aid and naval support, the Continental Army was too weak to capture the British strongholds of Charlestown, Savannah, and New York. The British also still possessed St. Augustine, Florida, and Penobscot, Maine. After winning at Yorktown, Washington kept close watch on the British Army occupying New York. In the South, Nathanael Greene continued to drive the Tories to Charlestown and confine them there. In London, even though Prime Minister North's government fell, George III still refused to surrender.

In January 1782 Greene sent the brave and impetuous General Anthony Wayne with a regiment of dragoons to Georgia. Wayne swam on horseback across the Savannah River and waged a war of attrition against Savannah. Defending against Greene, Loyalist Thomas Brown recruited a regiment of King's Rangers and appealed to the Cherokee and the Upper Creeks to come to his aid. When the British evacuated Savannah on July 11, 1782, Wayne's troops paraded victoriously into the city. Georgian Elijah Clarke returned home from his refuge in the Carolinas to harass the Cherokee and the Creeks. Ludicrously, Georgia still intended to convince the incredulous Creeks that the newly independent state of Georgia had rights to an empire that stretched to the Mississippi River, one the Creeks and their ancestors had claimed, inhabited and hunted on for centuries.

When Wayne, under General Greene, forced the British to evacuate Savannah, the ousted Tories headed toward Charlestown, the last British stronghold in the South. In late 1782 Charlestown was evacuated. Carlton, the British commander in chief of New York, refused to evacuate British troops until all Loyalist refugees had found a place of safety. Awaiting vessels to carry them home, the British, Hessians, exiled Loyalists and all forces paid by the British government remained in New York on Staten Island and Long Island until November 1783.

The peace treaty required that the English withdraw troops and relinquish all forts within the interior of the United States as well as the seacoast. Yet the British continued their extensive trade with American Indians in territories stretching from the Mississippi to the Appalachian Mountains on the Ohio.[1]

In the interval between the surrender of Cornwallis at Yorktown in 1781 and the ratification of the Peace Treaty of Paris in 1784, several skirmishes pitted Patriot militiamen against British and Loyalist troops and British-allied Indians. Rather than the Battle of Yorktown, some consider the August 19, 1782, Battle of Blue Licks in Kentucky County, Virginia, to be the last major battle of the war. Israel Boone, the second son of Daniel and Rebecca Boone to lose his life in the Revolution, was killed at Blue Licks. This battle erupted when a group of 150 Kentucky militiamen left Bryan's Station near Lexington in pursuit of a larger force of British soldiers and Wyandot Indian warriors. The militia rode headlong into a British-Indian ambush. Commenting on the Blue Licks Battle, in which his son Israel was one of 70 militiamen killed, Daniel Boone said, "So valiantly did our small party fight that, to the memory of those who unfortunately fell in the battle, enough of honour cannot be paid. Had Col. Logan and his party been with us, it is highly probable we should have given the savages a total defeat."[2] A big, handsome Scots-Irishman, Benjamin Logan, founder of Logan's Fort at Crab Orchard, Kentucky, arrived in time to bury the dead. Nathan Boone said, "My father went with Logan's party to bury the dead. He recognized his son Israel.... My poor brother's face was blackened and swollen, as were all the others on the battleground.... Father used to be deeply affected, even to tears, when he spoke of the Blue Licks defeat and the death of his son."[3] George Rogers Clark was absent at the Battle of Blue Licks, but in November he retaliated against the Ohio Indians because he was responsible for the defense of the Northwest Territory.

On September 11, 1782, a month after the Blue Licks battle, British soldiers allied with Shawnee, Wyandot and Mingo warriors carrying a British flag sprang an attack on Fort Henry, Virginia (now Wheeling, West Virginia), on the Ohio River between Point Pleasant and Pittsburgh. Some regard this siege as the last battle of the Revolution.

Betty Zane, a 13-year-old girl, knew that the fort was short on gunpowder and the men and boys could not defend it. So she made a dangerous dash out through the fort's gate and entered a storage house 70 yards away. It was the cabin of Colonel Ebenezer Zane, Betty Zane's brother. Much to the astonishment of the besieging British and Indians, she emerged with a large bundle of gunpowder wrapped in her apron. Her lightning speed back to the fort helped her dodge their gunfire. Women inside the fort loaded rifles to defend against the attack. Within a few days, the enemy abandoned the siege.

At about the same time, September 1782, John Sevier launched a Chickamauga expedition against Dragging Canoe. Following the expedition, Indian attacks on western overmountain settlements of Tennessee Country in Sullivan and Washington counties ceased for a short time. But the Chickamauga did not stop their attacks on Cumberland settlements. Far from ceasing when the Revolutionary War ended, the war between settlers and aboriginals continued for many years in what would become the State of Franklin and then the State of Tennessee. Dragging Canoe died in 1792. By 1794 many Chickamauga had started migrating across the Mississippi and by 1799 the migration was complete. Open warfare between Americans and Cherokee then ended.

Two women, both of whom were direct descendants of Mayflower Pilgrims, surfaced in 1783 after the war. They are the only female Mayflower descendants who are recognized by the Daughters of the American Revolution as Patriots. One was Mercy Raymond Bedford, who, as mentioned in the preface, fought her battles in court. The other, Deborah Samson, a secret soldier, fought on the battlefield and kept her female identity hidden until the war ended. Two years earlier, in early 1781, Deborah, disguised as a young man, took

19. The Last Pockets of Revolution and the Treaty of Paris

the name Robert Shurtliff and enlisted for three years. This young woman masquerading under a male pseudonym marched with her detachment to Yorktown. There, with blistered hands, she dug trenches and joined her fellow soldiers storming a British redoubt. She sustained a thigh wound in October 1782, but evaded medical attention. In order to keep her identity secret, she avoided bathing with the troops. In 1783, though hostilities had ceased, she was sent to Philadelphia to quell a riot of disgruntled soldiers. When Deborah contracted an infectious disease and lost consciousness, she was carried to the hospital. where a doctor uncovered her disguise. After her discharge, she married and gave birth to three children. In need of income, she petitioned the Massachusetts General Court for military back pay. Investigating her claim, Paul Revere wrote (to Willam Eustis), "When I heard her spoken of as a Soldier, I formed the idea of a tall, masculine female ... without education, & one of the meanest of her sex— When I saw and discoursed with her I was agreeably surprised to find a small, effeminate, and conversable woman, whose education entitled her to a better situation in life." Deborah received an honorable discharge in 1783 from General Henry Knox. Having told her story on lecture tours throughout New England, she "received both an invalid's pension and a veteran's pension. After her death, her husband had the unusual distinction of being granted a "widow's" pension as the surviving spouse of a veteran.[4]

Finally ending the war, the Peace of Paris comprised three separate peace treaties signed by Britain. The first, the 1783 Treaty of Paris, was an agreement with the United States and the only part actually signed in Paris. An agreement between Britain and the United States of America, it heralded the ending of the Revolutionary War. In it, America achieved independence from Great Britain as well as control over the eastern one-third of North America—the territory east of the Mississippi River—without making any major concessions to the British. Britain retained Canada and ceded Florida to Spain. Mitchell's map of North America, issued in 1755 at the onset of the French and Indian War, was used by negotiators to establish the boundaries set by the Treaty of Paris in both 1763 and 1783. This made Mitchell's map the "most significant map in the history of the United States."[5] The other two peace treaties signed by Britain—one with France, the other with Spain—were signed in Versailles. The Dutch Republic made peace separately in 1781.

Congress appointed John Adams, John Jay and Benjamin Franklin, who was already minister to France, as peace commissioners. They signed the treaty in Paris on September 3, 1783. British plenipotentiary David Hartley signed as representative of King George III. Article 10 of the treaty stipulated that in order for the document to take effect Congress must ratify and return the approved document to England within six months. After being delayed by a monstrous snowstorm and the illness of one of its delegates, the United States Congress met at the senate chamber of the Maryland statehouse. A vote was taken. Congress issued an official broadside notifying all the good citizens of these United States that on January 14, 1784, the Continental Congress ratified the Treaty of Paris. The United States was now an independent and sovereign nation. After almost nine years, the American Revolutionary War was formally and officially over.

After many years of bloodshed, the South longed to return to ordinary life, but the war had left plantations and farms in ruins. New York and New Jersey cities suffered the scars of prolonged enemy occupation. New England experienced "economic depression, farm foreclosures and unemployment." Throughout the country a small number of both male and female intellectuals discussed "the woman question."⁶ The debate began with a zealous rejection of the traditional notion that women were mentally and morally inferior to men. During the war, women, by demonstrating their ability to think rationally, manage the farm, and cope with adversity, had proved their point. Their unstinting, self-sacrificing participation in the Revolution was essential for winning American independence. Women writers argued that the stereotyped, pre-Revolution, perceived defects—vanity, superficiality, materialism, frivolous behavior—did not stem from natural defects but from poor education.

Abigail Adams wrote to her husband, John: "I can not say that I think you very generous to the Ladies, for whilst you are proclaiming peace and good will to Men, Emancipating all Nations, you insist upon retaining an absolute power over Wives." She complained that the legal position of a woman made her totally dependent, like a child and the insane. John considered his masculine system benign, rather than oppressive. "There was no room in John Adams's masculine system for female legal or economic independence."⁷ Her views on teaching diverged from those of her husband and son, John Quincy, especially on the importance of the Latin and Greek languages and literature in public formal education. Knowledge of the classics was required for admission to Harvard. Having no formal education, Abigail was self-taught and able to read the classics only in translation. John Adams loved Latin and Greek literature. During their courtship the 26-year-old John addressed his 17-year-old sweetheart, Abigail, as "Ever Dear Diana," referring to the Roman goddess of the hunt, nature and the moon. He signed his love letters "Lysander," referring to the fiery Spartan statesman and general of the Peloponnesian War.

After marriage Abigail eschewed the classics and signed her letters "Portia" when writing to John and intimate friends. She, like Shakespeare's Portia, was bright, beautiful and very feminine. Also like Portia, she could "turn two mincing steps into a manly stride."⁸ She was convinced that "classical education divided the sexes."⁹ The Adamses had difficulty in affording boarding schools for their five children. Abigail was concerned that there were no grammar schools in Braintree, Massachusetts. On October 13, 1810, John Adams wrote an explanatory letter to Benjamin Rush: "Mrs. Adams says she is willing you should discredit Greek and Latin because it will destroy the foundation of all the pretensions of the gentlemen to superiority over the ladies and restore liberty, equality, and fraternity between the sexes." Abigail's sentiments presaged the sharp decline in popularity of the classics in the 19th century.

Both Abigail Adams and her contemporary scribbler Judith Sargent Murray fought not only for female economic independence but also for equal education of girls and boys. Judith Murray, daughter of a wealthy merchant, was self-taught through reading books of geography, philosophy and literature from her father's large library. She set the stage for woman's entrance into the political world by insisting that women were as capable as men "of supporting with honour the toils of government." Stories of the Revolution abounded with valiant females who risked their lives on the battlefields or avoided bullets on their home farms. Murray's essays recounted the deeds of heroic queens and female warriors "who ruled wisely and led their warriors into battle courageously." And yet Judith Murray, like Abigail Adams "was ultimately more comfortable calling upon women's ability to influence and persuade than upon their powers to legislate or command."¹⁰

After the war, Murray published her lengthy essay *On the Equality of the Sexes*. Below is an excerpt:

> Will it be said that the judgment of a male of two years old, is more sage than that of a female's of the same age? I believe the reverse is generally observed to be true. But from that period what partiality! how is the one exalted, and the other depressed, by the contrary modes of education which are adopted! the one is taught to aspire, and the other is early confined and limited. As their years increase, the sister must be wholly domesticated, while the brother is led by the hand through all the flowery paths of science. Grant that their minds are by nature equal, yet who shall wonder at the *apparent* superiority....[11]

Judith Murray campaigned for opening women's schools with a rigorous curriculum that focused on geography, political philosophy and history rather than fine needlework. "Critics warned that formal education would create masculine women, unattractive in their appearance, negligent in their duties and 'disgustingly slovenly in person.'"[12] Yet, in 1787, due to the efforts of Judith Murray, Abigail Adams, Mercy Warren and other reformers, the Philadelphia Young Ladies Academy opened, ushering in a revolution in female education. It was the greatest achievement of its time for American women.

The odyssey continues.

Chapter Notes

Preface

1. Kierner, Cynthia A., *Southern Women in Revolution*, 1776–1800, Introduction, xx.
2. "Abigail Adams, Remember the Ladies," in *America in Class, National Humanities Center*, http://americainclass.org/abigail-adams-and-remember-the-ladies/.
3. Richards, *Mercy Otis Warren*, 143.
4. "Property," in *The Jefferson Monticello*, https://www.monticello.org/site/plantation-and-slavery/property.
5. Richards, *Mercy Otis Warren*, 142.
6. Passed December 29, 1785, *North Carolina State Records*, vol. 34, 761, 762.

Prologue

1. *Letters of Horace Walpole*, vol. 3, *1761*, 434.
2. McCullough, *John Adams*, 333.
3. McCullough, *1776*, ch. 1; O'Shaugnessy, *The Men Who Lost America*, 19.
4. Fiske, *American Revolution*, 1:40.
5. O'Shaugnessy, *The Men Who Lost America*, 47, 49, 51–52.
6. Speck, W.A., "The Structure of British politics in the mid-eighteenth century," Greene, Jack P., and Pole, J.R., eds., *A Companion to the American Revolution*, 3.

Chapter 1

1. Richards, *Mercy Otis Warren*, 126.
2. Thomas Jefferson's Library, Library of Congress, https://www.loc.gov/exhibits/thomas-jeffersons-library/interactives/history-of-the-american-revolution/.
3. Warren, Mercy, *History of the Rise, Progress and Termination of the American Revolution*, 394.
4. Ramsay, J.G.M, *Annals of Tennessee*, 721.
5. Richards, *Mercy Otis Warren*, 3.
6. Ibid., 5–6.
7. Ellet, *Women of the Revolution*, 76.
8. Warren, Mercy, *History of ... the American Revolution*, vol. 1, ch. 1.
9. Hosmer, *Samuel Adams*, 42.
10. McCullough, *John Adams*, 49, 62.
11. "Otis's Speech on Writs of Assistance," 17, in *American History Leaflets: Colonial and Constitutional*, issues 25–33, edited by Albert Bushnell Hart, Edward Channing of Harvard University, New York, 1896.
12. Hosmer, *Samuel Adams*, 44.
13. Fiske, *American Revolution*, 1:14.
14. Dickens, *Child's History of Englan*d, 747–48.
15. Adams, John, "Letters to Hezekiah Niles on the American Revolution 1818," teachingamericanhistory.org.
16. Cobb, *Rise of Religious Liberty in America*, ch. 8.
17. Parker, *Historic Americans*, 163.
18. McCullough, *John Adams*, 61.
19. Hosmer, *Samuel Adams*, 18.
20. Hurwitz, Mark, guest contributor, March 30, 2016, "This Old Pew: # 49—The Wells Family Connections," in *The Old North Church*.
21. McCullough, John Adams, 18, 55, 56, 59–61.
22. Morison, *Oxford History of the American People*, 201.
23. Warren, Mercy, *History of the ... American Revolution*, vol. 1, ch. 2.
24. Schrader, David E., "250 Years Ago: The Stamp Act," *SAR* 110, no. 2 (Fall 2015), 18, 19.
25. *American Heritage Pictorial Atlas of United States History*, 91.
26. Warren, *History of the ... American Revolution*, ch. 2.
27. Churchill, *Great Republic*, 57; Churchill, *Great Republic*, large print, 101.
28. Hosmer, *Samuel Adams* 48, 47.
29. Morison, *Oxford History of the American People*, 185.
30. Red Hill National Memorial, "Patrick Henry, Voice of the American Revolution," redhill.org.
31. Wood, *Americanization of Benjamin Franklin*, 119, 122, 70, 114, 150.
32. Lossing, *Pictorial Field Book of the Revolution*, vol. 1, ch. 20.
33. Ellet, *Women of the American Revolution*, vol. 1, 143, 144.
34. Hosmer, *Samuel Adams*, 8.
35. Chesterton, *A History of the United States*, 49.
36. Warren, Mercy Otis, *History of the ... American Revolution*, vol. 1, ch. 2.
37. Morison, *Oxford History*, 193.
38. Lossing, *Pictorial Field Book of the Revolution*, ch. 20.
39. Morison, *Oxford History*, 193.
40. Memorial Hall Museum, Deerfield, MA, "Flax Wheel," online collection.
41. Warren, Mercy, *History of ... the American Revolution*, ch. 2.
42. Morison, *Oxford History*, 192–93.
43. Fiske, *American Revolution*, vol. 1, ch. 2.
44. Hosmer, *Samuel Adams*, 152.
45. McCullough, *John Adams*, 62.
46. Warren, *History of ... the American Revolution*, vol 1, ch. 4.

47. Morison, *Oxford History*, 200–201.
48. McCullough, *John Adams*, 68.
49. Churchill, *Great Republic* (Large Print), 107.
50. Morison, *Oxford History*, 192, 201

Chapter 2

1. Ellet, *Women of the American Revolution*, vol. 1, 94.
2. Franklin, Benjamin, *Autobiography*, 89.
3. Hosmer, *Samuel Adams*, 188–189.
4. Morison, *Oxford History*, 201–202.
5. Warren, Mercy Otis, *History of the ... American Revolution*, vol. 1, ch. 4.
6. *Ibid*.
7. Note from Wells, *Life of Samuel Adams*," Hanover Historical Texts Project, regarding Adams, "Rights of the Colonists: The Report of the Committee of Correspondence to the Boston Town Meeting, Nov. 20, 1772," vol. 7, 417–28.
8. Ellet, Woman of the Revolution, 93,
9. Morison, *Oxford History of the American History*, 203.
10. Churchill, *Great Republic* (large print), 109, 110.
11. Ellet, *Women of the Revolution*, 78.
12. Commager and Morris, *The Spirit of 'Seventy-Six*, 1.
13. "Mystery of the Green Dragon Tavern and the Boston Tea House," www.boston-tea-party.org.
14. Morison, *Oxford History*, 204.
15. Warren, Mercy Otis, *History of the ... American Revolution*, vol. I, ch. 4.
16. Ellet, *Women of the American Revolution*, vol. 1, 94.
17. Morison, *Oxford History*, 204.
18. Great Britain: Parliament, Quartering Act, June 2, 1774, Yale Law School, "The Avalon Project"
19. Garraty and Gay, *Columbia History of the World*, 757.
20. Wade, William (King University professor emeritus), "The British Monarchy: 1603 to the Present," Lectures and handouts at Virginia Highlands Community College, Abingdon, Virginia, April 2006.
21. *American Archives*, "Documents of the American Revolution, 1774–1776," Lincoln.lib.niu.edu.

Chapter 3

1. Franklin, *Autobiography*, 188.
2. Commager and Morris, *The Spirit of 'Seventy-Six*, 274.
3. Chesterton, *History of the United States*, 47.
4. Chernow, *Washington*, 172.
5. "The Suffolk Resolves, Joseph Warren, 1774," Articles 11 and 14.
6. Griffin, *History of Old Tryon and Rutherford Counties*, 25–26, quoting Ashe, 1:475.
7. Sharp, Arthur G., *Not Your Father's Founders* (MA, Adams Media, 2012), 40.
8. Garrison, *Great Stories of the American Revolution*, 76, 77.
9. Kierner, *Southern Women in Revolution, 1776–1800*, 173.
10. O'Shaughnessy, *The Men Who Lost America*, 53, 54.
11. Summers, *History of Southwest Virginia*, 202–203.
12. Henry, "Give Me Liberty or Give Me Death," proceedings of March 23, 1775, Virginia Convention.
13. Churchill, *Great Republic*, 63.
14. Morison, *Oxford History*, 214.
15. Ellet, *Women of the Revolution*, vol. 1, 95.
16. Roth, D.W., "Israel Bissell," in *Art and Paintings of the Revolutionary War*.
17. Commager and Morris, *The Spirit of 'Seventy-Six*, 89–90.
18. Ellet, *Women of the American Revolution*, 114.
19. Casey Susan, *Women Heroes of the American Revolution*, 89–97.
20. Chernow, *Washington*, 191.
21. McCullough, *1776*, 34–35.
22. Ellet, *Women of the American Revolution*, 113."
23. National Park Service, "U.S. Navy."
24. Dept. of the Navy, Navy Historical Center, "Navy Birthday Information," history.navy.mil/birthday.htm.
25. Churchill, *Great Republic*, 66.
26. Bobrick, Benson, *Angels in the Whirlwind*, ch. 5 (Simon & Schuster, 1997).
27. O'Shaughnessy, *The Men Who Lost America*, 85.
28. Thane, *Fighting Quaker: Nathanael Greene*, as quoted by Connecticut Sons American Revolution "Connecticut's Response to the Lexington Alarm" Historical Series, no. 1 (July 1997).
29. Ellis, Joseph, *First Family Abigail and John Adams*, 39–40, 56,62.
30. O'Shaughnessy, *The Men Who Lost America*, 86.
31. Churchill, *Great Republic*, 66.
32. "Elizabeth Wells Adams; Wife of Samuel Adams," In Green and Green, *Wives of the Signers*.
33. O'Shaughnessy, *The Men Who Lost America*, 57.
34. Commager and Morris, *The Spirit of 'Seventy-Six*, 276.
35. Chernow, *Washington*, 183.
36. *Ibid*., 118, 191.
37. *Ibid*., 29, 123–24, xviii, 195.
38. Randall, *George Washington*, 283.
39. Chernow, *Washington*, 185.
40. Ellis, Joseph, *First Family Abigail and John Adams*, 47.
41. Randall, *George Washington*, 284, quoting George Washington.
42. Ellet, *Women of the Revolution*, 24.
43. Chernow, Washington, *A Life*, chpt. 1.
44. Ellet, *Women of the Revolution* 29–30.
45. *Ibid*., 28.
46. *Ibid*., 34.
47. *Ibid*., 80, 81.
48. Wright, Robert K., Jr., *The Continental Army*, Washington, DC., Center of Military History United States Army, 19–28.
49. McCullough, *1776*, 28.
50. Ellet, *Women of the American Revolution*, 117.
51. O'Shaughnessy, *Men Who Lost America*, 86.
52. McCullough, *1776*, 28.
53. McCullough, *John Adams*, 93–96.
54. Berkin, Carol, *Revolutionary Mothers*, 137.
55. Casey, Susan, *Women Heroes of the American Revolution*, 17.
56. *Ibid*., 23.
57. Chernow, *Washington: A Life*, 217–219.

58. Loan, Nancy K., *Following the Drum: Women at the Valley Forge Encampment* (Washington, DC: Potomac Books, 2009), 78.
59. Berkin, *Revolutionary Mothers*, 74.
60. Drake, Francis Samuel, *Life and Correspondence of Henry Knox*, 129.
61. Knox, Henry, December 17 Knox letter to George Washington from Lake George, New York.
62. McCullough, *1776*, 73.
63. O'Shaughnessy, *The Men Who Lost America*, 86–7.
64. Lossing, *1776*, 190.
65. Chernow, *Washington*, 227.
66. Abigail Adams, as quoted by McCullough, *John Adams*, 76.
67. Brakeley, Sam, *In the Wake of American's Hannibal* (Raleigh, NC: LuLu Press, 2015), 118, 119
68. Schuyler, as quoted by Donald M. Moran, "Major General Richard Montgomery," *Liberty Tree* (June 2006).
69. Ellet, *Women of the Revolution*, 89–91.

Chapter 4

1. McCullough, *1776*, 111–12.
2. *Ibid.*, 129–134.
3. Lossing, *1776*, 185–200; Chernow, *Washington*, 244.
4. Chernow, *Washington*, 259.
5. O'Shaughnessy, *The Men Who Lost America*, 97.
6. McCullough, *1776*, 243.
7. Berkin, *Revolutionary Mothers*, 139.
8. Fischer, David Hackett, on Book TV, discussing *Washington's Crossing*, C-SPAN 2, February 26, 2004.
9. *Ibid.*
10. *Ibid.*
11. "Guide to Freedom: A Jockey Statue Marked Underground Railroad," *Lexington Herald-Leader*, February 22, 1998.
12. Chernow, *Washington: A Life*, 278, 279.
13. *Ibid.*, 200, 231, 224, 291.
14. *Ibid.*, 288.
15. Trescott, Jacquelin, "Smoking Gun Surfaces in Washington Spy Scandal: 1777 Letter Finds Home at New Spy Museum," *Washington Post*, June 20, 2002.
16. Birken, *Women Heroes of the American Revolution*, 74–79.
17. Bergin, Sylvia, *The Mahopac Story*, Mahopac (NY) Public Library.org.
18. *American Heritage Pictorial Atlas of United States History*, 99.
19. Chernow, *Washington*, 302.
20. *Ibid.*, 306.
21. Unger, *Lafayette*, 50.
22. Chernow, *Washington*, 305.
23. Ellett, *Women of the Revolution*, vol. 1, 18.
24. Lengel, *General George Washington*, 251, as quoted by Chernow, Washington.
25. Randall, *George Washington*, 338, 339.
26. Library of Virginia.
27. George Washington Papers at the Library of Congress, 1741–1795: series 3 C Varick transcript.
28. Cunningham, John T., *New Jersey America's Main Road* (Garden City, 105).
29. Sharp, Arthur G., *Not Your Father's Founders* (MA, Adams Media, 2012), 67.

Chapter 5

1. O'Shaughnessy, *The Men Who Lost America*, 3, 124.
2. Williams, *The History of American Wars*, 63.
3. Churchill, *Great Republic*, large print, 131–133.
4. Williams, *The History of American Wars*, 64.
5. Churchill, *Great Republic*, 74, 75.
6. O'Shaughnessy, *The Men Who Lost America*, 149.
7. Fowler, *Empires of War*, 31, 32.
8. Berkin, *Revolutionary Mothers*, 110.
9. Axelrod, *A Savage Empire*, 260.
10. Colmmager and Morris, *The Spirit of 'Seventy-Six*, 1000.
11. U.S. Department of the Interior, NPS, "Teaching with Historic Places: The Battle of Oriskany."
12. Williams, *The History of American Wars*, 69.
13. O'Shaughnessy, *The Men Who Lost America*, 146.
14. Pell, S.H.P., *Fort Ticonderoga*, eprinted for the Fort Ticonderoga Museum, 1970, 85.
15. Williams, *History of American Wars*, 22.
16. Coburn, *Centennial History of the Battle of Bennington*, 12, 52.
17. Chernow, *Washington*, 182.
18. Morison, *Oxford History*, 248, 249.
19. Ellet, *Women of the American Revolution*, vol. 1, 59.
20. *Ibid.*, 97.
21. Churchill, *Great Republic*, 76.
22. Saratoga National Historic Park, New York, Archive.org.
23. Snell and Wilshin, *Saratoga*, 28.
24. Commager and Morris, *The Spirit of 'Seventy-Six*, 581, 583.
25. *American Heritage Pictorial Atlas of the United States*, 98.
26. Wood, *Americanization of Benjamin Franklin*, 197.
27. Chernow, *Washington*, quoting Revolutionary War surgeon Benjamin Rush, 317.
28. Idzerda and Smith, *France and the American War for Independence*, 17–20.
29. Churchill, *Great Republic* (large print), 137
30. Franklin, *Autobiography of Benjamin Franklin*, 49
31. Wood, *the Americanization of Benjamin Franklin*, 33.
32. *Ibid.*, 154
33. Franklin, *Autobiography*, 187–88.
34. Wood, *Americanization of Benjamin Franklin*, 148.
35. *Encyclopaedia Britannica Premium Service*, s.v., "Franklin, Benjamin."
36. Wood, *Americanization of Benjamin Franklin*, 277, 98.
37. Cole, "In Paris, Taking the Salons by Storm," *U.S. News*, July 7–14, 2008, 49.
38. Wood, *Americanization of Benjamin Franklin*, 198.
39. Idzerda and Smith, *France and the American War for Independence*, 1, 19.
40. Churchill, *Great Republic* (large print), 137.
41. Kingsbury, "Allied with the enemy of Our Enemy," *U.S. News*, July 7–14, 2008, 48.

42. Cole, "In Paris, Taking the Salons by Storm," *U.S. News*, July 7–14, 2008, 49.
43. Wood, *Americanization of Benjamin Franklin*, passim, 241–244.
44. Ibid., 240.

Chapter 6

1. Summary of several Valley Forge markers: "Log City," "To Build a Redoubt," "Artillery Park," "Training for Victory and Grand Parade."
2. Rees, John U., "An Overview of Continental Army Female Camp Followers," *The Continental Soldier* 8, no. 3 (Spring 1995), 51–58 (Journal of the Continental Line).
3. Warren, *History of the ... American Revolution*, vol. 1, ch. 10.
4. Bordewich, Fergus M., Flora Fraser's *The Washingtons*, book review, *Wall Street Journal*, November 14–15, 2015.
5. Wharton, Anne Hollingsworth, *Martha Washington*, 121–125.
6. Chernow, *Washington*, 354, 204.
7. Loane, Nancy E., *Following the Drum Women at the Valley Forge Encampment* (Washington, D.C., Potomac, 2009), 4.
8. Morison, *Oxford History*, 229.
9. Carbone, Gerald, *Nathan Greene: A Biography* (New York: Palgren McMillan, 2008), 80.
10. Chernow, *Washington*, 328–29.
11. Ibid., 378.
12. Ibid., 332.
13. Chernow, *Alexander Hamilton*, 109.
14. Lockhart, Paul, "The Rich Legacy of a Forgotten Founder," *U.S. News*, July 7–14, 2008, 45.
15. Valley Forge Visitor Center exhibit, "The American Soldier at Valley Forge."
16. Commager and Morris, *The Spirit of 'Seventy-Six*, 676, 693.
17. McCullough, *John Adams*, 189.
18. Ellis, Joseph, *First Family: Abigail and John Adams*, 73–79, 87–90.
19. Chernow, *Washington*, 338.
20. Ellet, *Women of the American Revolution*, 39.
21. Ibid., 44.
22. Ibid., 344.
23. Hanaford, Phebe A., "Women of the Century," *Daughters of America* (Journal published in Augusta, ME, by True, 1883).
24. *American Heritage Pictorial Atlas of United States History*, 91.
25. Commager and Morris, *The Spirit of 'Seventy-Six*, 705.
26. William S. Baker, *Pennsylvania Magazine of History and Biography* 15, no. 1 (1891), 26–34.
27. Chernow, *Washington*, 347.
28. Ellet, *Women of the American Revolution*, vol. 1, 82.
29. Idzerda and Smith, *France and the American War for Independence*, 32.
30. Chernow, *Washington*, 349–50.
31. *SAR* 85, no. 3 (Winter 1991).
32. Palisades Parks Conservancy, site information at Stony Point Battlefield State Historic Site, New York.
33. Berkin, Carol, *Revolutionary Mothers*, 43.
34. Casey, Susan, *Women Heroes of the Revolution*, 55.
35. George Washington to the president of Congress, 25 December 1779, Papers of the Continental Congress.
36. *American Heritage Pictorial Atlas of United States History*, 101.
37. Berkin, *Revolutionary Mothers*, 117.
38. Morgan, *League of the Iroquois*, 27.
39. Mann, Barbara Alice, *General Washington's War on Native Americans* (ebook) (University of Nevada Press, 2008).
40. Brewster, Michael, "The Story of Catherine's Town, NY," Exploring Upstate.com.
41. Ibid., s.v. "Iroquois Confederacy."
42. O'Shaughnessy, *The Men Who Lost America*, 232–233.
43. Warren, Mercy, *History of the ... American Revolution*, vol. 1, ch. 16.
44. Religion and the Founding of the American Republic, "Religion and the American Revolution."
45. Simms, *Life of Nathanael Greene*, 96.

Chapter 7

1. George Bancroft letter to D.L. Swain, Esq., July 4, 1848.
2. Ramsey, J.G.M., *Annals of Tennessee*, 97–98.
3. "Regulator Movement," *Encyclopedia of North Carolina*, University of North Carolina Press.
4. "Memorial of Jonas Bedford Esqr. Late of Tryon County, No. Carolina."
5. Henderson, *Conquest of the Old Southwest*, ch. 12.
6. Clayton, *History of Davidson County Tennessee*, 12.
7. Governor Tryon from Great Alamance Camp, May 16, 1772, to "the People now Assembled in Arms who Style themselves Regulators."
8. *The Commemorative Souvenir Program Bi-Centennial of the Battle of Alamance*.
9. Johnson, Lloyd, "Sandy Creek Baptist," *North Carolina History Project*; Jonas, Glen, "Sandy Creek Baptist Association," *NC Pedia*.
10. West Nashville's Founders' Museum, "Fort Nashborough on the Cumberland," wnfoundersmuseum.org.
11. Tennessee State Library and Archives, "Haywood, John (1762-1826), Papers (1768-1796)."
12. Haywood as quoted in Clayton's *History of Davidson County*, 13.
13. Alderman, *Overmountain Men*, 18.
14. Summers, *Annals of Southwest Virginia*.
15. Ramsey, *Annals of Tennessee*, 106.
16. Taylor, Oliver, *History of Sullivan County*, ch. 5.
17. Turner, Frederick Jackson, "Significance of the Frontier in American History," 15.
18. Ramsey, *Annals of Tennessee*, 102–103.
19. Folmsbee, Stanley J., "Annotations Relating Ramsey's *Annals of Tennessee* to Present-day Knowledge" (754, 755), in *Annals of Tennessee*, J.G.M. Ramsey, M.D., 1853.
20. Ramsey, *Annals of Tennessee*, 107.

Chapter 8

1. Howard's 1906 *Preliminaries of the Revolution, 1763-1775*, as published in *The American Nations: A His-*

tory, ed. Albert Bushnell Hart, Harvard University, 241 (e-book).
   2. "Nonhelema (Grenadier Squaw) (Ca 1720-1786)," in *Women and War: Historical Encyclopedia from Antiquity to the Present*, vol. 1, Bernard A. Cox, 434 (ebook).
   3. Ramsey, J.G.M., *Annals of Tennessee*, 72 fn.
   4. *Ibid.*, 75.
   5. Merk, *History of the Western Movement*, 69.
   6. Bergmann, "Commerce and Arms," PhD diss., University of Cincinnati, 19.
   7. Bogan, Dallas, "First Recorded Massacre on Powell's River Claims the Lives of Daniel Boone's Son and Others," *LaFollette Press*, reprinted in *History of Campbell County, Tennessee*, TNgenweb.org.
   8. "Dunmore's War, Primary Documents," in *Documentary History of Dunmore's War*, ed. Reuben Gold Thwaites and Louise Phelps Kellogg (Madison: Wisconsin Historical Society, 1905), xi (hereafter Thwaites and Kellogg, *Dunmore's War*).
   9. Boone, Nathan, *My Father, Daniel Boone*, 39.
   10. Kincaid, *Wilderness Road*, 83
   11. Chernow, *Washington*, 165.
   12. Unger, *Lions of Liberty: Patrick Henry*, 74.
   13. Thwaites and Kellogg, *Dunmore's War*, xiii.
   14. *The Preston and Virginia Papers of the Draper Collection of Manuscripts*, Calendar Series, vol. 1, Publications of the State Historical Society of Wisconsin (Madison: State Historical Society of Wisconsin, 1915) (hereafter Preston Papers).
   15. Washburn, Wilcomb E., *Indians of the American Revolution*, American Revolution.org.
   16. Thwaites and Kellogg, *Dunmore's War*, xv.
   17. Summers, *History of Southwest Virginia*, 148-49.
   18. Boone, Nathan, *My Father, Daniel Boone*, 43.
   19. Thwaites and Kellogg, *Dunmore's War*, 149-150.
   20. Taylor, *Historic Sullivan*, 45*n*.
   21. Williams, *Dawn of Tennessee Valley*, 399.
   22. Craig, Neveille, ed., *Olden Time* 2 (Pittsburgh: Wright & Charlton, 1848), 60.
   23. Quinn, *Arthur Campbell*, 124.
   24. Thwaites and Kellogg, *Dunmore's War*, 98.
   25. "Fleming's Journal," Thwaites and Kellogg, Primary Documents, *Dunmore's War*, 281-91.
   26. *Ibid.*, 257.
   27. Thwaites and Kellogg, *Dunmore's War*, introduction, xx.
   28. Lewis, Virgil, *History of the Battle of Point Pleasant*, 40.
   29. Isaac Shelby letter to John Shelby from the "Camp Opposite to the mouth of the Great Canaway October 16th 1774," in Thwaites and Kellog, *Dunmore's War*, 269-77.
   30. Hale, John P., *History of the Great Kanawah Valley*, 128.
   31. Lewis, Virgil A., "Anne Bailey," *Magazine of History* 11, no. 3 (March 1910) (West Virginia Archives and History).
   32. Thwaites and Kellogg, *Dunmore's War*, introduction xix, 426.
   33. *Ibid.*, 384.
   34. *WV Archives and History*, "First Biennial Report of department of Archives and History, 1906," 236-39, 289-291.
   35. "Dunmore's Account," in Thwaits and Kellog, *Dunmore's War*, 386.

   36. "Simon Girty Memorial Stone," United Empire of Loyalists' Association of Canada.
   37. Ohio Department of Natural Resources, Ohio State Parks, "Who Mourns for Logan?"
   38. Thwaites and Kellogg, *Dunmore's War*, 432.
   39. West Virginia Society, *SAR* (Summer 2015), 47.
   40. "Nonhelema (Grenadier Squaw) (Ca 1720-1786)," in *Women and War: Historical Encyclopedia from Antiquity to the Present*, vol. 1, Bernard A. Cox, 434.
   41. Sadler, Lynn Veach, *Not Dreamt of in Your Philosophy* (Bards & Sages, 2008), 102-105.
   42. Thwaittes and Kellogg, *Dunmore's War*, xxv-vi.

Chapter 9

   1. Kincaid, *Wilderness Road*, 93, 94.
   2. Walker, Felix, *Memoirs*, 8, excerpted in Samuel Cole Williams, *Tennessee During the Revolutionary War*, 294 fn.
   3. Alderman, *Overmountain Men*, 38.
   4. *Ibid.*, 24.
   5. *Ibid.*, 54.
   6. Boone, Nathan, *My Father, Daniel Boone*, 44.
   7. Summers, *History of Southwest Virginia*, 278.
   8. Walker, Felix, "Memoirs of a Southern Gentleman," *Journal of American History* 1 (January 1907), 49-60.
   9. Kincaid, *Wilderness Road*, 105.
   10. Hudson, Charles M., ed., *4 Centuries of Southern Indians*, 58.
   11. Chernow, *Washington*, 177.
   12. Unger, *Lion of Liberty*, 103.
   13. Summers, *History of Southwest Virginia*, 204-5.
   14. George Washington, quoted in Chernow's *Washington*, 202.
   15. Cheney, Lynn, *James Madison*, 50.
   16. O'Shaughnessy, *The Men Who Lost America*, 227, 260-61.
   17. Raphael, *A People's History of the American Revolution*, 245-247.
   18. Mayer, Henry, *A Son of Thunder Patrick Henry and the American Republic*, 251.
   19. Kierner, *Southern Women in Revolution, 1776-1800*, 4.
   20. U.S. Library of Congress, "The American Revolution, 1763-1783: First Shots of War, 1775," "King George III's Address to Parliament, October 27, 1775."
   21. English, William Hayden, *Conquest of the Country Northwest of the Ohio*, quotes from pp. 457-463.
   22. *Ibid.*

Chapter 10

   1. Griffin, *History of Old Tryon and Rutherford Counties*, 30.
   2. Moss, Bobby Gilmer, *Roster of the Patriots in the Battle of Moore's Creek Bridge*, 195
   3. *Ibid.*, vii.
   4. Walker, Felix, "Memoirs of a Southern Gentleman," *Journal of American History*, 1 (January 1907), 49-60.
   5. Lampman, Charles, "Battle of Cowpens, SC: Jan 17th, 1781," *SAR* 100, no. 3 (Winter 2006), 5.
   6. "Journals of the Continental Congress," Commager and Morris, *The Spirit of 'Seventy-Six*, 1068-1070.

7. Kierner, *Southern Women in Revolution, 1776–1800*, 20, 21.
8. Walker, Felix, *Memoirs of a Southern Gentleman.*
9. Letter from Abigail Adams to John Adams, datelined Braintree, 31 March 1776.
10. Supreme Court Justice Ruth Balder Ginsberg, *Charlie Rose*, aired October 8, 2016 on PBS, WETP.
11. Griffin, *History of Old Tryon and Rutherford Counties*, 33.
12. Constitutional Rights Foundation, "Foundations of Our Constitution," http://www.crf-usa.org/Foundation_docs/Foundation_home.html.
13. Commager and Morris, *The Spirit of 'Seventy-Six*, 320.
14. Hosmer, *Samuel Adams*, 349.
15. Chernow, *Washington*, 237.
16. Casey, Susan, *Women Heroes of the American Revolution*, 31.
17. Williams, *Tennessee During the Revolutionary War*, 48–49; Rea, *Washington County Tennessee Deeds, 1775–1800*, 9; Dixon, *Wataugans*, 38; Ramsey, *Annals of TN*, 160–63; Folmsbee, "Annotations," 757–758.
18. "Lieut. Timberlake's Memoirs," *London*, February 1766, as quoted by Hoig in *Cherokees and Their Chiefs*, 14.
19. Brown, John, *Eastern Cherokee Chiefs: Chronicles of Oklahoma March, 1938*, 20.
20. Taylor, *History of Sullivan County*, Ch. 6.
21. Ramsey, *Annals of Tennessee*, 150.
22. Williams, *Tennessee in the Revolutionary War*, 45.
23. *Ibid.*, 46.
24. Alderman, *Overmountain Men*, 33.
25. Williams, *Tennessee During the Revolutionary War*, 47.
26. *Ibid.*, 38.
27. Kierner, Cynthia, *Southern Women in Revolution, 1776–1800*, 36.
28. Brown, John, op. cit., 21.
29. Kierner, *Southern Women in Revolution*, 6.
30. Prucha, Francis Paul, *American Indian Treaties*, 35.
31. Taylor, *Historic Sullivan*, 68–70.
32. Brown, John, op. cit., 21.
33. Alderman, Pat, *Nancy Ward/Dragging Canoe* (Johnson City, TN: Overmountain, 1978), 38.
34. Brown, John, op. cit., 20, 21.

Chapter 11

1. Cheney, Lynne, *James Madison*, 86.
2. Journals of the Continental Congress, "The Articles of Association," October 20, 1774, Yale Law School, Avalon Project documents in law, history and diplomacy.
3. *American Heritage Pictorial Atlas of United States History*, 101.
4. Commager and Morris, *The Spirit of 'Seventy-Six*, 1035.
5. Summers, *History of South West Virginia*, 295–98, quoting Bickley's *History of Tazewell*.
6. Hoig, *The Cherokees and Their Chiefs*, 65.
7. Donelson, *Journal of a Voyage*, in Ramsey, *Annals of Tennessee*, 197.
8. Alderman, *Overmountain Men*, 147–148.
9. Bucy, Carole Stanford, "Charlotte Reeves Robertson," Volunteer State Community College, *Tennessee Encyclopedia*, Tennessee Historical Society, Nashville, 2002–2016.
10. Williams, *Tennessee During the Revolutionary War*, 167–170.

Chapter 12

1. Churchill, *Great Republic*, 41.
2. Sweet, Julie Anne, *William Stephens: Georgia's Forgotten Founder*, Baton Rouge: Louisiana State University Press, 162–165
3. Commager and Morris, *The Spirit of 'Seventy-Six*, 1073.
4. Cashin, Edwin J., "Revolutionary War in Georgia," Augusta State University, *New Georgia Encyclopedia of History and Archeology.*
5. Greene, Francis Vinton, *The Revolutionary War and the Military Policy of the United States*, 193–195.
6. Commager and Morris, *The Spirit of 'Seventy-Six*, 1081–2.
7. Georgia Historical Marker, "Battle of Kettle Creek, 157–15," located at the battle site.
8. Killion, Ronald G., and Waller, Charles T., *Georgia and the Revolution* (Cherokee, 1975), 76.
9. Casey, *Women Heroes of the American Revolution*, 186–194.
10. Berkin, *Revolutionary Mothers*, 142.
11. Henry, William, Georgia Southern University, "An Unfortunate Affair: The Battle of Brier Creek and the Aftermath in Georgia" (2012) Electronic Theses and Dissertations Paper, 875.
12. Greene, Francis Vinton, *The Revolutionary War and the Military Policy of the United States*, 193–195.
13. *Ibid.*, 194.
14. "Battle of Stono," *South Carolina* 5, no, 2(April 1904); Wilson, David K., *The Southern Strategy*,116–130; Commager and Morris, *The Spirit of 'Seventy-Six*, 1085.
15. Ellet, *Women of the American Revolution*, 208–217.
16. Hanaford, Phebe Anne, *Women of the Century* (Boston, BB Russell, 1877), 62.
17. "Deposition of Richard Doggett taken at Joseph Hudnuts tavern in the town of Washington Mason County Kentucky on the 14th day of June 1832," http://revwarapps.org/blwt1983-300.pdf.
18. Commager and Morris, *The Spirit of 'Seventy-Six*, 1090–91.

Chapter 13

1. Draper, *Kings Mountain and Its Heroes*, 20–21
2. *Ibid.*, 37–39.
3. *Ibid.*
4. Excerpt from Chambers' pension papers, courtesy of his descendant, DAR member Billie Whisnant.
5. O'Shaughnessy, *Men Who Lost America*, 256.
6. Chernow, *Washington*, 374, quoting British politician and writer Horace Walpole.
7. Burstein, *Passions of Andrew Jackson*, excerpted from ch. 1.
8. Commager and Morris, *The Spirit of 'Seventy Six*, 1170.
9. Scoggins, Michael C., *The Day It Rained Militia: Huck's Defeat and the Revolution in the South Carolina*

Backcountry, May-July 1780 (Charleston: History Press, 2005), 41–49. 65–83, 83–96.
   10. Casey, Susan, *Women Heroes of the American Revolution*, 154–161: Ellet, *Women of the American Revolution*, 237–249.
   11. Anthony, Lena, *American Spirit* (*DAR* magazine), "Francis Marion" (May/June 2012), 25.
   12. Warren, Mercy, *History*, vol. 1, ch. 16.
   13. O'Shaughnessy, *The Men Who Lost America*, 249, 250–51, 283, 259, 166.
   14. Taylor, *Historic Sullivan*, 101.
   15. Commager and Morris, *The Spirit of 'Seventy-Six*, 1117.
   16. Draper, *Kings Mountain and Its Heroes*, 298.
   17. Sons of the American Revolution, Gainesville, Florida, Chapter Home Page, "Camden (1780)."
   18. Chernow, *Washington*, 375.
   19. Keiner, *Southern Women in Revolution, 1776–1800*, 30.

Chapter 14

   1. Ellet, *Women of the Revolution*, vol. 1, 263–273.
   2. Letter from Tryon to Hillsborough, 12 December 1768, *State Records of North Carolina*, vol. 7, ed.Walter Clark, 878.
   3. Griffin, *History of Old Tryon and Rutherford Counties*, 52, citing *Political* magazine, March 1781.
   4. Draper, *Kings Mountain and Its Heroes*, 72.
   5. Graves, William T., "Col. Isaac Shelby's Account of His Exploits During the Revolutionary War," *Southern Campaign of the American Revolution* 2, no. 3 (March 2005).
   6. Draper, *Kings Mountain and Its Heroes*, 85–89.
   7. Ramsey, *Annals of Tennessee*, 217.
   8. Francis Rawdon Letter to Colonel McMahon, Donnington, 19 January 1801, re "the circumstances which preceded the defeat of Gates at Camden."
   9. "Thomas Sumter to Capt. Joseph McJunkin re: Patriot Victory at Hanging Rock," *Southern Campaigns of the American Revolution* 2, no. 3 (March 2005).
   10. Draper, *Kings Mountain and Its Heroes*, 124.
   11. Williams, *Tennessee in the Revolution*, 148.
   12. Ramsey, *Annals of Tennessee*, 219.
   13. Draper, *Kings Mountain and Its Heroes*, 106–8, 114.
   14. *Ibid.*, 144.
   15. *Ibid.*, 145, 146.
   16. *Ibid.*, 151–153.
   17. *Ibid.*, 198.

Chapter 15

   1. George F. Jex, *Notable Quotes*.
   2. O'Shaughnessy, *The Men Who Lost America*, 243.
   3. *Lieutenant Allaire's Diary*, in Griffin, *History of Old Tryon and Rutherford Counties*, 75.
   4. Draper, *Kings Mountain and Its Heroes*, appendix, 527, 527, 528, regarding Col. Arthur Campbell's "Kings's Mountain—A Fragment."
   5. Ramsey, *Annals of Tennessee*, 225.
   6. Shelby, "Pamphlet to the Public," in appendix of Draper, *Kings Mountain and Its Heroes*, 560–573.
   7. Draper, *Kings Mountain and Its Heroes*, 174.
   8. *Ibid.*, 173.

   9. Ramsey, J.G.M., *Annals of Tennessee*, 226.
   10. Alderman, *Overmountain Men*, 83.
   11. Williams, *Tennessee During the Revolutionary War*, 60 fn, 160.
   12. Alderman, Pat, *One Heroic Hour at Kings Mountain*, 28.
   13. Griffin, *History of Old Tryon and Rutherford Counties*, 63.
   14. Moss, *The Patriots at Kings Mountain*, 280.
   15. Draper, *Kings Mountain and its Heroes*, 229.
   16. "North Carolina Promotes Historic Preservation," *Daughters of the American Revolution Newsletter* 9, no.1 (January/February 2009).
   17. Draper, *Kings Mountain and Its Heroes*, 252.
   18. *Ibid.*, 524.
   19. Shelby, "Statement of Isaac Shelby: Kings Mountain."
   20. Williams, *Tennessee During the Revolution*, 155–158.
   21. Rose, Alexander, *American Rifle*, 64, 65.
   22. Draper, *Kings Mountain and Its Heroes*, 273, 576.
   23. Harper, *Fort Defiance and the General*, 19.
   24. Draper, *Kings Mountain and Its Heroes*, 314, 282–83.
   25. Joseph Starnes' American Revolutionary War Pension Application.
   26. Williams, *Tennessee in the Revolutionary War*, 158.
   27. Draper, *Kings Mountain and Its Heroes*, 291.
   28. Allaire, "Allaire's Diary."
   29. Draper, *Kings Mountain and Its Heroes*, 305, 308.
   30. Rea, *Washington County Tennessee Deeds, 1775–1800*, 15.
   31. Bailey, J.D., *Commanders at King's Mountain* (Gaffney, SC: Ed H. Decamp, n.p.s, 1926).
   32. Dykeman, Wilma, *Battle of King's Mountain with Fire and Sword* (NPS Govt. Printing Office).
   33. Draper, *Kings Mountain and Its Heroes*, 51.
   34. Starnes, *Pension Application*.
   35. Alderman, *Overmountain Men*, 115.
   36. Shelby, "Statement of Isaac Shelby: Kings Mountain."
   37. Brooks and Newton, *Bridges to the Past*, "Army's First Court Martial," 1:71–72.
   38. Draper, *Kings Mountain and Its Heroes*, 344.
   39. Richards, *Mercy Otis Warren*, 141.
   40. Ramsey, *Annals of Tennessee*, 264.

Chapter 16

   1. Pension application of William Holland; Brooks and Newton, "Capt. Holland Led Fight against Indians, British."
   2. Draper, *Kings Mountain and Its Heroes*, 74 fn, 468.
   3. Fink, Paul M., *Jonesborough: The First Century of Tennessee's First Town*, 23.
   4. McCullough, *1776*, 22
   5. Chernow, *Washington*, 203.
   6. *Ibid.*, 376.
   7. Williams, T. Harry, *History of American Wars*, 78.
   8. Bearss, *Battle of Cowpens*, 10–11.
   9. *Ibid.*, 17.
   10. *Ibid.*, 15.
   11. O'Shaughnessy, *The Men Who Lost America*, 266.
   12. Bearss, *Battle of Cowpens*, 30.
   13. Higginbotham, Don, *Daniel Morgan* (University of North Carolina Press, 1961), 142.

14. Bearss, *Battle of Cowpens*, 45–46.
15. Reid, Courtland T., *Guilford Courthouse*, 9.
16. O'Shaughnessy, *The Men Who Lost America*, 268.
17. Henry, *Narrative of the Battle of Cowan's Ford*, 7.
18. Ellet, *Women of the Revolution*, vol. 1, 297–299.
19. Mayer, *A Son of Thunder*, 343.
20. Draper, *Kings Mountain and Its Heroes*, 392.
21. *Ibid.*, 392.
22. South Carolina Historical Society, SCHistory.org, "Copy ... Earl Cornwallis to Lord George Germain."
23. "Battle of Guilford Courthouse," National Park Service, nps.gov.
24. Alderman, *Overmountain Men*, 60.
25. Ellet, *Women of the American Revolution*, 308.
26. Kierner, Cynthia, *Southern Women*, 31.
27. Corlew, *Tennessee*, 70.
28. Ellet, *Women of the American Revolution*, vol. 1, 284–291.
29. *Ibid.*, vol. 2, 341
30. *Ibid.*, vol. 1, 274–280
31. Swager, Christine R., *The Valiant Died: The Battle of Eutaw Spring*, 115, 124, 126.
32. Clement, Jessee, *Noble Deeds of American Women*.
33. Williams, Samuel C., *Tennessee during the Revolutionary War*, 219.
34. *Ibid.*, 183, 11 fn.
35. *Ibid.*, 201; Alderman, *One Heroic Hour*, 78–79.
36. Haywood, *Civil and Political History of the State of Tennessee from Its Earliest Settlement up to the Year 1796*, 501–4.
37. Ellet, *Women of the American Revolution*, vol. 1, 62–73.

Chapter 17

1. Gerson, *Statue in Search of a Pedestal*, 1, 10, 13.
2. Chernow, *Washington*, 296.
3. Warren, Mercy, *History*, vol. 2, ch. 17.
4. Churchill, "The Great Republic," 82; large print, 147.
5. Moran, Donald N., "George III's Soldiers General William Phillips," May 2007, *Liberty Tree Newsletter*, revolutionarywararchives.org.
6. Ellet, *Women of the American Revolution*, 304–330.
7. Phillips, Donald T., *On the Wing of Speed* (Illinois: DTP Companion Books, 2006), ch. 7.
8. *Ibid.*, 33, 34.
9. Landers, "Virginia Campaign and the Blockade Siege of Yorktown, 1781," Army War College, 106.
10. O'Shaughnessy, *The Men Who Lost America*, 275.
11. Draper, *Kings Mountain and Its Heroes*, 257, 391–400.
12. Bernier, *Lafayette: Hero of Two Worlds*, 123.
13. O'Shaughnessy, *The Men Who Lost America*, 255–56.
14. Cornwallis, "Answer to Sir Henry Clinton's Narrative of the Campaign in 1781 in North America by Charles Cornwallis," John Campbell, 1866 (Google ebook), 135.
15. Lafayette, Marquis de, *Memoirs, Correspondence and Manuscripts of General Lafayette with an Account of His Visit to America and His Reception by the People of the United States* (Project Gutenberg ebook).

Chapter 18

1. Wood, Gordon S., *The American Revolution* (New York: Random House, 2002), 67–8.
2. Churchill, *Great Republic* (large print), 137.
3. Wood, *The Americanization of Benjamin Franklin*, 196.
4. Chernow, *Washington*, 372.
5. George Washington to John Laurens, April 9, 1781, Library of Congress.
6. Williams, T. Harry, *History of American Wars*, 46–49.
7. Lewis, Charles E., *Admiral de Grasse and American Independence* (New York: Arno, 1980), 4, 40.
8. Bowen, "1781 Saw Patriot Defeat Turn to Final Victory," *SAR* (Summer 2006), 29.
9. Linder, Bruce, *Tidewater Navy*, 14.
10. Morgan, William James, "The Pivot Upon Which Everything Turned," History.Navy.Mil., Navy Historical Foundation, Washington, D.C., 1981.
11. *American Heritage Pictorial Atlas of United States History*, 112; Moran, Donald N., "The Long March to Yorktown," Sons of Liberty Chapter, Sons American Revolution.
12. Lewis, Michael, "The History of the British Navy," as quoted by NPS, "Battle of the Capes."
13. Idzerda and Smith, *France and the American War for Independence*, 43. 45.
14. Chernow, *Washington*, 412.
15. Rees, "Continental Army Female Camp Followers," *Journal of the Continental Line* 8, no. 3 (Spring 1995), 51–58.
16. Chernow, *Washington*, 418, 419.
17. Warren, Mercy, *History*, vol. 2, ch. 28.
18. Chernow, *Washington*, 770.
19. O'Shaughnessy, 243.
20. *American Heritage Pictorial Atlas of United States History*, 112.
21. U.S. Department of the Interior, National Park Service, Colonial National Historic Park, "Lafayette and the Virginia Campaign 1781."
22. O'Shaughnessy, 1-14, 120, 19.

Chapter 19

1. Warren, Mercy, *History*, vol. 2, 30.
2. Filson, John, *Adventures of Daniel Boone: Narrative of Wars of Kentucke by Daniel Boone* (ebook).
3. Boone, Nathan, *My Father, Daniel Boone*, 78.
4. Pilgrim Hall Museum.org; Keiter, Jane, *Women's National Health Museum*.
5. Ehrenberg, *Mapping the World*, 136.
6. Berkin, *Revolutionary Mothers*, 149.
7. *Ibid.*, 159.
8. Shakespeare, *Merchant of Venice*, Act 3, Scene 4.
9. Manning, Katherine, "The Adams Family as a Classical American Dynasty," *SAR* 110, no. 4 (Spring 2016), 16.
10. Berkin, *Revolutionary Mothers*, 159.
11. Murray, Judith Sargent, "On the Equality of the Sexes," *Massachusetts* 2 (For 1790), Boston, Thomas Andrews and E.T. Andrews, 133.
12. Berkin, *Revolutionary Mothers*, 153.

Bibliography

Archives and Primary Sources

Adams, Samuel. "The Rights of the Colonists, a List of Violations of Rights and a Letter of Correspondence: List of Infringements 20 Nov 1772, adopted by the Town of Boston, November 20, 1772."

Allaire, Anthony. "Diary of Lieut. Anthony Allaire." In Draper, appendix, *Kings Mountain and Its Heroes*, Sullivan County Archives, Blountville, Tennessee, and Griffin, *History of Old Tryon and Rutherford Counties*.

"Battle at Lindley's Mill." Revolutionary War Photo Archive.

Coale, Charles B. *The Life and Adventures of Wilburn Waters, the Famous Hunter and Trapper of White Top Mountain.* Richmond, VA: G.W. Cary, 1878; Repr., Radford, VA: Commonwealth Press, 1976 (Reference Section, Bristol Public Library).

Commager, Henry Steele, and Richard B. Morris. *The Spirit of 'Seventy Six: The Story of the American Revolution as Told by the Participants.*

Donelson, John. "Journal of a Voyage." Repr. in Ramsey, J.G.M., *The First American Frontier: The Annals of Tennessee to the End of the Eighteenth Century*, 1853. Compiled by C. Hammett (Sullivan County Archives, Blountville, TN).

Fink, Paul M. *Jonesborough: The First Century of Tennessee's First Town.* Tennessee State Planning Commission, Department of Housing and Urban Development, National Technical Information Service, publication no. 394, Springfield VA, June 1972.

Gaspee Virtual Archives. *The Writings of Samuel Adams.* Vols. 2, 3. Edited by H.A. Cushing (c. 1904-08).

George Washington Papers at the Library of Congress. http://memory.loc.gov/ammem/gwhtml/1775.html.

Haywood, John. *Haywood's History of Tennessee: The Civil and Political History of the State of Tennessee's Earliest Settlement to the Year 1796.* Repr. of 1823 ed. Nashville, TN: Publishing House of the Methodist Episcopal Church, 1891.

Henry, Patrick. "Give Me Liberty or Give Me Death." Proceedings of the March 23, 1775, Virginia Convention.

Henry, Robert. *Narrative of the Battle of Cowan's Ford, February 1st, 1781.* Greensboro, NC: D. Schenck Sr., 1891.

Journals of the Continental Congress 5 (June 7, 1776).

Memorial of Jonas Bedford. English Records, British Public Records Office, Office Papers, 1765-1790. Bedford AO Class 13 Bundle 117. "This section was typed from a photo static copy of the original pages 309-324 of the [Public Records Office Papers] named above. The Photostats were made in November and December 1973 by Department of Archives and History, State of North Carolina, from records in the department's archives."

Papers of George Washington. *Articles.* gwpapers.virginia.edu.

Pension Application of Joseph Starnes. "White Historical Collection." *Revolutionary War Soldiers of Western North Carolina, Burke County.* Vol. 1. Easley, SC: Southern Historical Press, 1984-98.

Pension Application of William Holland. Filed in Rutherford County, North Carolina, September 10, 1832 (GSA National Archives file No. W-4698).

The Preston and Virginia Papers of the Draper Collection of Manuscripts. Calendar Series, vol. 1. Publications of the State Historical Society of Wisconsin (Madison: State Historical Society of Wisconsin, 1915).

Rea, Loraine. *Washington County Tennessee Deeds, 1775-1800.* Greenville, SC: Southern Historical Press, 1991; repr. 2001 (Sullivan County Archives, Blountville, TN).

Shelby, Isaac. "Pamphlet to the Public" on the Battle of Kings Mountain. In Draper, appendix, *King's Mountain and Its Heroes* (Sullivan County Archives, Blountville, Tennessee).

_____. "Statement of Isaac Shelby: Kings Mountain." Repr. in the appendix of Draper, Lyman C. *King's Mountain and Its Heroes.* 1881; repr. Johnson City, TN: Overmountain Press, 1996.

Tennessee State Library and Archives. "Haywood, John (1762-1826), Papers (1768-1796)." http://www.state.tn.us/tsla/history/manuscripts/findingaids/ths448.pdf.

United States Library of Congress. The American Revolution, 1763-1783: First Shots of War, 1775. "King George III's Address to Parliament, October 27, 1775."

_____. George Washington Papers at the Library of Congress, 1741-1795. Series 3 C Varick Transcript.

_____. "Religion and the Founding of the American Republic: The Fighting Parson."

_____. Thomas Jefferson Timeline: 1743-1827.

Warren, Mercy (Mrs.). *History of the Rise, Progress and Termination of the American Revolution, Interspersed with Biographical, Political and Moral Observations in Three Volumes.* Boston, Manning and Loring, 1805 (ebook reprinted by Google).

Books

Abbott, John S.C. (1875) *Lord Dunmore's War.* Ohio Statewide Files. History (ch. 8). files.usgwarchives.net/oh/history/abbott/chapt8.txt.

Albright, Edward. *Early History of Middle Tennessee*. Nashville: Brandon, 1909.

Alderman, Pat. *One Heroic Hour at Kings Mountain*. 2nd ed. Johnson City, TN: Overmountain Press, 1990.

———. *Overmountain Men*. Johnson City, TN: Overmountain Press, 1970.

Alexandeer, John Edmiston. *A Historical Sketch of the Synod of Tennessee*. Philadelphia, Mac'Calla, 1890.

American Heritage Pictorial Atlas of United States History. New York: American Heritage, 1960.

Anderson, Fred. *Crucible of War*. New York: Vintage, 2001.

———. *The War That Made America*. New York: Penguin, 2005–2006.

Allaire (Lieutenant). "Allaire's Diary." In Griffin, *History of Old Tryon and Rutherford Counties*.

The Annals of America: 1755–1783. Chicago: Encyclopedia Britannica, 1976.

Arnold, Isaac Newton. *The Life of Benedict Arnold*. 1880; repr. New York: Arno, 1979.

Ashe, Samuel A. *History of North Carolina*. Greensboro, NC: C.L. Van Noppen, 1908–1925.

Ashe, Samuel A., Stephen B. Weeks, and Charles Van Noppen. *Biographical History of North Carolina*. Vol. 2. Greensboro, NC: Charles L. Van Noppen, 1905.

Auchter, Dorothy. *Dictionary of Literary and Dramatic Censorship in Tudor and Stuart England*. Westport, CT, and London: Greenwood, 2001.

Axelrod, Alan. *A Savage Empire: Trappers, Traders, Tribes and the Wars That Made America*. New York: Thomas Dunne Books, St. Martin's, 2011.

Bailey, J.D. *Commanders at King's Mountain*. Gaffney, SC: n.p., 1926.

Babits, Lawrence. *Cowpens Battlefield: A Walking Guide*. Johnson City, TN: Overmountain Press, 1993.

Barnes, Ian. *Historical Atlas of the American Revolution*. New York: Routledge, 2000.

Bearss, Edwin C. *Battle of Cowpens*. Johnson City, TN: Overmountain Press, 1996.

Bellesiles, Michael A. *Revolutionary Oulaws*. Charlottesville: University of Virginia Press, 1998.

Berkin, Carol. *Revolutionary Mothers*. New York: Vintage, 2005.

Bernier, Olivier. *Lafayette: Hero of Two Worlds*. New York: E.P. Dutton, 1983.

Bobrick, Benson. *Angel in the Whirlwind: The Triumph of the American Revolution*. New York: Penguin, 1998.

Boone, Nathan. *My Father, Daniel Boone*. University Press of Kentucky. The Draper Interviews, 1999. http://books.google.com/books.

Brooks, Noah. *Henry Knox: A Soldier of the Revolution*. New York and London: G.P. Putnam's Sons, 1900.

Brooks, Roy, and Mrs. Ernest Newton. *Bridges to the Past*. 2 vols. n.p., 1969–1978. Originally published as a series of columns in the *Forest City This Week*.

Brown, John P. "Eastern Cherokee Chiefs." *Chronicles of Oklahoma* 16, no. 1 (March 1938).

Buchanan, John. *The Road to Guilford Courthouse*. New York: John Wiley & Sons, 1997.

Burstein, Andrew. *The Passions of Andrew Jackson*. New York: Alfred A. Knopf, 2003.

Campbell, Arthur. "Campbell's Statement." In Draper, *Kings Mountain and Its Heroes*.

Casey, Susan. *Women Heroes of the American Revolution*. Chicago: Chicago Review Press, 2015.

Cashin, Edward J. *The King's Ranger: Thomas Brown and the American Revolution on the Southern Frontier*. New York: Fordham University Press, 1999.

Cecil. *History of the United States*. New York: George H. Doran, 1919. Digitized by Google. http://books.google.com/books (accessed September 7, 2008).

Chernow, Ron. *Alexander Hamilton*. New York: Penguin, 2004.

———. *Washington: A Life*. New York: Penguin, 2010.

Chesterton, Cecil. *History of the United States*. New York: George H. Doran, 1919. Digitized by Google.

Churchill, Winston S., ed. *The Great Republic: A History of America*. London: Cassell, 2002.

———, ed. *The Great Republic: A History of America (Large Print)*. New York: Random House, 1999.

Clayton, W.W. *History of Davidson County, Tennessee*. Philadelphia, 1880; repr., Nashville: Charles Elder, 1971.

Cobb, Sanford H. *The Rise of Religious Liberty in America*. New York: McMillan, 1902.

Coburn, Frank W. *The Centennial History of the Battle of Bennington*. Boston: George E. Littlefield, 1877.

Coleman, Kenneth. *History of Georgia*. Athens: University of Georgia Press, 1977, 1991.

Commager, Henry Steel, and Richard B. Morris. *The Spirit of 'Seventy-Six*. New York: Harper & Row, 1958, 1967.

Cornell, William Mason. *History of Pennsylvania from the Earliest Discovery to the Present Time*. Philadelphia: John Sully, 1876.

Cunningham, John T. *New Jersey: America's Main Road*. Garden City, NY: Doubleday, 1966.

Cutter, William. *Life of Israel Putnam, Major General in the Army of the American Revolution*. New York: 1850.

DAR Patriot Index. Washington, D.C.: NSDAR, 1966, 1967.

David, James Corbett. *Dunmore's New World*. Charlottesville: University of Virginia Press, 2013.

De Fonblanque, Edward Barrington (1821–1895). *Political and Military Episodes of the Last Half of the 18th Century*. Repr. of 1876 ed., google books (accessed October 15, 2013).

Dickens, Charles. *The Works of Charles Dickens*. Vol. 7. New York: P.F. Collier, undated.

Dixon, Don Higginbotham. *Daniel Morgan: Revolutionary Rifleman*. Chapel Hill: University of North Carolina Press, 1961 (Published for the Institute of Early American History and Culture at Williamsburg, VA).

Dixon, Max. *The Wataugans*. Johnson City, TN: Overmountain Press, 1989.

Donelson. *Journal of a Voyage*. Full text published in Ramsey, *Annals of Tennessee*, and Clayton, *History of Davidson County, Tennessee*.

Drake, Francis Samuel. *Life and Correspondence of Henry Knox*. Harvard College Library. E-Book digitized by Google (accessed October 13, 2013).

Draper, Lyman C. *King's Mountain and Its Heroes*. 1881; repr. Johnson City, TN: Overmountain Press, 1996.

Dykeman, Wilma. *The French Broad River*. Knoxville: University of Tennessee Press, 1987.

Ehrenberg, Ralph E. *Mapping the World*. Washington, D.C.: National Geographic, 2006.

Elder, W. Cliff. *Commemorative Souvenir Program, May 9–16, 1971*. Alamance County Historical Association, 1971.

Ellet, Elizabeth Fries. *Women of the American Revolution*. Vol. 1. Bedford, MA: Applewood, 1849.

Ellis, Joseph J. *First Family, Abigail & John Adams*. New York: Alfred A. Knopf, 2010.

English, William Hayden. *Conquest of the Country Northwest of the River Ohio, 1778–1783, and Life of Gen. George Rogers Clark*. Indianapolis and Kansas City: Bowen-Merrill, 1897.

Fairbanks, Charles H., John H. Goff. Commission Findings, Indian Claims Commission. *Cherokee and Creek Indians*. New York: Garland, 1974.

Faragher, John Mack. *Daniel Boone*. New York: Henry Holt, 1992. http://books.google.com/books (accessed October 16, 2008).

Ferguson, Patrick. "Denard's Ford, Broad River, Tryon County, Oct. 1st, 1780." In Griffin, *History of Old Tryon and Rutherford Counties*.

Filson, John. *Adventures of Daniel Boone*. "With a narrative of the Wars of Kentucky, by Daniel Boone." http://www.worldwideschool.org/library/books/hst/northamerican/TheAdventuresofColDanielBoone/Chap1.html (accessed May 29, 2007 & June 10, 2009).

Fischer, David Hackett. *Albion's Seed: Four British Folkways in America*. New York: Oxford University Press, 1989.

Fiske, John. *The American Revolution*. 2 vols. Boston and New York: Houghton, Mifflin; Cambridge: Riverside, 1891.

Folmsbee, Stanley J. "Annotations Relating Ramsey's Annals of Tennessee to Present Day Knowledge." In J.G.M. Ramsey, *Annals of Tennessee*.

4 Centuries of Southern Indians. Edited by Charles M. Hudson. Athens: University of Georgia Press, 1975.

Franklin, Benjamin. *Autobiography of Benjamin Franklin*. 1923; repr., Atlanta, Communication and Studies, 1st ed. of the Programmed Classics.

French, Allen. *Siege of Boston*. New York: McMillan, 1911. Gutenberg E-book. http://www.gutenberg.org/files/29199/29199-h/29199-h.htm (accessed October 10, 2013).

Garraty, John A. Gay, Peter, ed. *The Columbia History of the World*. New York: Harper & Row, 1972.

Garrison, Webb. *Great Stories of the American Revolution*. Nashville: Rutledge Hill, 1990.

Gerson, Noel B. *Statue in Search of a Pedestal*. New York: Dodd, Mead, 1976.

Gray. Mary Preston. *Family Tree*. n.p., 1980.

Green, Harry Clinton, and Mary Wolcott Green. *Wives of the Signers: The Women Behind the Declaration of Independence*. Aledo, TX: Wall Builders Press, 1997. Originally published as vol. 3 of *The Pioneer Mothers of America: A Record of the More Notable Women of the Early Days of the Country, and Particularly of the Colonial and Revolutionary Periods*. New York: G. P. Putnam's Sons, 1912.

Greene, Francis Vinton. *The Revolutionary War and the Military Policy of the United States*. New York: Charles Scribner's Sons, 1911.

Griffin, Clarence W. *The History of Old Tryon and Rutherford Counties, 1730–1936*. 1937; repr., Spartanburg, SC: Reprint Company, 1977.

_____. *Public Officials of Rutherford County, N.C., 1779–1934*. 1934; repr., Raleigh: North Carolina State Library, 1982.

Hale, John P. *History of the Great Kanawah Valley*. Madison, WI: Brant, Fuller, 1891.

Hamilton, Henry. "Henry Hamilton's Journal." In *Henry Hamilton and George Rogers Clark in the American Revolution with the Unpublished Journal of Lieut. Gov. Henry Hamilton*. Edited by John D. Barnhart. Crawfordsville, IN: R.E. Banta, 1951.

Harper, Margaret E. *Fort Defiance and the General*. 2nd ed. Huntington, WV: Aegina, 1997.

Hart, Albert Bushnell. *Epochs of History: Formation of the Union, 1750–1829*. 3rd ed. New York and London: Longmans, Green, 1893.

Hawthorne, Nathaniel. *Grandfather's Chair*. 1840 (available online).

Haywood, John. *Civil and Political History of the State of Tennessee*. Knoxville: n.p., 1823.

Henderson, Archibald. *The Conquest of the Old Southwest: The Romantic Story of the Early Pioneers into Virginia, the Carolinas, Tennessee, and Kentucky, 1740–1790*. New York: Century, 1920.

Hosmer, James K. *Samuel Adams*. Boston: Houghton, Mifflin, 1885.

Howard's 1906 *Preliminaries of the Revolution*, 1763–1775, as published in *The American Nations: A History*. Edited by Albert Bushnell Hart, p. 241 (e-book, accessed March 13, 2013).

Idzerda, Stanle J., Smith, Roger E. *France and the American War for Independence*. Lafayette Papers, Cornell University.

Indian Nations of North America. Washington, D.C., National Geographic.

Jackson, Michael, and Dot Hembree. *Keowee: The Story of the Keowee River Valley in Upstate South Carolina*. n.p., 1997.

Jacob, John J. *Biographical Sketch of the Life of the Late Captain Michael Cresap*. Cincinnati: Stearn, 1866.

Josephy, Alvin M., Jr. *500 Nations*. New York: Alfred A. Knopf, 1994.

Kajencki, AnnMarie Francis. *Count Casimir Pulaski from Poland*. New York: Rosen, 2005.

Kierner, Cynthia A. *Southern Women in Revolution, 1776–1800*. Columbia: University of South Carolina Press, 1998.

Kincaid, Robert L. *Wilderness Road*. 1947; Middlesboro, KY: Mrs. R.L. Kincaid, 1966.

Lewis, Charles E. *Admiral de Grasse and American Independence*. New York: Arno, 1980.

Lewis, Virgil A. *History of the Battle of Point Pleasant*. Charleston, WV: Tribune, 1909.

Linder, Bruce. *Tidewater Navy*. Maryland Naval Institute Press, 2005.

Loane, Nancy E. *Following the Drum Women at the Valley Forge Encampment*. Book review by Bill Hudgins. *American Spirit* (March/April 2010).

Lossing, Benson J. *Our Country: A Household History of the United States for all readers*, 1878. https://archive.org/details/ourcountryahous04lossgoog.

_____. *Pictorial Field Book of the Revolution*. Vol. 1 (1860). https://archive.org/details/pictorialfieldb00lossgoog.

_____. *Pictorial Field-Book of the Revolution*. Vol. 2. http://books.google.com/books.

_____. *1776*. New York: Edward Walker, 1847.

Mayer, Henry. *A Son of Thunder: Patrick Henry and the American Republic*. New York: Grove, 1991.

MacKenzie, George C. *Kings Mountain*. National Park Service Handbook, Series No. 22. Washington, D.C., 1955 (Rrepr. 1961).

McCullough, David. *John Adams*. New York: Simon & Schuster, 2001.

_____. *1776*. New York: Simon & Schuster, 2005.

Morgan, Lewis Henry. *The League of the Iroquois*. Originally published 1851, North Dighton, MA: JG, 1995.

Morgan, William James. "The Pivot Upon Which Everything Turned." History.Navy.Mil. Navy Historical Foundation, Washington, D.C., 1981.

Morison, Samuel Eliot. *Oxford History of the American People*. New York: Oxford University Press, 1965.

Morrison, Denise Pratt. *Joseph Martin and the Southern Frontier*. Danville, VA: Womack, 1976.

Moss, Bobby Gilmer. *Roster of the Patriots in the Battle of Moores Creek Bridge*. Blacksburg, SC: Scotia-Hibernia, 1992.

O'Shaughnessy, Andrew Jackson. *The Men who Lost America*. New Haven: Yale University Press, 2013.

Paine, Thomas. *Common Sense*. Pamphlet, 1776.

_____. *The Crisis*. A collection of articles written between 1776–1783. ushistory.org.

Parker, Theodore. *Historic Americans*. 2nd ed. Boston: H.B. Fuller, 1871.

Pell, S.H.P. *Fort Ticonderoga*. Reprinted for the Fort Ticonderoga Museum, 1970.

Perry, Marvin. *Western Civilization*. Vol. 1, 8th ed. New York: Houghton Mifflin, 2007.

Prucha, Francis Paul. *American Indian Treaties*. Berkeley: University of California Press, 1997.

Quinn, Hartwell L. *Arthur Campbell: Pioneer and Patriot of the "Old Southwest."* Jefferson, NC, and London: McFarland, 1990.

Ramsey, J.G.M. *The First American Frontier: The Annals of Tennessee to the End of the Eighteenth Century*. Compiled by C. Hammett. 1853; repr., Johnson City, TN: Overmountain Press, 1999.

Randall, William Stearns. *George Washington*. New York: Henry Holt, 1998.

Raphael, Ray. *A People's History of the American Revolution*. New York: New Press, 2001.

Regulators and the Battle of Alamance. "The Commemorative Souvenir Program Bi-Centennial of the Battle of Alamance, 1971,"

Reid, Courtland T. *Guilford Courthouse*. National Park Service Historical Handbook, Series no. 30. Washington, D.C., 1959.

Richards, Jeffrey H. *Mercy Otis Warren*. New York: Twayne, 1995.

Roosevelt, Theodore. *The Winning of the West*. Vol. 2. *From the Alleghenies to the Mississippi, 1777–1783*. Gutenberg e-book.

Rose, Alexander. *American Rifle*. Digitized by Google.

Selig, Robert A. *March to Victory: Washington, Rochambeau, and the Yorktown Campaign of 1781*. Government Printing Office. Google e-book.

Shelby, Isaac. "Pamphlet to the Public" on the Battle of Kings Mountain. In Draper, *King's Mountain and Its Heroes*.

Snell, Charles W., and Francis F. Wilshin. *Saratoga*. United States Dept. of Interior, National Park Service Handbook. Series no. 4, Washington 25, D.C., 1955.

Snowdon, Yates, and H.G. Cutler, ed. *History of South Carolina*. Vol. 1. Chicago and New York: Lewis, 1920.

Speck, W.A. "The Structure of British Politics in the Mid-Eighteenth Century." Edited by Jack P. Greene, and J.R. Pole. In *A Companion to the American Revolution*. http://books.google.com.

Spoden, Murial Millar Clark. *Kingsport Heritage: The Early Years, 1700 to 1900*. Kingsport, TN: Spoden, 1991.

Stark, James H. *Loyalist of Massachusetts*. "Andrew Oliver." Cambridge: Harvard University, 1907. Digitized by Google.

Summers, Lewis Preston. *History of Southwest Virginia, 1746–1786; Washington County, 1777–1780*. Johnson City, TN: Overmountain Press, 1989.

Swager, Christine R. *The Valiant Died: the Battle of Eutaw Spring*. Westminster, MD: Heritage, 2007.

Taylor, Oliver. *Historic Sullivan*. Bristol, TN: King, 1909.

Tennessee Historical Markers. n.p.: Tennessee Historical Commission, 1996.

Thane, Elswyth. *The Fighting Quaker: Nathanael Greene*. New York: Hawthorn, 1972.

Thom, James Alexander. *Follow the River*. "A Novel Based on the True Ordeal of Mary Ingles." New York: Ballantine, 1983.

Thwaites, Reuben Gold, and Louise Phelps Kellogg, ed. *Documentary History of Dunmore's War, 1774*. Bicentennial ed., 1905; repr. Harrisonburg, VA: C.J. Carrier, 1975.

de Tocqueville, Alexis. *Democracy in America and Two Essays on America*. Translated by Gerald E. Bevan. London and New York: Penguin, 2003.

"Treaty with the Cherokee, 1806." *Indian Affairs: Laws and Treaties*. Vol. 2. Edited by Charles J. Kappler. Washington, D.C.: Government Printing Office, 1904.

Turner, Frederick Jackson. *The Significance of the Frontier in American History*. New York: Henry Holt, 1921. books.google.com (accessed September 21, 2011).

Unger, Harlow Giles. *Lion of Liberty: Patrick Henry*. Philadelphia: Da Capo, 2010.

Walker, Felix. *Memoirs of a Southern Gentleman*. Reprinted from *The Journal of American History* 1 (January 1907).

Weig, Melvin J. *Morristown*. National Park Service Historical Handbook. Series no. 7. Washington, D.C., 1955.

Wells, William V. *The Life and Public Services of Samuel Adams, Being a Narrative of His Acts and Opinions, and of His Agency in Producing and Forwarding the American Revolution*. Boston: Little, Brown, 1866.

Wharton, Anne Hollingsworth. *Martha Washington*. New York: Charles Scribner's Sons, 1897.

Wheeler, John H. *Historical Sketches of North Carolina*. Vols. 1 and 2. Philadelphia: Lippincott, Grambo, 1851.

White, Anne Terry. *The American Indian*. Adapted from William Brandon, *The American Heritage Book of Indians*. Edited by Alvin M. Josephy, Jr. New York: Random House, 1963.

Williams, Samuel Cole. *Dawn of Tennessee Valley and Tennessee History*. Johnson City, TN: Watauga, 1937; repr. Nashville, Tennessee, Blue & Gray, 1972. A copy can be found in Sullivan County Archives, Blountville, Tennessee.

_____. *Tennessee During the Revolutionary War*. Knoxville: University of Tennessee Press, 1974 (originally published 1944, TN Historical Commission).

Williams, T. Harry. *History of American Wars from 1745–1918*. New York: Alfred A. Knopf, 1983.

Wills, Garry. *James Madison*. New York: Henry Holt, 2002.

Wilson, David K. *The Southern Strategy*. Columbia: University of South Carolina Press, 2005.

Wood, Gordon S. *The Americanization of Benjamin Franklin*. New York: Penguin, 2004.

Wright, Esmond. *Franklin of Philadelphia*. Harvard University Press, 1986.

Wright, Robert K., Jr., and Morris J. MacGregor, Jr. "James McHenry, Maryland." In *Soldier-Statesmen of the Constitution*. Washington, D.C.: Center of Military History, U.S. Army, 1987.

_____. "Thomas Fitzsimons, Pennsylvania." In *Soldier-Statesmen of the Constitution*. Washington, D.C.: Center of Military History, U.S. Army, 1987.

Yates Snowdon, and H.G. Cutler. *History of South Carolina*. Vol. 1. Chicago and New York: Lewis, 1920.

Index

Abingdon, VA (Wolf Hills) 124, 141, 148, 187
Abram of Chilhowie (Old Abram Ooskwha) 139–40, 143
HMS *Acteon* 135
Adair, John 186
Adam (Negro) 108
Adams, Abigail 1–2, 11, 16, 25, 32, 37, 44, 46, 51, 53, 68, 85, 88, 136–7, 242–3
Adams, Elizabeth "Betsy" Wells (2nd wife of Samuel) 15–16, 24, 45
Adams, Elizabeth Checkley (1st wife of Samuel) 15
Adams, Hannah (Samuel's daughter) 16
Adams, John 12,15–16, 18, 21, 23–4, 27, 33; in congress 136–7; as congressman 44, 46, 48, 50, 53, 57, 64, 68, 85; as minister to France and Amsterdam 90; peace commissioner 241–2
Adams, Samuel 12, 14–16, 18, 20–32, 35–6, 43, 45–6, 90
Adams, Samuel, Jr. 16
Adirondack Mountains 74, 79
Adventure (Donelson's flat boat) 151
African American *see* Black American
Alamance County, NC 211, 216
Alamance, battle of 101
Albany, NY 55, 73–4, 76, 79–80
Albemarle Sound 128
Alexandria, VA 127
Algonquian language 77
Algonquin Indians 74
Allaire, Anthony 183, 191, 195
Alleghany Mountains 112
allegiance (oath) 38, 60, 75, 93, 100–02, 162, 173, 175, 181–2, 185, 211; *see also* pledge
Allen, Ethan 42, 52, 54, 79
Alligator (Creek Bridge) 16, 182
American Army 53, 58, 62, 69, 79–80, 87, 89, 91, 120, 161, 171, 180, 202–3, 209, 220–1, 225, 227, 237; *see also* Continental Army
American colonies 9, 16–17, 24, 34, 38, 45, 77, 137, 147; *see also* British Colonies

American-French 232
American General Gazette 132
American (Patriot, Whig, Central) Government 48, 91, 131, 137, 145, 214; *see also* Continental Congress
André, John 72, 221–2
Anglicans 13–15, 37; *see also* Episcopal
Ani-Yunwiya "Real People" 143; *see also* Cherokee
Annapolis, Maryland 222–3
Anson County, NC 181
Appalachian (Mountains, Plateau, Valley) 3, 74, 106–10, 123, 177, 239
Arbuckle's company 116
Archbishop of Canterbury 14
Aristarchus (slave) 50
Armistead, Maria Carter 129
Armstrong, Anne 141
Armstrong, John 69, 141
Army, Continental *see* Continental Army
Arnette, Hannah White 60
Arnold, Benedict 42, 52, 54–5, 66, 72, 78, 80–2, 91, 170, 202–3, 219–23, 225
Arnold, Peggy Shippen 82, 221
arsenal 14, 26, 28, 31, 41–2, 127, 225–6; *see also* magazine
Articles of Association (the Association) 37–8, 154
Articles of Confederation 85, 145
Articles of Surrender 236
artillery train, Knox 52, 60–1
Ashley River 164
assembly *see* legislature
the Association *see* Articles of Association
Attacullaculla *see* Attakullakulla
Attakullakulla 123, 125, 138, 143; *see also* Cherokee Peace Chief; Little Carpenter
Attucks, Crispus (former slave) 25
HMS *Augusta* 71
Augusta, Georgia 154, 158, 181, 189, 211
Augusta Academy 113
Augusta Battalion 117
Augusta County 116
Augusta Division 117

Augusta of Saxe-Gotha, Mother of George III 34

Bache, Sarah Franklin 91–2
backcountry 109, 142, 154, 157, 160, 167–8, 178–9, 196, 200, 204, 207, 214; *see also* Piedmont, upcountry
Bailey, Anne Hennis Trotter 118
Bailey, John 118
Baker, Isaac 102
Bald Eagle (Delaware chief) 108
Balfour, Nisbet 211
Baltimore, Maryland 60, 137, 235
Baptist 37, 100–01
Barbados 64
Barker, Penelope 37–8
Barras, Jacques-Melchior, Comte de 232, 234
Barry, Andrew 205
Barry, Catherine Moore 205
battalion 42, 48, 71, 117, 150, 154, 159–60, 196, 204; *see also* division; regiment
battery, batteries 53–6, 80, 193, 223
Bean, John 105
Bean, Lydia 140
Beaufort (Port Royal Island), battle of 157
Beaulieu 162
Beaumarchais, Pierre-Augustin Caron de 83–4
Beaver Creek 3
Beaver Wars 74, 107
Beckham, Mrs. 205
Bedford, Jonas 3, 100, 176, 195, 197
Bedford, Mercy Raymond 3–4, 240
Bedford Hill 183, 185, 188–9, 191
Beloved Woman Ghi Ghu (Ghigau) 138–40, 150, 217; *see also* Ward, Nancy (Nanyuhi)
Bemis Heights, battle of *see* Saratoga, battle of
Bennington, battle of, 80
Bernard, Francis 22–3
Big Camp Meet 102; *see also* Bristol; Fort Shelby; Sapling Grove
Big Doe river 188
Big Fool, Chief 150
Big Jim, Indian 108
Big Levels of the Greenbrier 116–17

259

Index

Big Lick (Roanoke) 103
Biggerstaff, Aaron 197
Biggerstaff, widow Martha 197
Biggerstaff farm, hangings 197–8
Bissell, Israel 40
Black, Elizabeth (widow of Robert Black) 136
black American 3, 50, 63, 71, 88, 127–9, 142, 159, 162, 164–5, 167–8, 204; *see also* black slaves
Black Haitian troops (Chasseurs) 162
Black Mountain 181
Black sailor 25
Black slaves *see* Aristarchus; Attucks, Brom; Crispus; Jocko; Jupiter; Lee, William; Mammy Kate; Ned; Oscar; Phillis; Salem, Peter
Black soldier 63, 204
Black Swamp 160
Blackmore's Fort *see* Fort Blackmore
Black's Fort 141
Blacksnake, Seneca Chief 77
Blackstock Plantation, battle of 201
Bledsoe, Anthony 117
Block Island 218
Blockson, Charles 63
Bloody Scouts *see* Cunningham's Bloody Scouts
Blue Book *see* Regulations Order and Discipline of the Troops of the United States
Blue Jacket (Shawnee chief) 121
Blue Licks, Kentucky, battle of 121, 240
Blue Ridge (chain of Appalachian Mountains) 99, 101, 105–6, 116–7, 135, 140–1, 143, 152, 173–5, 177, 181–6, 188–9, 191, 200–1, 209
Bonnie Kate *see* Sevier, Catherine Sherrill
Boone, Daniel 103, 108, 110, 112, 115, 121, 124–6, 134, 171, 199, 226, 240
Boone, Israel 240
Boone, James 108, 114
Boone, Nathan 108, 111, 240
Boone, Rebecca Bryan 108, 111, 123, 139, 240
Boone's Creek 140
Boone's Trace 125
Boonesborough *see* Fort Boonesborough
Boozy Creek 113
border war 110, 138, 187, 198, 216–7; Indian border 38, 104, 106, 109–10, 126, 153, 187, 191, 199, 216
Boston, MA 4; siege of 35, 42, 46, 48, 50, 53, 56, 203
Boston Gazette 28
Boston Harbor 13, 21, 34–5, 43–4
Boston Massacre 24–5, 33, 53
Boston Port Bill 35
Boston Record 28
Boston Tea Party 21, 32–3, 85, 238

Botetourt County, VA 109, 11, 116, 129
Botetourt militia 116–17,
Boundary Lines *see* hard labor; Lochaber; Proclamation Line 1763; Stanwix; Tryon's
Bouquet, Henry 106
Bowling Green, New York 8, 137
Boyd, James 157–8
Boyd's Creek, battle of 198
Braddock's Campaign 112, 116, 203
Brandywine Creek, battle of 67–9, 71, 83, 196, 202, 220
Brant, Joseph (Mohawk Chief Thayendanegea) 75–7, 95–6
Brant, Molly 75–6, 78
Bratton, Martha Robertson 167–8
Bratton, William 167–8
Bratton Plantation 167–8
Breach Inlet 135
Breed's Hill 43–4; *see also* Bunker Hill, battle of
Brest, France 231–2
Brewster, Caleb 65
Brier Creek, battle of 157, 159–60
Bristol 102, 105, 113, 148, 187; *see also* Fort Shelby; Sapling Grove
HMS *Bristol* 135
British-allied American Indians 129, 131, 149, 160, 216, 240
British base 94, 128, 160, 167, 200–1, 203, 213–4
British colonies (colonists) 1–3, 14, 106–7, 147, 206; *see also* American colonies
British East India Company *see* East India Company
British Expedition 133
British fleet 56, 128, 135, 155, 234–5
British Gazette 195
British Government 17, 22, 26, 35, 50, 109, 131–2, 138, 176, 185, 239; *see also* British Parliament
British-instigated Cherokee 175, 198
British Legion 204
British naval force 138
British Navy *see* Royal Navy
British outposts 69, 146–7, 211
British Parliament 8, 13, 17–26, 28–9, 31–39, 43, 50, 54, 57, 85, 91,129, 147, 169, 237–8
British Superintendent of Indian Affairs in the North 75–6, 106–7; in Province of Quebec 146; in the South 116–7, 126, 138, 149, 216; in State of Virginia 149
Broad River 165, 174, 177, 179, 191–2
Broadsides, War of *see* Golden Hill
Brom (slave) 3
Brooklyn, battle of *see* Battle of Long Island
Brown, Jacob 102
Brown, Thomas 154–6, 182, 189, 191, 211, 214, 216, 239

Brown Bess Musket 80, 184, 193, 196
Brown Mountain 189
Brown's (King's) Rangers *see* Florida Rangers
Brownsborough, Georgia 154
Bryan's Station 240
Buford, Abraham 166, 192
Bull, Captain (Delaware chief) 108
Bull, William, II 37
Bulltown massacre 108
Bumpass Cove (Unicoi, TN) 186
Bunker Hill, battle of 43–5, 48, 50, 91, 101
Burgess *see* Legislature
Burgin, Elizabeth 94–5
Burgoyne, John 3, 43, 73–4, 78–82, 194, 203, 238
Burke, John 180
Burke, Thomas 216
Burke County, NC 170, 175, 181, 187, 191, 195
Burlington, NC 101
Burr, Aaron 61
Burr's Mill 205
Bushy Run, battle of 106
Butler, John 216
Butler, William 101
Byrd, William 109

Cahokia 146–7
Caldwell, James 97
Caldwell, Mrs. James 97
Calloway, Richard 139
Cambridge, Mass. 16, 30, 40–1, 43, 49–54, 64, 81–2, 88
Camden, SC 166–7, 169–71, 175, 200, 207, 211–14
Camden, battle of 171–3, 180, 187, 190, 200, 202–3, 209–10
Camden, 2nd Battle of *see* Hobkirk's Hill, battle of
Cameron, Alexander 105, 114, 138, 142–3, 149, 216
Camp Charlotte 119–21; *see also* treaties, Camp Charlotte
camp fever *see* typhus
Camp Followers (laundress, cook, seamstress, nurse, women) 1–2, 52, 59, 69, 79, 81, 88–9, 195
Camp Union (Lewisburg) 116–7
Campbell, Archibald 156–9, 162
Campbell, Arthur 109–15, 117, 121, 123, 130, 139, 148, 150, 187, 198–9, 217
Campbell, Margaret 114
Campbell, William (Patriot) 110–11, 114, 122, 127, 141, 186–7, 190, 192–3, 195, 198, 209–10, 227
Campbell, Lord William (Crown Governor) 131, 135
Camuse, Jane Mary 153–4
Canada Campaign 53–5
Candler, William 190
Cane Creek 183, 185, 191, 216
Cape Charles 223, 234
Cape Fear River 211, 215
Cape Henry 223

Index

Capes, battle of: First 223; Second 234
Caribbean 8, 17, 235
Carleton, Sir Guy 54, 82, 237
Carmel, NY 65
Carolina Gamecock *see* Sumter, Thomas
Carpenters' Hall 36
Carr, Patrick (Paddy) 179
Carter, John 103
Carter's Valley Settlement 102–3, 139
Castle's Woods (Castlewood) VA 108, 110–12, 115
Caswell, Richard (first governor of the state of N.C.) 122, 143, 149
Catawba Nation, Reservation, Indian warriors, women, children 115, 171, 174, 189, 216
Catawba River 167, 174, 177, 198, 201, 204, 207–9
Cayuga Nation, People, Tribe 74–5, 77–8, 95–6, 112
Cedar Spring: 1st Battle of 176; 2nd Battle of (Battle of Wofford's Iron Work) 178
HMS *Cerberus* 43
Chadds Ford 67, 202
Chambers, Robert 165
Chambers, Samuel 189, 191
Champion, Deborah 50
Champion, Henry 50
Chapel Hill, NC 100, 216
Charles (Negro) 108
Charles I, King of England 14
Charles River 39
Charlestown (Charleston), SC 8, 31, 37–8, 68, 96, 99, 132, 134–6, 141–2, 156–7, 160–2, 169–70, 172, 175, 200, 203, 211, 213, 215, 219–20, 239; siege of 99, 164–5, 169–70, 173–6, 209, 214, 221, 225, 236
Charlestown Campaign 97, 164–9; *see also* Charlestown, SC, siege of
Charlestown Harbor, SC 8, 131, 133, 135, 165, 203
Charlestown, MA 39, 43–4
Charlotte (queen of George III) 7, 119
Charlotte, NC 170–2, 178, 180, 183
Charlottesville, VA 226
Chasseurs *see* black Haitian troops
Chattanooga, TN 125, 149–50
Chatterton Hill, NY 58
Cheraw Hill, SC 203
Cherokee Billy 114
Cherokee Border War of 1781, 216
Cherokee Country 107, 126, 132, 142
Cherokee Expedition, Dec.–Jan. 1780–81, 217
Cherokee Ford crossing on Broad River 177
Cherokee Four State Retaliatory Expedition *see* Four State Retaliatory Expedition

Cherokee Lower Towns 112, 142
Cherokee Middle Towns 216
Cherokee Nation 3, 104–5, 107, 114, 123–6, 131, 138, 141–3, 150, 175, 199, 217
Cherokee Overhill (Upper) Towns 143
Cherokee Path 175
Cherokee Peace Chief 123, 138; *see also* Attakullakulla; Little Carpenter
Cherokee Settlements 216
Cherokee towns 126, 132, 141, 143, 174, 186, 199
Cherokee War of July 1776, 103, 130–1, 136, 138–43, 175
Cherokee War of 1780 198, 216
Chesapeake Bay 3, 67, 73–4, 92, 128–9, 219, 222–3, 230–2, 234–6
Chester County, SC 167
Chestnut Hill, PA 69
chevaux de frise see frizzy horses
Chew, Benjamin 69–70
Chew House (Cliveden) 69; *see also* Germantown, battle of
Chickamauga 122, 125–6, 138–9, 141, 143–5, 149–51, 198, 240; Campaign 122; Creek 125, 143; Expedition of 1779 149–50; Expedition of 1782 240; Migration 240
Chickasaw 126, 216
Chilhowie *see* Abram of
Chiswell Lead Mines 183–4
Choctaw 126, 216
Chota (Echota) Cherokee Nation capital 114, 124, 138–41, 150, 216; Council House 150
Christ Church of Boston 39
Christenbury, Ann 170
Christenbury, Nicholas C. 170
Christian, Anne Henry 111
Christian, William 109–11, 115–17, 121–22, 142, 217, 232
Chronicle, William 189
Church, Benjamin 29
Church, Willard 94
Church of England (Anglican Church) 14
circular letters 22, 30, 92
City Tavern, Philadelphia 36
Clark, George Rogers 129–30, 145–7, 148–9, 151–2, 240
Clarke, Elijah 156, 158–9, 168–9, 177–83
Clarke, Hannah Harrington 181
Clark's Orchard 64
clergy 13, 21, 97; *see also* parson; preacher
Cleveland, Benjamin 167, 186–94
Cleveland County, NC 180
Clifford Farm 12
Clinch River forts and settlements 108–13, 115–16, 121, 123, 139, 141, 148–9
Clinton, Sir Henry 43, 61, 74, 80–1, 91–4, 96–7, 99, 127, 133–5, 141, 156–7, 164–5, 169, 180, 183, 196,

216, 219–23, 225, 227–8, 230–1, 233–8
Cliveden (Chew House) *see* Germantown, battle of
Coastal Carolina 99, 170, 175
Coercive (Intolerable) Acts 27, 33–9, 50, 85, 129, 237
Colonial Assembly *see* Legislature
Colonial Government 3, 13, 20
Colonial laws during the Revolution 2
Columbia, SC 132, 170, 200, 226
Committee (Committees) of Safety 32, 36–43, 131–2, 139, 142, 154
Committee or Committees of Correspondence 27–36, 42, 85
common law 2, 28, 84, 88
Common Sense 59
Concord village, arsenal and battle of 39–41, 43–4, 50, 131, 154, 218
Confederation Congress 145
Congaree River 132, 173
Congregational ministers 14, 21
Congressional Headquarters at Philadelphia 197
Connolly, John 113
Constitutional Convention 237
Continental Army (American Army, Continentals, National Army) 2, 41, 46, 48–9, 40, 52, 54, 58, 61, 63–5, 67–9, 71, 74, 80, 89, 92, 96, 118, 121–2, 155–7, 165–6, 168, 170, 176, 190, 194, 200–02, 204, 206, 208–9, 218–21, 226, 238–9
Continental Congress 34; First 35–8, 126, 154; Second 38, 42, 45–6, 48–50, 54, 57, 59–60, 64, 66–8, 77, 83, 85, 95, 126, 131, 136–7, 142, 145, 154–6, 171, 197, 220, 225–6, 235, 241
Continental forces *see* Continental Army
Continental Hospital in Williamsburg 129
Continental Navy 42, 57, 232
Continentals, Continental Line 49, 53, 61, 64, 67, 87, 92, 155, 157, 159, 165, 170–1, 202, 204–7, 210, 213, 231, 236
cook, laundress, nurse *see* camp followers
Cool Faction of Congress 50
Cooper River 164
Corbin, John 59
Corbin, Margaret "Captain Molly" Cochran 59
Cornstalk (Keigh-tugh-qua) (Shawnee chief) 106, 108, 113, 117–21
Cornstalk, Chieftess Nonhelema (Kate) "Grenadier Squaw" 106, 120–1
Cornwallis, Charles, 1st Marquess, 2nd Earl Cornwallis 59–61, 63–4, 67, 69, 71, 91–2, 96, 99, 134–5, 164–72, 175, 178, 180, 183–4, 186,

191–2, 195–8, 200–4, 207–11, 213–16, 219, 223–30, 232, 234–9
Coronoh *see* Raven, Chief of Chota or Echota (Savanooka)
cotton gin 218
Council of Cherokee Chiefs 138–9
Council of Safety *see* Committee of Safety
county lieutenant 109–11, 114, 121, 123, 139, 150, 187
court martial 79, 90, 93, 160, 170, 198
Coventry, RI 218
coverture 2, 133
Cowan's Ford (Cowan's Crossing) 208
Cowpens, SC 122, 177, 190–2, 197; Battle of 204–8
Crab Orchard, Kentucky 240
Crabtree, Isaac 108, 114
Crawford, James 189, 191
Creek Indians 126–7, 138, 153, 239
Creole 162
Cresap, Michael 112–13, 120
The Crisis (Paine) 59, 61
Crockett, Davy 86, 171
Cronkite, Maria 236
Cross Creek (Fayetteville) NC 123, 133
Crown Government 131; *see also* British Government
Crown governor 154, 174, 35, 65, 107, 126
Crowtown 150
Cruger, John Harris 182, 211, 213
Culpeper 161
Culper, Jr. (Townsend) 65
Culper, Samuel: Abraham Woodhull & Robert Townsend 65
Culper, Sr. (Woodhull) 65
Culper Spy Ring (Network) 65, 95
Cumberland Compact of Government 152
Cumberland Expedition 151; Gap 108, 125, 148, 151; Mountains 108; Plateau 152; River 123, 125, 151; settlements 152, 240; Valley 150–1
Cummings, Charles the "fighting parson" 141
Cunningham, "Bloody" Bill 205, 212
Cunningham, John 206
Cunningham, Patrick 132, 176
Cunningham, Richard, 179
Cunningham, Robert 132, 175–6
Cunningham's Bloody Scouts 212
Curry, Abigail *see* Morgan, Abigail Curry
Custom House 25
customs commissioner 24, 30; customs duties 19, 22, 26–8; officials 13, 21; *see also* Sugar, Stamp and Townshend acts

Dan River *see* Race to the Dan
Danbury, CT 65–6
DAR *see* Daughters of the American Revolution
Darragh, Lydia 71–2
HMS *Dartmouth* 31
Dartmouth, William Legg, Earl of 38, 53, 77, 112, 127
daughters 1, 3, 7, 27, 33, 139, 153, 186, 203, 212, 214, 240; *see also* ladies
Daughters of Liberty 23
Daughters of the American Revolution (DAR) 4, 240
Davidson, Mrs. 181
Davidson, William Lee 152, 168, 178, 190, 200, 204, 207–8
Davidson County, NC 152
Davie, William Richardson 168, 171, 178–9, 200–1
Dawes, William 39
Deane (ship) 42
Deane, Silas 43–4, 46, 89–90, 220
Declaration of Independence from Great Britain 15, 21, 25, 29, 45–6, 57–8, 85, 137–9, 155, 226, 237
Declaration of Rights of the Colonists¬ 22, 28–9
Declaratory Act 269
Dedham, MA 40
Deist 27
Delaware Continentals 204, 213
Delaware Historic Commissions Iron Hill marker 67
Delaware Indians (Lenape Indians) 107–8, 110, 112, 120
Delaware River 67, 71, 74, 91; Crossing 60–1; Forts 71
Denard's Ford 191
DePeyster 183, 193, 195
d'Estaing, Count Charles Henri 91, 93–4, 162
Detroit 106, 113, 148
DeWitt's Corner 142
Diana, Roman goddess 44, 242
Dickinson, John 50
Dillard, James 201
Dillard, Mary 201
diseases 2, 21, 44, 56, 65, 165, 241; dysentery 44, 55, 170; gout 148, 161; malaria 56, 236; mumps 177, smallpox 15, 44, 56, 64, 84, 91, 124, 165, 167, 177, 201, 205, 218; typhoid fever 56; typhus fever (aka putrid or camp fever) 165
District Ninety Six S.C. *see* Ninety Six district
division 48, 60, 70, 80, 117–8, 202; *see also* battalion; regiment
Doak, the Reverend Samuel 188
Dockyard Act 29
Doggett, Richard 161
Domestic, Molly (Draper?) 40
Donelson, John 104–5, 151–2
Donelson, Rachael (future wife of Andrew Jackson) 151
Don't Tread on Me 128
Dooly, John 158–9
Dorchester Heights 43, 53, 56
Doty, Edward Pilgrim 12
Dragging Canoe 122, 124–6, 138–45, 149–51, 198–9, 240

dragoons 38, 79, 136, 166–7, 169, 172, 179, 196–7, 201, 204–7, 224–6, 232, 239
Drake (youth at Wallen Ridge) 108
Draper, Kate 40
Draper, Lyman 110–11
Draper, Mary 40
Draper, Militia Captain (Mary's husband) 40
Draper Collection at the Wisconsin Historical Society 110
Draper's Meadows Massacre 112
Drayton, William Henry (Anglican lay minister) 37
Dunmore, Gov. John Murray 34, 38, 105; Battle of Great Bridge (Norfolk) 128–9; confiscates gunpowder 126–7; declares liberty to slaves 128; disapproves Transylvania purchase 125–6; Dunmore's War (Shawnee Expedition) 106–23, 125–8; ousted 128–9, 131
Dutch Republic 230–241
Dutch smugglers 31
duties *see* tax

East India Company 8, 31; London merchants and financiers 32
East India Tea Company *see* East India Company
East India Trading Company *see* East India Company
East Tennessee Country 101, 104, 121, 124, 134, 138–9, 141, 145, 153, 174–5, 187, 192, 217, 240
Eaton's Fort (Station) on Island Road 140–1
Edenton in the Albemarle–Pamlico Sound, NC 38
Edenton Tea Party 38
education 1–2, 4, 11, 16, 21, 41, 47, 51, 75–6, 113, 137, 188, 201, 241–3
Elbert, Samuel 156, 159–60
Elder Settlement 212
Electoral College 237
Elizabeth River 129
Elizabethton (Sycamore Shoals) 102, 125, 185
Elizabethtown (Elizabeth, NJ) 60, 97
Elizabethtown, NC, battle of 215
Elk Creek, VA 116
Elk Garden, VA 112
Elk Hill, VA (Jefferson's plantation) 226
Elk River (Charleston, WV) 116–17
Elk River, DE 67
Elkton, ME 235
Ellet, Elizabeth Fries 4, 47, 89, 133–4, 158, 205, 214, 223
Elliot, Jane 215
English Common Law *see* common law
English East India Company *see* East India Company
English imports 25

Index

entailment 3
Episcopacy 14
Episcopal Bishops *see* clergy
espionage 65, 212, 221, 232
Ethiopian Regiment 128
Eutaw Springs 167; Battle of 215
Evangelical Christianity 100
Evans, Mrs. Jesse 149
Expeditionary forces 57, 91, 142, 219, 231
extralegal provincial congress *see* Provincial Congress

Fair Forest Creek 176; night fights 176; settlements 176
Fairfax militia 45
Fairforest Shoals 179
Faneuil Hall 25
Fanning, David 216
Father of Middle Tennessee *see* Robertson, James
Fayetteville, NC *see* Cross Creek
Federal Government *see* Continental Congress
Federal Hill, NJ 231
Ferguson, Patrick: aftermath of death 200–1, 207, 216, 219; bio 196; at Brandywine 67–68; at Gilbert Town and Kings Mountain 183–96; in Old Tryon County 169, 173–82
Ferry Farm 47
Fighting Elder *see* Pickens, Andrew
Fincastle Committee of Safety 38; Resolution 38
Fincastle companies, battalion, regiment 115–17,
Fincastle County, VA 38, 108–12, 114–15, 117, 123, 127, 130, 139
First Continental Congress *see* Continental Congress
Fishing Creek 168; Battle of 172–3, 200–1
Fleming, William 116–18, 120
Florida Campaign 156
Florida coast 154–5
Florida Expedition 155
Florida Rangers (Thomas Brown's King's Rangers) 154–7, 182, 214, 239, 242
flying camp: Greene's 203; Morgan's 204
Folkmoot *see* town meeting
Folmsbee, Stanley J. 104
Forbes, Widow Elizabeth 211
forensic medicine 45
Forks of the Ohio 106, 109, 113, 116, 203; *see also* Fort Pitt, Fort Dunmore
Fort Anderson *see* Thicketty Fort
Fort Billingsport 71
Fort Blackmore 112–13, 115
Fort Boonesborough 125, 139, 199
Fort Cahokia 146–7
Fort Caswell *see* Fort Watauga
Fort Charlotte, SC 131; *see also* Camp Charlotte, Ohio Country

Fort Chiswell, VA 107, 109, 124, 139, 174, 183, 203
Fort Congaree (Columbia, SC) 131–2
Fort Cornwallis (Augusta, GA) 214
Fort Crown Point 42, 52, 82
Fort Defiance 193
Fort Detroit 146–8
Fort Dunmore (the site of Fort Pitt) 113, 115–6, 119
Fort Eaton *see* Eaton's Fort
Fort Edward 79–81
Fort Fincastle (Wheeling, WV) 119
Fort George 157
Fort Gower 119
Fort Graham (Graham's Fort) 181
Fort Granby (Cayce) 213
Fort Grindall *see* Grindall's Fort
Fort Hanging Rock 178; Battle of 178–9
Fort Henry (now Wheeling WV) 240
Fort Henry at Long Island on the Holston 143, 150–1
Fort Jackson 113
Fort Kaskaskia, IL 147, 151
Fort Lee at Limestone on the Nolichucky 139
Fort Lee NJ 58–60
Fort Massac 147
Fort Mercer, NJ 71
Fort Mifflin, PA 71
Fort Moore *see* Moore's Fort
Fort Motte 213
Fort Moultrie *see* Fort Sullivan
Fort Murray 128
Fort Nashborough 152
Fort Niagara 96, 106
Fort Ninety Six 131–2, 171–6, 180, 182, 190–1, 200–1, 203–4, 211–14
Fort Pitt *see* Fort Dunmore
Fort Preston 112
Fort Randolph 120–1
Fort Sackville (Vincennes) 147–9
Fort St. John 52, 54, 79, 154
Fort Shelby (Shelby's Fort, Plantation) 102–3, 113, 115, 124, 139, 148, 185, 187
Fort Stanwix 74–5, 77; Siege of 75, 77–8, 104, 107; Treaty of 74–5, 77, 107–8, 125; Map 104; Line 107
Fort Sullivan (renamed Fort Moultrie) 135–6, 162
Fort Ticonderoga 42, 52, 54, 79
Fort Tonyn 155–6
Fort Vincennes *see* Fort Sackville
Fort Washington, 58; Battle of 59
Fort Watauga (Fort Caswell) 124, 139–40, 185, 187
Fort Watson 211, 213–14
Fort West Point 73, 81, 94, 202, 221–2
forts along the Clinch River *see* Clinch River forts or specific names
Forts in Holston Valley 112

Four State Retaliatory Expedition of 1776 against Cherokee 131, 142
HMS *Fowey* 127
Francisco, Peter "Giant of Virginia" 171
Franco-American (French-American) Agreement, Alliance 84, 86, 89–90, 219; attempt to seize Rhode Island 94; Franco-American siege of Savannah 162; planned attack on New York 220, 225, 227, 231–2; Yorktown attack 235–6
Franklin, Benjamin: Loyalist 9, 15, 19–21, 25, 27; Patriot 35, 57, 82, 84–7, 89–90, 92, 137, 220, 230, 234, 240–1
Franklin, Deborah Read (wife of Benjamin) 84
Franklin, Sara (Benjamin's daughter) *see* Bache, Sara
Franklin, William (son of Benjamin) 27
Fraser Highlanders (a Scots Infantry Regiment) 133, 159, 161, 204, 207, 215
Frederick the Great 57, 89
Fredericksburg, VA 47–8
Freeman, Elizabeth ("Mum Bett") 3
Freeman, John (Loyalist) 80
Freeman Farm *see* Saratoga Campaign
French and Indian War (Seven Years War) 7, 15, 18, 31, 35, 40, 76, 83–4, 100, 102, 106–7, 109, 111–13, 116, 118, 120, 147, 157, 160, 167, 203, 231, 241
French black American woman (Creole) 162
French Broad River 198, 217
French Canadian 54, 79
French financial aid 85–6, 90, 95, 231; supplies 86, 230, 234
French government 83, 230
French Lick settlement (Nashville, TN) 151
French military forces 91, 94, 231, 235; Army 91, 162, 171, 222, 231, 234, 236; Fleet 96–7, 215, 223, 230, 231–2, 234–6, 239
French Revolution 86
French settlers 147
French victory 234
frizzy horses (*chevaux de frise*), 71
frontier warfare: Carolina—upcountry, backcountry, Piedmont 99–101, 107, 132, 134, 166–7, 169, 174–5, 196–7, 199–200, 217; Northwest Territory (Ohio Country) 95, 108–11, 115, 117, 119–20, 145–9, 153, 240; Southwestern frontier 96; Western frontier 4, 38, 100, 104, 108–11, 121, 147, 149–50, 156, 169, 174–6, 187, 194, 196, 203, 216–7

Gage, Thomas 23, 29, 33, 35, 39, 43–5, 49–50
Gallant Six Hundred 177–9
Gallows Tree 198
Gamecock *see* Sumter, Thomas
HMS *Gaspee* 30; Affair 29–31
Gaston, Esther 178
Gates, Horatio: commander Northern Department Continental Army 60–1, 80–2; commander of Southern Department 170–3, 178, 180, 187, 190, 200, 202–3, 209–10
Gaylord, Aaron 95
Gaylord, Katherine Cole 95
Geiger, Emily 214
General Court of Massachusetts 14, 17–8, 31, 39, 241 *see also* assembly; House of Burgess; Legislature
George II, King of Great Britain 153
George III, King of Great Britain 7–8, 26, 33–4, 38, 43, 50, 57,73, 77, 106, 120, 129, 137, 156, 167, 181, 185, 196, 209, 237, 239, 241
Georgetown 213
Georgia committees of safety *see* Committees of Safety, GA
Georgia Trustees 163–4; *see also* proprietors and Lord proprietors
Gérard, Conrad Alexandre 83–4
Germaine, Lord George 73–4, 82, 225, 235
German Army *see* Hessian
German Dragoons *see* Hessian, Hessians
German Princes 57, 77
Germantown, battle of—Cliveden 69–71, 83, 87, 152, 165
Germantown, PA 69
Ghi Ghu (Beloved Woman) *see* Ward, Nancy
Giant of Virginia *see* Francisco, Peter
Gibbs, Mary Anna 161
Gibbs, Robert 161
Gibbs, Sarah Reeve 161
Gibbs Plantation 161
Giever, Philip 194
Gilbert Town (Rutherfordton, NC) 141, 183–4, 189–91, 187, 207
Gilkey Creek 179
Gilmer, Enoch 192
Girty, Simon 120
Gist, Nathaniel 142–3, 195, 217
Gloucester 236
Gloucester Point, VA 230
Glover, John 60
Glover's Marblehead Continental Regiment, Black Americans 60, 63
Goddard, Mary Katherine 137
Golden Hill, battle of (aka War of the Broadsides) 24
gout *see* diseases
government *see* American (Patriot Central); Articles of Confederation; British, Continental Congress; Colonial; Confederation; House of Burgesses; House of Commons; Provincial Congress; Provincial Government
Graham, Williamo 178, 180, 189
Grasse, Francois-Joseph Paul, comte de 232, 234–6, 239
Graves, Thomas 231, 234–5
Graves, Tom (a young Black) 63
Great Alamance Creek 101
Great Bridge, battle of *see* Dunmore
Great Britain 1, 13–14, 17, 19–20, 22–8, 30–1, 33–5, 37–8, 50, 54, 57, 59, 73, 75–6, 83–4, 90, 93–4, 99, 127, 134, 136–8, 143, 146, 153–4, 219–21, 228, 232, 235, 238, 241
Great Indian War Path 139
Great Kanawha *see* Kanawha
Great Lakes 75
Great Pennsylvania Wagon Road *see* Great Wagon Road
Great Road from Camden to Waxhaw 213
Great Smoky Mountains (Great Smokies) 138, 216
Great Valley *see* Valley of Virginia
Great Wagon Road 106, 115
Great White Marsh of NC 168
Green Dragon Tavern 32
Green Dragoons, Tarleton's 166, 169, 172, 197, 201, 204–7, 224–6
Green Mountain Boys of New Hampshire Grants (now VT) 42, 52, 79
Green Mountain Continental Rangers (reorganized Green Mountain Boys) 79
Green Mountains of Vermont 79
Green Spring, VA 230; Battle of 228
Green Spring Plantation 228
Greene, Catherine (Caty) 56, 88–9, 218
Greene, Nathanael: bio 201–2; as commander of Cont. Army in South 202–5, 207–19, 222, 226, 228; in the North 41, 49, 53, 56, 59–60, 62–4, 67, 69–71, 88–9, 97; in the South 190, 199
Greeneville, TN 188
Greensboro, NC 209, 216
Greer, Joseph 197
Grenadier Squaw *see* Cornstalk, Nonhelema (Kate)
Grenville, George 8, 18, 91
Grier, Suzannah (wife of Sgt. Joseph Grier) 54
grievances 19, 23, 27, 29, 101, 147
Grindal Shoal 204–5
Grindall's Fort 204
Groton, MA 41
Ground Hog Sausage *see* Oconostota
guerrilla *see* partisan
Guilford Courthouse 189; Battle of 209–11, 216, 219, 225, 227
Gwinnett, Button 155, 163
Gwynn' Island engagement, Andrew Lewis 129

Habeas Corpus Act 30
Haigler, King, Catawba Chief 171
Hair Buyer *see* Hamilton, Henry
Haitians (Chassaurs) *see* Black Haitian Troops
Hale, Nathan 58
Halifax, Novo Scotia 23, 53, 56
Halifax VA 209, 223, 225
Halifax Resolves 137
Hall, Harriet Prudence 164
Hall, John 164
Hall, Lyman 154–5
Hambright, Frederick 189, 192–3
Hamilton, Alexander 61–2, 67–8, 81, 89, 171, 231
Hamilton, Henry "Hair Buyer" 146–50
Hampton, Andrew 177, 185, 190
Hampton, Wade 215
Hampton Grants 40
Hampton Roads, VA 127, 219, 230, 232
Hancock, Dorothy (wife of John) 21
Hancock, John 15, 20–1, 23, 32, 39, 41–3, 45, 51, 68, 137
Handel, George Frederick 8
Hanging Maw 139
Hanging Rock Battle of *see* Fort Hanging Rock
Hannah's Cowpens *see* Cowpens
Hanover Square, Boston 21
Hard Labor Line 104, 107
Hardeeville 157
Harrington, Hannah *see* Clarke, Hannah
Harrison (John Hancock's brig) 20
Harrison, Benjamin 45
Harrod, James 114–15, 117
Harrodsburg, KY 114, 129, 145, 148
Hart, Benjamin 158–9
Hart, Nancy Ann Morgan 158
Hart, Captain Nathaniel 123
Hart, the Rev. Oliver 37
Hart, Sukey 158
Hart, Susannah (future wife of Isaac Shelby) 123
Hartley, David 241
Harvard College 12, 15, 21, 242
Hawthorn, Nathaniel 31, 84
Hawthorne, James 189
Haydn, Joseph 7–8
Haywood, John 102
Hazel Patch 125
Head of Elk, MD 67, 69, 235
Heard, Stephen 159
Heard, Stephen Plantation 159
Heights and Plains of Abraham *see* Plains of Abraham
Hemphill, Thomas 181
Henderson, Judge Richard 99–100, 123–6, 129–30, 149, 150–2

Index

Henderson Plantation 101
Henry, Patrick 9, 18–19, 30, 35–6, 38, 45, 109–11, 118, 120, 122, 126–30, 143, 145, 149–50, 209
Henry, Robert 208
Herbert, William 115, 117
Hercules of the Revolution *see* Francisco, Peter
Herkimer, Nicholas 77–9
Heroine of the Battle of the Bluff *see* Robertson, Charlotte
Hessians (German mercenaries) 44, 57–9, 61–3, 65, 68, 71, 77, 79–82, 84, 87, 96–7, 160, 164, 178, 210, 223, 228, 239
Hiawassee (Cherokee Upper Town) 139
Highland soldiers 54
Highlanders 133, 154, 157, 159–61, 176, 204, 206–7, 215
Hill, William 189
Hillsborough, Lord 22, 25
Hillsborough, NC 37, 166, 170, 198, 216; Superior Court of 100, 152
historical marker *see* Brant; Brier Creek; Howe's Landing; Iron Hill; Trading Ford
Hite, Abraham Jr. 110
Hobkirk's Hill, battle of (the 2nd Battle of Camden) 213–5
Hockhocking River (Athens County, Ohio) 117, 119
Holland 83
Holland, William 200
Holston Peace Treaty 143
Holston River and Valley 74, 102–5, 110, 112, 124, 127, 130, 136, 139–41, 148, 151, 177, 185–6, 188, 217; North Fork of Holston 148
Holston Settlement *see* North Holston Settlement
Honeycutt (Watauga settler) 102
Hood, Samuel 234
Hooks, Mary 133; *see also* Slocumb, Mary Hooks
Hopkins, Stephen, Pilgrim 12
hornet's nest 170, 180, 200, 207, 225
Hosmer, James K. 15
hospital 59, 81, 129, 179, 207, 218, 231, 241
hounds 72; greyhound 89
House of Burgesses 18–19, 30–1, 34, 46, 104, 109–11, 126; *see also* Assembly; General Court; House of Commons
House of Commons, British 8, 14, 18, 20, 23, 29–30, 38, 83, 91; *see also* British Parliament
housewife, Whig 40–1, 72, 181
Houstoun, John 155–6
Howard, John Eager 204, 206, 215
Howe, Admiral Lord Richard 1, 57, 67–8, 94, 238
Howe, Robert (Continental Army commander in the South) 155–7
Howe, Gen. William 1, 43–4, 50, 53, 56–61, 64–9, 71–4, 79–82, 87, 90–3, 133, 238
Howell, Rednap 101
Howe's Landing; Maryland Historical Society marker 66
Hubbardton, battle of 79
Huck, Christian 162, 168
Hudson Heights, NY 233
Hudson River 43, 46, 58, 73–4, 79–8, 92, 94, 96, 220–1, 232, 255
Hudson Valley 40, 57, 74, 221
Huger, Gen. Isaac 161, 165–6
Hunter, James 101
Husband, Herman 100–1
Hutchinson, Gov. Thomas 19, 27–8, 30, 32–3, 51

Illinois Indians 74; Territory 147
Indian 3, 7, 15, 18, 31–2, 35, 38, 40, 44, 58, 69, 74–9, 81, 83–4, 91, 95–6, 100, 102–27, 129–32, 136, 138–43, 146–7, 149–55, 157, 160, 164, 167, 171, 174–5, 178, 180, 182, 184–7, 190–1, 193, 197–9, 203, 206, 209–11, 216–7, 220, 231, 239–40; *see also* Algonquin; Catawba; Cherokee; Chickamauga; Creek; Delaware; Iroquois; Lenape; Ohio Country; Santee; Seminole; Susquehanna; Wyandotte; Yamacraw
Indian-British alliance 138, 145, 153
Indian-Buffalo path 102
Indians of Ohio Country 110, 240
Indians, Southern 126
Indigenous People 77, 109
Inman, Shadrack 180
insurrection 19, 35; mutiny 231; Regulator 100–1, 123; slave 127
Intolerable Acts *see* Coercive Acts
Ireland 37, 43, 72, 113, 134, 237
Iron Hill Marker, Delaware Historic Commissions 67
Iroquoian Society (Confederacy) of Six Nations 3, 74–7, 95–6, 107–8, 120
Iroquois 74–6, 112; Towns 96; *see also* Mingo
Iroquois "give-away" 107
Isle of Palms SC (Long Island, SC) 135

Jackson, Andrew 151, 161, 166–7, 178–9, 237
Jackson, Elizabeth Hutchinson 166–7
Jackson, John 163
Jackson, Miss Nancy 178
Jackson, Robert 166–7
Jaegers (Hessian sharpshooters) 210, 223
James City Court house 149
James Island 135
James River 128, 219, 223, 226, 228
James River Plantation 226
Jamestown, VA 2, 228, 234
Jasper, William 136, 162

Jefferson, Thomas 1, 3, 9, 11–12, 15, 21, 29–30, 45–6, 68, 86, 113, 148, 187, 194, 219–20, 226, 235
Jefferson's James River Plantation *see* James River Plantation
Jefferson's Monticello Plantation *see* Monticello
Jesuit 113
Jewett Bridge 41
Jocko (slave) 63
John Bull (Englishmen) 33
Johns Island in Santee Swamp, SC 173; at Charlestown, SC 173; on Stono River SC 160
Johnson, Guy 76–7
Johnson, Sir John 76–7
Johnson, Sir William 75–6, 106–7
Jones, John Gabriel 129–30
Jones, John Paul 232
Jonesborough, NC (now TN) 102, 152, 185, 187–8
Judd's Friend *see* Ostenaco Outacite
judges' salary 18, 27–9
Jupiter (slave, Jefferson's valet) 45

Kanawha (Great) River 112, 115–8; Little Kanawha 108, 116
Kanawha Valley 116, 118
Kaskaskia 146–7
Kentucky Country 103, 106, 108–10, 117, 121, 124–5, 129, 134, 145, 150; *see also* Transylvania
Kentucky County, VA 123, 130, 146–8, 151, 177, 195, 240
Kentucky militiamen *see* Militia of Kentucky
Kentucky River 124–6, 139
Keowee 175
Kerr, Joseph 192
Kettle Creek, battle of 157–9
Keywood Settlement 101, 139
King, Mrs. Elizabeth 38
King George III *see* George III
Kingfisher, Nanyehi's husband 138
King's Bridge on the Harlem River 46
King's Friends 33, 154, 170; *see also* Loyalists; Tories
King's Men *see* Tory
King's Mill Fort 113
Kings Mountain, battle of 4, 117, 122, 166, 180, 183, 191–202, 204–5, 207, 219, 227
King's Proclamation of 1763 *see* Boundary Lines, Proclamation of 1763
King's Rangers *see* Florida Rangers
King's Royal Regiment of New York 77
King's troops 23; *see also* Redcoats, British and Hessian Soldiers
Kip's Bay on Manhattan 57
Knights of Malta 232
Knox, Henry 1, 12, 49, 51–3, 56, 61–2, 64, 70, 88–90, 202, 235, 241

Knox, Lucy Flucker 1, 51–3, 56, 62, 88–9, 236
Knoxville in Tennessee Country 124
Knyphausen William von, Baron 67, 96–7

Lacey, William 189, 193
Ladies of Edenton 38
Ladies of Mecklenburg County, NC 132
Ladies of Valley Forge 87; *see also* daughters
Lafayette, Andrienna de La 92, 220, 229
Lafayette, Marquis de 48, 67–8, 81, 92, 94, 220–3, 225–9, 231–2, 234–7
Lake Champlain 42, 54, 79
Lake Erie 113
Lake Ontario 74–5
land grant (warrant) 96, 107, 109, 152, 195
Lane, Anna Maria (soldier) 70
Lane, John 70
Langston, Laodicea (Dicey) 212
Laud, William (Archbishop of Canterbury) 14
Laurens, Henry 94, 142, 237
Laurens, John 93, 231
law 2–3
Lead Mines, Chiswell 109, 111, 183–4, 186–7, 203
Leather Shirts 128
Leatherwood Plantation 209
Lee, Arthur 84, 90
Lee, Charles 48, 60–1, 92–3, 142
Lee, Henry "Light Horse Harry" 210–1, 213–5, 224
Lee, Mary Digges 202
Lee, Richard Henry 30–1, 45
Lee, William "Billy" (Washington's slave) 46, 50, 88, 92
Legge, Lord William 2nd Earl of Dartmouth 38, 53, 77, 112, 127
Legion, Tarleton's British dragoons 204, 206
Legislature: Assembly (Colonial, Provincial, General Court) of NC 4, 14, 175, 191; of MA 18, 22–5, 27, 39; of NC 10, 123; of NY 22, 24, 50, 53; of RI 30; of SC 37, 131; Superior Court of MA 13–14, 28; of VA (House of Burgesses) 30, 129–30, 226
Lenape *see* Delaware Indians
Lenoir, William 189, 193
Leslie, Alexander 207–8, 225
Lewis, Andrew: in Dunmore's War 109–11, 114–122; at Gwynn's Island 129
Lewis, Charles 115–18
Lewisburg *see* Camp Union
Lexington 240
Lexington, battle of 16, 29, 32, 39, 40–2, 50, 91, 101, 126, 137, 154, 218
liberty 1, 5, 12, 13, 15, 20–3, 29–30, 39, 46, 48, 59, 63, 126, 128, 165, 183, 186, 220, 227, 238, 242; *see also* natural rights
Liberty (Hancock's merchant ship) 21
liberty to slaves 128
Liberty Tree (pole) 21, 24–5,
life *see* natural rights
Light Horse Harry *see* Lee, Henry
Limestone (now TN) 102, 139, 187
Lincoln, Benjamin 81, 156–7, 159–62, 164–6, 170, 209, 219, 236
Lincoln County, NC 170, 175, 189, 192, 208
Lindley's Mill, NC, battle of 216
Little Carpenter 104–5, 123–6, 138–9, 141, 143, 149–50; *see also* Attakullakulla; Cherokee Peace Chief
Little Eden, Ninety Six District 212
Little Kanaway (Parkersburg, now WV) Little Kanawha River 108, 116
Little Pee Dee Swamp 168
Little River 175
Little Tennessee River 124, 140, 216
Lochaber Line 103–5, 107
Lochaber Treaty of 1770 102–4
Lock, Francis 170
Locke, John, British philosopher 22, 29
Logan, Benjamin 240
Logan, James 112
Logan, John Mingo Chief 108, 112–3, 120; Logan's Lament 120
Logan's Fort 240
HMS *London* 234
Long Island, a Chickamauga Town 150
Long Island (NY) 56, 65–6, 239; battle 57
Long Island, SC *see* Isle of Palms
Long Island Flats (TN) Battle of 140–1
Long Island of the Holston River (TN) 103–5, 125, 139–40, 142–3, 150–1, 217
Long Island Sound (NY) 65
Longhouse 74
long-hunters 110
Lookout Mountain at Chattanooga 143, 150
Lookout Town 150
Lord Dartmouth *see* Legge, William, 2nd Earl of Dartmouth
Lord North's Tea Act *see* Tea Act
Lord Proprietors 84, 152
Louis XVI, King of France 83, 85, 230
Lower Clinch River *see* Clinch River
Loyalist (American Tory): definition 9
Loyalist refugees 239
Loyalist tribes *see* Cayuga; Mohawk; Onondaga; Seneca
Loyalist wives 3
Lucas, Robert 24, 103
Ludington, Colonel 66
Ludington, Sybil 65–6
Lying Fish 143
Lynnhaven Bay 234
Lytle, Mrs. Thomas 181
Lytle, Thomas 181

Macaulay, Catherine (English historian-philosopher) 1, 37, 48
Machias, battle of 42
Madam Sacho 96
Madison, James 61
magazine: at Charlotte 202, 204; at Savannah 154; at Williamsburg 126; *see also* Arsenal
HMS *Magdalene* 126
Magna Carta 18, 29–31
Maitland, John 160–1
malt house 15–16
Mammy Kate (slave) 159
Manchester 223; Manchester to Rockingham Road 79, 223
Manhattan 56–59, 137
Marblehead MA *see* Glover's Marblehead
HMS *Margaretta* 42
Marie Antoinette (queen of France) 85
Marine Corps 126, 421
Marion, Francis "Swamp Fox," brigade of partisans 2, 167–9, 172–3, 200, 211, 213, 215
Marion, Mary Esther Videau 2, 169
Marion, VA 114, 141, 148, 187
Market Square at Germantown 70
Mars 196
Marshall, John 46, 61–2, 68, 128
martial law 39, 127
Martin, Elizabeth 214
Martin, Grace 214
Martin, Joseph 139, 149–50, 167, 216–7
Martin, Rachel 214
Martin, William 214
Maryland Journal 137
Massachusetts Assembly *see* Legislature, of Massachusetts
Massachusetts Bay Colony 12
Massachusetts Committee of Safety *see* Committee of Safety
Massachusetts General Court *see* Legislature
Massengill, Solomon 201
Mayflower (Pilgrims' ship) 12
Mayflower Compact 12
Mayflower descendants 4, 12, 240
Mayflower pilgrims 12
Mayhew, the Reverend of Boston 14
Mayson, James 131–2
McCrae, Jane 3
McDonald, Angus 115, 119, 122
McDowell, Charles 171, 174, 176–85, 187–93, 206
McDowell, Ellen 197

Index

McDowell, Jane 197
McDowell, Joseph 206
McIntosh, Lachlan 154–5
McJunkin, Miss Jane 177
Mecklenburg County, NC 132, 135, 171, 174, 178, 200, 204, 208
Medway River, GA 157
Mellon, Thomas 86
Mendenhall brothers 108
mercenaries *see* Hessian
Mercer, Dr. Hugh 63
merchant ships (merchantmen), vessels 42, 155, 232, 235
Miami tribes 74
Middle Towns *see* Cherokee Middle Towns
Mifflin, Thomas 53, 56
militia: definition and organization 37, 39, 49; nucleus of Continental Army 48–9
Miller, Phineas 218
Mingo (Iroquois of the Ohio) 107–8, 112, 115, 117, 120–1, 240
minutemen 22, 32, 39, 41, 128, 181, 198
Mississippi River 146, 152, 185, 239, 241
Mitchell's Map 241
Mobile, AL 126, 138
Mohawk Nation 76–7, 93, 96
Mohawk River 74
Mohawk Valley, NY 74–7, 79, 95, 107, 112
Molly (the Drapers' domestic) 40
Molly Pitcher 93
Moncks Corner 213; battle of 165–6
Monmouth Courthouse, battle of 90, 92–3
Monongahela River 108, 113; Monongahela Valley 116
Monroe, James 59, 61–2
Montague, John Earl of Sandwich 238
Montgomery, Janet 55
Montgomery, Richard 54–5
Montgomery County, VA 130
Monticello 45, 226
Montour, Catherine Iroquois Queen 96
Montour, Esther Iroquois Queen 95–6
Montreal, Quebec Province 54, 74, 79
Moore, John 170
Moore's Creek Bridge, battle of 131, 133–4, 223
Moore's Fort 111, 115
Moravian 100; missionaries 119; settlement 209
Morgan, Abigail Curry 203
Morgan, Daniel "the Old Waggoner" 49, 55, 80, 82; biography and Cowpens 203–9; War in the South 115, 122, 170, 190, 199
Morgan, Daniel's Independent Rifle Company 55, 81
Morristown, NJ (Washington's Winter Headquarters) 64–6, 95–7
Motte, Rebecca 213
Moultrie, William 135–6, 157, 160–1
Mt. Independence, VT 79
Mount Vernon 47–8, 87, 235–7
Mozart, Wolfgang Amadeus 8
Mulberry Grove Plantation 218
Mum Bett *see* Freeman, Elizabeth
Murray, John 4th Earl of Dunmore, Viscount of Fincastle *see* Dunmore, Gov.
Murray, Judith Sargent 242–3
Muscle Shoals 151
Musgrave, Thomas 169–70
Musgrove, Beaks 179
Musgrove, John 153
Musgrove, Mary 153, 179
Musgrove Mill 179–80
Musgrove Mill, battle of 180–3, 185, 193, 227
musket *see* Brown Bess Musket
mutiny 231
Mystic River 41

Nanye-hi (Nanyehi) *see* Ward, Nancy
Narragansett Bay 218
Nashborough (Nashville) 152; *see also* French Lick Settlement
national army 204; *see also* Continental Army
natural rights of the colonists as men 13, 15, 18, 22, 29
Navy, U.S. birth at Battle of Machias 42
Ned (black slave) 162
Nelson's Ferry 213
Netherlands 85, 232, 235
Neuse River 133, 223
New Bern, NC 35, 100, 123
New Brunswick, NJ 60
New Haven, CT 40
New River 109, 112, 115–6, 124, 139, 183
New River, General (Catawba warrior) 171
New River group, raised by Herbert, Dunmore's War 115
New River Valley 104, 127
New River, Sally (Queen of the Catawbas) 171
New World 85, 153
New York City 24, 30, 33, 43, 46, 53–4, 56, 58–61, 64–6, 81, 91, 94, 96–7, 137, 231–2, 234–5, 239; Washington plans defenses of 46
New York Colonial Assembly *see* Legislature of New York
New York Gazette 100
New York Harbor 1, 31, 53, 57, 73, 93, 96–7, 219
New York ladies 23
Newark, NJ 51, 59–60
Newport, RI 30, 222–3, 231–2, 234
Nickajack 150
Ninety Six District SC 131–2, 141, 155, 175–6, 180, 191, 200, 204, 211–2; *see also* Fort Ninety Six
Nionne, Ollie (wife of Attakullakulla) 123
No-tea Party 37
Noble Train of Artillery *see* artillery train, Knox
Nolichucky River 102, 105, 139–40, 143, 185–7, 216
Nolichucky Settlement 101–2, 105, 115, 139, 177, 198
Nonhelema *see* Cornstalk, Chieftess, "Grenadier Squaw,"
non-importation, non-exportation and non-consumption 154
Norfolk as a British base *see* Dunmore, Dunmore's War
Norfolk Harbor in Chesapeake Bay *see* Dunmore, battle of Great Bridge
North, Lord Frederick 8, 31, 33, 38, 237
North Bridge at Concord 39
North Carolina General Assembly *see* Legislature of NC
North Carolina State Legislature *see* Legislature of NC
North Carolina Superior Court *see* Legislature
North Edisto River 212
North End Caucus 32
North Fork of the Holston 148
North Holston Settlement 102–3, 105, 113, 115, 124, 139, 150, 176, 181, 184–5, 198
Northwest Territory (Ohio Country) 95, 108–11, 115, 117, 119–20, 145–9, 153, 240
Northwestern Indians *see* Ohio Country Indians
Norwalk 65
Nova Scotia 53, 56

Oath of Allegiance (loyalty) 60, 93, 101–2,173, 175, 180–2, 185
Oconistoto *see* Oconostota
Oconostota, Cherokee War Chief 14–5, 124, 126, 138, 141, 143, 149–5, 216
Oglethorpe, James Edward 153
O'Hara, Charles 208, 236
Ohio Country (Northwestern) Indians 106, 108, 110–12, 115, 117, 119, 240
Ohio River 74, 108, 112–3, 116–20, 123, 126, 145–8, 155, 185, 203, 239–40
Ohio Valley 75, 106, 117
Okefenokee Swamp 155
Old Abram (Ooskwha) *see* Abram of Chilhowie
Old Hickory *see* Jackson, Andrew
Old North Church Boston 15
Old South Church Boston 15
Old Tassel, Chief 142–3
Old Tryon County *see* Tryon County
Olive Branch Petition 50

Index

Oliver, Andrew 19, 51
Ollie, Nionne (wife of Little Carpenter) 123
Oneida Carry 74
Oneida Creek 77
Oneida Indians 74–5, 77–9, 96, 112
Onondaga Indians 74–5, 77, 96
Orange County, NC Regulators 100, 102
Orangeburg British Post on Edisto River, NC 212, 214–15
Oriska (Oriskany, NY) 77, 79
Oriskany, battle of 78
Osborn, Sara 236
Oscar (Marion's slave) 168
Ostenaco Outacite (Judd's friend, war chief under Oconostota) 107, 141, 143, 167
Oswego on Lake Ontario 74, 77–8
Otis, Col. James 11
Otis, James, Jr. Esq. 11, 13–15, 20, 22–4, 28–9, 32–3
Ottawa (Taway) 106, 117
HMS *Otter* 128–9
Otter Creek 125
Outacite *see* Ostenaco
over the mountain 102, 185, 188, 194, 209
Overhill (Upper Town) *see* Cherokee Towns
Overhill Towns *see* Cherokee Towns
Overmountain Country 134, 174–5, 183, 185, 187; march 117, 185–6; militiamen 115, 121, 126, 150, 166, 173–4, 176–7, 180, 185–91, 198, 204, 209, 211, 215–16, 227; people 182, 184; settlements 101–3, 181, 240
Oxford University 204

Pacolet River 177, 179, 201, 204
Paine, Thomas 59, 61
Paint Clan 123
Palmetto 135, 157
Paoli Massacre 68–9
Parker, Commodore Sir Peter 133, 135, 138, 141
Parker, Theodore (historian) 15
Parker, William 103
Parliament *see* British Parliament and House of Commons, British
parson 141; *see also* preacher, clergy
partisan (guerrilla) 167–9, 172, 178–90, 200, 207–8, 211, 214–5, 225
Path Deed 125
Patriot (rebel, Whig) government 131, 162, 214, 216; *see also* Provincial Congress
Patton, James 102, 109, 112
Patton, Mary 186
Paul, Virginia 195
Peace of Paris *see* Treaty, Peace of Paris
Peaceful Retreat Plantation 161
Pee Dee River 203
Pemberton Oak 187

Pendleton, Edmund 45
Penn, William 20, 112
Pennsylvania Wagon Road *see* Great Wagon Road
Pennypacker's Mills near Skippack Creek 68
Penobscot, ME 239
Pensacola, FL Panhandle 126, 138
pension 1–2, 4–5, 59, 70, 75, 95, 121, 165, 176, 194, 199–200, 236, 241
Pepperell, MA 40–1; covered bridge 41
Perth Amboy 57
petition 2, 19–20, 22–3, 25, 42, 70, 100–1, 107, 112, 116, 136, 141, 145, 165, 211, 241; Olive Branch Petition 50; petition from Wataugans 136
petticoat courier *see* Hall, Harriet Prudence
pewter melted for bullets 49
Philadelphia, PA 31, 35–6, 38, 44–5, 47–8, 51, 56–7, 60–2, 64, 66–71, 73–4, 76, 79, 81, 83–4, 87–8, 91–5, 112, 131, 139, 154–5, 196–7, 220, 222, 226, 235, 241, 243; City Hall 40; Congressional Headquarters 197
philanthropy 20, 84, 91, 153
Phillips, Samuel 95, 191
Phillips, William 223, 225
Phillis (slave, poet) *see* Wheatley, Philis
HMS *Phillis* (slave ship) 51
Phrygian cap 21
Pickaway County OH 121; Plains 119, 121
Pickens, Andrew ("the Fighting Elder"; "Wizard Owl") 158–9, 167, 200, 204–7, 211–12, 214–15
Piedmont Carolinas 95–101, 132, 166, 169, 174, 196–7, 199–200, 217; *see also* backcountry; up-country
Pitcairn, John 44
Pittsburgh, PA 96, 113, 119, 121, 240
Plains of Abraham 54
Pleasant Green plantation 223
pledge 32, 38, 50, 60, 120, 132, 173, 175, 179, 183
Plymouth Colony 11–12; Division of Land & Cattle 12
Pocahontas of the West *see* Ward, Nancy
Point Comfort, VA 230
Point Pleasant 104, 240; battle of 110–11, 116–22; *see also* Dunmore's War
Polk, Thomas 135
Polk, William 208
Polk County, NC 107
Polly (ship, American Merchantman) 42
Pompton Mutiny 231
Pontiac (Ottawa chief) 106
Pontiac's War 106, 176
Port Gower 117

Port Royal Island *see* Beaufort, battle of
Portsmouth, NH 21
Portsmouth, VA 127, 219, 227–8, 230
Postmaster General 27
Potomac River 47; Valley 116
Potter, Mrs. 205
Potts House, Isaac Potts House 88
Powell Mountain 108; Valley 108, 148, 152
prayer 24, 34, 42, 62, 88, 188, 211
preacher 37, 97; *see also* clergy; parson
Presbyterian 14, 37, 97, 100, 117, 158, 178, 186, 188
Prescott, Dr. Samuel 39
Prescott, William 43
Preston, William (Fincastle county lieutenant) 109–11, 114–16, 118, 123, 125–6, 139, 209–10, 217
Preston Papers 110–1, 113, 116, 118, 125, 210
Prevost, Gen. Augustine 156–7, 159
Prevost, Col. James Marc 156, 159–61
primogeniture law *see* law
Princeton, NJ 60, 62–3; College 188
Princeton, battle of 63–4
prisoner 41, 54–5, 58, 62, 70, 77, 79, 81–2, 84, 93–5, 101, 113, 120, 129, 142, 146, 148–9, 157, 159–61, 165–7, 170–3, 178, 180, 184, 191, 195, 197–8, 203, 207–8, 215–17, 222, 224, 237
prisoner exchange 54, 81, 93, 149, 165, 171, 175, 203, 217, 222, 237
privateers 42, 52, 164, 232
Proclamation Line of 1763 106–7, 109, 123, 147
property 2–4, 18, 22, 29, 42, 47, 60, 85, 120, 136, 168, 223–4, 226; *see also* natural rights
proprietors 84, 152; *see also* lord proprietors; trustees
Providence, RI 218
Provincial Council 37, 45, 136; *see also* Provincial Congress
Provincial (extralegal) Congress 29, 35–7, 40, 100, 131–2, 154–5, 175, 195, 127, 131, 137; *see also* assembly; General Court; House of Burgesses; Legislature; Patriot (Whig) government
Provincial (Rebel) Government 100, 131–2; *see also* Provincial (extralegal) Congress
Provisional Congress *see* Continental Congress
Pulaski, Count Casimir 68, 160, 162
Pulaski Square 162
Puritan 12–14, 16, 27
Purrysburg 157, 160
Putnam, Israel ("Old Putt") 41, 43–4, 49, 60, 67
Pyrrhic victory 21, 215

Quaker 13, 49–5, 59, 72, 84–5, 100–1, 112, 201–2, 218; Quaker woman 71, 89
Quaker Meadows (Morganton NC) 176, 184, 186, 189, 198, 206
quartering 25, 27, 42, 188; Act of 1765 8, 22, 24; Act of 1767 (Part of Townshend Acts) 22–5; Act of June 2, 1774 33–4, 36
Quebec, battle of (besieged by Montgomery and Arnold) 54–5, 122, 203
Quebec District (Province) 52, 54, 74, 146–7, 237
Queen Elizabeth I 31
Queen of the Catawbas *see* New River, Sally
Queen's Own Loyal Regiment 128
Quincy, Samuel 53

Race to the Dan 207–8
Raleigh, Sir Walter: *History of the World* 12
Raleigh Tavern 34
Ramsey, J. M.G. 102, 104, 198
Ramsour's Mill 170
Randolph, Peyton 36, 45
Randolph County, NC 100
Rappahannock River 47
Raven (Savanooka) Chief of Chota (Echota) 125, 139, 141–3, 216–7
Rawdon, Lord Francis 167, 169, 178, 211–15, 225
Rawlings, Margaret 129
Red Bank Plantation 71
Redstone Creek 113
Reed, Esther de Berdt 91
Reedy Creek 113, 151, 210
refugee 140, 173, 185–6, 239
regiment 23, 25, 43, 48–9, 56, 60, 62–3, 66, 69–71, 77, 81–2, 94, 109, 115–8, 121–2, 128, 135–6, 158, 162, 165–6, 169, 173, 177, 186–7, 190–2, 195, 202, 204–5, 212–13, 219, 232, 236, 239; *see also* battalion; division
Regulations Order and Discipline of the Troops of the United States (the Blue Book) 90
Regulator Movement (1766–1771) 102, 123, 175
Regulator (Regulators) 99–102, 104, 109, 123, 152, 177, 182
religion 12, 37, 45, 100, 188
Revere, Paul 22, 25, 32, 36, 39, 41, 64, 241
Rice Boats, battle of 155, 162
Richardson, Dorcas 173
Richardson, Capt. Richard (husband of Dorcas) 173
Richardson, Col. Richard 132
Richardson Plantation 173
Richelieu River 79
Richmond, VA 38, 126, 148, 187, 219–20, 223, 226–8
Ridgefield, battle of 66
Rifle Company, Daniel Morgan's 55, 203

right of conquest 74, 107, 126, 178
rights of colonists as men and as British subjects 4, 13–15, 22, 18–19, 25, 29–30, 34
rights of Parliament to tax and govern colonists 8, 14, 18, 22, 28–9, 36, 38
Roach, Jordan 201
Roan Mountain, NC 188–9, 191
Roanoke River 148
Robertson, Ann 140
Robertson, Charles 177
Robertson, Charlotte Reeves 152
Robertson, James (of now WV) 116
Robertson, James of Watauga 102–3, 105, 117, 123, 151–2
Rochambeau, Count de 220, 222, 227, 231–2, 234–7
Rocky Mount 167; Battle of, 178
Rodney, Sir George 234–5, 238
Rousseau, Jean-Jacques 45
Rowan County, NC 132, 141, 170
Roxbury 41
Royal Navy, British 30, 57–8 232, 235, 238
Royal Oak, Marion, VA 114–5, 148, 187
Royal Regiments of Loyalists, NC & SC 158
Running Water, Chickamauga Town 150
Rush, Dr. Benjamin 36, 45
Russell, Henry 108
Russell, William 110–12, 115, 117
Rutherford, Griffith 142, 170–1
Rutherford County, NC 175–6, 183, 185, 187, 191; militia 177
Rutledge, Edmund 57
Rutledge, John 168, 200

Sackett, Nathaniel 65
safe houses for Underground Railroad 63
St. Augustine, Florida 155–6, 162, 239
St. Clair, Arthur 79
St. Clair, Sally 162
St. Eustatius 235
St. George's Island, MD 129
St. John, Canada 52, 54, 79
St. John Parish 154
St. Lawrence River 74–5
St. Leger, Barrymore 74–5, 77–80
St. Louis 148
St. Luke's, London 91
St. Mary's River 155
Sal, Virginia *see* Virginia Sal
salaries 18, 24, 27–9, 91, 225
Salem, Peter (former slave) 44
Salem Church 188
Salisbury, NC 170–1, 108–9; Salisbury Wagon Road 210
Salter, Sally 215
Saluda River 175
Samson, Deborah (aka Robert Shurtliff) 236, 240–1
Sandy Creek Baptist Church 100–1

Sandy Hill, SC 215
Sandy Hook, NJ 56, 66, 93–4, 164, 234
Santee Indian Mound 211
Santee River 167–9, 173, 213, 215; Swamp 173; Valley 167
Santo Domingo 83
Sapling Grove 102–3, 105, 113–4, 124, 127, 139, 150, 185, 187
Saratoga, battles of 4, 73–4, 77, 80–4, 86, 90, 170, 194, 203–4, 219, 221, 230, 238
Savannah, GA 8, 21, 99, 154–62, 181, 214–5, 239; siege 162, 214
Savannah magazine 154
Savannah River 113, 154, 157–60, 162, 164, 218, 239
Savanooka *see* Raven of Chota
HMS *Scarborough* 155
Scarsdale, NY 58
Schuyler, Catherine 81
Schuyler, Elizabeth 81
Schuyler, Gen. Philip 52, 55, 78–81
Schuylkill River 60, 68–9, 87
Scioto River 112; Valley 119; villages 106, 119
HMS *Scorpion* 131
Scott County, VA 111
Scovil 99; Scovilite 99, 131–2, 175, 212
Second Continental Congress *see* Continental Congress
Selectmen 15, 32, 39
Seminole Indians 126, 155
Seneca Indians 74–7, 95–6, 112, 120
Sequoya (Sequoyah) 142, 195, 217
Sessions, Darius 30
Seven Mile Ford 141
Seven Years War *see* French and Indian War
Sevier, Catherine Sherrill ("Bonnie Kate of Tennessee") 140, 177, 185, 187
Sevier, James 187
Sevier, John "Nolichucky Jack" 103, 135–40, 143, 150, 176–7, 182–3, 185–7, 189–90, 192–4, 197–9, 211, 216
Sevier, Joseph 187
Sevier, Valentine 117
Shawnee Expedition (Dunmore's War) *see* Dunmore
Shawnee Nation 38, 77, 105–9, 125, 139, 148, 171, 240
Shelby, Evan (founder of North Holston Settlement) 102–3, 105, 109, 114–5, 117–8, 121–2, 127, 149–50
Shelby, Evan (son of Evan, brother of Isaac) 194
Shelby, Isaac 117–18, 122–3, 150, 173, 176–87, 189–95, 198–9, 204, 211, 215
Shelby, Letitia Cox (wife of Evan the founder) 102
Shelby, Moses 186
Shelby's 600 178–9

Shelby's Fort, Plantation, Station *see* Fort Shelby
shelving rock 188–9
Sherrill, Catherine *see* Sevier, Catherine "Bonnie Kate" of Tennessee
Shippen, Dr. William, Jr. 64
Shirtmen 128
Shurtliff, Robert *see* Samson, Deborah
Siege of Boston *see* Boston, Siege of
Siege of Charlestown SC see Charlestown, Siege of
Siege of Yorktown *see* Yorktown, Siege of
Six Nations *see* Iroquois Society (Confederacy)
Skippack Creek, PA 68–70, 87
slaves, slavery 3, 8, 25, 38, 39, 44–5, 47, 50–1, 63, 120, 126–8, 157, 159, 161–2, 167, 213, 224; *see also* African Americans; black Americans; black slaves
Slocumb, Ezekiel 133, 223–4
Slocumb, Mary 133–4, 223–5
Slocumb Plantation 133, 225
smallpox *see* diseases
Smallwood, William 69
Smith, Daniel 110–12
Smith Ford on the Broad River 179
Smithfield 110, 112
smugglers, smuggling 8, 13, 17, 21, 30–1, 139, 164, 173
Snickers, William 207
Snow Campaign (Expedition) 131, 167, 175, 212
Society of Working Women *see* Daughters of Liberty
Somerset Court House, PA 64
Sons of Liberty 9, 14, 19–25, 29, 32–3, 39, 41, 45, 99, 109, 154–5
South Carolina Provincial Congress *see* Provincial (extralegal) Congress, SC
South Carolina Gazette 132
South Fork Boys 192
Spain 83–4, 90, 230, 232, 241
Spanish aid to America 83
Spanish Florida 153–4
Spanish territory of Louisiana 154, 185; of St. Louis 148
Spartanburg city and county, SC 141, 158, 175–9, 201, 204–5
Spartanburg-Greenville 107
Spencer, Joseph 42
Spinning Wheels 23, 41, 71
spoils of war 59, 99, 126, 165, 177, 195
Spruce Pine 189
Spurgeon, John 158
spy 29, 58, 62, 65, 72, 78, 192, 221–2; female 50, 94, 158, 205, 212, 214–15; network 64–5; spyglass 50, 61, 226; spymaster 64–5, 71–2, 83, 95; *see also* Culper Spy Ring

Stamp Act 1765 8, 14, 16–21, 32–3, 39, 85, 91, 99, 137, 169
Standing British Army in America 8, 23, 30
Star Fort at Ninety Six 211, 213–14
Stark, John 41, 49
Starnes, Joseph 194, 197–9
State House (Independence Hall) 36
state of rebellion 37–8
Statecraft 33
Staten Island, NY 57, 97, 239
Staunton, VA 113, 167
Steele, Mrs. Elizabeth 208–9
Stephen, Adam 70
Steuben, Friedrich Wilhelm August von 89–90, 222–3, 226–7
Stewart, Alexander 214–5
Stirling, Lady Sarah 88
stock company 31
Stoner, Michael 110
Stono River 160
Strong, Anna Smith, Patriot spy 65
Stuart, Henry 138
Stuart, John "Bushyhead" 106–7, 126, 138
Stuart Kings 14
The Sucks 150
Suffolk Resolves 36–7, 39, 45
Sugar Act 8, 17
Sullivan, John 3, 49, 53, 57, 62, 69, 70; Sullivan's Raid 95–6
Sullivan County, NC (TN) 112, 141, 150, 176–7, 184, 186–7; militia 150, 177
Sullivan's Island, battle of 131, 135–6, 138, 157, 167
Sumner, Jethro 215
Sumter, Mary Jameson 167
Sumter, Thomas "Gamecock" 2, 167–9, 172–3, 177–9, 183, 200–1, 204, 207, 211, 213–14
Sumter, Thomas, Jr. 167
Sumter Plantation 167
Sunbury, GA 157
Sunshine, NC 189
superintendents of Indian Affair *see* Johnson (in the North); Stuart (in the South)
Supreme Court *see* Legislature
Surry County, NC 187–9
surveyor 109–10, 122, 129, 150, 167
Susquehanna Indians 112; River 95
Swamp Fox *see* Marion, Francis
swan's wing (of beloved woman, Nancy Ward) 138, 140
Sycamore Shoals (now Elizabethton, TN) 102, 124, 139, 144, 161, 184–9, 197

Taliwa, 1755 Battle of 138
Tallmadge, Benjamin 65, 95
Tame Doe of the Wolf Clan 138
Tarleton, Banastre 61, 165–9, 172–3, 175, 178, 183, 190–2, 194–5, 197–8, 200–1, 203–9, 223–6, 228
Tarleton Quarters 166

Tassel *see* Old Tassel, Young Tassel
tax, taxation 8, 20–2, 28, 31, 34–5, 38, 99–100, 162, 172; collector 15, 19–20; colonial property, business and poll 18; relief 172, 211, taxation without representation 13–14, 20, 188; tea 22, 27, 31–2; trade (import duties) 12, 13; *see also* Stamp Act; Sugar Act; Townshend Acts
Tazewell County, VA 111
Tea Act 1773 8, 31, 33
teamsters 203, 231
Tecumseh 118
Teedyuscung, King of the Delawares 108
Tennessee Country 101, 104, 121, 134, 138–9, 141, 145, 153, 174–5, 187, 192, 217, 240
Tennessee River 150–1, 217; Valley 127, 150
terms of service 60
Ternay, Charles Louis d'Arsac, Chevalier de 231–2
HMS *Terrible* 234
Thayendanegea *see* Brant, Joseph
Thicketty Creek 177, 179, 205
Thicketty Fort (originally Fort Anderson) 177–8
Thomas, Isaac 139–40, 216
Thomas, Jane 176
Thomas, John, Jr. 176
Thomas, Margaret (free Black; wife of Billy Lee) 88
Thompson, William "Old Danger" 135
Thomson, Charles 36
Ticonderoga, NY 42, 51–4, 79–80
Tidewater 100, 109, 127, 129,
Tidewater Plantations 128
Timberlake, Henry 167
Timberlake, Richard 143
Tobago 232
Tomochichi, Yamacraw chief 153
Tonyn, Patrick 154
Tory, Tories (Loyalists, Royalists, King's Men): definition 9
Tower of London 237
town meeting (folkmoot) 17–18, 21, 23, 28–9
Townsend, Robert (Culper Jr.) 65
Townshend, Charles 221–2
Townshend Acts 1767 14, 22, 23–7, 31
Trading Ford on the Yadkin, Historical Marker 209
transitional governments 35
Transylvania Land Company 124, 151
Transylvania Purchase: agreement 124; treaty 124–5, 139, 143, 150, 152
treason speech *see* Henry, Patrick
Treaty Alliance 1778 with France 84
Treaty of Camp Charlotte 119–21
Treaty of DeWitt's Corner 142–3

Index

Treaty of Fort Stanwix 108, 125
Treaty of Lancaster 125
Treaty of Logstown 125
Treaty of Long Island on Holston (1777) 143, 217, 219
Treaty of Long Island on Holston (1781) 217, 219
Treaty of Paris 1783 (part of Peace of Paris Treaty) 241
Treaty, Peace of Paris 1783 (three separate treaties) 241
Trenton, battle of 62–3, 84
Tribal alliance by Shawnee 108
Triplett, Francis 204
Trotter, Anne Hennis 119; *see also* Bailey, Anne Hennis Trotter
Trotter, Richard 119
trustees *see* Georgia trustees; *see also* proprietors
Tryon, Royal Gov. William 65–6, 100–1, 104, 107, 174
Tryon County, NC 100, 132, 170, 174–7, 180–1, 186–7, 189, 191
Tryon Mountain, Polk County, NC 107, 174
Tryon's Line 104, 174
Tuckaseegee River 216
Turkey Cove 189
Turner, Frederick Jackson 104
Tuscarora 74–5, 77, 96
Tusculum College, TN 188
Twiggs, John 183
Twitty, Mr. (trailblazer with Boone) 126
Twitty, Susan 180
Twitty, William 180
Tybee Island 156, 164
Tyger River 141, 176, 201, 212, 237
typhus (camp fever) *see* diseases
tyranny 13–14, 20, 24, 28, 85, 102, 141, 183, 185
tyrant 88, 101, 129, 136, 141, 237

Unaka 140
Underground Railroad Safe Houses 63
Union County, SC 102
Union Jack (British flag) 8, 57, 147, 257, 240
United Kingdom 14; *see also* Great Britain
United States Congress *see* Continental Congress
United States Navy birth 42
United States Marine Corps birth 42
Unity (American merchant ship) 42
upcountry 99, 132, 168, 175; *see also* backcountry; Piedmont
Upper Creeks *see* Creeks
Upper Towns (Overhill Towns) *see* Cherokee towns

Valerius Poplicola 28
Valley of Virginia 183
Valley Towns (Cherokee) 142
Van Nest's Mill 64

Vergennes, Charles Gravier, Comte de 70, 83–4, 86, 90, 230–1
Vernon River 162
Versailles 241
Versailles, Palais de 85
veterans of Dunmore's War 38, 121, 177; of French and Indian War 40, 100, 102, 107, 109, 111, 157; of Revolutionary War 59, 96, 167, 175, 199, 204, 241
veteran's pension *see* pension
Vincennes Expedition 146–8
Vindex 23, 28
Virginia Assembly *see* Legislature; of Virginia
Virginia Beach 234
Virginia Campaign 200, 207, 219–20, 222–3, 225, 232–3
Virginia Convention 38, 126, 136, 142
Virginia Gazette 129, 141
Virginia House of Burgesses *see* Legislature of Virginia
Virginia legislature *see* Legislature of Virginia, Burgesses
Virginia Paul 195
Virginia Sal 195
von Riedesel, Prussian Baroness Frederika 79, 81
von Riedesel, General Friedrich Adolf 81

Wabash River 147
Walker, Felix 124–5, 134–6
Wallen Ridge 108
Walnut Grove Plantation 205
Walpole, Sir Robert 33
Walton, George 155
War Woman *see* Hart, Nancy Ann Morgan
Ward, Artemas 41, 43
Ward, Betsy 139, 150
Ward, Brian 138–9
Ward, Nancy (Nanyehi, Ghigue "Beloved Woman") 138–40, 150, 217
Warner, Pvt. James 54
Warner, Jemima 54
Warren, Dr. Joseph 28–9, 32, 36, 39, 45
Warren, James (husband of Mercy Otis) 12, 28
Warren, Mercy Otis 1, 3–4, 11–13, 17, 22–4, 28, 30, 32–3, 35, 37, 40, 51, 55, 82, 87, 93, 97, 169, 198, 243
Warren, Richard (pilgrim) 12
Warrior's Path 125
warships, British 21, 53, 66, 128, 134, 154, 165, 223
Washington, Augustine (father of GW) 47
Washington, George 1–2, 9, 36, 45–6; appointed Nathanael Greene to replace Gates in the South 190; at Brandywine 67–8; in Canada Campaign 53–5; crossed the Delaware 60–3;

elected commander in chief of Continental Army 46–9; at Germantown 69–71; met with Rochambeau and sends Lafayette to VA 220; at Monmouth Courthouse 92–3; at Morristown 64–6; at Morristown and NY 94–6; in NY and NJ campaigns 56–60; rallied support for Saratoga Campaign 82; reached stalemate with Clinton in the North 156; at Shippack Creek 69; in siege of Boston 49–53; at Trenton and Princeton battles 63–4; at Valley Forge 87–90; victory at Yorktown 231–237; at White Marsh 71
Washington, Lawrence (half-brother of GW) 47–8
Washington, Martha Dandridge Custis (wife of GW) 51, 87–90
Washington, Mary Ball (mother of GW) 47
Washington, Col. William 204, 206–7, 210, 215, 224
Washington College, TN 188
Washington County, NC (now TN) 150, 152, 177, 184–7, 195, 198, 201
Washington County, VA 113, 150, 176, 186–7, 198
Washington's army *see* Continental Army
Watauga, Wataugans 99, 101–2, 104–5, 110, 114, 124, 127, 143, 151, 153, 175, 181–2, 194, 198, 217
Watauga Association 105, 134, 152; drafted Articles for civil government 105
Watauga River 102, 105, 114, 124, 140, 144, 184–8, 191, 198
Watauga Settlement (Elizabethton, TN) 101–3, 105, 123–6, 151–2, 177, 184, 186, 197; *see also* Fort Watauga
Watauga settlements 102–3, 105, 113, 115, 125, 139
Wataugan women 139, 151, 186
Wateree River 175, 213–14
Watertown, MA 40
Watson, Col. John 211, 213; *see also* Fort Watson
Watts, John (Young Tassel) 143
Waxhaw Presbyterian 178–79
Waxhaws 166, 192; battle of 165–6, 194
Wayne, Anthony 64, 68–71, 93–4, 226–8, 239
Webley, Mary 128
Wells, George 163
West Indies British, Dutch and French 17, 21, 37, 94, 129, 165, 232, 234, 236, 239
West Point *see* Fort West Point
Western Waters 183, 185, 187, 210
Westover Plantation 219, 226
Westward expansion 101

Wetzel's (Whitesell's) Mill 209–10; battle at 210
Wheatley, John 51
Wheatley, Mary 51
Wheatley, Phillis (Black American poet) 50–1
Wheatley, Susanna (wife of John) 51
Wheeling (now WV) 112, 115, 119, 240; River 112
Whig (Rebel, Patriot) definition of Whig 9
Whipple, Prince 62
White Eyes (Koquethagechton, Delaware chief) 119
White Plains, NY 58–9
Whitemarsh, PA (Washington's encampment) 71–2
Whiting, Leonard 41
Whitney, Eli 218
Wilderness Road 103, 113, 124–5, 145, 148, 187
Wilkes County, NC 186
Williams, James 175, 179–80,183, 189, 191–3, 195–7
Williams, Otho Holland 209–10, 215
Williams Plantation 176
Williamsburg 19, 34, 112, 125, 127, 129–31, 141, 145, 147–9, 223, 226–8, 230, 235–6
Williamsburg magazine *see* magazine, Williamsburg
Williamson, Andrew 132, 142, 155, 159
Williamson Plantation 168
Wilmington, NC 38, 211, 215–6, 219, 223; Road 134
Winchester, VA 115, 203
Winnsboro, SC 198, 200–1, 203, 207
Winston, Joseph 189–90
Winthrop, Hannah 1, 27, 30, 33, 40, 82
Winthrop, Dr. John 30
Wisconsin Historical Society 110; Northwest Territory 145; Oneida migration 96
Wizard Owl *see* Pickens, Andrew
Wofford's Iron Works *see* Cedar Spring, 2nd Battle of
Wolf Clan, Cherokee 123, 138
Wolf Hills *see* Abingdon, VA
women camp followers *see* camp followers
women, general contributions of 1–4, 11
Wood Creek 74
Woodhull, Abraham, Culper, Sr. 65
Woods, Michael 116
Wright, David 41
Wright, Gov. Sir James 154, 162
Wright, Prudence 41
Wright's Bluff 211
Wright's plantations 162
Writs of Assistance 13–14
Wyandot, Wyandotte Indian 106, 113, 117, 121, 240
Wynnesborough *see* Winnsboro

Yadkin River 108, 193, 209
Yamacraw Chief *see* Tomochichi
Yamacraw creek 156
Yankees 56, 81, 236
Yellow Creek 112–13; Massacre 112
Yellow Mountain 189
York County SC 168
York River 127, 230, 236
Yorktown, VA 127, 222, 226; Battle of 160, 165, 194, 207, 215, 230–41
Young, Robert 194
Young Tassel *see* Watts, John

Zane, Betty 240
Zane, Ebenezer 240

www.ingramcontent.com/pod-product-compliance
Lightning Source LLC
Chambersburg PA
CBHW081545300426
44116CB00015B/2765